1986

WORLD BROADCASTING
IN THE
AGE OF THE SATELLITE

COMMUNICATION AND INFORMATION SCIENCE

A series of monographs, treatises, and texts
Edited by
MELVIN J. VOIGT
University of California, San Diego

Recent Titles:

Alan Baughcum and Gerald Faulhaber • Telecommunications Access and Public Policy
Herbert Dordick, Helen Bradley, & Burt Nanus • The Emerging Network Marketplace
Sara Douglas • Labor's New Voice: Unions and the Mass Media
William Dutton & Kenneth Kraemer • Modeling as Negotiating
Fred Fejes • Imperialism, Media, and the Good Neighbor
Glen Fisher • American Communication in a Global Society
Howard Frederick • Cuban-American Radio Wars
Edmund Glenn • Man and Mankind: Conflict and Communication Between Cultures
Gerald Goldhaber, Harry Dennis III, Gary Richetto, & Osmo Wiio • Information Strategies
Bradley Greenberg, Michael Burgoon, Judee Burgoon, & Felipe Korzenny • Mexican Americans and the Mass Media
W. J. Howell, Jr. • World Broadcasting in the Age of the Satellite
Heather Hudson • When Telephones Reach the Village
Robert Landau, James Bair, & Jean Siegman • Emerging Office Systems
James Larson • Television's Window on the World
John Lawrence • The Electronic Scholar
Kenneth Mackenzie • Organizational Design
Armand Mattelart and Hector Schmucler • Communication and Information Technologies
Robert Meadow • Politics as Communication
Vincent Mosco • Policy Research in Telecommunications: Proceedings from the Eleventh Annual Telecommunications Policy Research Conference
Vincent Mosco • Pushbutton Fantasies
Kaarle Nordenstreng • The Mass Media Declaration of UNESCO
Kaarle Nordenstreng & Herbert Schiller • National Sovereignty and International Communication
Everett Rogers & Francis Balle • The Media Revolution in America and in Western Europe
Dan Schiller • Telematics and Government
Herbert Schiller • Information and the Crisis Economy
Herbert Schiller • Who Knows: Information in the Age of the Fortune 500
Jorge Schnitman • Film Industries in Latin America
Jennifer Daryl Slack • Communication Technologies and Society
Keith Stamm • Newspaper Use and Community Ties
Robert Taylor • Value-Added Processes in Information Systems
Sari Thomas • Studies in Mass Media and Technology, Volumes 1–3
Barry Truax • Acoustic Communication
Georgette Wang and Wimal Dissanayake • Continuity and Change in Communication Systems
Frank Webster & Kevin Robins • Information Technology: A Luddite Analysis

In Preparation:

Susanna Barber • News Cameras in the Courtrooms
Lee Becker, Jeffrey Fruit, & Susan Caudill • The Training and Hiring of Journalists
Thomas Lindlof • Natural Audiences
David Paletz • Political Communication Research
Jennifer Daryl Slack & Fred Fejes • The Ideology of the Information Age
Lea Stewart & Stella Ting-Toomey • Communication, Gender, and Sex Roles in Diverse Interaction Contexts
Tran Van Dinh • Communication and Diplomacy in a Changing World
Tran Van Dinh • Independence, Liberation, Revolution

World Broadcasting
in the
Age of the Satellite:

Comparative Systems, Policies, and Issues
in Mass Telecommunication

W. J. HOWELL, Jr.

Canisius College

ABLEX PUBLISHING CORPORATION
NORWOOD, NEW JERSEY

Cover illustration by Kathleen Collins Howell

Library of Congress Cataloging in Publication Data

Howell, W. J., Jr.
World broadcasting in the age of the satellite.

(Communication and information science)
Bibliography: p.
Includes index.
1. Broadcasting.   2. International broadcasting.
3. Artificial satellites in telecommunication.
I. Title.   II. Series.
HE8689.4.H69   1986   384.54   86-3380
ISBN 0-89391-340-5
ISBN 0-89391-390-1 (pbk.)

Ablex Publishing Corporation
355 Chestnut Street
Norwood, New Jersey 07648

CONTENTS

I dedicate this book to

Kate and Wally, my parents
Kathy, my wife
Wilbur Samuel Howell, my uncle and mentor

Acknowledgments

Writing a book is never a solo effort. Every author receives help from a variety of professional and personal sources. Of the many people who assisted me in this project, I wish to publicly thank the following:

In keeping with my belief that gratitude, like charity, begins at home, I want to thank my wife Kathy for putting up with me these past 3 years and for letting me convert our dining room into my base of operations.

At Canisius College, I am particularly indebted to: the Administration for granting me a sabbatical leave during the spring of 1982, which allowed me to travel, interview, and collect information for this book; our librarian, Peter Laux, whose unflagging moral support and professional staff were with me every step of the way; and to Janet Holler, Irene Ehde, and the wonderful women in the Secretarial Center—especially Rosemary Sortino—who typed and word-processed the manuscript.

To those august colleagues around the country who met with and encouraged me, critiqued my prospectus and offered valuable suggestions, I wish to express my genuine appreciation to five fellow professors: Henry Breitrose and Elie Abel at Stanford University; Tony Giffard at the University of Washington; and Don Browne and Burton Paulu at the University of Minnesota.

Finally, I am grateful to my editor, Mel Voigt, and the entire Ablex publishing team, for transforming over 500 pages of raw type into a beautifully crafted and readable book.

PART I

FRAMES OF REFERENCE IN WORLD BROADCASTING

Understanding World Broadcasting: A Rationale, Framework, and Methodology for Analysis

In the beginning, Planet Earth had only one satellite, a natural one called the Moon. Then man added another in 1957 and called it Sputnik. Today, several hundred communication satellites encircle the globe, performing countless telecommunication tasks. These orbiting "birds" relay and distribute broadcast signals to earth stations whose transmissions have made much of the world's population privy to such live events as humankind's first lunar landing, the Olympic Games, championship boxing matches, international soccer contests, and Britain's 1981 Royal Wedding—the latter seen by 600 million viewers in 60 countries.[1] And this is just the beginning.

We are presently on the threshold of direct satellite-to-home broadcasting, a revolutionary technology with the potential to bring programming from stations and nations around the world directly to individual TV sets regardless of their locations. Direct satellite broadcasting, together with two-way cable, will provide many of tomorrow's viewers with over 100 channels of diverse services as well as international programming.

The FCC formulated rules governing satellite broadcast services in America during 1982. To date, the Commission has received DBS applications from about a dozen private firms.[2] Hence, several channels of satellite TV programming will be available directly to homes in all 50 states by the end of the decade.[3] Elsewhere in the world, Japan, France, West Germany, Australia, Great Britain, and Luxembourg are likewise preparing to operationalize DBS. And Canada has been a pioneer in communication satellites with its Anik series.[4] Little wonder that the United Nations, in recognition of these dramatic developments, declared 1983 "The Year of World Communication."

Abroad, however, the concerns over these technological advances go beyond their possible effects on national systems of traditional braodcasting. For instance, the developing countries feel that their national independence and authentic cultures will be threatened with extinction from media domination by the richer Western nations. Some national leaders have voiced opposition to the intrusion of uninvited broadcasts and alien information into their sovereign territories. Others worry about the effects that consumer-oriented advertising and programs depicting Western values in entertainment, news coverage, and materialistic life styles might have on the beliefs and expectations of peoples living in drastically different circumstances.

Perhaps the overriding impact of the emerging technologies of mass telecommunication will be psychological—forcing humankind to rethink many time-honored concepts like nationalism, sovereignty, patriotism, independence, cultural integrity, progress, education, and transportation. The list of anxieties is long; the time to address them is short. In the age of the satellite, broadcasting means world broadcasting. Hence, the list of reasons for studying the broadcasting systems and cultures of other nations is likewise long.

A RATIONALE FOR STUDYING WORLD BROADCASTING

Studying world broadcasting is a lot like travelling. But as an ancient proverb warns: "If you don't know where you want to go, any road will take you there." Just as the seasoned traveller always draws up an itinerary before leaving home, embarking upon an unfamiliar course of study requires similar advance planning. The course charted in this chapter offers reasons why the study of broadcasting in other nations is important, defines the central conceptual and technical information needed to be conversant in the field, and constructs a framework and method for analyzing and comparing foreign broadcasting systems within their national and global contexts.

Radio and television are endowed with a number of unique distribution and production qualities which have always set them apart from other forms of mass communication. These include the ability to:

- instantaneously transcend national boundaries;
- reach distant and undifferentiated mass audiences;
- command simultaneous public attention with direct sounds and images of persons and events;
- set the agenda for a large measure of public debate and private discourse;
- and disseminate compelling aural and visual messages, whose comprehension is often independent of geopolitical, cultural, and literacy considerations.

Such attributes have made radio and television the preeminent vehicles of shared social expression and cultural transmission within and between countries. With cable and satellites added to the mass telecommunication arsenal, the practice and study of broadcasting have become dramatically altered.

A FRAMEWORK FOR ANALYZING WORLD BROADCASTING

Qualified professionals in all highly specialized fields inevitably share a technical vocabulary and authoritative expertise. No less is true of the scholars, policy-makers, and practitioners involved in world broadcasting. Analyses and comparisons of broadcasting within and between divergent nations require frames of reference concerning the process, technologies, concepts, systems, and relative contexts of mass telecommunication.

Public telecommunication technology may be classified on the basis of size and purpose. Mass telecommunication is mainly dependent upon *Delivery Systems*. These are complex, usually interconnected, and have organizational infrastructures. They may be described as large, costly enterprises that require technical, managerial, and creative expertise. They operate within a legally regulated environment and are licensed by government to produce, procure, and distribute programming intended for reception and use by the general public. Prime examples of Delivery Systems of mass telecommunication are radio, television, cable, and satellite. These are operational in some combination and degree in virtually every nation, and are the main interest of this book.

The other category of public telecommunications may be called *User Systems*. These are smaller, less sophistocated units of telecommunication technology whose pricing makes them available for ownership by individuals and groups for their private use. Their operation requires little or no technical training, no licensing, and is subject only to copyright regulation. The most common types of the new technologies are the home computer and the video cassette recorder (VCR). The worldwide impact that the VCR as a user technology is having on television delivery systems will be described in the final chapter.

Delivery and User technologies are both dependent upon electromagnetic energy, and therefore must utilize the spectrum. Existing as a phenomenon of nature, the spectrum is regarded worldwide as a public resource which cannot be privately owned. Like the seas, it must be managed by national governments and international authorities who regulate its use through laws and conventions agreed upon voluntarily by, and for the benefit of, all nations. This function is discussed in the next chapter.

Table 1-1 summarizes world broadcasting services in terms of how they use the electromagnetic spectrum.

Broadcasting services of some description are found in virtually every country on earth. Radio is the most universal medium of mass telecommunication, especially the Medium Wave and Shortwave varieties. Television tends to be a creature of modernization; thus, it is most likely to be present in developed settings in general and urban areas in particular. Satellites have the capacity to reach nearly all points on the globe. Cable, on the other hand, is a capital-intensive technology. It is therefore limited at present to wealthy, developed, and densely populated nations, with the exception of a few wired radio systems still operating in some communist and Third World locales.

Table 1-2 illustrates the growth and diffusion patterns of radio and television receivers throughout the world over the past quarter century.

Several noteworthy differences exist among radio and TV services around the world. For instance, American radio is dominated by AM and FM stations, with Long Wave and Shortwave virtually unknown. Outside of North America, how-

Table 1-1 Summary of Electromagnetic Spectrum Utilization by World Broadcasting Services

Band designation	Frequency range expressed in:			Broadcast service	Allocated frequencies	Type of wave propagation
	Kilohertz (thousands of cycles per second)	Megahertz (millions of cycles per second)	Gigahertz (billions of cycles per second)			
VLF =	Below 30	—	—	N/A	N/A	
LF =	30-300	—	—	Long Wave	160-255 kHz	Ground
MF =	300-3,000	—	—	AM	535-1605 kHz	Ground (daytime) & Sky (Nighttime)
HF =	3,000-30,000	3-30	—	SW	12 Bands: 2,300 kHz–26,100 kHz (See Table 8-1, Chapter 8)	Sky
VHF =	30,000-300,000	30-300	—	TV	54-76 MHZ (channels 2-6)	Direct
				FM	88-108 MHZ	
				TV	174-216 MHZ (channels 6-13)	
UHF =	300,000-3,000,000	300-3,000	—	TV	470-806 MHZ (channels 14-69)	Direct
SHF =	3,000,000-30,000,000	3,000-30,000	3-30	Satellite	3-30 GHZ (DBS 4/6 & 11/14 & 18/30 GHZ)	Direct
				Microwave		Direct
EHF =	30,000,000-300,000,000	30,000-300,000	30-300	Satellite	41-43 GHz	Direct
				Microwave	84-86 GHz	Direct

Sources: Head and Sterling, 1982, pp. 43, 50 and 73.
BBC Handbook 1980, pp. 198-199.
WRTH 1982, pp. 10, 44 and 386-7.

Table 1-2 World Radio and Television Receivers—1982

	Population in Thousands, 1982	Number of Radio Sets (excluding wired receivers) in Thousands				Number of Television Receivers in Thousands		
		1955	1965	1975	1982	1965	1975	1982
World Figures (approx.)	4,513,000	237,000	529,000	1,010,000	1,500,000	177,000	398,000	622,000
Europe								
Western Europe	421,000	65,310	116,500	186,600	281,800	49,400	103,400	149,100
USSR and European Communist Group	385,000	20,260	59,700	92,600	141,800	24,000	87,000	113,500
Middle East (including North Africa)	206,000	2,200	12,300	29,300	47,000	1,250	6,000	15,100
Africa								
South Africa	29,000	875	2,600	4,800	9,000	—	500	3,000
Other African countries	344,000	360	4,800	18,500	36,600	100	600	7,200
Asia								
Chinese People's Republic	1,000,000	1,000	6,000	35,000	80,000	70	750	15,000
India	690,000	1,000	4,800	24,000	40,000	2	300	2,000
Japan	119,000	12,000	27,000	87,000	100,00	18,000	42,000	65,000
Other countries	673,000	1,800	13,300	49,700	94,900	700	8,950	25,900
Western Hemisphere								
United States of America	229,000	111,000	230,000	380,000	500,000	68,000	110,000	160,000
Canada	24,000	5,500	14,000	23,000	30,000	5,000	9,500	13,000
Latin America	358,000	12,600	29,400	62,800	112,900	7,400	22,600	14,300
West Indies	10,000	190	860	4,000	5,500	100	1,200	1,800
Australasia and other Ocean Territories	25,000	2,760	7,800	13,000	20,600	3,200	5,000	7,500

Source: *BBC Annual Report and Handbook 1984*, p. 142.

ever, AM is called Medium Wave, FM is VHF Stereo, and both LW and SW radio signals are widely heard. And because high frequency broadcasting uses sky waves during both daylight and nighttime hours, shortwave signals thus have the ability to skip off of the ionosphere and travel great distances back to earth— spanning oceans and continents with ease. This makes the SW medium ideally suited for international (i.e., external) broadcasting and propaganda purposes, subjects to be further explored in Chapter 8. Moreover, American television has from its start relied principally upon VHF channels (2–13), while most other nations developed their TV systems using mainly UHF channels (14–69).

The study of world broadcasting is again complicated by the fact that national policy-makers have adopted 14 different technical standards and three separate color technologies in developing their domestic *television* systems. Table 1-3 enumerates the world's five principal TV standards, citing examples of nations using each type.

One can detect politics at work in the historical evolution of multiple TV standards. After World War II, the United States rushed to capitalize on a new consumer market by developing the world's first nationwide television service. In doing so, however, America committed its domestic communications industry to a 525-line system, a state-of-the-art technology in 1946. Then, in 1953, the FCC adopted the color standards of the National Television Systems Committee (NTSC), a consortium of electronics firms having competing color systems.[5] Meanwhile, the European nations were slower in developing the new medium in the context of post-war economic recovery. This proved advantageous, enabling

Table 1-3 Generic Types and Characteristics of World Television Standards

System designation	Lines per frame	Channel width (MHz)	Sound modulation	Frames per second	Examples of users
A	405	5	AM	25	Great Britain (being phased out)
B(CCIR)	625	7	FM	25	Most of Western Europe
D	625	8	FM	25	China, Eastern Europe, USSR
E	819	14	AM	25	France
M	525	6	FM	30	Canada, Japan, Latin America, United States

Comment: Counting minor variations, there are 14 different basic (black-and-white) standards, plus three different color systems. Outside the American sphere of influence, the most widely used is System B, also known as the CCIR System (referring to a committee of the International Telecommunication Union). To find out which system each country uses, consult the annual *World Radio-TV Handbook,* edited by J. M. Frost.

Source: Sydney W. Head, with Christopher H. Sterling, *Broadcasting in America: A Survey of Television, Radio, and New Technologies* (Boston: Houghton Mifflin, 1982, Fourth Edition), p. 72.

them to improve upon both American standards by establishing a 625-line image standard and two color systems: the Phase Alternate Line (PAL) from West Germany, and France's Sequential Color and Memory (SECAM) system.

Each of the above color systems is well represented in the international marketplace. For example, PAL is found throughout Western Europe and Anglophone Africa, in most of the nations of the Near East and Asia, and in some Latin American nations (e.g., Uruguay, Brazil, and Argentina). SECAM is used in France, of course, and throughout Francophone Africa, much of the Middle East, parts of the Caribbean, and in most communist countries except Yugoslavia and the Peoples Republic of China, which use the PAL system. The NTSC standard operates in North America, Japan, most of the Caribbean, many of the Central and South American nations (like Mexico, Guatemala, Costa Rica, Nicaragua, Bolivia, Chili, Peru, and Venezuela) and in those Asian areas under U.S. military and trade influence—such as South Korea, the Philippines, Guam, and associated Pacific islands.[6] Reasons for a given nation choosing a particular line standard and color system are tied to such factors as ideology, international trade agreements, cost of implementation, technical compromises, and the state of the art at the time of decision.

Defining World Broadcasting as a Field of Study

World broadcasting can be examined from both comparative and international perspectives: COMPARATIVE BROADCASTING through the analysis of the organization and function of broadcasting systems in two or more nations; INTERNATIONAL BROADCASTING through the study of the patterns, purposes, extent, and effects of the flow of radio and television programming across national borders. These broadcasts may be designed for reception abroad and *intentionally* transmitted by a nation's *external service*, or may occur *accidentally* in the form of programming *spillover* between countries in geographic proximity.[7]

Implicit in both species of broadcasting research are the profound implications that radio and television programming have for national cultures. Engaging in comparative analyses of national broadcasting systems requires an open mind and, hopefully, nurtures a sensitivity to foreign cultures and ideologies. The enemy of this process, however, is *ethnocentrism*—the value judging of another culture as being inferior by the standards of one's own culture. Culture mapping figures prominently in comparative broadcasting analysis, as do crosscultural communication principles.

Crosscultural (sometimes known as trans- or intercultural) *communication* takes place between members of whole cultures, or when leaders of cultures are in contact with each other. It also is used in making a comparative base between cultures. Crosscultural communication tends to be formal; collective, planned, and one-way—usually from a small formalized group (like broadcasters) to a large informal group (such as the audience).[8] Since radio and television programming routinely crosses national borders and is traded in the international marketplace, it stands to reason that broadcasting from one culture can have substantial impact upon any alien cultural setting in which it is received. Edelstein makes an important distinction when he concludes that the study of the *transfer* of programming across national boundaries is international communication, while the study of the *effects* of this flow is crosscultural.[9]

When several distinct cultures (and languages) exist within a single nation, the culture having greatest access to the airwaves is in a position of dominance over the minority cultures relatively deprived of broadcast exposure. This tendency of members of one culture to seek such dominance over members of the same or a different culture is called *Cultural Imperialism*. It is characterized by the expansion or imposition of one culture's values, beliefs, assumptions, and language upon another culture; hence, cultural imperialism and cultural dependency always occur simultaneously.[10] These issues—together with the impact of technology on culture, and cultural stability and change—are serious world concerns. Nowhere is this truer than in developing nations and multi-cultural societies. These relationships will be discussed in later chapters.

Classifying Broadcasting Systems

A number of scholars have classified the various systems of national broadcasting found throughout the world according to typologies based on *ownership, control,* and *financing.*[11] OWNERSHIP, for example, may be by: (a) Government, (b) Public Corporation, (c) Private Enterprise, (d) Hybrid Arrangement (e.g., semi-state).

Regardless of ownership genus, all broadcasters are chartered by their own national governments to operate legally according to assigned frequencies, powers, and times. Those who operate without such authorization are called "clandestine broadcasters." CONTROL, therefore, may be thought of in terms of *social* control (the process of government regulation and licensing of broadcasters) and *operational* control (the fiduciary agent responsible for daily broadcast activities). The process of formal enfranchisement in effect makes these two facets of control inseparable.

Perhaps the most utilitarian typology is that proposed by Albert Namurois, based upon four *Modes of Control*. These are:[12]

1. State-operated directly by a government ministry, department, or administrative agency;
2. Public Corporation operated autonomously under state charter;
3. Public interest partnership (viz., semi-state) operated by legally chartered private corporations with state stock interests;
4. Private enterprise operated by private individuals or companies under government license with generally weak regulations.

This indicates that, with respect to telecommunications, governments always hold the power of social control. It also ultimately decides the *kinds* and *condi-*

tions of ownership; that is, the organizational or market structure of the system. For instance, shall there be only one broadcasting service (a monopoly), two (a duopoly), or a number in competition with each other (an oligopoly)? This means that more than one type of system may co-exist within a given nation.

From these kinds of decisions, consequently, flows national broadcasting policy with respect to programming and methods of FINANCING systems. No matter the country, broadcasting has only five possible *sources of revenue:*

1. State subsidization through taxes;
2. Annual license fees levied on receivers;
3. The sale of airtime to advertisers;
4. Direct payment from individuals and corporations in the form of memberships, subscriptions, donations, gifts, grants, and underwriting;
5. Any combination of the above.

But the most prominent feature of any broadcasting system is its *programming*. This is the public's principal contact with the broadcaster—a tangential one at best. Public consciousness about broadcasting is typically limited to conversations regarding program likes and dislikes, celebrities, and the occasional reaction, either random or organized, to specific broadcasts. In essence, broadcasting sets the agenda for significant proportions of both public debate and private discourse. To the broadcaster, however, programming is regarded as the end product of a system whose operational policies and structures are shaped by human will and national conditions.

UNESCO has developed a system of program classification which is recognized throughout the world.[13] Seven types were identified:

1. *Information*—news, commentary, public affairs, sports
2. *Advertising*—commercial and publicity announcements
3. *Education*—formal (in-school) and informal (at home) enlightenment
4. *Light Entertainment*—pop music, comedy, drama, serials, games
5. *Arts, Letters, and Sciences*—serious music, drama, documentaries, talk
6. *Ethnic Minority Broadcasts*—language courses, cultural programs, forums
7. *Special Audience Broadcasts*—children, religion, women, handicapped.

Programming Theories and Philosophies of Broadcasting

All classifications of the world's broadcasting systems are ultimately the handmaids of each nation's political and economic ethos. No matter the type of programming being broadcast, it is comprised of ideas. The question is: *whose* ideas? The answer lies in classical philosophical suppositions about the nature and degree of free expression a state should accord its citizens and media of mass communication.

The reason for differences in mass communication theories is tied to the existence of competing political and social structures among nation-states. All societies have laws which determine basic relationships between their citizens and their institutions, especially the mass media, as well as appropriate mechanisms of social control to enforce and adjust these interactions. Other reasons for a given nation adopting a specific media philosophy relate to its ability to financially support mass communication systems; its relative level of industrialization, urbanization, technological development, health care, education, and literacy; and the salience of its cultural heritage, folklore, and traditional values.

The classic Four Theories of the Press—Authoritarian, Libertarian, Soviet Communist, and Social Responsibility—attempted to classify the relative freedom of the world's media systems as they existed in 1956.[14] However, a more relevant global perspective on national media freedom in the geopolitical and technological environment of the 1980s has been provided by William A. Hachten, whose derivative Five Concepts of the World's Media are better suited to this book's purposes. The five are: *Authoritarian, Western, Communist, Revolutionary,* and *Developmental.*[15]

The AUTHORITARIAN media concept today governs broadcasting in many noncommunist dictatorships and is especially prevalent in Latin America. Authoritarianism is the world's oldest and most pervasive political ideal. The media can be owned either privately or by the state, with the government maintaining control over content through patenting media monopolies, licensing editorial gatekeepers, and prosecuting violations of censorship laws. Thus, under authoritarianism, the mass media function as instruments of the state by advancing the policy objectives of the government in power and by manipulating the information and entertainment received by its citizens. The leadership typically regards the media as its agents for establishing social order, keeping the public peace, squelching dissent, and discouraging diversity.

The WESTERN concept is the mirror image of authoritarianism. It synthesizes the libertarian ideals of the Age of Enlightenment with the 20th century notion that freedom and responsibility go hand in hand. The advent of broadcasting imposed new constraints on the libertarian principle of absolute freedom in that governments, as legitimate proprietors of the spectrum, inevitably became involved in regulating it in the public interest as they would other natural resources. Thus was born the social responsibility interpretation of freedom as being a privilege that carries with it an obligation to tell the truth and offer the public the widest possible range of opinions on all subjects. Whereas the libertarians believed in "freedom period," the proponents of social responsibility qualified it as "freedom if."

Today, this amalgam of ideals is primarily practiced in the affluent, literate, industrial democracies of North America, Western Europe, and Japan, where personal rights and free expression are protected by law and the mass media are allowed to operate independent of government. Ownership of the media is chiefly private, although public and some government communication services may exist—especially in the area of telecommunication. The main functions of the media under the Western concept are to supply the public with information and entertainment, to assist the free-market economy and media self-sufficiency through advertising, to insure that the media are editorially independent of government controls over news and programming, and to provide a public forum for political debate and for responsible criticisms of government.

Mass communications in the Soviet Union and the Eastern Bloc nations operate under the COMMUNIST concept, a modified form of authoritarianism. Its philosophical assumptions were provided by Hegel and Marx, but its implementation bears the markings of Lenin and Stalin. Although contemporary communism is more manifold than monolothic, the mass media in Marxist societies function according to totalitarian principles. These principles are often couched in libertarian language, however. The Soviet Constitution, for instance, guarantees its citizens "freedom of speech, of the press, and of assembly, meetings, street processions, and demonstrations." Sound familiar? The catch is that freedom, as defined here, means freedom to say what the state considers to be true. Hegel put it this way: "Man is free to know that he is not free; his actions are determined by history, society, and the state. Freedom exists *within* the state rather than *from* it." In practice, to speak or act against the state is, by definition, "irresponsible."

Communist ideology requires that all communication outlets be owned by the government and run by state ministries, with the top administrative and gatekeeping positions occupied by Party officials. Accordingly, the mass media function as instruments of state power and policy, Party leadership and information, social unity and official knowledge, and propaganda, agitation, and organization.

The REVOLUTIONARY concept of mass communication applies to illegal and underground media that are owned and operated by people intent on overthrowing the government they live under because their political, religious, and/or cultural interests are not being served. Revolutionaries of every ideological stripe have used outlaw media as anti-authoritarian tools for subverting the established order; yet there is irony in the fact that the new order which follows is often, though not always, itself authoritarian.

Revolutionary media reside outside of the target country more often than not. In a sense, all shortwave radio services whose propaganda is directed at adversary states or audiences can be thought of as adhering to Revolutionary precepts. Contemporary versions of revolutionary media come in several intriguing forms, including the use of photocopying machines, typewriters, and mimeographs for duplicating and distributing unlawful information by way of underground networks of dissidents—as in the case with the self-publishing (*samizdat*) press inside the Soviet Union. The ousting of the Shah of Iran by the Ayatollah Khomeini has been called "the first cassette revolution" because his recorded revolutionary speeches were smuggled into the country and played in the sactuary of the mosques.

Clandestine radio stations, illegally operated by political and religious groups, flourished during World War II,[16] and more recently were involved in the coups d'etat of many black African nations. Today, they are active throughout the Middle East. The "pirate" stations of Western Europe represent a kind of socioeconomic media revolt in which unlicensed broadcasters have attempted to circumvent the authorized radio and TV services by offering new programming formats and commercial competition. There is also an element of the Revolutionary concept at work when cultural minorities protest and even sabotage national broadcasting systems that restrict or banish them and their languages from the airwaves.

The DEVELOPMENTAL media concept grew out of authoritarianism, but its underlying purpose is demonstrably more positive and important than merely serving the power interests of totalitarian regimes or the market interests of advertising and entertainment industries. This theory, as its name denotes, has been operationalized mainly in the developing nations of the Third World. With nationbuilding as their shared goal, these newly formed states regard information as a vital resource best managed by a benevolent government toward the ends of improving the living conditions of their peoples and gaining national independence. It is also relevant in those societies where ethnic minorities wish to mobilize the mass media, particularly broadcasting, as a means of keeping their ancestral languages alive and achieving cultural independence from national media domination.

The mass media typically are owned by government and operated under the guidance of a central authority. This arrangement allows the media to be used as official instruments for forging social unity, political stability, economic growth, cultural pride, and national sovereignty. Television and especially radio are enlisted in the political leadership's fight against disease, poverty, illiteracy, and factionalism. Perhaps the most controversial aspects of the Third World's implementation of the Developmental concept are a penchant for censoring internal dissent and a desire to control the flow of international news both into and out of their sovereign territories.

These five concepts, regardless of the differences between them, all share the common purpose of serving the political and economic principles of the nations which adopt them. Each country's principles are then translated into an operational broadcasting policy. It is important, however, to distinguish between *regulation* and *policy*. According to communication scholar and attorney Don Le Duc, "*regulation* is that form of government that compels those entities over which it has legal jurisdiction to act or refrain from acting in the manner in which they would otherwise tend to act." By contrast, *policy* is "a long-term and continual process of legal guidance towards a clearly defined communication goal."[17] Regulation is therefore restrictive, prescribes through law what can and cannot be done legally, and offers enforcement measures. Policy, on the other hand, is goal-oriented, establishes procedures for attaining goals, and identifies the resources necessary to achieve the desired goals. In other words, a policy is implemented through laws, making regulation the *means* and policy the *end*.

A nation's broadcasting policy thus is shaped by its political economy and, in turn, determines the general orientation, gatekeeping attitudes, selfinterested goals, and programming of its radio and television services. Generally speaking, type of ownership is the most telling manifestation of a country's broadcasting policy. Table 1-4 summarizes world broadcasting systems by ownership typology and descriptive criteria.

The study of broadcasting on a world scale involves two fields of focus. One might be called the Micro-view, a close-up examination of a single broadcasting system within its national context. The other is the Macro-view, a wide-angle perspective of broadcasting as it occurs between nations and within the global arena. From these two levels of analysis, we are able to classify, compare, contrast, and evaluate national systems of broadcasting in terms of their respective structures, domestic functions, and operative philosophies. Simultaneously, we may acquire an understanding of broadcasting as a transnational phenomenon with the potential to envelop the entire planet.

The National Context: Political, Economic, and Sociocultural Dimensions

Broadcasting is perhaps a nation's most conspicuous social institution and cultural manifestation. So, too, is broadcasting an explicit reflection of a nation-state's political and economic order. To properly understand broadcasting as it occurs in a given country, one must begin by acquiring reliable information about the nation's location, size, climate, geography, population, ethnic composition, language(s), religions, heritage, indigenous culture, polity, degree of freedom, economy, industrial development, educational level, literacy rate, achievement in the arts, and geopolitical alignment in the world.

Any analysis of a given nation's broadcasting system may begin by asking four seminal questions: Who owns it? Who controls it? Who pays for its operation? Whose interests are best served by its programming? The answers, of course, will differ from country to country depending on their respective political philosophies, economic imperatives, levels of industrial-technological development, and a number of other sociocultural factors. One thing, however, is universal: broadcasting requires money and expertise. Accordingly, a nation's capacity to (a) purchase and maintain the requisite equipment, (b) financially support the system's operation, and (c) produce indigenous programming of professional quality and cultural relevance are measurable indicators of the effectiveness and sophistication of its broadcasting.

The Global Context: A Geopolitical Assessment of Broadcasting

Historically, broadcasting has been studied either on a country by country basis or according to region or continent. While these are entirely legitimate frames of reference, they do not necessarily take into account the impact of the working world's geopolitical alignments and machinations on national broadcasting endeavors. As the decade of the 1980s approached, increased attention was being

Table 1-4 Typological Synthesis and Summary

Analytical Criteria	Systemic Options by Ownership Type			
	Government	Public	Private	Hybrid
Market Model	Monopoly	Duopoly: Public Private	Public & Oligopoly:Private Mixed	Monopoly or Duopoly
Operational Control	Directly by government ministry	By Autonomous corporation chartered by government	By private entity with a government license	Semi-state corporation: State-owned transmission facilities operated by public/private company
Sources of Income	Subsidized by state funds (Taxes)	Receiver License fees and/or public funds and advertising	Advertising with some public funds	Combination of any two or more: Ads, gifts, fees or taxes
Programming Orientation	Elitist	Democratic	Popular	Survival of authentic & minority cultures
Prevalent Theory(ies)	Soviet Communist Authoritarian	Social Responsibility & Libertarian	Libertarian and S.R.	As per national theory public responsiveness
Gatekeeping Attitude	Authoritarian	Paternalistic	Permissive	Pluralistic
Policy Interests	Ideological	Enlightenment	Mass Appeal	Cultural and Marketplace
Programming Priorities by Type	1. Propaganda 2. Information 3. Education 4. Entertainment	1. Information 2. Education 3. Entertainment 4. Commercial	1. Commercial 2. Entertainment 3. Information 4. Education	1. National culture 2. Minority cultures 3. Entertainment 4. Information

paid to broadcasting as a cultural and diplomatic extension of national alliances based upon shared political strategies and economic status.

One reputable method of describing contemporary international relationships is the "three worlds" taxonomy.[18] For our purposes, a so-called "fourth world" will be added. These are defined as follows:

The First World—the industrialized democracies of the West;
The Second World—the Eastern bloc communist countries;
The Third World—the developing nations of Africa, Asia, and the Middle
    East, Central and South America;
The Fourth World— the stateless cultures existing within nations.[19]

The Four World's rubric imposes both logic and organization upon the global telecommunications context by collating ideologically-similar nations into rational groupings whose broadcasting theories, structures, and functions can be compared and contrasted.

Our framework for analyzing broadcasting around the world involves a description of each of the Four Worlds using the following criteria: (a) Prevailing Media Theory (b) Associated Ownership Typologies, (c) Financial Support Mechanisms (d) Dominant National Models, (e) Program Policy Orientation, (f) Programming Priorities, (g) Relative Operational Autonomy, (h) Organizational Structure.

The industrialized democracies of the Western alliance generally have free market economies, substantial aggregate and per capita wealth, and advanced levels of education and literacy. They also enjoy extensive civil and media liberties in the Libertarian tradition, although Social Responsibility modifications have been instituted, primarily in North America and Britain. First World broadcasting systems favor public and private modes of ownership, and are financed largely by license fees and advertising. Its dominant national models are the state-run French, the noncommercial British, and the advertiser-supported American. Considerable amounts of disposable income and leisure time have precipitated programming policies which support economic and diversionary goals. These are met through commercial messages, mass appeal entertainment and news, and some cultural or educational specials. Thus, broadcasters take full advantage of journalistic and creative freedom to the extent allowed by the marketplace. Most Western systems are organized along national and regional lines, with local stations prominent throughout North America. Examples of all three market models—monopolies, duopolies, and oligopolies—can be found in the First World.

Broadcasting in the Second World is owned and operated as a government monopoly according to Marxist principles. Financial support comes mainly from tax revenues, although advertisements by state enterprises contribute additional income. The Soviet broadcasting model can be seen in familiar form in most communist countries, thus accounting for programming policies which yield information and entertainment high in ideological content. Because all state activities, including broadcasting, are centralized under Communist Party authority, the concept of autonomy is one which turns on itself. In practice, programmers promote Party doctrine and government policy, yet are free to criticize state services that fail the public.

The *Third World* nations constitute a continuum of development ranging from the less developed countries (LDC) to those whose natural resources are hastening industrialization. Many are newly independent states engaged in the mission of nation-building. Colonialism and imperialism have left the Third World a legacy of poverty, illiteracy, and institutional debilitation. Responsibility for establishing political and economic independence has been assumed by cadres of the educated elite who necessarily have adopted Authoritarian means to forge national identity and facilitate development. Broadcasting policy throughout the Third World is, therefore, oriented toward the goals of social and economic advancement through programming designed to educate. Nevertheless, entertainment programming, largely imported, is both plentiful and popular.

Broadcasting in the emerging nations of Africa and Asia is almost entirely in the hands of government, modelled after British and French colonial systems. Their radio and TV services are typically organized as monopolies, and rely upon license fees and public subsidization. In Latin America, however, broadcasters have adopted the US model of private ownership and commercialization. While these operations often give the appearance of being either duopolies or competitive oligopolies, governments throughout the Third World exercise tight controls over content and have structured their broadcasting systems in a unitary fashion. As a result, autonomy is marginal.

It is more difficult to apply our eight criteria to the stateless cultures of the *Fourth World* in that they may be found in nations throughout the First, Second, and Third Worlds. Ideology thus yields to a pragmatic responsiveness in most pluralistic broadcasting situations, since it presupposes that all national governments have singular responsibility for serving all their constituents, including the cultural and linguistic needs of indigenous minorities. In fact, few countries of the world are ethnically homogeneous. The number, size, and salience of racial and ethnic groups differ from nation to nation. Where bilingual and specialized broadcasting services have been established, their operations are usually regional or localized, their programming evidentially cultural. Fourth World broadcasting policy is inherently devoted to the survival of authentic cultures and ancestral languages.

Table 1-5 summarizes national broadcasting within its global context by applying our eight selected criteria to the Four Worlds geopolitical framework.

A METHODOLOGY FOR ANALYZING AND COMPARING NATIONAL BROADCASTING SYSTEMS

World broadcasting, as an institution and as a process, may be studied on a *case* (country by country) basis, a *comparative* (country with country) basis, or an

Table 1-5 Descriptors of National Broadcasting Vis-a-Vis Geopolitical Context

Telecommunication Criteria	First World	Second World	Third World	Fourth World
Prevailing Media Theory	Western	Communist	Authoritarian Developmental	Developmental Revolutionary
Associated Typologies	Private Public	Government State	Government Some private	Regional Authority or Public/Private
Financial Support Mechanism	Advertising License Fees Taxes	Taxes Government rev. Some advertising	Advertising & Taxes Fees, Ads & Taxes Government Revenue US (in So. America)	Taxes Fees Advertising
Dominant National Model(s)	British (noncommercial/ public) French (commercial/ state-run) American (commercial/ private)	USSR	British & French (in Africa and Asia)	The national system
Program Policy Orientation	Economic and Diversionary	Political and Ideological	National Development (Pol. Soc-ec. Cul)	Cultural Protection Survival of Authentic culture & language
Programming Priorities By Type	Commercial Mass Entertainment Mass Information Educational & cul.	Propaganda Informational Educational Cultural	Educational Mass entertainment Informational commercial	Cultural Informational Educational Entertainment
Degree of Freedom/Content	High	Low	Marginal	Moderate
Organizational Structure	Multi-level: National Regional Local	Centralized: Gov't control	Unitary: Direct or Indirect Gov't control	Regional Authority or Local Surrogate

international (country to countries) basis. What follows is a methodology for the systematic analysis and comparison of broadcasting as it occurs in nations from all corners of the globe.

Before national broadcasting systems can be compared and contrasted, a case study must first be completed on broadcasting in each country selected for analysis. This approach recognizes that virtually all national broadcasting is affected to some degree by international factors—be they geographic, cultural, political, or economic in nature. The significance that national and global contexts hold for all of the world's broadcasters, therefore, must be documented. This method of comparative analysis prescribes the following four-step sequence:

1. Ascertain the national context of each system chosen for analysis;
2. Determine each nation's appropriate global alignment;
3. Conduct a case study of each nation's broadcasting system using a set of descriptive criteria;
4. Compare the data of selected case studies and generalize about significant similarities and differences.

But several requirements must be met in implementing such a methodology. First, criteria must be established as a basis for identifying and evaluating similarities and differences existing among national broadcasting systems. Second, the researcher must strive for "equivalence" (in terms of concepts, semantics, data analysis, situations, measurement, and reporting) when selecting the key variables used for comparison and contrast.[20] In other words, the same set of conditions and units of measurement chosen to describe and analyze broadcasting in one country must be similarly applied to all other countries selected for study if meaningful generalizations about commonalities and variances between them are to be made. Or, following the often repeated advice, "only compare apples to apples, not apples to oranges."

Several chronic problems, nevertheless, confront comparative broadcasting research. One is that uniform, accurate, and up-to-date information on broadcasting activities is not available for all nations. The UN and UNESCO regularly compile and publish data on mass communications worldwide. These, however, are often based upon information provided by national governments that is not always reliable or current. Then, too, some governments, notably totalitarian ones, simply refuse to cooperate with outsiders attempting to obtain even the most innocuous literature and descriptive facts about their mass media.

A second problem area, alluded to above, hinges on the notion of equivalence. An example of some gravity to this field is the concept of *freedom*. The Western democracies relate freedom to individual civil liberties and political rights—such activities as voting, free speech, privacy, and fair trials. While these ideals may be said to exist in practically all societies, at least in rhetorical fashion, the Western concept of freedom allows for the people to criticize with impunity the political, economic, and religious systems under which they live. Also allowed are open public discussion, a free and adversary press, opposing and competing political parties, an independent judiciary that often decides against the government, and an absence of political imprisonment. By contrast, the concept of freedom in totalitarian settings often is cast in rhetorical expressions like "freedom from want or freedom from fear."[21] Or, in the Hegelian sense, freedom *within* rather than *from* the state; freedom to know that one is not free.

Such disparities make equivalence difficult when using a concept like freedom as a comparative criterion. Difficult, but not impossible. By assessing *relative freedom* between and among countries, it is possible to gain equivalence in terms of degree if not always in absolute or semantic terms.

The Methodology

In an attempt to ameliorate problems of equivalence and other constraints endemic to comparative broadcasting scholarship, the criteria and data employed in the following methodology have been drawn from authoritative international sources such as UNESCO, Freedom House, the *World Radio TV Handbook*, official almanacs, *The Europa Year Book, Political Handbook of the World*, and the works of reputable broadcast scholars. These political, economic, sociocultural, and broadcasting indicators are cited in Table 1-6 for the purpose of serving as guidelines of analysis.

Freedom House has identified and defined seven POLITICAL SYSTEMS in existence throughout the world. These are:

1. *Decentralized Multiparty*—powers are held by people at two or more levels of the political system and dissent is legitimated through opposition parties (Examples: USA, Switzerland, and Brazil);
2. *Centralized Multiparty*—central government organizes lower levels of the government for reasons of efficiency (Examples: Japan, Finland, and Ireland);
3. *Dominant Party*—allows democratic forms but structures the process so that opposition groups realistically cannot achieve power (Examples: South Korea, Egypt, and Mexico);
4. *Communist One-Party*—states having only the Communist Party (Examples: USSR, Vietnam, and Cuba);
5. *Socialist One-Party*—states ruled by Marxist-Leninist elites but not entirely communist (Examples: Iraq and The Congo);
6. *Nationalist One-Party*—the state is controlled by a single party but usually rejects revolutionary ideologies and totalitarian controls (Examples: Kenya and Liberia);
7. *Nonparty*—states which may be governed democratically, but more commonly are ruled by either Nonmilitary (Jordan and Saudi Arabia) or Military

Table 1-6   A Methodological Schema for Analyzing National Broadcasting in Context

National Criteria	Political, Economic, and Social Indicators

Capital City: _____   Population: _____

Political system: ___Decentralized Multiparty; ___Centralized Multiparty;
___Dominant Party; ___Communist One-Party; ___Socialist
One Party; ___Nationalist One-Party; ___Nonparty

Geopolitical Alignment: ___First World; ___Second World; ___Third World

Political Rights: ___Free; ___Partly Free; ___Not Free

Civil Liberties: ___Free; ___Partly Free; ___Not Free

Comparative Freedom: Less Free Than_____
As Free As_____
Freer Than_____

Economic System: ___Capitalist; ___Noninclusive Capitalist; ___Capitalist Statist;
___Mixed Capitalist-Socialist; ___Socialist; ___Noninclusive
Socialist; ___Mixed Socialist-Capitalist

Gross National Product (GNP) in US $_____

Per Capita Income in US $_____ Monetary Unit per US Dollar_____

Major Ethnic Groups: _____

Official Language(s): _____

Religions: _____

Literacy Rate: _____%   Deaths/1,000 Births: _____   Life Expectancy:___M/___F

National Criteria	Broadcasting Indicators

Market Model: ___Monopoly; ___Duopoly; ___Oligopoly / Ownership:_____

Major Broadcasting Organization(s): _____

Sources of Income: ___Advertising; ___Government; ___License Fee(s)

Number of Receivers: Radio_____/TV_____(% in Color _____)

Fee per Year in US $: Radio_____/ B&W TV_____/ Color TV_____

Regulatory Body: _____

Operative Legislation: _____

Programming Priorities: e.g., 1. Information / 2. Entertainment / 3. Education

Percentage of Imported Programming: _____ %

Principal Language(s) Broadcast: _____

Minority Language(s) Broadcast: _____

TV Systems Adopted: *Lines*: ___525/___625/___819 *Color*: ___NTSC/___PAL/___SECAM

(Argentina and Pakistan) persons having no formal affiliation with a political party.[22]

The seven ECONOMIC SYSTEMS of the world classified by Freedom House are:

1.   *Capitalist*—developed states that rely on the operation of the market and on private provision for industrial welfare (Examples: USA and Canada);

2. *Noninclusive Capitalist*—societies in which less than half of the population is included in modern capitalist economy, while the remainder is living in their traditional economy (Examples: Liberia and Thailand);

3. *Capitalist Statist*—nations having a large productive enterprise owned by government because of either development philosophy or dependence on a major resource, like oil (Examples: Brazil and Saudi Arabia);

4. *Mixed Capitalist-Socialist*—nominally capitalistic states whose governments or other nonprofit institutions provide large scale social services for egalitarian purposes (Examples: Israel, The Netherlands, and Sweden);

5. *Socialist*—states whose entire national economy is under direct or indirect government control (Examples: USSR and the Peoples Republic of China);

6. *Noninclusive Socialist*—states with small, socialized, yet modern economies, and large preindustrial economies organized around tradition (Examples: India and Madagascar);

7. *Mixed Socialist*—proclaimed socialist states with large portions of their economies in private hands (Examples: Egypt and Poland.[23]

Having classified a nation's political and economic systems, it is a simple task to assign it to its proper geopolitical status within either the first, second or third world. A systems analysis of a nation's broadcasting arrangement requires using criteria and measurement indicators to ascertain ownership, control, financing, regulation, extent of services, programming policy and the like.

The final step entails comparing compiled data, criterion by criterion, of two or more nations in order to form generalizations about how, to what degree, and why their broadcasting systems match or differ. Naturally, the national and international contexts of all broadcasting situations selected for comparative analysis must be taken into consideration in formulating one's generalizations. The process further leaves some latitude for interpretation, but most of the descriptive data, if accurate, normally should yield results that are academically valid and reliable. This Methodological Schema will be used to organize national and broadcasting data on the countries chosen for comparative analysis in Chapters 3, 4, and 5.

CHAPTER 1 NOTES

[1] Joe Roizen, "As the World Turns . . . Televising The Royal Wedding", *Broadcast Communications*, October 1981, p. 50.

[2] "DBS: Sailing Through", *Broadcasting*, June 14, 1982, p. 7.

[3] "Satellite-To-Home TV Gets Backing of FCC", Buffalo (NY) *Courier-Express*, April 22, 1981, p. 2.

[4] "Broadcasting: TV By Satellite", *InterMedia*, January 1980, vol. 8, No. 1, pp. 7–8.

[5] Sydney W. Head, with Christopher H. Sterling, *Broadcasting in America: A Survey of Television, Radio, and New Technologies* (Boston: Houghton Mifflin Company, 1982), Chapter 2.

[6] *World Radio TV Handbook 1982*, (Annual), vol. 36 (New York: Billboard, 1982), pp. 386–432.

[7] These definitions are the author's own. See also: Heinz-Dietrich Fischer, "Forms and Functions of Supranational Communication", in Heinz-Dietrich Fischer and John C. Merrill, eds., *International and Intercultural Communication* (New York: Hastings House Publishers, 1976), pp. 9–11; and, Alex S. Edelstein, *Comparative Communication Research* (Beverly Hills, CA: Sage Publications, 1982), pp. 13–15.

[8] Michael H. Prosser, *The Cultural Dialogue: An Introduction to Intercultural Communication* (Boston: Houghton Mifflin Co., 1978), pp. 42ff. and 293ff.

[9] Edelstein, *op. cit.,* pp. 14–15.

[10] Prosser, *op. cit.,* pp. 8–9 and 295.

[11] Chief among these are, in alphabetical order: John R. Bittner, *Broadcasting: An Introduction* (Englewood Cliffs, NJ: Prentice-Hall, 1980), ch. 10; Giraud Chester, Garnet R. Garrison, and Edgar E. Willis, *Television and Radio in Society* (Englewood Cliffs, NJ: Prentice-Hall, 1978), pp. 170–171; Fred Fedler, *An Introduction to the Mass Media* (New York: Harcourt Brace Jovanovich, Inc., 1978), pp. 381–385; Eugene S. Foster, *Understanding Broadcasting* (Reading, MA: Addison-Wesley Publishers, 1978), pp. 405–409; Sydney W. Head, with Christopher H. Sterling, *Broadcasting in America: A Survey of Television, Radio and New Technologies* (Boston: Houghton Mifflin Co., 1982), p. 9; Alan Wells, ed., *Mass Communications: A World View* (Palo Alto, CA: Mayfield Publishing Co., 1974), pp. 3–9.

[12] Albert Namurois, *Structure and Organization of Broadcasting in the Framework of Radio Communications,* EBU Monograph No. 8, Legal and Administrative Series (Geneva, Switzerland: European Broadcasting Union, 1972).

[13] Sydney W. Head and Thomas F. Gordon, "Programming Around the World", in Charles Sherman and Donald Browne, eds., *Issues in International Broadcasting,* BEA Monograph No. 2 (Washington, DC: Broadcast Education Association, 1976), pp. 46–47.

[14] Fred S. Siebert, Theodore Peterson and Wilbur Schramm, *Four Theories of the Press* (Urbana: University of Illinois Press, 1956 and 1963). The following discussion is drawn from this source.

[15] William A. Hachten, *The World News Prism: Changing Media, Clashing Ideology* (Ames, Iowa: The Iowa State University Press, 1981), Chapter 5. All information and quotes in this section come from this and the above source.

[16] J. Herbert Altschull, "Government Dialogue Through the Mass Media", in Fred L. Casmir, ed., *Intercultural and International Communication* (Washington, DC: University Press of America, Inc., 1978), p. 687.

[17] Don R. LeDuc, "Transforming Principles into Policy", *Journal of Communication* 30(2), Spring 1980, pp. 197–198.

[18] Marc U. Porat, "Communication Policy in an Information Society", in Glen O. Robinson, ed., *Communications for Tomorrow: Policy Perspectives for the 1980s* (New York: Praeger Publishers, 1978), p. 45. The "three worlds" taxonomy was employed also by UNESCO's International (MacBride) Commission for the Study of Communication Problems, as well as for other international communication events—like "World Communications: Decisions for the Eighties", a conference held at the University of Pennsylvania's Annenberg School of Communicatios, May 12–14, 1980.

[19] For this definition of "fourth world", see William F. Mackey, "Language Policy and Language Planning", *Journal of Communication* 29:2 (Spring 1979), p. 50. It should be noted that the expression "fourth world" also has been used by political scientists to mean the poorest of the poor nations. However, the former definition is operative throughout this text.

[20] Edelstein, *op. cit.,* pp. 15–17.

[21] Raymond D. Gastil, ed., *Freedom in the World: Political Rights and Civil Liberties 1980* (New York: Freedom House, 1980), pp. 4–5.

[22] *Ibid.,* pp. 44–45.

[23] *Ibid.,* pp. 42–43.

Intergovernmental and Nongovernmental Organizations in World Broadcasting

The world of mass telecommunication is populated with organizational acronyms, an alphabet soup of international and regional bodies concerned with a host of legal, technical, policy, developmental, and professional matters pertinent to broadcasting. One way through this bureaucratic maze is to divide the world's plethora of communication associations into two functional classifications. These have been termed INTERGOVERNMENTAL and NONGOVERNMENTAL organizations.[1]

Intergovernmental. As the word implies, Intergovernmental agencies are formed from agreements entered into by groups of nations, with each government sending an official delegation to represent its national policy. This type of organization typically addresses a specific facet of telecommunication, such as (a) political, (b) technical, or (c) proprietary concerns. The involvement of national governments through written contracts means that the actions and decisions taken by Intergovernmental organizations often carry the weight of law and/or perform regulatory functions.

Nongovernmental. These unofficial organizations usually are created by national representatives from common trade, industrial, or professional fields within broadcasting. Lacking the legal authority to enact laws or to formulate official policy, their interests are confined therefore to (a) administrative, (b) technical, or (c) programming areas of broadcasting. Unlike their Intergovernmental counterparts, the members of Nongovernmental associations come together voluntarily to pursue shared professional objectives rather than through official accords established between governments. Although such groups are clearly not governmental entities, their memberships may nevertheless include officials from national telecommunications organizations. And despite the fact that many call themselves "unions," the word denotes administrative rather than labor activities.

Fairly formal lines of procedural demarcation exist between Intergovernmental and Nongovernmental organizations. For instance, members of Nongovernmental organizations may not participate in Intergovernmental proceedings, but on occasion they may be invited to sit in as nonvoting observers or be asked to file written briefs on issues under consideration. Similar protocol obtains for representatives from Intergovernmental agencies attending Nongovernmental meetings. Generally speaking, relations between the two types of broadcasting organizations are cordial, with Nongovernmental bodies often referring specific problems to Intergovernmental authorities for action.

This chapter describes the histories, objectives, and roles of four Intergovernmental organizations critical to the international regulation and development of mass telecommunications, and nine Nongovernmental confederations representative of the major broadcasting regions the world over. The amount of attention

Table 2-1   A Taxonomy of World Broadcasting Organizations

Classification	Political	Technical	Proprietary	Administrative		Programming	
Intergovernmental	UN *UNESCO	*ITU *INTELSAT CEPT	*UNESCO *WIPO				
Nongovernmental		ISO IEC		EBU OIRT ABU URTNA ASBU CBA	URI IAAB IBI NANBA CBU	CISAC IFPA UNDA WACB OTI/SIN Prix Italia	OOC FIFA IMMI IIC

Alphabetical Key To Above Organizations:
ABU—Asian-Pacific Broadcasting Union
ASBU—Arab States Broadcasting Union
CBA—Commonwealth Broadcasting Union
CBU—Caribbean Broadcasting Union
CEPT—European Conference of Post and Telecommunications Administrators
CISAC—International Confederation of Societies of Authors and Composers
EBU—European Broadcasting Union
FIFA—International Federation of Football Associations
IAAB—Inter-American Association of Broadcasters (from Central & South America)
IBI—International Broadcasting Institute (scholars and professionals)
IEC—International Electrotechnical Commission (standards for equipment)
IFPA—International Federation of the Phonograph Industry
IIC—International Institute of Communications, Ltd. (research and scholarship)
IMMI—International Mass Media Institute (consultancy, education and research)
INTELSAT—International Telecommunications Satellite Organization
ISO—International Standards Organization (for film, video, acoustics and pitch)
ITU—International Telecommunication Union (specturm regulation and allocation)
NANBA—North American National Broadcasters Association
OIRT—International Radio and Television Organization
OOC—Olympic Organizing Committee
OTI/SIN—Organization of Latin American Television/Latin American News Service
Prix Italia—Italian award for excellence in cultural programming in Europe
UN—United Nations
UNDA—International Catholic Association for Radio and Television
UNESCO—United Nations Educational, Scientific and Cultural Organization
URI—International Radio and Television University (an OIRT affiliate)
URTNA—Union of National Radio and Television Organizations of Africa
WACB—World Association for Christian Broadcasters
WIPO—World Intellectual Property Organization (copyright enforcement)

given each is commensurate with its status and significance within the totality of world broadcasting.

Table 2-1 categorizes an inventory of significant broadcasting organizations by assigning each to its most relevant domain within either the Intergovernmental or the Nongovernmental realm.[2]

INTERGOVERNMENTAL ORGANIZATIONS: REGULATION AND DEVELOPMENT

The United Nations, despite its chronic inadequacies and political impotence, nevertheless must be considered the closest that humankind has come to creating a viable world government. Its humanitarian programs have contributed to peace and tangible socioeconomic progress throughout much of the world. The UN's direct involvement in world broadcasting, however, has been limited largely to the political issues and implications attending satellite communication. These are necessarily complex, given that satellites use international orbital space, transcend national frontiers, and can be used for militaristic purposes. Hence, much UN attention has been devoted to sponsoring a series of global conferences on "the peaceful uses of outer space." But world broadcasting is most vitally affected by the work of three Specialized Agencies of the UN—the ITU, UNESCO, and WIPO. A fourth, INTELSAT, is a UN-formed telecommunication service.

The International Telecommunication Union (ITU)

Each nation has a state agency for licensing and regulating its own wired and wireless media. The U.S. has the FCC. Canada has its Canadian Radio-television and Telecommunications Commission. Britain relies on the Home Office. In most countries, such authority resides in their PTT (post-telegraph-telephone or telecommunications) administrations. Worldwide telecommunication regulation is carried out by a similar but more constrained body called the International Telecommunication Union. The ITU's development parallels that of the telegraph and telephone. In 1865, 20 European nations conferred in Paris and signed an agreement called the International Telegraph Convention. A decade later, the International Telegraph Union was formed to coordinate telegraph (and, later, telephone) transmissions across national borders. When wireless emerged at the turn of the century, 27 governments adopted a similar pact at the 1906 International Radio-Telegraph Conference in Berlin, and later formed their own union. In 1932, the wired and wireless unions merged under a single International Telecommunication Convention, and the current ITU was created.[3]

But it was not until its 1947 Atlantic City conference, shortly after becoming a special UN agency, that the ITU articulated its overall aims and purposes. Specifically, its members agreed:

- to maintain and extend international cooperation for the improvement and rational use of telecommunications of all kinds;
- to promote the development of technical facilities and their most efficient operation with a view to improving the efficiency of telecommunication services, increasing their usefulness, and making them, so far as possible, generally available to the public;
- to harmonize the actions of nations in the attainment of those common ends.[4]

The tasks of the ITU fall under five main headings: Regulation, Research and Standards, Information, International Frequency Register, and Development. The means for attaining the above objectives were specified through the functions that the ITU set forth for itself in its 1965 Convention. These are:

1. Effective allocations of the radio frequency spectrum and registration of radio frequency assignments;
2. Coordinating efforts to eliminate harmful interference between radio stations of different countries and to improve the use made of the radio frequency spectrum;
3. Fostering collaboration with respect to the establishment of the lowest possible rates;
4. Fostering the creation, development, and improvement of telecommunication equipment and networks in new or developing countries by every means at its disposal, especially its participation in the appropriate programs of the United Nations;
5. Promoting the adoption of measures for ensuring the safety of life through the cooperation of telecommunication services;
6. Undertaking studies, making regulations, adopting resolutions, formulating recommendations and opinions, and collecting and publishing information concerning telecommunications matters benefiting all Members and Associate Members.[5]

The ITU today offers technical expertise, conducts research, and arranges financing to assist emerging nations in building telecommunication systems. It also trains personnel to operate and manage national communication facilities. By 1984, 158 nations were ITU members.[6]

The organization of the ITU is structured around six components: (a) The Plenipotentiary Conference, (b) The Administrative Conferences, (c) The Administrative Council, (d) The International Consultative Committees, (e) The International Frequency Registration Board (IFRB), and (f) The General Secretariat.[7]

The supreme authority of the ITU is *The Plenipotentiary Conference*. It is comprised of representatives from all member nations, and meets every 5 to 8 years to review and, if need be, revise the entire International Telecommunication Convention. It is empowered to establish ITU's budget and approve all accounts. It also elects the Administrative Council, the International Frequency Registration Board, the Secretary General, and the Deputy Secretary General.

The Administrative Conferences are either international or regional in scope, meeting periodically to consider specific telecommunications matters. World administrative conferences address specific telecommunication questions, placed on their agenda by the Administrative Council, that have worldwide implications for any of the four areas of ITU jurisdiction—viz., Radio, Telegraph, Telephone, and Additional Radio Regulations. Worldwide administrative conferences also review and prescribe the activities of the IFRB. Regional conferences deal only with questions affecting a specific geographic area.

Of critical importance to world broadcasting are the World Administrative Radio Conferences (WARC). General WARCs are held at 20-year intervals, giving the representatives from all member states the opportunity to discuss and act upon global telecommunication issues. The most recent general WARC, held in Geneva in 1979, reviewed international use of the entire frequency spectrum and established long-range policy covering marine, mobile, aeronautical, broadcast, and satellite communication activities. (Specific aspects and results of the 1979 WARC will be dealt with in future chapters as their relevance to topics under discussion warrants.) In addition, limited-subject WARCs are convened more frequently, as the timeliness and urgency of an issue demands. For instance, in 1977 WARC negotiated an international treaty which placed the operation of DBS and conventional communication satellites in the 12 GHz band of the electromagnetic spectrum.

The Administrative Council meets for a month every spring to conduct the ITU's administrative affairs in between meetings of the Plenipotentiary Conferences. At the time of its creation in 1947, the Council was comprised of 18 members. It later grew to 25. During the 1970s, four more members were added in response to demands from Third World governments for better representation. By 1984, 41 member nations were represented on the Administrative Council, each having one vote. Its work may be divided into three categories: external relations, coordination, and administration. The first entails maintaining good relationships between the ITU and other specialized agencies of the UN involved in allied international endeavors. Then, the Council meets to coordinate the work of the Union's permanent organs, such as arranging conferences and preparing the annual report. Lastly, it is responsible for writing regulations for ITU's administrative and financial activities, reviewing and approving budgets, and supervision the functions of the Secretariat, the consultative committees, and the IFRB.

The International Consultative Committees set the technical specifications for all telecommunication equipment. These responsibilities are split between the International Telephone and Telegraph Consultative Committee (CCITT) and the International Radio Consultative Committee (CCIR), which meet every 3 to 5 years. Of most import to world broadcasting is the CCIR, whose duties are "to study technical and operating questions relating specifically to radio communication and to issue recommendations on them.'' Its supreme organ is a Plenary Assembly, which meets every 3 years and includes a Director and the following chaired Study Groups: (a) Spectrum utilization and monitoring, (b) Space research and radioastronomy, (c) Fixed service at frequencies below 30 MHz, (d) Fixed service using communication satellites, (e) Propagation in nonionized media, (f) Ionospheric propagation, (g) Standard frequency and time-signal services, (h) Mobile services, (i) Fixed service using radio-relay systems, (j) Broadcasting service (sound), including audio-recording and satellite applications, and (k) Broadcasting service (television), including video-recording and satellite applications.

The Plenary Assembly chooses questions for the Study Groups to deal with, although they also may be submitted by an ITU conference, another consultative committee, or the IFRB. The Study Groups prepare a ''study program,'' which is sent out to ITU members for comment. The returned comments are discussed, and a report or recommendation is drafted and sent to all participating parties. The final draft is then forwarded to the Plenary Assembly, who may reject it, modify it, or accept it and pass it on to the administration as a recommendation.

The International Frequency Registration Board (IFRB) functions, ideally, as an arbitrator of the spectrum's use by all nations of the world. It does so by maintaining an international Master Register of frequency use, a kind of clearing-house process that enables individual nations to activate frequencies without creating interference for other users. Having 11 members originally, the Board's membership was reduced to five, along with its budget, in 1965. The individuals who sit on the IFRB are required to be highly qualified by virtue of technical training in radio and practical experience in frequency assignment and utilization. Its five members are elected by the Plenipotentiary Conference—one from each of the world's major geographic sections. Although they must be knowledgeable about their respective regions, they are not representatives of their home countries. On the contrary, as custodians of an international public resource, a high degree of objectivity is demanded of all IFRB members. The IFRB elects its own chair and vice chair for 1-year terms and has its own specialized secretariat.

The General Secretariat makes the organization run on a day to day basis. Its executive consists of a Secretary General and a Deputy Secretary General who are elected by the Plenipotentiary Conference. The Secretary General, an agent also of the Administrative Council, is responsible for all aspects of the Union's managerial and financial affairs. His duties include appointing and supervising the work of a 1200-person staff. The Secretariat has six departments; Personnel, Finance, Conferences and Common Services, Computer, External Relations, and Technical Cooperation. Lastly, the Secretary General may participate in all ITU conferences and is the Union's legal representative and official welcomer.

Like nearly all organizations in world broadcasting, the ITU publishes several official organs, in addition to innumerable rules, regulations, and documents. Chief among these is the TELECOMMUNICATION JOURNAL, published monthly in English, French, and Spanish editions. It covers news of the activities of the ITU and its members, technical advances, reception conditions, forthcoming meetings, articles on space communications, and the regulatory aspects of telecommunication—as well as a bibliography of telecommunication articles appearing in the scientific press. Further, the IFRB furnishes data for another important ITU publication, the INTERNATIONAL FREQUENCY LIST, containing all requirements recorded in the Master Register and the weekly IFRB circulars.

The ITU's operating funds come from the contributions of its member governments, each of which selects a contributory fee-class based on an amount appropriate to its national wealth and ability to pay. In terms of governance, the member nations of the ITU agree upon the rules for using telecommunications worldwide. These rules become a matter of record in the International Telecommunication Convention and the four Regulation documents covering telephone, telegraph, and all forms of radio communication. Nations who ratify these agreements vow in principle to abide by them. In practice, however, many countries, like the U.S., require separate treaties for specific regulations; other nations may have signed the ITU Convention with certain "reservations" stipulated or conditions waived.

A review of ITU practices and policies over the past three decades reveals some interesting trends. Its traditional role was to facilitate the interconnection of national telegraph, telephone, and radio systems. This entailed convening international conferences, discussing problems, and establishing rules and regulations to solve them. The ITU's more recent role has expanded into assisting in the national development of telecommunication systems.

This transition is due mainly to the entrance of the developing nations into the ITU. The accompanying demands of the Third World newcomers eventually led to changes in the organizational structure and function of the ITU. For example, the emerging nations became a majority within the Union and gradually realized the importance of telecommunication technology to their national development missions. The two main structural changes that occurred in the ITU were: (a) the addition of more member nations to the Administrative Council—from the original 18 to 36, and (b) the reduction of the IFRB from 11 to five members, though its complete elimination had been proposed. The ensuing changes in the Union's functions centered around Article 4 of the 1965 Convention (see page 28), which expanded ITU's role in development assistance.

A string of events makes these modifications clearer in retrospect. The first was the linking of telecommunications to the national development process. Second was an awakening by ITU's Third World parties to their collective political strength within the organization. Next came the developing nations' push in the UN for a redistribution of the world's resources from the rich North to the poor South under the aegis of the New International Economic Order, which translated into demands for a similar reallocation of communication and knowledge—i.e., the New World Information Order. The most recent event has been the Third World's call for equal access to and more equitable allocation of the electromagnetic spectrum and orbital positions for prospective satellites.[8]

In *summation,* ITU's principle tasks are:

1. to establish binding rules and regulations concerning the use of telecommunication systems;
2. to conduct research and set nonbinding standards for telecommunication technology;
3. the dissemination of information relative to the legal and technical use of telecommunications;
4. providing aid to developing nations engaged in building domestic telecommunication systems.

A succinct description of how the ITU works has been offered by George A. Codding, Jr., who writes:

> delegates from member countries meet to revise the rules and regulations as the need has arisen and study committees composed of experts from member countries carry out the necessary research and set standards. The Secretariat provides the infrastructure necessary for holding conferences and meeting and for dissemination of information; the IFRB helps administrations to select and use radio frequencies without causing harmful interference with the stations of other countries. And the cost is relatively small for the services rendered.[9]

The role of the ITU in world broadcasting policies and practices is vital yet incomplete. It has done an admirable job of coordinating, moderating, logging, and reporting on a multiplicity of telecommunication activities, issues, and problems. It also has maintained the delicate balance between the concern for communication autonomy by sovereign nations while providing leadership in maximizing international access to the spectrum in a fair and effective manner.

But two needs must be redressed. One is a better spirit of cooperation and compromise on the parts of both the industrial and developing countries within the ITU. Another is for the ITU to have legal jurisdiction and enforcement powers—granted to it by international law—over all nations engaged in telecommunication activities, not just consensual authority over those belonging to the United Nations.

A new International Telecommunication Convention was signed by ITU's member states at the 12th Plenipotentiary Conference in Nairobi during the fall of 1983. Taking effect on January 1, 1984, the new agreement creates a regulatory framework to take the ITU well into the 1990s. Significant changes were made to help the ITU to better regulate global telecommunications. These included:

- electing the directors of the international consultation committees at the Plenipotentiary Conferences;
- changing the ITU financial structure so that rich nations can contribute more money, and the LDCs less, than before;
- increasing ITU's Administrative Council from 36 to 41 members;
- adopting Arabic as an official language—thus joining English, Chinese, Spanish, French, and Russian;
- reviewing the long-term future of the IFRB as well as ITU policies for planning and allocating frequencies.

The 1983 Plenipotentiary also recommended ways to strengthen technical cooperation and assistance to developing nations through a better regional ITU presence in the Third World. It plans to achieve the latter goal by offering more funding through the UN Development Program. The ITU hopes to raise its status by taking these measures and thereby placing itself on an equal footing with other specialized agencies of the UN. The Nairobi conference concluded by choosing new officers and scheduling 15 global (WARC) and regional (RARC) meetings to be held throughout the 1980s. These WARCs and RARCs will be dealt with fully in the contexts of Chapters 6 (the Third World) and 9 (satellite broadcasting).[10]

United Nations Educational, Scientific and Cultural Organization (UNESCO)

UNESCO was established on November 4, 1946, when its constitution was ratified by 20 nations. By the early 1980s, it had grown to an organization having 154 member states, a $200 million annual budget, and modern headquarters in Paris. UNESCO's daily work is carried out by a Secretariat. Its various programs are determined by the full membership and supervised by a 45-member Executive Board.[11] UNESCO's involvement in world communication is implicit in its name; but as one examines its constitution, organizational structure, and many activities, that role becomes more explicit.

Article 1 of UNESCO's Constitution defines part of its mission as being to "collaborate in the work of advancing the mutual knowledge and understanding of peoples, through all means of mass communication, and to that end recommend such international agreements as may be necessary to promote the free flow of ideas by word or image."[12] That document—predicated on UNESCO's belief in universal educational opportunity, free inquiry, and open expression—continued by pledging that its signatories

> are agreed and determined to develop and to increase the means of communication between their peoples and to employ these means for the purposes of mutual understanding and a truer and more perfect knowledge of each other's lives.[13]

The organization of UNESCO further demonstrates the importance of communication in serving its end. Within its Communication Sector are the two areas most directly concerned with UNESCO's endeavors in world broadcasting—designated the Free Flow of Information and International Exchanges, and the Development of Communication Systems.[14] Their activities involve research, training, field projects, facility and policy development, publications, and sponsorship of innumberable regional conferences and educational seminars. Specifically, UNESCO's research and publications are the responsibility of its Department of Mass Communication in Paris. These include the annual UN STATISTICAL YEARBOOK and UNESCO STATISTICAL YEARBOOK; sporadic editions of a 200-nation media survey, WORLD COMMUNICATIONS (1951, 1956, 1964, 1975); commissioned books; and a series of monographs entitled, "Reports and Papers on Mass Communications," issued regularly since 1952. In addition, other communication functions are performed by various UNESCO offices and departments: Public Information, Statistics, Documentation, Libraries and Archives, Book Promotion and Development. The success of UNESCO's publications is due to its ability to collect meaningful data from most of the world's communication systems, and the integrity of its field work.[15]

Like ITU, UNESCO has changed discernibly during the course of its history of nearly four decades. In its first 10 years, for example, it served as a "low-budget catalyst" for the reconstruction of communication facilities and networks ravaged by World War II. Next, UNESCO devoted its energies to the development of communication facilities and the training of personnel in the emerging nations through the generous aid of UN sources. Called the Second Development Decade, its success can be measured tangibly by the dramatic increases in the number of radio and TV receivers throughout South America, Africa, and Asia. During its third decade, UNESCO enthusiastically promoted the new technologies of communication—especially satellites. Its participation in space communication has revolved around problems relating to uninvited satellite transmissions into sovereign territories, as well as the benefits accruing from the creation of INTELSAT and the use of satellites for developmental purposes like education.

Now, in the twilight of its fourth decade, UNESCO has shifted its emphasis away from material assistance and toward helping nations and regions to develop communication policies and standards, identify long-range objectives, and formulate decision-making mechanisms. Some reasons for this change in mode of assistance may be traced to the weakened world economy and the emergence of the Third World as a political force within the UN itself. Evidence of the latter can be seen in the 1974 election of Mahtar M'Bow to serve as UNESCO's first African Director General.

Attention in the present phase has centered on two communication issues: the concept of freedom of information; and, the concept of responsibility of mass media vis-a-vis national governments. From these have arisen UNESCO's most political proposal—the New World Information Order.[16] This will be discussed in Chapter 6, relative to the USA's 1984 withdrawal from UNESCO.

To summarize, UNESCO's greatest contribution to world broadcasting has been in the area of development. It has provided substantial assistance to the world's neediest nations by helping them to: (a) plan, finance, and build media facilities; (b) train personnel to operate and manage them; (c) help in the use of media in national development; and (d) generate communication policies tailored to their specific needs.

The World Intellectual Property Organization (WIPO)

One of the most litigious aspects of public communication is protecting the rights of the creators and proprietors of the various informational, educational, cultural, artistic, and entertainment products mediated to the public in order to prevent their unlawful use, expropriation, or exploitation by other parties. Just as manufactured goods and products are patented in the commercial marketplace, so too must the products of the mind be similarly registered. The mechanism for doing this is called *copyright,* and, besides offering protection, may be seen as promoting the free and legal flow of ideational material among nations.[17]

WIPO was established on April 26, 1970 as the successor to a series of copyright associations—e.g., the 1883 International Bureau of Paris Union, the 1886 Berne (International Copyright Convention) Union, and the more recent United International Bureau for the Protection of Intellectual Property. In December of 1974, WIPO became a specialized agency of the UN, with headquarters in Geneva, Switzerland. Its stated purpose is "to promote legal protection of intellectual property, including artistic and scientific works, artistic performances, sound recordings, broadcasts, inventions, trademarks, industrial designs, and commercial names."[18]

UNESCO also has provided a valuable service to world broadcasting in the area of copyright and what it calls "neighboring rights." Its 1952 Universal Copyright Convention offered a more liberal approach to copyright than the older Berne Union, and it revised it in 1971 so that developing nations could get just compensation, compulsory translation rights, and compulsory reproduction rights in only 1 year, rather than the 7 required of the industrialized nations. This allows developing nations to print needed books quickly and at favorable royalty rates, conditions needed in nations poor in wealth and information. But of most relevance to world broadcasting is the concept of *neighboring rights,* a protection for programming similar to copyright. Three agreements attempt to achieve this: the 1964 International (Rome) Convention for the Protection of Performers, Producers of Phonograms and Broadcasting Organizations; the 1973 Convention for the Protection of Producers of Phonograms Against Unauthorized Duplication of their Phonograms; and the 1974 Convention Relating to the Distribution of Program-Carrying Signals Transmitted by Satellite. The latter case does not concern direct broadcasting (DBS), but is an attempt to prevent signatory nations from distributing program signals carried by satellites but not intended for their use.[19] In other words, national broadcasters should not take programs they haven't paid for off satellites. The issues relating to the transnational flow of television programming via DBS will receive fuller treatment in a later chapter.

The International Telecommunications Satellite Organization (INTELSAT)

The concept of communication satellites was first introduced to the public by Arthur C. Clarke, reknown writer of science fiction and fact, in an October 1945 article, "Extraterrestrial Relays," published in *Wireless World* magazine. It would be another decade and a half, however, before his idea became reality. That occurred in August 1960, when the United States launched Echo I into orbit to relay telephony, facsimile, and data transmission to and from earth stations. Telestar and Relay satellites followed 2 years later, designed for intercontinental wideband communication and television transmission.[20]

At the same time, the US Congress passed the Communications Satellite Act of 1962, creating the Communications Satellite Corporation (COMSAT). Its ownership structure became half public and half private; that is, 50% of the stock belonged to the public COMSAT, and the remainder was split between AT&T (25%) and a consortium of telecommunication corporations (25%)—including ITT, RCA, and Western Union International.[21]

Meanwhile, attention was being given to this revolutionary technology at the UN, whose General Assembly unanimously adopted Resolution 1721 on December 20, 1961, declaring in part that

> international law, including the Charter of the United Nations, applies to outer space and celestial bodies . . . which are free for exploration and use by all States in conformity with international law and are not subject to national appropriation.[22]

This was reaffirmed 2 years later, when the UN General Assembly adopted, again unanimously, a "Declaration of Legal Principles Governing the Activities of States in the Exploration of Outer Space." Further progress was made during the summer of 1964, when the United States and 18 other UN governments signed the "Agreement Establishing Interim Arrangements for a Global Commercial Communications Satellite System." A second "Special Agreement" allowed public or private telecommunications entities to sign. Thus, on August 20, 1964, the International Telecommunications Satellite Consortium (INTELSAT) came into being.

Next, the Consortium formed the Interim Communication Satellite Committee (ICSC) to direct policy and to contract with COMSAT to manage, build, and operate the satellites. The Agreements called for COMSAT to capitalize 61% of the project, with the West European members contributing 30.5% and the rest coming from Canada, Japan, and Australia.[23] Other countries belonging to the ITU signed the agreements subsequently, bringing the number of international partners to 46 by 1965.[24]

In April of that year, INTELSAT put its first communication satellite, "Early Bird," into geosynchronous orbit over the Atlantic Ocean, connecting North America and Europe. Three more satellites were launched during 1967, two in fixed orbit over the Pacific Ocean and another over the Atlantic, all having multiple access (distribution) capacity instead of only point-to-point (relay) like Early Bird. In 1968, an Intelsat III was placed over the Atlantic, followed a year later with three more—two over the Pacific and a third over the Indian Ocean. The INTELSAT system paid dividends to over 500 million TV viewers in July of 1969, enabling them to witness man's first landing on the moon.[25]

Earlier in 1969, a Plenipotentiary Conference to Establish Definitive Arrangements for the International Telecommunications Satellite Consortium was convened in Washington. Two years of debate and negotiations ensued, with INTELSAT and Operating Agreements finally opened for signature by ITU members in mid-1971. Both Agreements were subsequently approved on February 12, 1973 by over two-thirds of the INTELSAT membership. This paved the way for converting the Consortium into the International Telecommunications Satellite Organization—a legal international entity providing wide-ranging telecommunication services to all ITU member countries through its own global satellite system.[26]

The prime objective of INTELSAT "is the provision, on a commercial basis, of the space segment required for international public telecommunications services of high quality and reliability, to be available on a non-discriminatory basis to all areas of the world." Each INTELSAT member's investment share is based upon its use of the system. Revenues come from utilization charges and, after deducting operating costs, are distributed among members in proportion to their investments, plus a 14% return.[27]

The INTELSAT global satellite system has two essential elements: (a) the *space* segment (all satellites owned by INTELSAT), and (b) the *ground* segment (all earth stations, owned by the telecommunication entities of the countries in which they are located).

INTELSAT's organizational structure features four interacting groups, which forward recommendations and resolutions to one another for discussion and action. These are:

1. The Assembly of Parties meets every 2 years to formulate policy and long-term objectives;
2. The Meeting of Signatories (to the Operating Agreements) occurs periodically to consider financial, technical, and operational aspects of the system;
3. The Board of Governors, composed of 27 members having the largest investments in INTELSAT, is responsible for all major decisions concerning the design, development, construction, establishment, operation, and maintenance of the INTELSAT space segment;

4. The Executive Organ is headed by a Director General, appointed for 6 years
    by the Board of Governors, who supervises an internationally recruited staff
    and is responsible for the day to day management of INTELSAT from its
    Washington, D.C. headquarters.[28]

At the beginning of the 1980s, INTELSAT was serving 105 member countries, 24 national nonsignatory users, and 14 other territory users with voice,
telegraph, telex, data, and television transmissions through its 11 satellites and
224 earth stations in 125 locations. Its INTELSAT V generation of satellites,
each having a capacity of 12,000 to 15,000 audio circuits and two television
channels, was being phased into operation, and contracts for the larger
INTELSAT VI series were being let.[29]

In conclusion, communication satellite technology is being developed and
deployed at a rate so awesome that attempts to describe it are often dated by the
time they appear in print. Less mercurial, perhaps, but just as awesome, are
reflections on the likely impacts that satellite communication pose for national
broadcasting systems and policies the world over. These impacts and the multi-
lateral issues accompanying the arrival of direct broadcast satellites will be
identified and analyzed in Chapter 8.

NONGOVERNMENTAL ORGANIZATIONS: REGIONAL
BROADCASTING GROUPS

Among the most practical Nongovernmental organizations in world broadcasting
are the confederations of regional broadcasters which function as mechanisms for
nations to discuss and solve common telecommunication problems, as well as to
exchange programming with one another. Ironically, there is no global organization of national broadcasting services. This is due largely to irreconcilable differences in political ideology and media philosophy throughout the world, particularly between the Western democracies and the Communist bloc. In recent
years, however, the major regional associations have held international meetings
to address programming matters of universal interest—such as the costs of
broadcasting rights and intercontinental satellite tariffs.[30]

Nongovernmental groups serve the common interests of broadcasting professionals from different nations through a forum allowing them to share information and resources relative to the administrative, technical and programming
facets of broadcasting. Table 2-2 outlines the key features of nine major professional organizations representing broadcasting systems in Europe, Asia and the
Pacific, Africa, the Middle East, the Americas, the Caribbean and the historical
British Commonwealth of nations.

The regional broadcasting confederations cited in Table 2-2 have similar
operational objectives and organizational structures. All have goals that serve:

Table 2-2 A Compendium of Major Nongovernmental Broadcasting Organizations

Group (Began)	Principle Area Served	Headquarters	Number of Members Active/Associate	Special Activities	Publications
EBU (1950)	Western Europe	Geneva, Swtizerland	35/69	Eurovision TV Network	EBU Review (monthly)
OIRT (1946)	Eastern Europe	Prague, Czechoslovakia	28/2	Intervision TV Network	RADIO-TELEVISION (bi-monthly)
ABU (1964)	Asia & Pacific	(NHK) Tokyo, Japan	42/25	Institute for Broadcasting Development	ABU Newsletter and Technical Review
URTNA (1962)	Africa	Dakar, Senegal	41/9	Center for Rural Radio Studies	URTNA Review Studies and Reports
ASBU (1969)	League of Arab States	Cairo, Egypt* & Tunis, Tunisia	15/4	Damascus Training Center / News feeds	ASBU Review Research Reports
NANBA (N/A)	US, Canada, and Mexico	Ottawa, Ontario, Canada	8/0	Annual meetings of N. American broadcasters	Occasional Reports
IAAB (1946)	North & Latin America	Montevideo, Uruguay	14/0	Medals of Merit to private broadcasters	AIR Bulletin Monographs
CBU (N/A)	The Carribean	Kingston, Jamaica	25/0	Co-Productions and Copyright advice	NEWSLETTER (quarterly)
CBA (1945)	Ex-British Commonwealth	London, England	55/0	Collective research Mutual assistance	COMBROAD (quarterly)

*Original HQ not recognized by Arab League since the 1979 Egyptian-Israeli (Camp David) peace accord. (See: Douglas A. Boyd, *Broadcasting in the Arab World: A Survey of Radio and Television in the Middle East* (Philadelphia, PA: Temple University Press, 1982), pp. 273–276.

Source: All information in Table 2-2 came from the *World Radio Television Handbook* 1984 (pp. 62–66) and from material sent to the author by the respective broadcasting unions and organizations.

1. to promote and coordinate broadcasting development within and among member nations;
2. to discuss common problems and serve the collective interests of their memberships;
3. to resolve conflict and ensure that all their members abide by international agreements;
4. to exchange information and programming among themselves and with broadcasting services in other regions;
5. to encourange and conduct research, and to disseminate relevant information and knowledge through regular publications of their unions.

Likewise, all regional broadcasting bodies are structured in like fashion, usually having the following common elements:

1. A General Assembly comprising all members, full-time active and nonvoting associate, and meeting once every year or two;
2. an Administrative Council of a dozen or two representatives who meet more frequently than the General Assembly to conduct policy and recommend changes;
3. a Secretariat and staff who run the organization on a daily basis year-round from a central headquarters;
4. optional committees responsible for specific areas like programming, legal and technical matters, research, training—sometimes operating from autonomous locations;
5. an Executive Board and/or officers, such as President, Director General and the like.

Although the landscape of world broadcasting is strewn with a mind-numbing assortment of acronyms and jargons, these nevertheless provide a universal shorthand through which policymakers, proprietors and students of world broadcasting are able to communicate with each other.

CONCLUSION

The world of broadcasting is inherently international and interdependent. Radio and television signals travel at the speed of light across national borders via airwaves and space that do not belong to any nation, corporation, or individual. Such characteristics make telecommunication technology difficult for sovereign governments to effectively control. Neither do broadcasters operate autonomously nor in a vacuum. Broadcasting, whether from the standpoint of the politician or the practitioner, necessarily takes place in an environment of symbiotic interaction.

And so, governments and broadcasting institutions have had to cooperate and compromise, among themselves and with one another. A complex of Intergovernmental and Nongovernmental organizational arrangements has helped accomplish this rapport.

CHAPTER 2 NOTES

[1] See, Charles E. Sherman, "An Approach to Analyzing the International Organizations in Broadcasting," in Charles E. Sherman and Donald Browne, eds., *Issues in International Broadcasting*, Broadcast Monographs, No. 2, (Washington, DC: Broadcast Education Association, 1976), pp. 114–121.

[2] The inventory of organizations in Table 2.1 was formulated from: Sherman, *Ibid.; World Radio TV Handbook 1984* (New York: Billboard Publications, 1984), pp. 62–66. See also, William L. Rivers, et. al., eds., *Aspen Handbook on the Media, 1977–79 Edition: A Selective Guide to Research Organizations and Publications in Communications* (New York: Praeger Publishers, 1977).

[3] George A. Codding, Jr., "The New Nations and the International Telecommunication Union: Some Policy Implications for the Future," in Herbert S. Dordick, ed., *Proceedings of the Sixth Annual Telecommunications Policy Research Conference* (Lexington, MA: Lexington Books/D. C. Heath and Co., 1979), pp. 357–360. For a full history and systems analysis of the ITU, see David M. Leive, *International Telecommunications and International Law: The Regulation of the Radio Spectrum* (Dobbs Ferry, NY: Oceana Publications, 1971).

[4] *Ibid.,* p. 361.

[5] From the International Telecommunication Convention (Montreux, 1965), as quoted in John R. Bittner, *Broadcast Law and Regulation* (Englewood Cliffs, NJ: Prentice-Hall, 1982), p. 92.

[6] *World Radio TV Handbook* 1982, *op. cit.,* p. 54 (Hereinafter cited as WRTH).

[7] The following description of ITU's structure is from: George A. Codding, Jr., "International Constraints on the Use of Telecommunications: The Role of the International Telecommunication Union," in L. Lewin, ed., *Telecommunications: An Interdisciplinary Survey* (Dedham, MA: AR-TECH House, 1979), pp. 1–34. See also: Leive, *op. cit.;* Bittner, *op. cit.;* and Codding in Dordict, *op. cit.*

[8] Codding, in Dordick, *op. cit.,* pp. 357–373.

[9] Codding, in Lewin, *op. cit.,* p. 33.

[10] "ITU: A New Convention is Agreed," *InterMedia,* 11(1), January 1983, pp. 6–8.

[11] Thomas L. McPhail, *Electronic Colonialism: The Future of International Broadcasting and Communication* (Beverly Hills, CA: Sage, 1981), pp. 90–91.

[12] As quoted in Warren K. Agee, et. al., *Introduction to Mass Communications* (New York: Harper and Row, 1982, 7th ed), p. 426.

[13] Robert P. Knight, "UNESCO's Role in World Communication," in Heinz-Dietrich Fischer and John C. Merrill, eds., *International and Intercultural Communication* (New York: Hastings House, 1976, 2nd ed.), p. 377.

[14] WRTH 1982, p. 54. See also: Alan Hancock, "UNESCO," in John A. Lent, ed., *Broadcasting in Asia and the Pacific: A Continental Survey of Radio and Television* (Philadelphia, PA: Temple University Press, 1978), pp. 369–370.

[15] Knight, *op. cit.,* pp. 381 and 391.

[16] This analysis of UNESCO is from *Ibid.,* pp. 371–391. See also, Rivers, *Aspen Handbook on the Media, op. cit.,* pp. 253–254.

[17] Knight, *loc. cit.*

[18] *Information Please Almanac 1982 (Atlas and Yearbook),* 36th edition (New York: Simon and Schuster, 1981), p. 328.

[19] Knight, *op. cit.,* pp. 381–382.

[20] UNESCO, *A Guide to Satellite Communication,* No. 66 in the Reports and Papers on Mass Communication series (Paris: UNESCO Press, 1972), p. 8.

[21] Henry Goldberg, "International Telecommunication Regulation," in Glen O. Robinson, ed., *Communications for Tomorrow: Policy Perspectives for the 1980s* (New York: Praeger, 1978), pp. 166–172.

[22] As quoted in Walter B. Emery, *National and International Systems of Broadcasting: Their History, Operation and Control* (East Lansing, MI: Michigan State University Press, 1969), p. 654.

[23] *Ibid.*, pp. 652–660.

[24] *The Intelsat System* (Washington, DC: INTELSAT, 1977), pp. 1–4.

[25] *Ibid.*, pp. 18–22.

[26] *Ibid.*, p. 5.

[27] *Ibid.*, p. 6.

[28] *Ibid.*, p. 28.

[29] From the Intelsat "Facts Sheet," April 1980; and COMSAT Magazine, No. 6, 1981, p. 3. See also: Rivers et al., *Aspen Handbook, op. cit.,* pp. 235–236.

[30] Sherman, *op. cit.,* pp. 117–118.

PART II

FOUR WORLDS OF NATIONAL BROADCASTING

Chapter 3

The First World: Broadcasting in the English-Speaking West

Broadcasting throughout the Western world takes place within settings that are generally parliamentary, capitalistic (with some elements of socialism), technologically advanced, highly educated, pluralistic, affluent, and hedonistic. Radio and television services in developed nations typically are owned and operated by nongovernment public corporations and privately-owned commercial enterprises, existing either alone or in competition. Funding is by license fees and/or advertising proceeds, sometimes with government aid.

Substantial levels of personal freedom, disposable income, and leisure time make mass media both highly valued and supported as diversions and industries. A libertarian environment yields programming that meets popular appetites for entertainment and information as well as such institutional goals as education and culture.

Trends in First World broadcasting include (a) a growing acceptance of advertising and private competition on national and local levels, (b) efforts to make programming more pluralistic and representative, (c) public demands for greater access to telecommunication channels, and (d) evidence of mass audience fragmentation in the wake of rapid diffusions of new technologies like cable and DBS.

By way of illustrating the variety in national broadcasting systems operating in the West, a dozen case studies of varying complexity and length are presented, using the methodology described in the opening chapter.

These may be classified according to the three market structures most common to broadcasting throughout the world. Thus a *monopoly* means that only one broadcasting agent is present, a *duopoly* has two separately-owned programming services in parallel, and an *oligopoly* features three or more broadcasters in competition with one another. The following combinations and permutations of ownership and financing are found among 12 case models within each market type:

MONOPOLIES:	*Ireland*	—Semi-State
	Sweden	—Private Noncommercial
	France	—State Commercial
	New Zealand	—Public Statutory
DUOPOLIES:	*Britain*	—Public Noncommercial & Private Commercial

	Australia	—State-Supported Public & Private Commercial
	Canada	—Commercial-State-Supported Public & Private Commercial
	Italy	—Fee-Commercial Public & Private Commercial
	Japan	—Fee-Commercial Public and Private Commercial
OLIGOPOLIES:	The Netherlands	—Fee-Commercial Private & Pluralism
	The U.S.A.	—Private Commercial with some Noncommercial
	West Germany	—Federalized Semi-Commercial

This chapter examines broadcasting in the United States, Canada, Great Britain, Ireland, Australia, and New Zealand. Broadcasting in Western Europe and Japan is analyzed in the next chapter. The American model of broadcasting is summarized only briefly in these pages, on the assumption that the reader is most familiar with it. Fuller attention is devoted to broadcasting in the other five countries. The special bilingual and multicultural services found in Canada, Ireland, Wales, and Australia are taken up in detail in Chapter 7.

The historical positions of the United Kingdom and the United States make the study of broadcasting in the English-speaking world compelling. Today, Anglo-American communication systems and media institutions dominate the global arena of information, mass entertainment, popular culture, and the arts. The reasons for this lie in the fact that both countries have free press traditions, were in the forefront of the industrial revolution, and contributed to the worldwide presence of their mother tongue, English, through British colonial rule and American economic imperialism.

ENGLISH: THE WORLD LANGUAGE FOR WORLD BROADCASTING

English was being spoken by 386 million people throughout the world by 1980, more than any other language except Mandarin Chinese (701 million).[1] The reasons for the widespread presence and usage of English are several. It is, of course, the mother tongue of Great Britain, the United States, and the white Commonwealth nations. During the British Empire's rule, English was adopted as the working language, the lingua franca, of the former British colonial nations in West Africa, Asia, Latin America, the Caribbean, and countless islands throughout the Pacific region of Oceania.

Its rich literary tradition and extensive vocabulary have helped make English a practical and popular storytelling medium as well as a highly functional language. These attributes also have contributed to making English well suited to modern mass media, especially radio and TV, which in turn have shaped its usage by millions of consumers of Anglo-American popular culture and entertainment around the world.[2] At the same time, more hours of informational programming are broadcast in English by the world's international shortwave radio services than in any other language.[3]

But the salience of English also has to do with political and economic factors. English is the basic international language for commerce, finance, science, technology, and travel. The dramatic spread of English is seen in its having become the chosen second language of most national groups. In Western Europe, for example, being bilingual in English is synonymous with being well educated. For these and other reasons, a working knowledge of English is now considered essential in most developing nations. And its use is no longer viewed as an affront to a person's cultural or national integrity, but rather is regarded as a necessary tool for competing in contemporary geopolitics and the global marketplace. No wonder it's been called "the language of access to modern life."[4]

But there are those who see English as an exploitative extension of economic imperialism and power by American multinational corporations which do, in fact, dominate much of the world's technology, especially information and communication systems. Thus, their language, English, has been adopted as the lingua franca of international business and promoted as the world's single language.[5]

Six Case Studies

Besides language, the Anglicized countries of the First World share a common political heritage and economic philosophy. Differences can be found among them, however, especially in terms of size, location, wealth, and ethnicity. Table 3-1 compares some vital national statistics for the United States, Canada, the United Kingdom, Ireland, Australia and New Zealand. Their broadcasting features are compared similarly in tabular form at the end of the chapter. It is fitting to begin with the American system, since it is the most powerful programming force in world broadcasting today.

THE AMERICAN MODEL OF BROADCASTING

The key descriptors for the broadcasting model developed in the United States are: *private, local, networked, autonomous, commercial,* and *populist*. Private ownership and localism have been two important premises underlying the American system, the rationale being that independently financed stations would be licensed for the purposes of serving their assigned areas with programming of local interest. The number and type of local stations on the air in the U.S. by 1984 were: 4726 AM, 4594 FM, 638 VHF-TV, and 506 UHF-TV. Three-fourths of the television outlets, and 88% of the radio stations presently licensed, are privately owned and advertiser-supported. The remaining stations are noncommercial, publicly-owned, and licensed to communities, universities, and state or

Table 3-1 A Comparative Summary of Political, Economic, and Social Descriptors for Selected English-Speaking Nations

Criteria	U.S.A.	Canada	United Kingdom	Ireland	Australia	New Zealand
Capital City	Washington, D.C.	Ottawa	London	Dublin	Canberra	Wellington
Population	226 Million	23.7 Million	56 Million	3.4 Million	14.3 Million	3.2 Million
Political System	Decentralized Multiparty	Decentralized Multiparty	Centralized Multiparty	Centralized Multiparty	Decentralized Multiparty	Centralized Multiparty
Political Rights Civil Liberties	Free Free	Free Free	Free Free	Free Free	Free Free	Free Free
Less Free Than	None	None	None	None	None	None
As Free As	Australia	U.S.A.	U.S.A.	Canada	United Kingdom	U.S.A.
Freer Than	Italy	Italy	West Germany	France	Italy	Japan
Economic System	Capitalist	Capitalist	Mixed Capitalist	Capitalist	Capitalist	Capitalist
GNP in US $	2,626 Billion	288.4 Billion	353.6 Billion	13.8 Billion	130.7 Billion	19.2 Billion
Per Capita Income	$9,458	$7,573	$4,360	$3,000	$6,830	$4,106
Monetary Unit (US Equivalence)	US Dollar 1 = $1	CN Dollar 1 = .73	Pound Sterling 1 = 1.40	Irish Pound 1 = 1.16	AUS Dollar 1 = .71	NZ Dollar 1 = .55
Ethnic Groups	78% White 11% Black 6% Hispanic	61.4% English 25.6% French 13% Other	81.5% Anglo 15.7% Celtic 2.8% Nonwhite	Irish Anglo-Irish	95% British 3% European 2% Aborigine	90% Anglo-Europ. 10% Maori & Polonesian
Official Lang(s)	English	English & French	English (Welsh)	English & Irish	English	English (Maori)
Religions	56.7% Protestant 37.3% Catholic 4.3% Jewish 1.7% Other	46.2% Catholic 39.7% Protestant 14.1% Other	55% Anglican 10% Catholic 4% Protestant 1% Jewish	95% Catholic 5% Protestant	36% Anglican 25% Catholic 20% Other Protestant	70% Protestant 16% Catholic
Literacy Rate	99%	98%	99%	99%	98%	98%
Deaths Per 1,000 Births	14.0	12.4	14.0	15.7	12.5	14.5
Life Expectancy	M68.7 F76.5	M69.3 F76.4	M67.8 F73.8	M68.7 F73.5	M67.6 F74.1	M68.5 F74.6

local education agencies.[6] However, station ownership by a single party is limited by law to 12 AM, 12 FM, and 12 TV, with only one of each kind allowed in any given market.

Nevertheless, private station ownership in the U.S. is becoming concentrated in fewer and fewer hands. For instance, a third of all radio stations and nearly three-quarters of the nation's TV stations are presently group-owned.[7] Most of the programming now aired by these local radio and television outlets comes from national sources, such as recording companies, news services, advertising agencies, and networks. This trend toward cross-media and multiple ownership of the production and distribution infrastructure by chains and conglomerates militates against program diversity and genuine competition, ideals nominally held by the American broadcasting industry.

Networking and advertising are also prominent features of America's broadcasting model. The market structure for private over-the-air television is an *oligopoly* comprised of three national networks—ABC, CBS, and NBC—each supplying up to 85% of the airtime of their respective 200-odd local affiliates. These networks function as tripartite brokers between their contracted affiliates (who have the audience), program producers and suppliers (who have the air product), and national advertising clients (who have money).[8] How much money? As of 1982, commercial broadcasting had annual advertising revenues estimated at $15 billion.[9] Now consider those less fortunate.

Most noncommercial stations belong to regional associations or networks and are members of the *Public Broadcasting Service*. PBS provides a satellite distribution system and national programming services via its Public TV and *National Public Radio* (NPR) networks. Congress established PBS with passage of the Public Broadcasting Act of 1967. In its collective wisdom, it thought of everything except how to finance the service. PBS thus has the distinction of being the world's only broadcasting system with no structural means of support. Public broadcasters in America consequently live a hand-to-mouth existence. Much of their airtime and human resources are necessarily wasted begging for dollars through ever-expanding membership drives and auctions. Such activities attempt to supplement the inadequate funding they receive from governmental allocations, private corporate underwriting, foundation grants, and other manners of gift-giving.

Broadcasting in the U.S. is loosely regulated by the Federal Communications Commission (FCC), which manages the spectrum, promulgates technical rules and regulations for wired and wireless telecommunication operations, grants construction permits, and licenses radio and TV stations for 5 and 7 years, respectively. Its authority flows from the out-dated Communications Act of 1934. A minimum of content and operational requirements are imposed on broadcasters, and the present climate of deregulation promises even less ahead.

Perhaps American broadcasting's greatest strength is its freedom from government interference, a legacy often attributed to private financing and ownership. Except for laws governing obscenity, the advertising of certain products, balance in presenting controversial issues, and free equal time for political candidates, U.S. broadcasters enjoy virtual autonomy in using the public airwaves. But they are not similarly free of marketplace interference from advertisers, stockholders, competitors, and the tyranny of ratings.

The overriding objective of private broadcasting in America is profit maximization through audience maximization. This is achieved by offering mass appeal entertainment, information, and sports programming as bait for attracting the largest audience possible to the commercial messages that interrupt and shape program schedules. Program success and profitability are determined solely by a quantitative system of "ratings," which purports to measure the number and proportionate share of sampled sets tuned to competing stations on a market by market basis. The most popular shows command the highest advertising rates, and therefore yield broadcasters the best revenues. In short, only profitable programs remain on the air; the public interest is reduced to that which most interests the public. Meaning entertainment.

Entertainment takes priority over all other program genres in American television. Its visual production values emphasize action and brevity; its thematic values stress youthfulness, affluence, competition, sex, criminality, and materialism. Broadcasting's fiercely competitive environment breeds duplicative schedules of slick, imitative, and diversionary programming. Even the personnel and content of TV news are selected on the basis of audience appeal and business criteria, rather than journalistic skill and newsworthiness. Serious documentaries, original drama, prosocial children's shows, education, and cultural presentations are relegated to public broadcasting.

The mass audience that has supported traditional broadcasting in the U.S. is in the process of fragmentation as low-power TV, cable, videotex, satellites, and home video recorders offer viewers enhanced user-control over an expanding selection of program options and channels. About 6,000 locally-franchised cable systems now provide from 12 to over 100 channels carrying local TV stations, imported signals from distant markets, and choices from among four "superstations" and 38 national pay-cable services distributed by satellites.[10] Nearly 40% of all TV households in the U.S. were wired by mid-1984, a total of 34 million homes.[11] As will be shown, the American broadcasting model is being adopted in those countries where local stations, entertainment, and advertising are in demand.

CANADA

America's neighbor to the north faces the multifaceted predicament of being the world's second largest country in land area, yet having a relatively sparse and multicultural population of approximately 25 million people. Nine of ten Canadians live within 100 miles of the U.S. border, and the remainder are scattered throughout the ten provinces and two territories that comprise this vast Dominion. Then, too, Canada recognizes two official languages, English and French, the latter spoken by a quarter of her citizens, notably in Quebec Province.

Proximity to a wealthier nation with an English-speaking population 10 times greater has resulted in the omnipresence of American programming, via airwaves and cable, and a disconcerting preference for it by Canada's Anglophone majority. The situation is further complicated by the fact that French and English Canada are effectively (and voluntarily) isolated from one another.

These geocultural conditions have had significant impact on Canada's communication needs and policies, compelling the propitious use of cable and satellites for program distribution. Also, a near-obsessive cultural concern has been expressed repeatedly in all official studies of Canadian broadcasting through the phrase "national unity and identity," watchwords that have become the twin objectives of broadcasting in Canada.

In an attempt to address if not redress these challenges to its bilingual sovereignty, Canada has created national radio and TV services in both English and French, imposed legal limits on the amount of foreign (read American) programming on its airwaves, required the deletion of commercials from U.S. broadcasts carried by Canadian cable systems, and disallowed income tax deductions by Canadian advertisers who buy time on neighboring American stations, so as to stem the flow of Dominion dollars south of the border.

Organization

Broadcasting in Canada is officially described as a single system having public and private elements.[12] This de facto duopoly accounts for the nation's approximately 3200 originating and rebroadcasting stations.[13] The public component is the *Canadian Broadcasting Corporation* (CBC), established by the Broadcasting Act of 1936 and owned by the federal government. It provides nationwide radio and television services through separate English and French networks of owned and operated stations and private affiliates. The extent of coverage of the CBC English services to the Anglophone population, as of 1982, was 99% by AM, 74% via FM Stereo, and 99% for TV. The comparable coverage patterns of the CBC service in French, called Radio Canada, were 99% for AM, 67% by FM Stereo and 99% with TV.[14]

Private sector broadcasting in Canada consists of all commercial radio and television stations not affiliated with the CBC nor recipients of government funding. There are no private radio networks in Canada, meaning all stations not connected with the CBC are local independents. Three private TV networks are in operation, however. The *Canadian Television Network*, Limited (CTV), was licensed in 1961 to broadcast in English only, and now reaches over 90% of the nation's Anglophone households. *Les Telediffuseurs* (TVA) has been enfranchised since 1971 to serve all of Quebec Province exclusively in French. Licensed a year later, *Global* Communications, Limited, today provides coverage to all of Ontario Province and parts of Western Canada in English.[15]

Educational broadcasting is administered on the provincial level. Among the most active are the Ontario Educational Communications Authority, whose TVO service delivers 16 hours of programming daily to nearly 90% of the province's homes;[16] the Société de radio-television du Quebec, known as *Radio Quebec;* and the Alberta Educational Communications Corporation (ACCESS). In addition, a small number of radio and TV stations, as well as several regional networks, are specifically licensed for multilingual, native (Indian) or bilingual service.[17]

Finances
Canada realized from the outset that its broadcasting would risk becoming a mere parasite on the U.S. system if it attempted to rely solely on advertising, since American sponsorship and network affiliation would be required for survival. On the other hand, direct government or public support also would be unfeasible, due to the nation's limited economy, tax base, and population. As a result, the CBC has been financed by Parliamentary stripends, receiver license fees (between 1923 and 1953), and supplementary advertising.[18]

Today, the CBC receives 80% of its support through an annual allocation of about half a billion dollars from Parliament, to which it must report periodically through the Secretary of State. The remainder of its income is realized from advertising sales on television only, since the CBC's radio services are noncommercial.[19] Private broadcasters in Canada, as in the U.S., depend entirely on advertising for their operating revenues.

Control
The reigning legislation currently governing all telecommunications in Canada is the Broadcasting Act of 1968. Its wording emphasizes the nationalistic purpose and cultural objectives of broadcast policy in Canada:

> the Canadian broadcasting system should be effectively owned and controlled by Canadians so as to safeguard, enrich and strengthen the cultural, political and economic fabric of Canada . . . [and should be] a national broadcasting service that is predominantly Canadian in content and character . . . [in order to] contribute to the development of national unity and provide for a continuing expression of Canadian identity.

The Act further stipulates that radio and television "be a balanced service of information, enlightenment and entertainment for people of different ages, interests and tastes . . . in English and French . . . to all parts of Canada."[20]

Perhaps the most important administrative feature of the 1968 law was the creation of the *Canadian Radio-television and Telecommunications Commission,* an independent public authority charged with regulating and licensing all broadcasters and cable operators for 5-year periods. The CRTC has nine full-time and ten part-time commissioners representing all parts of the nation and appointed by the Governor in Council for terms of 7 and 5 years, respectively. The Commission, whose responsibilities were expanded in 1976 to include federal jurisdiction over all telecommunication carriers, also sees to it that all policies of the 1968 Act are adhered to and implemented.

Perhaps the most conspicuous action taken by the CRTC to cope with the domination of Canada's airwaves by U.S. programming was its imposition of "Canadian Content" quotas on all domestic broadcasters in the early 1970s. These regulations now require that, between the hours of 6 pm and midnight, 60% of TV programming aired by the CBC and half of that telecast by private licensees must be made in Canada, with no more than 30% being imported from any one foreign country.[21] For radio, 30% of all recorded music played on AM stations must be Canadian in terms of either performer, composer, lyricist, or recording studio. FM stations need only meet the levels of Canadian Content specified by the conditions of their licenses.[22] The objectives of the content rulings are both cultural (i.e., limiting American programs) and economic (i.e. stimulating the production and recording industries in Canada).

How effective have these measures been? The CBC's performance outshines that of its private competitors, with over 70% of its prime time (6 pm to midnight) schedule being Canadian productions.[23] Private telecasters in English, on the other hand, tend to place their Canadian programming at each end of the prime-time block, filling most of the peak viewing hours (8 to 11 pm) with American shows. They rationalize the practice by arguing that audience maximization is crucial to their survival, being totally dependent on advertising, and that their daily programming averages legally meet the CRTC's mandates.[24]

Critics blame this disparity of compliance between broadcasters on the Commission's liberal parameters for prime time and on its laxity in applying content criteria to all parts of the program schedules.[25] Although the CRTC reaffirmed its commitment to content requirements for TV in early 1983, by year's end it had proposed several changes in defining and tabulating Canadian content in light of future cable and satellite services.[26] One new scheme involves a "six-minimum" standard in which values are awarded for various Canadian participants in productions. For example, each native writer or director is worth two points, while other key personnel equal a point apiece. All domestic programs must have a Canadian producer, however.[27] Another method would specify that certain amounts of home-grown programs be produced and scheduled during mid-evening (8 to 10 pm) as a condition of licensing, as was done in the renewal of CTV's franchise in 1979.[28] For Pay TV, content criteria would be based on the amount of money spent in program production rather than on percentages of air schedules. These rules allow for co-productions with foreign studios, meaning that Americanized programs could technically meet Canadian Content requisites, and that conditions and exemptions could vary among licensees.[29]

Working with the CRTC in the regulatory process is the Department of Communications, established in 1969 to carry out research and formulate national policy for all communication media. Its jurisdiction originally included the Post Office, but now is confined largely to telecommunication systems. Broadcast policymaking eventually fell under its purview as radio and TV became increasingly intertwined with cable and satellite technologies.[30]

Cable and Satellites

Canada has perhaps the world's most technically-advanced and cost-effective cable and satellite systems. It is also among the most highly wired nations, with well over 600 cable systems providing access to three-quarters of its households, of which over 65% had connected by 1984. A national videotex-teletext technology, called *Telidon,* is in the process of being operationalized.

Telesat Canada was established by a 1969 Act of Parliament as a commercial telecommunications carrier of mixed (public and private) ownership for the purpose of developing a domestic system of communication satellites to serve Canada's special needs. Likewise, in 1981, the CRTC gave permission to Canadian Satellite Communications, Inc. (CANCOM) to distribute a multiple-channel package of radio and TV signals by satellite to remote and underserved communities as a means of extending broadcasting services in lieu of cable.[31]

The nation's principal satellite system, *Anik,* which means "brother" in Eskimo, operates through the efforts of the Department of Communications and Telesat Canada. The *Anik* series of satellites (I, II, III, A, B, C, and D) perform a number of telecommunication services, including the distribution of regular television programs to scores of ground stations. Direct satellite broadcasting is beginning presently.[32]

Following the Canadian government's reluctant approval, Pay TV operations finally began in February 1983. Three national and five regional channels were the first to enter what promises to be a fiercely competitive but lucrative market. A national 24-hour service, *First Choice Canadian,* will offer recent movies, ad-free and uncut, to over 2.5 million potential subscribers through nearly 90 cable systems initially enlisted nationwide. Another national service, *C-Channel,* is committed to a nightly performing arts programming format, featuring award-winning international films, children's shows, and live performances. C-Channel had contracted with 68 cable systems by 1983, reaching over 2 million homes.

The five regional Pay TV services will emphasize various programming mixes. *World View Television* of Vancouver, the smallest, will offer international films and local programs in six ethnic languages to around 100,000 potential subscribers. The other regionals are: *Télévision de l'Est du Canada, Inc.* (TVEC), which will compete with Premier Choice mainly in Quebec Province;

Star Channel, serving part of Atlantic Canada from Halifax; and *Superchannel,* the combined service of two big companies in Alberta and Ontario Provinces.[33]

Programming

The public CBC does a better job of fulfilling the national identity mandates of Canadian broadcast policy than its private competition. The private telecasters tend to tailor their seasonal program schedules to yield annual content averages that meet the letter if not the spirit of the CRTC's requirements. This is done by airing more Canadian productions during summer's slack viewing time and saving the peak viewing months for the more attractive American programs. Their emphasis is therefore on mass entertainment content for achieving commercial objectives.

The CBC, on the other hand, concentrates on domestic production that is high in surveillance value, meaning programming that covers Canadian life. Commitment to this goal was strengthened in 1981 when the CBC moved its national TV newscast up one hour, from 11 pm to 10 pm. The change to prime time has proven popular with Canadian viewers, who historically have favored their own news and public affairs broadcasts to those from across the border.[34]

A content analysis of the English CBC-TV network in the early 1980s showed its largest programming category to be Informational (46.9%), followed by Light Entertainment (35.8%), Sports (14.2%), and Cultural (3.1%). The CBC's AM networks in both languages featured music, news, and "background content," defined by the CRTC as programming requiring only casual audience attention.[36] Both of their nationwide FM Stereo networks aired mainly international music, with backgrounding and news programs rounding out their schedules.

As much as Canadian audiences appreciate their own public affairs programs, they also have a healthy appetite for slick entertainment fare. Herein lies the chronic weakness of Canadian television, and the curse of living next door to the entertainment center of the world.

The looming presence and widespread popularity of American television programming in Canada is born out by a litany of facts. Consider these five:[37]

- 75% of the TV programming watched by English-speaking Canadians during the day, and 85% during evening prime time, is of American origin;
- 40% of the viewing time of French Canadians is spent watching dubbed American programs;
- Children under 12 years of age in both language groups devote less than half their viewing time to Canadian TV programs;
- two of every three TV programs in English aired in Canada yearly are foreign productions, mostly American;
- approximately 70 U.S. programming services are available on various Canadian cable systems and only a fraction of the total programming hours delivered weekly is made in Canada.

The cultural and economic implications of this evidence are obvious. Besides the lost opportunities for cultural self-expression that occur when a society loses the attention of its own people to foreign media, the $2 billion a year Canadian broadcasting industry is likewise threatened with lost advertising income and lost jobs as audiences defect and creative talents emigrate.[38]

The Canadian-American TV Border War

The popularity of American programming and its alleged intrusion into the national consciousness of Canada has been the focal point of a succession of official inquiries commissioned by the Canadian government down through the years.[39] Canadian rhetoric on the subject was couched largely in cultural terms until the 1970s, when their emphasis shifted to the real underlying issue— economics. Since advertisers follow audiences, the ability of U.S. border TV stations to attract large numbers of Canadian viewers naturally lured huge sums of Canadian advertising revenue south of the 49th parallel.

The situation eventually erupted into a so-called "television border war," involving 24 American stations in eight states.[40] The four major border TV markets, from east to west, are: Plattsburgh (NY)/Burlington (VT)-Montreal; Buffalo (NY)-Toronto; Detroit (MI)-Windsor; the Bellingham (WA)-Vancouver. Buffalo is the largest service area, with its stations serving over 5 million Canadians in the Niagara-Hamilton-Toronto corridor.

The origins of the conflict can be traced to the absence of the normal barriers to broadcast spillover between adjacent countries, such things as mountains, differing languages, and a lack of popular support for foreign programming due to either poor quality or cultural incompatibility. Just as Canada has tied the economics of the dispute to the lofty ideals of national culture and identity, so too has the United States linked it to the principles of free trade and free flow of information. This became apparent as both sides staked out their respective positions and took measures to address if not redress the border TV issue.

Canada's Viewpoint and Actions

The first point raised was that Canadian public and private television outlets pay about $35 million annually to American producers for the rights to air their programs in Canada. Second, Canadian advertisers spend an estimated $20 million a year buying time on U.S. border stations whose signals cover the most heavily populated sections of a country they are not licensed to serve. A third argument claims that multi-national corporations forego spending some $30–$40 million each year advertising on Canada's airwaves, since most Canadian viewers are already being reached by U.S.-sponsored programming either directly or through cable relays.[41]

The government of Canada has taken two courses of action in response to what they feel is an encroachment upon their national economy and sovereign culture. The *first* came in the early 1970s, when the CRTC authorized Canadian cable operators randomly to delete commercials from the TV signals received from U.S. border stations and replace them with public service announcements.[42] The *second* official measure came in 1976 with passage of Bill C-58, disallowing income tax deductions to Canadian businesses for the cost of advertising in U.S. media. The new law, coupled with the 52% tax rate on corporate profits in Canada, effectively doubled the cost of advertising on American stations.[43] The intention of C-58 was for Canadian TV stations to get the advertising money being spent in the neighboring U.S. markets and to use it to make more and better programs for the viewers in their own enfranchised areas.

The American Position and Response
The U.S. border broadcasters maintained that the Canadian cable industry's popularity and profitability is due precisely to the fact that their viewers prefer and are willing to pay for American television programming. They also claim that cable operators in Canada extract American programs free of charge and do not compensate U.S. border broadcasters for the money lost to them through deletion of their commercials. They further point out that restrictions placed upon Canadian broadcasters and advertisers by their own government are simply self-punishing, and that official cable policy in Canada has actually aided the spread of U.S. television further inland.

Nevertheless, many U.S. border stations have suffered economic damage due to Canada's Bill C-58. For instance, three network affiliates in Buffalo, New York, and one station in Bellingham, Washington, have lost in excess of $140 million in Canadian advertising proceeds since C-58 was enacted. Not surprisingly, it was the managers of these four stations who spearheaded the American retaliation. First, they successfully lobbied Congress in 1977 to block a business tax exemption to American firms and organizations holding their conventions and meetings in Canada.[44] Next, the border broadcasters led the effort in the U.S. Congress for "mirror" legislation that would deny income tax deductions to American advertisers buying time on Canadian stations as long as C-58 stands.[45] By fall 1984, such a measure had been passed by both houses of Congress and signed into law by President Reagan.[46] An amendment to the mirror legislation links the American future of Canada's highly-touted new videotex technology, Telidon, to the status of C-58. The U.S. videotex-teletext market is seen by Canadian officials as being critical to Telidon's financial success in that, without it, the venture could lose as much as $1 billion a year by 1990.[47]

The worst case scenario, however, is the threat by American broadcasters to jam their own signals at the border, a proposal given initial approval by the FCC.[48] If carried out, U.S. programming from border stations would be denied to Canadian viewers. This is not very likely, because of the expense involved in such an undertaking and because of the possibility of direct network distribution via satellite. The latter option, ironically, has validity and appeal to both Canadian broadcasters and American networks. With the border stations being by-passed, Canada would be advantaged by no longer having to pay royalties to U.S. copyright holders, and by virtually eliminating the incentive for Canadian advertisers to buy airtime south of the border.[49]

Likewise, the American networks would continue to distribute programs, without commercial deletion, and multination advertisers would continue to buy network time to directly reach viewers in the Canadian markets. Further, direct distribution is compatible with the U.S. policy of free information flow. Whatever the outcome, it is telling that the FCC gave CBS the go ahead in November 1983 to deliver its programming directly to TV stations in Canada.[50]

The Conflict's Status in 1984

A negotiated settlement had not been reached by the end of 1984. The results of the actions taken by both countries show that each has lost much and gained little by the TV border war. To illustrate, the four stations most deeply involved—three in Buffalo (NY) and one in Bellingham (WA)—collectively lost $140 million in Canadian advertising proceeds from C-58 between 1976 and 1984. Canada, by comparison, lost some $400 million in American tourist revenue in the 4 years following the U.S. Congress's retaliatory tax law.[51]

The practice of substituting Canadian PSAs for American ads on cablecasts virtually ended by 1978, having proved to be as ineffective as it was crude. C-58, however, was successful in reducing by half advertising purchases on U.S. border channels, from $20 to $10 million per annum—an amount roughly equal to the Canadian corporation tax.[52] In other words, the government of Canada profited by C-58, not Canada's broadcasters. On balance, television stations on both sides of the boundary were hurt by the legislation, Canadian program production was not significantly enhanced, and North American trade relations are about as healthy as acid rain. Only Canada's tax coffers seem to have benefitted.

Meanwhile, Canadian cable enterprises have become formidable competitors in the United States. By 1980, Canada's investment in the American cable market approached a quarter of a billion dollars, having won franchises in cities like Minneapolis, Atlanta, Syracuse, and Fort Lauderdale. A bitter irony is implicit in the fact that Canadian cable giants like the Toronto-based Rogers and Maclean-Hunter are reaping handsome rewards south of the border, while foreign ownership of cable systems in Canada is limited by law to 20%. Thus, some U.S. cable firms have asked the FCC to cap outside investment in American cable operations to 25%.[53]

The way these two North American neighbors resolve their cultural and economic differences is being closely observed by other nations as trans-national programming looms as a global phenomenon in the emerging age of direct satellite broadcasting.

A Review of Cultural Policy

The years 1982 and 1983 yielded a new CBC president, the first review of national cultural policy in three decades, an official green light for Pay TV and a bold new national broadcasting policy. The Report of the (Applebaum-Herbert) Federal Cultural Policy Review Committee was issued in 1982 following 3 years of inquiries and deliberations. The 18-person commission made 101 recommendations, nearly a quarter of which addressed broadcasting matters relating to the CBC, the CRTC, and governmental involvement in funding a program archives and local radio services. Specifically, the committee suggested a modified noncommercial CBC, more co-productions with foreign studios, better marketing of Canadian programs abroad, wider provincial input into decision-making, and a new broadcasting act for greater flexibility and autonomy in regulating content via the new technologies. Lastly, the Applebaum-Hebert Report appealed for the federal government to "develop a clear and coherent" satellite policy which would help fund and deliver a host of new Canadian productions.[54]

A Broadcasting Policy for the Future

The attention and respect bestowed upon broadcasting in Canada attests to the perceived value that officialdom attaches to it as a vehicle for national unity, cultural projection, and economic growth. Canada's cultural institutions, though markedly improved over the past three decades, are no match for the technical infrastructure of its broadcasting, cable, and satellite systems, which may be the best in the world. Inspired by the cultural policy review of the Applebaum-Hebert committee, the Minister of Communications, Francis Fox, released a dramatic document in early 1983 entitled *Towards A New National Broadcasting Policy*.[55] It set forth a sweeping new plan for giving Canadians a greater choice in programming and for making the nation's broadcasting industry more competitive in the burgeoning environment of global telecommunication. The policy's three goals are: (a) to maintain the broadcasting system as an effective vehicle for implementing Canada's social and cultural policies; (b) to improve the accessibility, quality and diversity of Canadian programming by strengthening the home-based broadcasting and production industries; and (c) to increase the choice among programs of all kinds, in both English and French, for all Canadians.

The 1983 Broadcasting Strategy for Canada was unveiled in two sections: a White Paper that spelled out four policies for immediate implementation, and a Green Paper outlining eight policy proposals, called "thrusts," for public consideration. The four mandatory initiatives have been adopted with the promise of enabling Canadian consumers, broadcasters, and entrepreneurs to participate in and profit from the new telecommunication technologies emerging in the coming decade. These four policy objectives are:

1. *Expand Programming Choice.* This will be achieved by providing Canadians with access to a variety of worldwide satellite programming through direct reception by home earth stations and via cable. Canada has given highest priority to its technically superior cable systems as the most cost efficient means of distributing the widest possible choice of TV programming to the majority of its residents in the future. The three-tiered delivery system places only Canadian stations on its basic service. The second level would carry specialised Pay TV programming, including American services like HBO. The third tier offers only Canadian Pay TV services and, at an additional fee, television signals from U.S. stations. Many nonprogramming options also will be available, such as videotex, data bank information, meter reading, and home alarm systems.

2. *Strengthening Canadian Programming.* The latest effort to improve the quality and expand the quantity of domestic TV products rests upon a government-established Canadian Broadcast Program Development Fund. Administered by the Canadian Film Development Corporation, the new fund supports private production companies and independent producers at an initial level of $35 million a year, rising to $60 million by the fifth year. The rationale for the investment is that Canada's public and private broadcasters cannot compete with the U.S. market in terms of production and per capita advertising revenue. The situation has been particularly critical in dramatic programs, a genre dominated by American studios. French TV has been less affected than its English language parallel, but even teen-aged Francophones have become increasingly attracted to U.S. dramas.

The goal of the Broadcast Fund is to stimulate quality production in all categories of TV programming, especially children's shows, drama, and variety. To illustrate, the fund will contribute one dollar for every two committed by a private producer, meaning an investment in Canadian TV production totaling $105 million in the first year and $180 million 5 years hence. Guidelines require that Canadians have creative control and are employed at all levels of production. The scheme should result in dramas that are suitable for prime time viewing and productions of such quality as to attract Canadian viewers, be exportable to foreign TV markets, and adhere to the ethical standards of the Canadian Association of Broadcasters and the CRTC.

3. *Government Direction of the CRTC on Policy Matters.* This initiative gives the Canadian government, through the Governor in Council, the power to issue only broad policy directives to the CRTC in order to be more responsive to the fast-changing environment of telecommunication technology. Although somewhat pernicious sounding at first glance, the measure does not give the politicians control over program content, freedom of expression, or licensing matters.

4. *Abolition of Satellite Dish Licensing Requirement for Individuals.* Canadians living in remote areas have not benefitted from the multiplicity of channels and programming afforded through cable to their more fortunate urban compatriots. Many have, therefore, invested in dish antennas capable of picking up TV signals directly from satellites, and also have had to pay a license fee for the privilege. The government has chosen to redress this programming imbalance and unfair fee penalty by no longer requiring individuals and certain commercial establishment (like bars) to have a license to operate a television receive-only (TVRO) earth station. The requirements for master antenna television (MATV) systems operated by apartments and condominiums also have changed, allowing them to receive and distribute satellite signals to their residents, so long as the local cable service suffers no economic harm as a result.

The eight policy proposals identified in the 1983 strategy's Green Paper were intended to encourage public debate and spur interest in Canada's telecommnication future prior to any final action by officials. In brief, the *first* of these recognizes the importance of the private sector in national broadcasting, and envisions that at least half of the programming developed by the Broadcast Fund will be aired over private television facilities. Private Licensees will be expected to invest their money and expertise in producing new programs of quality.

The *second* thrust is aimed at stimulating better French-language television programming for both national exhibition and exportation, with the possibility of a second private TV network in French for Quebec Province an idea to be explored. *Third,* a related need exists to create a mechanism for marketing worldclass Canadian TV programs abroad, and for facilitating more co-productions with European broadcasters. Such an export effort would include the sale of satellite programming for transnational airing, program exchanges with the United States, and the international distribution of video cassettes and discs.

A *fourth* proposal would attempt to equalize services nationwide through the use of the CANCOM satellite, in order to reach underserved communities now able to receive only two or three TV channels. *Fifth,* more broadcasting services also would be made available to Native People of the north, providing them with programs in their languages and reflective of their traditional cultures.

The *sixth* policy suggestion would make regulation more flexible, particularly with respect to Canadian Content quotas and priority-carriage obligations for the new tiered cable structure. The *seventh* initiative would offer revised legislation to streamline and simplify the regulatory process. A new act is needed to redefine broadcasting in light of the new technologies, and could thus empower the CRTC to compel cable operators to lease channels at reasonable rates to those wanting to provide innovative programming and informational services through videotex.

The *eighth* and final policy thrust would modify the mission and reduce the role of the CBC to broadcasting only national news, public affairs programs, cultural presentations, and special events of uniquely Canadian interest.

Canada's vast size, relatively small and clustered population, bilingualism, and location are facts of life that cannot be changed, yet also defy easy accomodation. Historic attempts to create cultural policy and fashion communication systems to minimize America's cultural and economic intrusions have proven to be frustratingly ineffective. Nevertheless, policymakers are pinning their hopes on a series of new proposals and strategies designed to stimulate debate and provide a blueprint for Canada's future role in the brave new world of global telecommunications.

UNITED KINGDOM OF GREAT BRITAIN
AND NORTHERN IRELAND

British radio and television have the enviable reputation of being the best in the world. This alleged status has been achieved through a public-private *duopoly* comprised of the noncommercial British Broadcasting Corporation (BBC) and the advertiser-supported Independent Broadcasting Authority (IBA).[56] The BBC was the monopoly public service broadcaster in Britain from 1922 until it was introduced to competition with passage of the Television Act of 1954 by Parliament. This legislation created the United Kingdom's first commercial system, Independent Television (ITV), which became IBA in 1973 when Independent Local Radio (ILR) was added to the Authority's charter.

The competition, however, was not exactly equal, since the BBC had two television channels to ITV's single service until 1982. With two national TV networks each—BBC-1 and BBC-2, ITV and Channel Four—the public and private components of the duopoly now enjoy relative parity as partners in British broadcasting.

Organizational Structure

The BBC is organized in a fashion that is at once *public, central,* and *national.* Although it maintains local radio stations and regional broadcasting centers, most of the system's programming and decision-making emanate from its London headquarters and studios. The main objectives of the BBC are: (a) to provide public broadcasting services to all parts of the UK; (b) to construct and operate transmission facilities for its home and external broadcasting services; (c) to produce, rent, buy, and sell radio and TV programming, films, tapes, and records; and (d) to disseminate to the public information about the Corporation's policies and operation, as well as news and information about Britain and the world.

The Independent Broadcasting Authority is perhaps best described by the words *private, plural, regional,* and *federal.* It is composed of a number of privately-owned radio and television programming companies enfranchised to serve various regions throughout the U.K., yet also contribute both operating money and programs to the Authority for its national network services. IBA's four functions are: (a) to select and appoint the radio and TV program companies; (b) to supervise program planning; (c) to control the frequency, amount, and nature of all advertising aired by its contractors; and (d) to plan, build, and allocate the use of the IBA-owned and operated transmitters.

The management structure of the two organizations is quite similar. Both have: Boards of Governors appointed by the Home Secretary; Director Generals, who, along with their Deputies, serve as the chief operating officers for supervising executive staffs; Broadcast Complaints Commissions to act upon negative public reaction to programs; and a host of advisory bodies to offer input on matters ranging from regional interests (namely, in Scotland, Wales, and Northern Ireland), education, religion, local radio, and the like.

Control

For years, broadcasting in Britain was under the control of the Postmaster General. The Post Office Act of 1969 transferred this authority to the Minister of Posts and Telecommunications. Since 1974, regulatory authority for all broadcasting activities has been vested in the Secretary of State for the Home Department. The Home Secretary, as he is known, appoints the boards of the BBC and IBA, licenses all broadcasting services, and sees that the relevant charters and laws are adhered to and correctly implemented by both broadcasting organizations.

The BBC has received five renewals and three extensions of its charter since the initial one in 1927. The IBA has been enfranchised through a succession of Parliamentary acts passed in 1954, 1964, 1974, 1978, and 1980. The current license periods of both broadcasters run through December 1996 by virtue of the IBA's Broadcasting Act of 1980 and the BBC's 1981 Charter.

Finances

As a noncommercial public body, the BBC is owned neither by the government nor by private interests. It, therefore, receives no money from advertising and only technical assistance from government. All funding comes from the public through the license fees it pays annually on TV receivers only. Fees in 1983 were 15 pounds (about $20) per black-and-white set, 45 pounds (about $75) for a color receiver.

The IBA, on the other hand, receives no share of the license fee revenue. The Authority's income is collected in the form of rental fees paid to it by the local radio and regional television franchises who use IBA's transmitters and, as privately-owned companies, make money by selling spot advertising time on their stations.

Although the IBA is supported entirely by advertising revenues, the relationship between its broadcasters and commercial clients differs markedly from that found in the United States. For starters, there is no program sponsorship; clients merely buy units of time, and the IBA broadcaster decides where to place the advertising spot in the daily broadcast log. It is, therefore, the Authority, not the advertiser or agency, who determines program schedules. The IBA controls all aspects of advertising through a strict Code of Advertising Standards and Practice. For example, commercial time on television may average only 6 minutes an hour over the broadcast day, and cannot exceed 7 minutes in any clock hour. In radio, the advertising limit is 9 minutes per hour. Further, all commercial copy must be approved by the IBA's Advertising Control Division before an ad is produced, as must the finished spot prior to being broadcast. All claims made within an ad must be supported by factual evidence and presented in a manner that does not give false, misleading, or careless impressions. About eight of ten advertisements meet these criteria; the other 20% are rejected. Finally, there must be a distinct break between the program and the commercials, rather than the direct segue so common in American TV.

Programming
The BBC and the IBA, despite their noncommercial and commercial distinction, are both publicly chartered corporations. Each, therefore, regards itself as a public service broadcaster. For this reason, as well as by tradition, they also claim the same programming objectives: that is, (a) to inform, (b) to educate, and (c) to entertain all segments of the public by providing balanced schedules of wide-ranging programs.[57] A generalized breakdown of their TV schedules for the 1980–81 season confirms how closely their programming performances match one another relative to the three stated categories:[58]

	BBC	ITV
Information (News, Current Affairs, Religion)	27.6%	25.75%
Education (Adult/Continuing, Schools, Children)	29.3%	19.75%
Entertainment (Series, Films, Drama, Music, Sport)	43.1%	54.50%

Regardless of this similarity in programming output, the BBC is still widely perceived as the "establishment" broadcaster (hence the nickname, "Auntie Beeb"), while the IBA has a more populist image.[59] Yet many of the most highly acclaimed British dramas seen on Public Television in America (e.g., "Masterpiece Theater"), although assumed to have come from the BBC, are often productions of private IBA companies. Two notable examples are "Upstairs, Downstairs," from London Weekend Television, and "Brideshead Revisited," produced by Granada Television, the IBA franchise for northwest England in Manchester.

This reputation for quality has made the U.K. one of the world's biggest exporters of TV programming. On the home front, however, Britain's airwaves have been limited by law to no more than 14% foreign content. This was amended slightly by IBA in 1983 to allow its ITV companies to import up to 15.5%, so long as the extra programming comes from Commonwealth nations.[60]

Both the BBC and the IBA have public charters which make them accountable to the public through Parliament, and invest professional broadcasters with sole authority over all programming, be it noncommercial or commercial, paid for directly by viewer taxation or indirectly by advertising consumers. Also, Britain's rich tradition in literature and theatre continues to supply a bountiful pool of artists whose talents have always been employed by radio and television rather than excluded from the airwaves for not being popular enough to meet commercial goals.

Lastly, consider the British way of producing and scheduling programs for television. The BBC and IBA each schedule their two channels with programs intended to complement rather than compete with one another. In this way, two shows of the same kind or of equal popularity are not aired at the same hour. This gives viewers a choice and implicitly places their interests above those of the advertiser or broadcaster. Downright cheeky if not subversive, what?

Relatedly, most British TV series run a predetermined number of weeks (typically 4 to 12) and then, no matter how popular, are replaced by new ones. Many productions are based on novels and historical biographies whose storylines are finite; but even original series are terminated as their writers begin to run dry. Again, internal reasons rooted in quality control prevail over external factors such as "ratings" in most program decision-making in the UK.[61]

BBC Services
The BBC presently operates two national television networks, four national radio networks, three regional broadcasting services, 30 local radio stations, and an external shortwave service.

National Networks.

TV: BBC 1—The mainstream programming service intended for a general audience and operating over 5300 hours annually.

BBC 2—Emphasizes minority preference programs and documentaries mixed with sports and other popular offerings; over 4300 hours a year.

Radio 1—A popular music service based on the US Top 40 and deejay format. This most popular radio network broadcasts nearly 6000 hours yearly.

Radio 2—A 24-hour MOR music, sports, and news service. It attracts an average of 8 million listeners daily and shares VHF frequencies with Radio 1.

Radio 3—This VHF stereo service features serious music, current affairs, and drama approximately 6900 hours each year. It also offers over 600 hours of courses annually through Open University.

Radio 4—The spoken word characterizes this service of public affairs, news, lectures, quizzes, plays. Operating over 7600 hours per annum, it also carries educational program for schools and nearly 400 hours of Open University courses.

Regional Broadcasters.   (these provide area program services on an opt-out basis from the national networks):

BBC Scotland: Annual output averages over 500 hours of TV and 6500 hours via radio.

BBC Wales: Averages over 800 hours of TV and nearly 7100 hours of radio yearly, with roughly 45% of each total broadcast in Welch.

BBC Northern Ireland: Provides over 300 hours of TV programming and about 4400 hours of radio in an average 12-month period.

Local Radio.   The BBC is responsible for 30 local radio stations as of 1984, with more planned for the future. All broadcast on both AM and FM. Collectively they transmit over 83,000 hours annually.

External Services.   The BBC operates a number of international shortwave radio services. These are classified accordingly: BBC World Service, English by Radio, Overseas Regional Services, and the Language Services to Western and Southern Europe, Eastern Europe, Africa, Asia, the Middle East, and Latin America. All tolled, these external services average over 700 hours of broadcasts per week in 39 foreign languages.

The BBC also provides a nationwide "university of the air" service, *Open University,* an average of 36 hours weekly via Radio 3 and 4 and both television networks, especially BBC 2. By 1982, over 90,000 adult part-time students were taking credit bearing courses through O.U., which offers undergraduate degrees in many subjects. The BBC opened a new $13 million educational production center at Open University's headquarters in central England in late 1982.[62]

On January 17, 1983, the BBC launched Britain's first early morning TV show, "Breakfast Time." Styled after America's "Today Show," this voyage into the uncharted waters of "breakfast telly" runs from 6:30 to 9:00 am.[63]

IBA Services

The IBA has contracts with 15 television and 69 radio program companies, two news organizations, and a production firm for its early morning TV show.[64] The TV franchises provide local program services to their respective regions, and also contribute programming to IBA's national networks, ITV, and Channel Four. However, the five largest companies supply most of the national programming and are therefore referred to as the "network companies." From largest to smallest, based on populations served, the names and locations of IBA's TV franchises are:

1. *Thames Television* (serves London weekdays until 5:15 pm Friday)
2. *London Weekend Television* (from 5:15 pm Friday until sign-off Sunday)
3. *Central Independent Television* (East and West Midlands, from Birmingham)
4. *Granada Television* (North-West England, from Manchester)
5. *Yorkshire Television* (serves Yorkshire region from Leeds)
6. *Television South* (South and South-West England, from Southhampton)
7. *HTV* (is two companies: *HTV Wales,* from Cardiff; *HTV West of England,* in Bristol)
8. *Anglia Television* (East of England, from Norwich)
9. *Scottish Television* (Central Scotland, from Glasgow)
10. *Tyne Tees Television* (North-East England, from Newcastle Upon Tyne)
11. *Television South West* (South-West England, from Plymouth)
12. *Ulster Television* (Northern Ireland, from Belfast)
13. *Grampian Television* (North Scotland, from Aberdeen)
14. *Border Television* (The Borders and Isle of Man, from Carlisle)
15. *Channel Television* (The Channel Islands, from St. Helier, Jersey)

The typical television franchise broadcasts just over 100 hours each week. About 60 hours of this programming comes directly from the ITV network, over four-fifths of which is produced by the five largest network companies. In addition, each regional station produces at least 8 hours of local programming weekly. News from ITN accounts for another 7 hours of airtime, and the remaining 25 hours of air product comes from a variety of outside sources. Below are all of the IBA's radio and TV services:

National Television Networks:

ITV: Initiated in 1955, this channel offers a program service that is two-thirds Mainstream (entertainment, films, drama, music, and sports) and one-third Informative (news, current affairs, education, and religion). It broadcasts over 100 hours a week via its 15 inter-connected regional franchises.

Channel Four: Its programming format reverses the mix found on ITV-1 and emphasizes innovative programming by independent producers. It operates about 4000 hours annually, having begun only in the fall of 1982. In Wales the service is run independently as S4C, with 22 hours of its weekly output in the Welsh language.

Independent Local Radio (ILR): There were 44 private commercial stations on the air by 1984. IBA has enfranchised another 25 ILR stations which are planned for activation during the 1980s, bringing the total of ILR outlets to 69 by 1990. About two-thirds of the UK's population is within the coverage of an ILR station. ILR contracts currently run for 8 years and require stations to serve their areas with high quality programming of local interest. Stations sell their own airtime and most have formats of deejayed popular music.

Other Services:

ITN: Independent Television News is a nonprofit organization that provides all ITV stations with national and international news specials and three network newscasts—News at One, News at 5:45 and News at Ten, a 30-minute nightly presentation. ITN is owned by the 15 ITV companies and is co-owner of UPITN, a newsfilm agency for foreign TV services.

IRN: Independent Radio News is a subsidiary of an IBA all-news station in London, LBC, the London Broadcasting Company. It supplies national and international news via hourly newscasts networked to ILR stations.

TV-am: This company was awarded an 8-year contract to provide IBA's early morning service via its national ITV network. Called "Good Morning Britain," the program debuted opposite the BBC's "Breakfast Time" in the spring of 1983 and features news, investigative reporting and topical interviews by David Frost.

Teletext and Videotex

The British pioneered the use of broadcasting to send textual and graphic information over the air for reception on home television screens. The IBA was the first to publicly demonstrate teletext in 1973, using its ORACLE system.[65] The BBC's system, called CEEFAX, took to the air a year later.[66] At present, both broadcasters transmit electronic pages containing various items of news, information, and entertainment. The most recent use of teletext, however, is for subtitling recorded programs and transcribing live broadcasts as an aid to the hearing impaired. Subtitles are also being developed for translating material (like foreign films or programs) from one language into another. The wired version, videotex, will find even greater applications as cable television is developed in the U.K. The main videotex system in Britain, PRESTEL (formerly VIEWDATA), is run by the Post Office, now called British Telecom.

Cable

As the decade of 1980s began, only 14% of British households were connected to cable and nearly half a million home video recorders were in use.[67] But ambitious plans for cable television in the UK unfolded during 1982 and 1983. The (Hunt) Committee of Inquiry into Cable Expansion and Broadcasting Policy, convened in early 1982 by the Home Secretary, issued its report in mid-October. The Committee concluded that multichannel cable would not threaten the high TV standards already set by the BBC and ITV; rather, that cable would complement, not compete, by offering a multiplicity of services.[68] The Hunt Report further recommended that a new public authority be established to award cable franchises and supervise their activities with a minimum of regulations. As specified, these included no limit on the amount of advertising, no program importation restrictions, no local access obligation, no prior scrutiny of programs or commercials, and no requirements regarding impartiality or balance in newscasts.[69]

Today, a seven-member Cable Authority, appointed by the Home Secretary, has sole responsibility for issuing separate licenses for cable systems (owners) and cable operators (programmers), though many companies hold both permits. Cable systems receive an initial 12-year license and renewals for 8 years. Cable operators also receive a 12-year franchise, but systems having switching (two-way) capability may receive a 20-year license.

The Cable Authority is empowered and encouraged to make decisions about matters of taste and decency in program content, but to do so with a "light touch." Cable operators must carry the UK's four terrestrial networks (BBC 1, BBC 2, ITV, and Channel Four) and the five planned DBS channels as they become activated. Carriage of additional terrestrial and satellite services is also permitted, be they foreign or domestic, but operators are banned from offering data communication services in major urban centers.

Licensees may choose the type of cable (optic fibre or coaxial) and delivery configuration (switched or tree-and-branch) wanted for their systems. Pay-TV channels and pay-per-view options are allowed on British cable.[70]

Satellites
Having been awarded five DBS channels by the 1979 WARC in Geneva, the UK became as interested in developing direct satellite broadcasting as with building a nationwide cable system.

The first question to be answered was: who should have access to the impending satellite channels—the BBC, the IBA, or both? The government, in March 1982, awarded the first two available satellite channels to the BBC instead of to Independent Television, in part because current law technically limits the IBA to terrestrial broadcasting. The BBC subsequently committed about $255 million (168 million pounds) to develop its DBS service, including the leasing of two transponders on Britain's UNISAT satellite.[71] Protests from the IBA and private interests interests during 1983 led the government to the conclusion that direct satellite broadcasting was too important and costly an enterprise to be undertaken by the BBC alone. By the end of 1984, a tripartite consortium had been authorized to operate UNISAT. The plan was to have given the BBC and ITV two DBS channels each, with the fifth going to private programmers, but finances killed the UNISAT project in 1985. This subject will be taken up more fully in Chapter 8.

The second issue to be resolved in 1982 concerned selection of a DBS transmission standard. The government created a study committee, led by Sir Anthony Part, to evaluate proposals and recommend one. It came down to the

BBC's Expended PAL (E-PAL) system versus the IBA's Multiplexed Analogue Component (MAC) standard. Based on the Part Committee's choice, the Home Secretary accepted at year's end the Authority's MAC standard over E-PAL on the grounds that it was (a) technically superior, (b) could be more flexibly adapted to future improvement, and (c) stood a good chance of becoming the common DBS standard for all of Europe—and thus benefit British manufacturing.[72] Indeed, the final version of C-MAC (the "C" indicating digital sound capacity) was field tested, found to be compatible with all existing color standards,[73] and subsequently endorsed by the European Broadcasting Union as the continent's DBS standard.[74]

Problems and Prospects

The principal problem facing British broadcasting is the fate of its national system of public service broadcasting, the BBC. Its survival depends on the ability to attract 50% of the viewing public, on average, if continuance of the license fee is to be justified after cable and DBS become established. As the new technologies fragment the mass audience, and as Pay TV entrepreneurs compete for the viewer's money and attention, public willingness to pay the license fees so critical to the BBC may erode. Indeed, a supplementary fee may be needed to finance its second DBS channel at the same time the BBC would be soliciting viewers to subscribe to its first satellite service. In case of dire money straits, the BBC may have to resort to some form of private financing to remain solvent.[75]

And radio's future? Looking ahead to the 1990s, the BBC hopes to reorganize its radio frequencies so that its national, regional, and local services can collaborate in providing five balanced and nonduplicative program choices to every listener. The four current radio networks would be joined by a fifth, Radio 5, comprised of 40 stations broadcasting mostly local fare but linked together to receive popular drama, continuing education, and programs of interest to ethnic groups and other minorities from the new network.[76]

IRELAND

The island of Ireland, a geographic entity about the size of Maine, is comprised of four provinces, 32 counties, nearly 5 million people, and two separate nations. The Republic of Ireland occupies the 26 counties of the Emerald Isle's three southern provinces—Connacht, Leinster, and Munster. The fourth, predominantly Protestant (65%) Ulster Province, also known as Northern Ireland, is part of the United Kingdom of Great Britain.

The Republic's three and a third million people are nearly all (95%) Roman Catholic. About 5% speak only Irish, and most of the rest know some Irish words but speak English almost exclusively. Broadcasting in Ireland, from the founding of Radio Eireann in 1926 until the late arrival of television in 1960, has been shaped by a hard-won political independence, cultural pride, religious fidelity, and bilingualism.

Irish broadcasting is the sole responsibility of a national monopoly, Radio Telefis Eireann (RTE), a semi-state corporation dependent upon advertising and receiver license fees for its operating revenue. RTE functions under the auspices of a nine-member board, the RTE Authority, appointed and commissioned by a bicameral parliament (the Oireachtas) as mandated in the seminal Broadcasting Authority Act of 1960.[77]

Control
While broadcasting policy and operations fall within the purview of the RTE Authority, regulatory control and licensing are responsibilities of the Minister of Posts and Telegraphs. The current law governing all broadcast activities in the Irish Republic is the Broadcasting Authority (Amendment) Act of 1976.

Financial Support
RTE's income comes from advertising sales (48.3%), TV license fees (41.3%), and other sources (10.4%) like cable fees, publications, and program rentals. Annual TV license fees currently are $38 for black-and-white and $63 for color sets.

Services and Programming
RTE operates two national radio networks, two nationwide television channels, a full-time Irish language radio service, one part-time and one experimental local radio service, and a mobile community radio facility. The national services are:

> *RTE Radio 1*—a comprehensive programming format of news and MOR music via VHF monaural and MF transmitters averaging 130 hours per week and over 6800 hours annually.
> *RTE RADIO 2*—Features Anglo-American and Irish popular music about 136 hours weekly (over 700 hours yearly) in VHF stereo to youthful (14–35) audiences. The service began in 1979 out of public demand.
> *RTE-TV-1*—Programs a varied schedule in excess of 60 hours each week, 48% of it imported, to a general audience. Operated 3278 hours in 1981.
> *RTE-TV-2*—Counterprograms opposite the first channel an average of 42 hours weekly. It was on the air 2157 hours in 1981, with 72% of its schedule imported. The channel began operations in 1978.

The combined broadcast total during the 1980–81 season for the two radio networks was 13,810 hours. The two TV channels aired 5435 hours together, of which 57% was imported.

Local Broadcasting. Cork Local Radio, which broadcasts approximately 1 hour at mid-day, is Ireland's only regularly scheduled local broadcasting service. It transmits daily on an opt-out basis from Radio 1 during the noontime hour for an annualized average of 324 hours. However, RTE offers a mobile remote facility called *Nationwide Community Radio* (Radio Pobal na Tire in Irish), which serves various locales throughout the Republic on a rotating schedule. The

service logged 282 hours of airtime in 1981. RTE has proposed installing regional studios to allow Community Radio to broadcast on a scheduled basis. An
experimental operation, Radio West, was undertaken in 1981 using one main and
four satellite studios in County Mayo.[78]

In the absence of local radio stations, Ireland, like other European nations,
has been plagued with a surfeit of pirate broadcasters. By 1982, over 50 illegal
radio stations were on the air. The RTE Authority applied to the Posts and
Telegraph Minister in 1977 for permission to operate commercial local radio
stations in areas with populations over 100,000 persons. The Minister eventually
introduced a compromise measure in 1981, the Independent Local Radio Authority Bill, which would have created an autonomous organization to own and
operate local outlets in the Irish Republic. The legislation was never enacted, due
to a change in governments, but the idea is expected to be revived in some form
in the future.

Irish Language Broadcasting.   RTE is required by law to serve the Republic's Irish-speaking citizens. To that end, *Radio na Gaeltachta* broadcasts
about 40 hours a week (2041 hours in 1981), exclusively in Irish, for the
monoglot population in the west and interested bilingualists nationwide. In addition, 11% of all television programs produced by RTE are in the Irish language,
with a 20% target set for the future. Bilingual broadcasting in Ireland is treated as
a case study in Chapter 7.

Cable and Satellites

Cable television began in 1961 on a limited scale in Ireland. Its early development was mainly along the eastern seaboard, from Dublin to Wexford, where
British TV signals were available over the air in varying degrees of receptability.
Private concessionaires were allowed to offer cable services with permission of
the P & T Minister, providing RTE's signals were carried and at least 500
subscribers were served. Statutory regulations for cable, enacted in 1974, abol-
ished subscription limits but allowed RTE, which was denied the cable monopoly, to compete through its subsidiary, RTE Relays.[79]

By the early 1980s, cable TV in Ireland has spread to most major cities, with
25% of all households wired. RTE sees the 1980s as the decade when its
programs will gain access to vast continental audiences through cooperation with
the EBU's satellite experiments and by sharing time on several European
DBSs.[80]

Problems and Prospects

Irish broadcasting's future will be challenged by difficult economic conditions,
the new technologies, and domestic demands for private local stations and greater cultural pluralism. At home, Radio Telefis Eireann faces chronic financial
problems and the threat of losing its monopoly status as the national broadcasting
institution if private stations are permitted.

Domestic broadcasting has been further complicated by a mountain range that cuts the geography and population of the Republic into two sections. Those living west of the divide can receive only the two RTE television channels, while most viewers in the eastern half have additional British TV services available to them directly or via cable. This imbalance is all the more exacerbated by the fact that all Irish residents pay the same TV license fee. It is likely that cable and satellite systems will extend coverage and equalize TV program services within a decade. While many will no doubt be pleased by this, Ireland's policymakers fear a future loss of control over the small country's cultural sovereignty and communication media.[81]

OCEANIA

Australia and New Zealand, two isolated nations in the South Pacific, are often lumped together in the thinking of outsiders; yet a close look reveals two quite distinct places. Whereas Australia is an enterprising nation eager to make its mark on world affairs, New Zealand is a retiring and agrarian welfare state of enormous scenic beauty. Ironically, the sense of geographic isolation shared by Australia and New Zealand has been a stimulant to them in developing two highly sophisticated systems of national broadcasting. In terms of hours of operation, program choice, and distribution, each has exceeded the performance levels usually associated with broadcasters in underpopulated countries.[82]

AUSTRALIA

Australia, continent and nation, is roughly the size of the United States but with a population 16 times less. Two thirds of its nearly 15 million people are clustered along the southeast seaboard in New South Wales and Victoria, two of the nation's six states. A recent influx of Europeans immigrants, together with indigenous aborigines and the natives of Papua New Guinea, a former Australian territory north of the state of Queensland, have created the need for a significant presence of ethnic diversity in local radio programming and for a new multi-cultural television service.

The broadcasting situation in Australia is one in which a state-supported national service competes with numerous private radio and television stations not interconnected into nationwide networks, although regional TV chains do exist. This duopoly has been joined in recent years by two smaller contingents of public and ethnic broadcasting stations.

Organizations and Services
For half a century, the Australian Broadcasting Commission (ABC) was responsible for all public radio and television services. The ABC grew out of a private company and was converted into a government body by virtue of a 1932 law.

The growth in the number of commercial radio satations in the following decade led to passage of the Australian Broadcasting Act of 1942, a comprehensive statute governing private broadcasting as well as the ABC. The new law required private stations to pay a yearly license fee and one percent of their gross advertising receipts to help finance the ABC, which was supported mainly by an annual grant from the Federal Parliament. The tax on private broadcasters, along with a small receiver license fee paid by the public, was eventually phased out. The legislation, through a series of amendments, became known as the Broadcasting and Television Act of 1942, and governed Australian radio and TV activities for four decades.[83]

A 1983 Act changed the ABC into the Australian Broadcasting Corporation. The new ABC has a BBC-like charter and a smaller Board of Directors, comprised of seven instead of eleven members, with authority to appoint the Managing Director. It continues to be financed by an annual parliamentary appropriation, making the ABC the only broadcasting organization in the West to be funded solely by government.[84] That distinction could be lost if Canada's CBC decides to drop advertising or if the TV license fee, discontinued in 1973, is reinstated. While the idea of corporate sponsorship has been rejected by the new ABC, a TV license fee remains a possibility.[85] At present, 90% of its operating income comes from Parliament, the remainder coming from the sale of programs, books, records, and concert tickets for performances by ABC's six regional symphonic orchestras. It also publishes weekly TV and radio guides and a monthly FM feature magazine.

Headquartered in Sydney, the ABC maintains radio and TV studios in the national capital of Canberra, in the six state capitals, and in Darwin, the seat of the Northern Territory. By 1983, its metropolitan and regional stations numbered 94 AM, 15 FM, 11 SW, and 69TV.[86] These formed the basis of the three national radio networks and *ABC-TV*, the nationwide television service. *Radio 1* broadcasts popular music, light entertainment, sports, information, and regular newscasts to a general audience via major AM stations in the state capitals. *Radio 2* offers classical music, drama, public affairs, science, and religion programming to select audiences of serious listeners. *Radio 3* is the regional network, whose 70 stations provide a balanced mix of music, news, community information, and programs of local interest from local, state, and national sources. The ABC also operates a contemporary station, 2JJ in Sydney, whose rock music and deejay format is relayed to 2CN in Canberra and to 2NC in Newcastle. *ABC-FM*, which began in 1976, is heard in stereo 24 hours a day via stations in Sydney, Melbourne, Canberra, and Adelaide, featuring serious music, concerts, and some drama. *Radio Australia*, the SW overseas service of the ABC, transmits around the clock in nine languages to international audiences.[87]

ABC's single television network is on the air 12 hours daily with programs originating from five metropolitan studio centers. Roughly 57% of its content is produced in Australia, the rest being imported from the BBC (16.1%), IBA and other Commonwealth broadcasters (9.9%), and the U.S. (17.5%).[88] The ABC also runs the nation's largest news organization, with over 300 journalists and 2000 part-time correspondents stationed across the country and abroad.[89] And the Parliamentary Proceedings Broadcasting Act of 1946 requires the ABC to air about 76 sessions of the federal parliament yearly on one of the radio networks.[90]

Operating along side the ABC is the better financed and more popular private broadcasting sector. The Federation of Australian Radio Broadcasters is comprised of the local proprietors of 123 AM and seven FM stations around the country. These commercial operations generally offer popular music and local news briefs in the style of American Top 40 radio formats. Their 43 local TV counterparts belong to the Federation of Australian Commercial Television Stations (FACTS).[91] Although there are no national private networks, most TV stations are tied in to one of several regional networks that reach the majority of the nation's viewers. This is fairly easy, since half the population lies within the combined coverage pattern of two stations in Sydney and Melbourne alone. The two largest such regional chains are the *Nine Network* and the *Seven Network,* so-named because their affiliate stations operate on channels 9 and 7 in their various cities.[92] Another commercial channel, TV3, began in 1984.

Two other types of stations were licensed for Australia during the 1970s. The *Special Broadcasting Service* (SBS) was established in 1978 as a statutory authority funded by parliament for the purpose of providing radio and television services in the languages of the country's major ethnic groups. The multicultural programming efforts of the SBS stations will be described more fully in Chapter 7.

Beginning in 1974, the government recognized a need for nonprofit radio stations designed to serve the special needs of communities and educational institutions. Licensed and designated as Public Stations, they are funded by their sponsoring organizations and through membership subscriptions.[93] There were 36 Public Stations on the air in 1983—10 AM and 26 FM.[94]

Control

While the ABC and SBS are responsible to Parliament under their charters, the private and Public broadcasters are licensed and regulated by the Australian Broadcasting Tribunal, an independent government authority. The Minister of Communications has oversight responsibility for implementing all broadcasting laws and for reporting directly to Parliament on the performance of all communication agencies.[95]

Programming

TV program schedules and policies in Australia are determined by historical conditions similar to those found in Canada. So large a territory with so small a population necessitates that Australia be both an importer and an exporter of programming. The main reasons for its heavy reliance on imports are an insufficient supply of local talent, the relative inexpense of buying foreign shows

($12,600 per hour from the U.S.) rather than producing them, and the tested popularity of U.S. and British productions with Australian audiences. The policy response has been to impose home content quotas. A 1979 ruling mandates that 50% of the programming telecast between 4 and 10 pm be made in Australia, though imports tend to dominate the peak viewing hours. In the 1979–80 season, for example, half the prime time (8 to 11 pm) offerings were imported, with 54 U.S. and 13 British shows scheduled on Australian airwaves. The ABC tends to favor British productions; the commercial stations, American.[96]

But a nation of only 15 million must also sell its production abroad if its own media are to survive financially. The Australian government has stimulated its film and TV industries in recent years through tax incentives and international marketing assistance. Both the ABC and private networks have co-produced programs with, and sold them to, the BBC, CBC, PBS, and others. By the summer of 1982, in fact, eight of the ten most popular shows on TV in Australia were domestic commercial productions—the other two being British imports.[97]

Problems and Prospects

The agenda of changes and innovations in Australian mass telecommunications emerged from the 1981 Dix Committee of Inquiry into the ABC,[98] the Australian Broadcasting Tribunal's 1982 report on cable and subscription TV, and the 1983 election of an activist Labor government. The central question is: how will the new technologies affect traditional broadcasting? This has vital implications for a tax-based national service like the ABC, whose expenses are climbing while its viewer support averages about 15% and it rarely has a program ranked in the top ten.[99]

Several developments are planned for the 1980s. First, the ABC may start a second TV channel on a subscription basis, and add a second regional radio service. Multicultural TV also is slated for expansion in all states.[100] And a teletext service, *Instant Information*, is being developed using the UK's standard.[101] Cable and pay-TV services are a certainty, but the roles of private operators, the national Telecom authority, the ABC, and commercial broadcasters in its ownership and operation await final decision as of 1983.[102] An independent regulatory agency for cable has been recommended, with 10-to 15-year licenses and content guidelines.[103] AUSSAT, a joint state-public enterprise, hopes to put a DBS in orbit by 1985, offering two channels (ABC and one private) to remote regions.[104] Lastly, the future of home video also looks promising in Australia, as over a million VCRs were in use by 1984.[105]

NEW ZEALAND

The four islands (North, South, Stewart, and Chatham) that constitute New Zealand, a nation about the size and shape of California, lie 1400 miles southeast of Australia across the rough Tasman Sea. With its political roots planted firmly in the soil of democratic socialism, New Zealand's broadcasting history is marked by direct and persistent government involvement in program policy and services as well as in technical matters. Indeed, New Zealand is perhaps the only Western nation to have created a cabinet-level portfolio with the title, Minister of Broadcasting. The position symbolizes the importance that New Zealand's government attaches to broadcasting as an instrument of national purpose and as a major social institution.[106]

Organization and Financing

Like Ireland and a number of Western European nations, New Zealand determined early on that its limited resources could be best put to use in broadcasting through a public service monopoly. The present organization, the Broadcasting Corporation of New Zealand (BCNZ), controls all public radio and television activities, manages the New Zealand Symphony Orchestra, and publishes a weekly broadcasting journal, the *New Zealand Listener*. The BCNZ was established by the Broadcasting Act of 1976 and consists of four services—TV 1, TV 2, Radio New Zealand, and Central Services Division, a support agency which provides transmission facilities and accounting services for the other three broadcasting units. Two thirds of the income to operate BCNZ's four services comes from radio and TV advertising revenues, and the remaining third from an annual license fee only on TV receivers.[107]

A 1973 law had established TV 1, TV 2, and Radio New Zealand as independent services, together with a Broadcasting Council to regulate them and a small number of private radio stations. This structure soon proved disastrous in that the two television networks engaged in a ratings war that resulted in low quality and duplicative programming.

Public dissatisfaction and poor morale in the broadcasting ranks led to a reorganization of television services, as formalized with passage of the 1979 Broadcasting Amendment Act. Accordingly, TV 1 and TV 2 were unified into a two-channel operation named Television New Zealand, headed by a Director General and administrated by two divisions. One, the *Production Service,* produces all local programming and news using each network's main and regional studio facilities. The other, the *Network Service,* is responsible for scheduling programs on both channels in a complementary fashion, for purchasing foreign programming, and for advertising sales.

Control

The Minister of Broadcasting implements national broadcast policy, oversees all radio and television operations in the country, and recommends appointments to the boards and executive positions within the BCNZ. In addition, the operative 1976 Act created a three-person Broadcasting Tribunal to consider applications and license private as well as public radio stations, and to adjudicate formal complaints about breaches of programming policy.

Services and Programming

Television New Zealand currently operates the nation's only two national channels, *Television One* and *Television Two*. TV 1, which opened in 1960, is now on the air from 11:30 am to 11 pm daily, providing universal national coverage with programming from its studios in Wellington and Dunedin. TV 2 began in 1975 and currently broadcasts daily from 2:30 pm until midnight, reaching over 90% of the country with transmissions from its studios in Auckland, Christchurch, and Hamilton.

TVNZ imports three-quarters of its programming, the highest amount among the Western nations. Most of it comes from the United States, but British imports tend to draw the highest praise and the largest audiences. Both of its networks are mandated to serve all segments of the public through counterprogramming a wide range of offerings and by airing programs intended for cultural tastes and minority audiences. No radio and television advertising is permitted on Sundays in New Zealand. In addition, each channel has one other noncommercial day: Mondays for TV 1 and Fridays for TV 2.

Radio New Zealand presently supplies programming to its 62 local stations. All are AM facilities and, with the exception of about a dozen, commerical or part-time commercial operations. Each of these stations is linked to one of three national services: the *National Network* (news, information, music, and drama), the *Cultural Network* (noncommercial service of classical music, lectures, drama, and parliamentary proceedings), or the *Commercial Network* (local stations designated by ZM call letters and originating local music/deejay formats with hourly newscasts inserted from the network studio).[108]

By 1983, a dozen private radio stations had been licensed in New Zealand.[109] The Minister of Broadcasting also had granted a private company, Northern Television Ltd., an hour of daily airtime on TV 1, thus sending a signal that private regional TV channels may be approved in the future.[110] The future will most likely see the introduction of FM stereocasting, but New Zealand has no definite plans for the development of cable or direct satellite broadcasting.

COMPARISONS, CONTRASTS, AND TRENDS

In the beginning of this chapter, it was noted that the greatest variety of broadcasting systems exist within the First World and that English is now the lingua franca of world broadcasting. Having profiled the national data of the six major Anglophonic nations of the West and examined their current broadcasting arrangements, a similar statistical and narrative summary will highlight the uniquenesses and commalities among them.

The following relationships and conclusions can be drawn from the foregoing case studies and data contained in Table 3-2:

• America's broadcasting marketplace is the most competitive.
• The U.S. is the only country whose present broadcast legislation pre-dates the advent of television.

Table 3-2 A Comparative Summary of Broadcasting Criteria in Selected English-Speaking Nations

Criteria	U.S.A.	Canada	United Kingdom	Ireland	Australia	New Zealand
Market Model	Private-Commercl Oligopoly	Public-Private Duopoly	Public-Private Duopoly	Semi-State Monopoly	Public-Private Duopoly	Public Monopoly
Major Broadcasting Organization(s)	Private: ABC, CBS NBC; Public: PBS	Public: CBC, TVO; Private: CTV, TVA Global	Public: BBC; Private: IBA	Radio Telefis (RTE) Eireann	Public: ABC; Private: FACTS	BCNZ-Brdcstng Corporation of New Zealand
Sources of Income	Private: Advertising; Public: Gifts	CBC: 80% Gov't 20% Adv.(TV); Private: Adv.	BBC: License Fee; IBA: Advertising	52% License Fee; 48% Advertising	ABC: 100% Gov't; Private: Adv.	Advertising 2/3; TV License Fee 1/3
Regulatory Body	FCC: Federal Communications Commission	CRTC–Canadian Radio-TV T-Comm Commission	Home Secretary	RTE Authority Minister of P&T	Australian Brdcstng Comm & Comm. Minister	BCNZ
Operative Legislation	Communication Act of 1934	Canadian Broadcasting Act of 1968	BBC: Parlmentry Charter–1966; IBA: Act of 1982	Broadcasting Authority (Amendment) Act, 1976	Broadcasting & Television Act	Statutory Corporation
Programming Priorities	Commercials Entertainment Information Education	Information Entertainment Culture Education	Information Education Enlightenment Entertainment	Information Entertainment Education Culture	Information Entertainment Education Enlightenment	Information Entertainment Education Enlightenment
% of Imported Programming	1% Private 2-3% Public	34% Public 46% Private	Limited to 14% by Law	57%	57%	75%
Principal Lang(s)	English	English & French	English	English	English	English
Minority Lang(s) Broadcast	Spanish Various Ethnic	Italian, Greek, German, Inuit	Welsh Scotch Gaelic	Irish	European (6)	Maori
Fee/Year: Radio	None	None	None	None	None	None
B & W TV	None	None	$20	$38	(TV License now being considered)	$20
Color TV	None	None	$75	$63		$30
No. of Sets: TV	140 Million	11.9 Million	19.5 Million	980,000	5.5 Million	890,331
(% in Color)	65%	65%	58%	58%	50%	74%
Radio	456 Million	27 Million	40 Million	960,000	14 Million	2.8 Million
TV Systems: Lines	525	525	625	625	625	625
Color	NTSC	NTSC	PAL	PAL	PAL	PAL

79

- The U.S. places the lowest priority on information programming among the Western Anglicized nations.
- The public broadcasting component is a major programming force in all countries but the United States, where it is weakest against the private competition.
- Only the U.S. has privately-owned national radio network services.
- The U.S. and Canada have the only independent regulatory commissions with jurisdiction over both private and public broadcasters.
- The U.S. and Britain have the least amounts of imported TV programming.
- The U.S. is the only country never to have had a receiver license fee.
- The regulation of both the content and amount of broadcast advertising is weakest in the U.S. and Canada, and most stringent in Britain and Ireland.
- Ireland and New Zealand have the only broadcasting monopolies in the English-speaking West.
- Among the duopolies of Canada, Britain, and Australia, the public-private partnership is most evenly balanced in the United Kingdom.
- The BBC is the only public broadcasting organization solely dependent on license fee revenue.
- Receiver license fees currently exist only in Britain, Ireland, and New Zealand.
- Canada's CBC and Australia's ABC are the only broadcasting systems in the Anglicized West to be dependent on direct government financing.
- Canada and Britain are the only nations with legal limits on foreign TV programming.
- New Zealand has the highest level of imported TV programming (75%), and America the lowest (less than 5%).

In addition, other comparisons and contrasts within the English-speaking West may be summarized in greater depth. Five are of particular interest.

Canada–America: Common Border, Conflicting Values
Winston Churchill once described the Soviet Union as a riddle wrapped in a mystery inside an enigma.[111] Were he describing the broadcasting structure in present day Canada, he might well call it a dichotomy inside a contradiction wrapped in compromise. Here's why. Nearly every aspect of Canada is divisible by two. This chronic condition has been termed "hyphenated Canadianism" because of the many *dichotomies* that plague the nation—such as English–French, western–eastern, rural–urban, provincial–federal.[112]

The *contradictions* inherent in Canadian broadcasting policy and practice are also numerous. For example, its broadcasting arrangement is described as a single system (monopoly?) having public and private elements (duopoly?). Then, too, the CBC is supposed to promote national unity and identity by separately addressing the two major language groups through parallel radio and television networks. And many policies and laws have worked at cross purposes, like promoting cable and private TV interests at the expense of the public service CBC, or initiating bilingual broadcasting in 1936 but not making French and English officially equal languages until 1969.

Lastly, consider these *compromises*. The CBC was originally modelled after the noncommercial BBC, but chose to finance the system through direct government funding and advertising rather than by the more autonomous license fee method. This decision in turn subverted Canadian broadcasting's nation-building mission, as American programming was eagerly purchased to fill air schedules and to attract larger audiences in order to meet commercial rather than nationalistic objectives.

On the regulation front, it took the Canadian government nearly half a century to establish a truly independent regulatory body and to set mandatory levels of imported and home-produced programming for both private and public broadcrsters. As for the future, the 1983 broadcasting policy signals a compromising trend *away* from traditional objectives of seeking national culture and identity through required Canadian Content quotas and a strong CBC *toward* the new populist goals of expanding program choice via the new technologies and a weakened CBC. The prospect of a diminished role by the national CBC undermines its previous plans to distribute two additional TV services—CBC-2 in English and Tele-2 in French—via satellite and cable.[113] Instead, Canada's skies will be opened up to American Pay TV, amid predictions that over 90% of the nation's prime time programming will be US-made by 1990.[114]

The American broadcasting model has always placed the private interests of advertisers and owners ahead of the needs and best interests of the public. The Canadian model, however, nominally places the interests of national culture first, but audience ratings obviously are important to sponsors and broadcast proprietors. This basic difference in design is a reflection of deeper differences in the two countries' value systems.

Canadian broadcasting from its beginnings was considered a public resource to be centrally guided by a benevolent government so as to serve national development and sovereignty. The mixed system of public and private broadcasters seemed the best way to balance the sometimes conflicting political and economic aspects of national development through both informational and diversionary programming services.

So, too, have the results been mixed. Besides the shortcomings cited previously, Canadian broadcasting has its strong points. The best evidence is seen and heard through the excellent radio services of the CBC and the high quality public affairs and newscasts aired by the nation's public and private TV networks. An area of clear Canadian superiority over American broadcasting is the professionalism and intelligence displayed by its on-the-air personnel. The educational and performance standards for radio and television announcers and news reporters are demonstrably more stringent in Canada than is the case in the

United States. In monitoring Canada's airwaves, one does not readily encounter poor grammar, sloppy diction, high-pitched voices, inarticulateness, and anti-intellectualism. In America, these traits are commonplace. Whatever criticisms may be leveled at Canadian broadcasting's intellectual pretentions, they stand in stark contrast to the contempt displayed by America's broadcasters for anything that smacks of intellectualism.

Britain-America: Public Service Versus Private Profit

The American and British models of broadcasting are the two most influential and imitated systems in the world, yet differ fundamentally in terms of structure, programming philosophy, and purpose. Programs in commercial broadcasting are made for the primary purpose of meeting the objectives of advertisers (audience maximization) and station or network owners (profit maximization). Entertainment and information goals are secondary. The needs and interests of the audience are decided solely by advertisers and program producers whose prior sponsorship and post facto ratings logic determine which programs get and remain on the air. In other words, radio and TV programs have only extrinsic value as means to private ends.

In Britain, however, another mentality ruled. The government took a proprietary interest in broadcasting as a valuable public resource to be used to enlighten its people, uplift popular tastes, and transmit the nation's rich cultural and historical heritage from generation to generation. Its purpose was seen as being too important to be placed in private hands for personal gain. The only alternative to government ownership was to structure broadcasting as a public corporation. Further, it would be regarded as a profession, not a business. The same graduates of Oxford and Cambridge who formed Britain's ruling elite would also administer and produce programs for a broadcasting service that would be national instead of local, fee-based rather than commercial, diversified rather than diversionary. Thus was born the concept of public service broadcasting.

Programming in public service broadcasting is designed by a professional elite for the primary purpose of meeting the needs and interests of various segments of society. With slight exception, this is true whether the service allows advertising or not. The seminal public service model, the noncommercial BBC, has no need to concern itself with pleasing sponsors or attracting audiences large enough to reach arbitrary ratings thresholds. This means that programming is regarded as having intrinsic value. Each program is an end in itself, not a means to anything other than meeting the aesthetic and professional standards of its creator and generally satisfying its target audience.

This is not to say that program popularity and audience numbers (ratings) are irrelevant. On the contrary, a broadcasting service that depends upon direct support from the public through license fees must be *more* not less responsive to its listeners and viewers. Thus the public service broadcaster can claim to be accountable to a far greater number of people than private broadcasters who are answerable only to advertisers and stockholders. This same principle applies to the IBA as well, since it is a publicly-chartered organization in which advertisers only buy units of time; they cannot sponsor programs and therefore cannot determine program schedules.

Ireland–Canada: National Culture Versus Foreign Spillover

These two countries shoulder many of the same obstacles and concerns as a result of having sparse populations, limited economies, and adverse locations. Their national broadcasting organizations, RTE and the CBC, are (a) financed by public funds and some advertising, (b) mandated by law to serve cultural objectives in two official languages, and (c) forced to compete with programming from neighboring British and American services for the attention of their own peoples.[115]

Besides the trans-border flow of broadcasts into their sovereign territories, Ireland and Canada have both become heavily dependent on imported TV programming as the most feasible way of expanding viewing choice and filling at least half of the schedules of their respective home channels. But the rationale behind their importation policies differs. For example, Ireland has chosen not to impose legal limits on imported TV programming, electing instead to freely purchase it as a less expensive substitute for costly home-production and to counterschedule it strategically on RTE's two channels vis-a-vis the broadcasts from Britain's proximal stations. By contrast, Canada has legislated quotas for home-production but has allowed its broadcasters to schedule imported programming predominantly during peak viewing hours.[116]

Australia–Canada: Duopolies, State Financing and Multiculturalism

Public broadcasting in Australia and Canada is carried out by a government funded organization, in competition with vigorous private companies whose entertainment-oriented programming is generally more popular. Public and private broadcasters in both countries import roughly half of their program schedules. The population in each nation continues to grow and become more culturally diverse, factors that place special requirements on their broadcasting service.

Several major differences exist and are worth noting. First, Australia's ABC allows no advertising, while the CBC was still selling time on TV as of 1984. Changes could occur in both cases as Australia contemplates a return to the TV license fee and Canada considers making the CBC completely noncommercial. In terms of production, Australia's television and film industries are emerging as major exporters of high quality entertainment throughout the West and elsewhere, thanks to an enlightened policy based on government subsidies and an aggressive international marketing strategy. Canada, however, lags far behind in the amount, quality and foreign placement of its TV programs and feature films.

New Zealand–Ireland: Small Island Monopolies

New Zealand and Ireland are small island nations with relatively homogeneous populations of roughly 3 million each. Their rather limited economies require that broadcast services be run as a national monopoly financed by a mixture of public and private funds. Both operate two national TV channels which are counterprogrammed with the aid of heavy doses of imported productions.

Distinctions between their broadcasting systems are more a matter of degree than kind. The BCNZ, for instance, receives two-thirds of its income from advertising and offers three national radio services in English only. RTE draws only half of its revenue from advertising sales, and programs two nationwide radio networks in English and one in Irish. Lastly, Ireland is confronted with the additional problem of spillover from nearby British stations, while New Zealand finds itself out of the reach of foreign signals.

CHAPTER 3 NOTES

[1] *The World Almanac and Book of Facts: 1981* (New York: Newspaper Enterprise Association, 1980), p. 272.

[2] Jeremy Tunstall, *The Media Are American* (New York: Columbia University Press, 1977), pp. 126–128.

[3] Donald R. Browne, *International Radio Broadcasting: The Limits of the Limitless Medium* (New York: Praeger, 1982), p. 359.

[4] Glen Fisher, *American Communication in a Global Society* (Norwood, NJ: Ablex, 1979), pp. 12–15.

[5] Herbert I. Schiller, *Communication and Cutlural Domination* (White Plains, NY: Industrial Arts and Sciences Press, 1976), pp. 6–8.

[6] *Broadcasting Yearbook 1984*, p. A-3.

[7] Peter M. Sandman, David B. Sachsman, and David M. Rubin, *Media: An Introductory Analysis of American Mass Communications* (Englewood Cliffs, NJ: Prentice-Hall, 1982), p. 114.

[8] Stephen A. Sharp, "The US Networks May Not Need Their Affiliates," *InterMedia* 11(2), March 1983, p. 6.

[9] *Profile: Broadcasting 1983* (Washington, DC: National Association of Broadcasters, 1983).

[10] Donald W. Wood, *Mass Media and the Individual* (St. Paul, MN: West, 1983), p. 147.

[11] *Broadcasting Yearbook 1984*, p. D-3.

[12] *Broadcasting Act of 1968* (Ottawa: Information Canada, 1968).

[13] "New Strategies Revealed," *TV World*, August 1983, p. 20.

[14] *CRTC Annual Report: 1981–1982* (Ottawa: CRTC Information Services, 1982) p. 53.

[15] E. S. Hallman, with H. Hindley, *Broadcasting in Canada* (Don Mills, Ontario: General Publishing, 1977), pp. 58–62.

[16] Gordon Martin, "Videotex Teams Up With Educational Broadcasting," *TV World*, July 1982, p. 36.

[17] Hallman, pp. 62–68.

[18] Frank W. Peers, *The Politics of Canadian Broadcasting: 1920–1951* (Toronto: University of Toronto Press, 1969), pp. 18 and 363.

[19] Canadian Broadcasting Corporation, *Annual Report 1979–1980* (Ottawa: CBC, 1980), p. 30.

[20] See Sections 2 and 3 of the Act.

[21] T. C. Seacrest, "The Davey Report: Main Findings and Recommendations," in *Communications in Canadian Society*, edited by Benjamin D. Singer (Toronto: Copp Clark, Second Edition, 1975), p. 181. See also, "Regulations Respecting Radio (TV) Broadcasting" (Ottawa: CRTC, June 1972), pp. 6–7.

[22] CRTC, *Annual Report: 1976–1977*, p. 5.

[23] Douglas Martin, "Canadian Broadcasters Win Awards But Not Big Audiences," *The New York Times*, May 15, 1983, p. 8E.

[24] W. Brian Stewart, "The Canadian Social System and the Canadian Broadcasting Audience," in Singer, *op. cit.,* pp. 54–56. Cf. Note 9.

[25] Frank W. Peers, "Canada and the United States: Comparative Origins and Approaches to Broadcast Policy." A paper prepared for the Canada-US Conference on Communication Policy, sponsored by the University of Toronto, Syracuse University and The Americas Society, Friday, March 11, 1983, Center for Inter-American Relations, New York, New York.

[26] Theodore Hagelin and Hudson Janisch, "The Border Broadcasting Dispute in Context." A paper prepared for the Conference on Canadian-US Telecommunication Issues and Policies (see above information), p. 31.

[27] "Cancon, Again!" *TV World*, October 1983, p. 9.

[28] Hagelin and Janisch, pp. 31ff.

[29] Gordon Martin, "Pay TV: Operators and Prospects," *TV World*, April 1983, pp. 36–38.

[30] Hallman, pp. 38 and 71.

[31] CRTC, *Annual Report 1981–1982*, pp. 26–27.

[32] "TV By Satellite," *InterMedia* 8(1), January 1980, pp. 7–9.

[33] Martin, *TV World*, April 1983, pp. 36–38.

[34] "CBC To Break Tradition, To Start Newscast at 10," *Buffalo* (NY) *Courier-Express*, March 29, 1980, p. 11.

[35] CBC, *Annual Report 1979–1980*, pp. 26–27.

[36] CRTC, *Annual Report 1980–1981*, p. 2.

[37] W. J. Howell, Jr., "Language Policy and Television Efficacy in Canada," *Mass Comm Review* 10(½), Winter 1982/Spring 1983, p. 6.

[38] Francis Fox, *Towards A New National Broadcasting Policy* (Ottawa: Department of Communications, Information Services, 1983). The following policy information comes from this source.

[39] These are: The Aird Report of the 1929 Royal Commission on Broadcasting; The Massey Report of the 1949–51 Royal Commission on National Development in the Arts, Letters and Sciences; The 1957 Fowler Report of the Royal Commission on Broadcasting; the 1965 Fowler II Report of the Advisory Committee on Broadcasting; the 1970 Davey Report of the Special Senate Committee on Mass Media; the 1977 CRTC Report of the Committee of Inquiry into the National Broadcasting Service; and The 1982 Report of the Federal Cultural Policy Review Committee.

[40] Barry Berlin, *The Canada-United States Television Advertising Border Dispute: A Case Study in the Politics of Broadcasting.* An unpublished Ph.D. dissertation, State University of New York at Buffalo, November 1983, pp. 12–13. The affected American stations are: KVOS-TV, Bellingham, WA; WIVB-TV, Buffalo, NY; WGR-TV, Buffalo, NY; WKBW-TV, Buffalo, NY; WCAX-TV, Burlington, VT; WPTZ-TV, North Pole, NY; WAGM-TV, Presque Isle, ME; WABI-TV, Bangor, ME; WICU-TV, Erie, PA; KBJR-TV, Superior, WI; WPBN-TV, Cheboygan, MI; WTOM-TV, Cheboygan, MI; WVII-TV, Bangor, ME; WDAZ-TV, Grand Forks-Devils Lake, ND; WDEE-TV, Erie, PA; WWNY-TV, Watertown, NY; KXLY-TV, Spokane, WA; KTHI-TV, Fargo, ND; KCFW-TV, Kalispell, MT; KFBB-TV, Great Falls, MT; WEZF-TV, Burlington, VT; WSEE-TV, Erie PA; KXMD-TV, Williston, ND; KXMC-TV, Minot, ND.

[41] Harry J. Boyle, "Survival," an address to the Men's Canadian Club of London, Ontario, December 3, 1975. (Reprinted by the CRTC, 1976).

[42] Hagelin and Janisch, pp. 11–19.

[43] Yale Braunstein and Kalba Bowen Associates, "The Economics of Advertiser-Supported Television in Adjacent Countries: Consumer Sovereignty, Advertising Efficiency and National Policy." A paper presented at the Canada-US Conference (see Note 25), March 11, 1983, pp. 4–5.

[44] Berlin, pp. 163–187.

[45] "Senate Bill 'Answers' TV Ad Tax Law in Canada," *Buffalo* (NY) *Courier-Express*, February 4, 1982, p. B-4.

[46] "Trade Bill," *Broadcasting*, November 5, 1984, p. 46.

[47] Hagelin and Janisch, pp. 19ff.

[48] Mary B. Cassata and Molefi K. Asante, *Mass Communication: Principles and Practices* (New York: MacMillan, 1979), pp. 241–242.

[49] Hagelin and Janisch, pp. 69ff.

[50] "CBS Telecasts to Canada OK'd," *The Buffalo* (NY) *News*, November 24, 1983, p. C-5.

[51] Berlin, pp. 254–255.

[52] "Call It Border Patrol," *Buffalo* (NY) *Courier-Express*, February 9, 1982, p. B-9. See also, Braunstein, et al., pp. 4–5.

[53] Stephen Banker, "For Cable TV, It's a One-Way Border," *TV Guide*, January 12, 1980, p. 32.

[54] "Challenge to the CBC," *InterMedia* 11(1), January 1983, pp. 8–9.

[55] Fox (see Note 38). All information on the 1983 policy strategies comes from this source.

[56] All information on the two broadcasting organizations, unless otherwise cited, was taken from the *BBC Annual Report and Handbook 1984* (London: The British Broadcasting Corporation, 1983); and , *Television and Radio 1984* (London: Independent Broadcasting Authority, 1983).

[57] Burton Paulu, *Television and Radio in the United Kingdom* (Minneapolis: University of Minnesota Press, 1981), p. 154.

[58] These figures were synthesized by the author from programming data published by the BBC and IBA (see Note 56). It should be noted that nearly half of the BBC's educational programming is via Open University; ITV airs more actually in-school programs. Also, as Channel Four's schedule stabilizes, ITV's overall programming profile will undoubtedly change.

[59] Paulu, p. 156.

[60] "British TV Increases Quote for Foreign Product," *TV World*, September 1983, p. 6.

[61] *Ibid.*, pp. 26–27.

[62] "New Production Center at the OU," *EBU Review* XXXIII(4), July 1982, p. 52.

[63] "Waking Up to Tea and Telly," *Newsweek*, January 31, 1983, p. 76.

[64] Paulu, pp. 166 and 202.

[65] IBA, *Television and Radio 1982*, p. 187.

[66] *BBC Handbook 1976*, pp. 14–15.

[67] Desmond Fisher, *Irish Broadcasting Review*, Summer 1982, p. 32.

[68] "More Support for Cable TV," *InterMedia* 10(6), November 1982, p. 4.

[69] Patrick Campbell, "What Level of Regulation for Cable TV?" *TV World*, December 1982/January 1983, pp. 54–56.

[70] "Proposals for Cable Television," *InterMedia* 11(3), May 1983, p. 7.

[71] Patrick Campbell, "Catching Up on Satellite Plans," *TV World*, April 1983, pp. 120–124.

[72] "Choosing a DBS Standard," *InterMedia* 11(1), January 1983, p. 6.

[73] Campbell, *TV World*, April 1983, p. 122.

[74] "MAC Prevails in Europe," *Broadcasting*, August 1, 1983, p. 56.

[75] Patrick Campbell, "A Sceptic of New Technology," *TV World*, September 1982, p. 15.

[76] "BBC Radio Looks to the Future," *EBU Review* XXXIV (1), January 1983, p. 49.

[77] *RTE Annual Report 1980–81* (Dublin: Radio Telefis Eireann, 1981). All information on RTE, except where otherwise notated, is from this source.

[78] Brendan McCarthy and Tom Manning, "Radio Goes West," *Irish Broadcasting REview*, No. 13, Spring 1982, pp. 35–39.

[79] Fachtna O'Hannrachain, "Cable Distribution in the Republic of Ireland," *EBU Review*, XXX(6), November 1979, pp. 48–53.

[80] Desmond Fisher, "Cable TV Looks Ahead," *Irish Broadcasting Review*, No. 12, Autumn-Winter 1981, pp. 48–52.

[81] W. J. Howell, Jr., "Ireland's Second TV Channel: Seeking National Culture and Viewer Choice, *Journalism Quarterly* 56(1), Spring 1979, pp. 77–86.

[82] Alexander F. Toogood, "Australia and Papua New Guinea," in John A. Lent (Ed.), *Broadcasting in Asia and the Pacific: A Continental Survey of Radio and Television* (Philadelphia: Temple University Press, 1978), pp. 273–274.

[83] Walter B. Emery, *National and International Systems of Broadcasting: Their History, Operation and Control* (East Lansing, MI: Michigan State University Press, 1969). See Chapter XXX.

[84] "Australia: Prelude to Changes," *InterMedia* 10(4/5), September 1982, p. 7.

[85] "Australian License?" *TV World,* August 1982, p. 8.

[86] *World Radio TV Handbook 1983,* pp. 237–239 and 423–425. (Also, WRTH 83).

[87] *ABC 47th Annual Report: 1 July 1978– 30 June 1979* (Sydney: Australian Broadcasting Commission, 1979).

[88] *Commonwealth Broadcasting Association Handbook 1981–82* (London: Secretariat of the CBA, 1982), pp. 51–54.

[89] *ABC 47th Annual Report,* p. 70.

[90] Peter Lucas, "Australian Broadcasting," in William E. McCavitt (Ed.), *Broadcasting Around the World* (Blue Ridge Summit, PA: TAB Books, 1981), pp. 318–320.

[91] WRTH 83, pp. 240–243 and 224–225.

[92] Myles P. Breen, "The Flow of Television Programs From America To Australia," *Journalism Quarterly* 58(3), Autumn 1981, pp. 388ff.

[93] Lucas, p. 323.

[94] WRTH 83, p. 243.

[95] Lucas, p. 320.

[96] Breen, pp. 389–392.

[97] "Australian TV '82," *TV World,* March 1983, p. 31.

[98] Although a change in government rendered much of The Dix Report moot, a cogent review of the inquiry can be found in: John Hartley, "Australia Plans New Broadcasting Moves," *Irish Broadcasting Review,* No. 12, Autumn-Winter 1981, pp. 32–36.

[99] Toogood, p. 24. According to *TV World* (April 1983, p. 132), not one of the top rated ten TV programs in Australia for the week ending March 19, 1983 was aired on ABC-TV.

[100] Christopher Day, "Commercial Broadcasters Out of Favor," *TV World,* April 1983, pp. 126–128.

[101] "Teletext for Australia," *TV World,* November 1982, p. 6.

[102] Christopher Day, "Cable and STV Debate," *TV World,* October 1982, p. 24.

[103] "Australia: Proposals for Cable," *InterMedia* 10(6), November 1982, p. 8.

[104] *InterMedia,* September 1982, p. 7.

[105] "Video in 1983: Who to Deal With in Major Territories," *TV World,* December 1982/January 1983, p. 19. See also: *TV World,* May/June 1984.

[106] Alexander F. Toogood, "New Zealand," in Lent, pp. 288–289. (See Note 84).

[107] *CBA Handbook 1981/82,* pp. 60–62. (See Note 90).

[108] The information on the BCNZ was supplied to the author by Mr. P. A. Fabian, Overseas Liaison Officer, BCNZ. For an interesting historical account, see: Toogood, pp. 288–298.

[109] WRTH 83, p. 248.

[110] "NZ Private Channel?" *TV World,* August 1982, p. 9.

[111] Kenneth Turan, "TV Bookshelf," *TV Guide,* December 31, 1983, p. 39.

[112] Howell, "Language Policy . . . ," p. 2. (See Note 37).

[113] *CRTC Annual Report 1981–1982,* pp. 17–18.

[114] Douglas Martin, *op. cit.* (See Note 23).

[115] W. J. Howell, Jr., "Canada's Border War With US Television: Implications for Ireland," *Irish Broadcasting Review,* No. 8, Summer 1980, pp. 62–66.

[116] ———, "Broadcast Spillover and National Culture: Shared Concerns of the Republic of Ireland and Canada," *Journal of Broadcasting* 24(2), Sprint 1980, pp. 225–239.

The First World: Broadcasting in Western Europe and Japan

Broadcasting in Western Europe and Japan historically has been performed by publicly-owned corporations financed primarily by license fees on receivers and chartered by their parliaments to provide a balanced menu of informational, educational, and entertainment programming via national radio and television services. This type of organizational structure and programming mandate was born of policy based upon two suppositions: (a) that spectrum space was scarce, and (b) that the use of this finite resource must be judiciously planned and allocated by government in order to ensure that the best interests of their respective publics and national cultural heritages were effectively served.

Most Western European broadcasting institutions began as centralized monopolies, allowing little or no advertising, though examples of duopolies or oligopolies now can be found in those nations that have sanctioned some level of public or private competition.[1] As technological societies operating on democratic principles, the governments have played paternalistic yet restricted roles in assisting the technical development of their broadcasting systems while adhering to libertarian ideals of programming freedom tempered by guidelines for social responsibility. Official involvement in broadcasting has, therefore, been confined largely to the control of transmission facilities by their ministries of posts and telecommunications (PTTs), political appointments to boards of governors, and parliamentary approval and oversight authority vis-a-vis the budgets and policies of their chartered broadcasting organizations.

In Western Europe, broadcasting has undergone distinct changes since the late 1960s due to: (a) the opening up of additional frequencies for the expansion of services; (b) increased exposure to foreign programming by way of importations and spillover from neighboring countries; (c) the emergence of cable, home video, and satellite technologies; and (d) demands for more pluralism by locales, regions, and various minority interests.[2] These developments have translated into the following policy issues:[3]

> *Decentralization:* Widespread support of local and regional stations to offer more choice and relevance in programming, particularly news;
> *Competition:* An end to monopoly broadcasting practices through the introduction of public and private commercial services;
> *Access:* to the airwaves, programming decisions, and policy-making for increased segments of society;

Public Accountability: through creation of program complaint boards and effective feedback mechanisms to make broadcasters more responsive to audience preferences;

New Programming Formats: such as deejayed popular music on radio for the younger listeners, mass appeal entertainment for the general TV audience, and commercials to facilitate the marketplace, enhance the advertising industry, and preclude the need for unpopular license fee increases;

Depolitization of Broadcasting: The realization by many politicians that attempts to control broadcasting may be more of a liability than an effective means of influencing public opinion.

These trends are very much in evidence in France, Italy, West Germany, The Netherlands, Sweden, and Japan—whose broadcasting systems are examined in this chapter. These nations were chosen for their representativeness of the types of systems found in Western Europe, and for their own merits and distinctiveness.

As a means of profiling their national contexts, Table 4-1 offers a comparative inventory of significant political, economic, and social descriptors.[4] A table at the end of the chapter compares (and contrasts) the defining characteristics of the six models of national broadcasting. Details on the development of direct broadcast satellites and cable TV are deferred to Chapters 8 and 9.

FRANCE

The French government has always been involved in the development and control of public utilities and those industries directly affecting national life. Although free enterprise and press freedom have generally been supported in modern France, broadcasting, until recently, has been a state-controlled monopoly whose programming reflected government policies of the day. Today, French broadcasting is in the process of adjusting to unprecedented freedom and welcome independence, resulting from a 1982 law that redesigned its structure and further decentralized its services.

France put an end to private broadcasting in 1944 with legislation that created its first centralized monopoly, Radiodiffusion-Television Francaise (RTF), a fee-supported public service which developed four national radio networks, and in 1948, the first French television channel.[5] RTF became a state entity in 1959 but, due to political interference in its programming, was replaced 5 years later by L'Office de Radiodiffusion-Television Francaise.[6] The new ORTF put a second nationwide TV channel on the air in late 1964 and reorganized radio into three national networks: *France-Inter* (a 24-hour general interest service), *France-Culture* (arts and letters), and *France-Musique* (opera, classical, and jazz in FM stereo).[7]

A July 1972 act reaffirmed broadcasting as a state monopoly in France at a

Table 4-1 A Comparative Summary of Political, Economic, and Social Descriptors for Selected Western Nations

Criteria	France	Italy	West Germany	The Netherlands	Sweden	Japan
Capital City	Paris	Rome	Bonn	Amsterdam	Stockholm	Tokyo
Population	53,950,000	57,100,000	61,400,000	14,250,000	8,330,000	117,650,000
Political System	Centralized Multiparty	Centralized Multiparty	Decentralized Multiparty	Centralized Multiparty	Centralized Multiparty	Centralized Multiparty
Political Rights	Very Free	Free	Very Free	Very Free	Very Free	Free
Civil Liberties	Free	Free	Free	Very Free	Very Free	Very Free
Less Free Than	United Kingdom	France	The USA	Belgium	Denmark	United Kingdom
As Free As	West Germany	Greece	France	Portugal	West Germany	West Germany
Freer Than	Spain	Morocco	Italy			Italy
Economic System	Capitalist-Socialist	Capitalist	Capitalist	Mixed Capitalist	Mixed Capitalist	Capitalist
GNP in US $	$531.5 billion	$394 billion	$717.7 billion	$143.2 billion	$98.6 billion	$1,020 billion
Per Capita Income	$8,759	$3,470	$9,278	$7,597	$14,340	$6,010
Monetary Unit (US Equivalence)	Franc (1 = 12.2¢)	Lire (1808 L = $1)	Mark (1 = 38¢)	Florin/Guilder (1 = 33¢)	Krona (1 = 12.5¢)	Yen (1 = $216.22)
Ethnic Groups	European and Mediterranean	Slovenes, Albanians, Greeks, Fr.	Spanish, Turks, Yugoslavs	Frisians and Indonesian	Finnish and Lapps	Korean
Official Lang(s)	French	Italian	German	Dutch	Swedish	Japanese
Religions	90% R. Catholic 8% Protestant 1% Jewish/Moslm	99% R. Catholic 1% Other	49% Protestant 45% R. Catholic 6% Other	40% R. Catholic 24% Dutch Refm. 36% Unaffil or Other	95% Lutheran 5% Other Protestant	99% Shintoist & Buddhist 1% Christian
Literacy Rate	99%	94%	99%	99%	99%	99%
Deaths per 1,000 Births	16.4	17.6	15.5	9.5	7.7	8.9
Life Expectancy	M=69.2 F=77.2	M 69 F 75	M 69 F 75	M 72 F 78	M 72 F 78	M 72 F 77

time when virtually all West European broadcasters were facing new demands for access to the airwaves from localities and from advertisers. The pressure on ORTF came particularly from four neighboring stations known as "Radio Peripherique"—*Radio-Television Luxembourg* (RTL), *Europe No. 1* (from bordering Saarland in West Germany), *Radio Monte Carlo* (RMC), and *Radio Sud*—as well as from pirate stations like *North France*, which used American deejayed music formats and aired commercials. Although *France-Inter* had adopted a similar, albeit noncommercial pop style in 1966, the idea of private local radio was officially resisted by ORTF.[8]

The irony, if not hypocrisy, herein is that the French government is involved in the ownership of these peripheral stations through its Societé Financière de Radiodiffusion (SOFIRAD), a state-owned corporation that promotes France's political, cultural, and commercial interests through a complex network of media subsidiaries. To illustrate, SOFIRAD is the sole owner of *Radio Sud*, had 83% interest in RMC, and controls a third of the stock and the majority of voting rights in *Europe No. 1*. SOFIRAD also holds financial interest in broadcasting operations in Morocco, Gabon (West Africa), Lebanon, Latin America, and Tele-France International, whose subsidiary, Tele-France USA, offers a national satellite service of French programming to many US pay-cable systems.[9]

The proliferation of illegal pirate stations and simultaneous emergence of cable in Europe during the early 1970s conspired to force another restructuring of French broadcasting. A sweeping new law dissolved the ORTF in 1975 and placed the production and operation of French broadcasting in the hands of seven nominally autonomous organizations—three national TV networks, a central radio company, a production service, a public body in charge of transmission facilities, and a national research and training agency.[10]

The new structure began a process of decentralization in French broadcasting, leading to experiments with local stations in Paris by 1977 and their eventual legalization under national control in 1981.[11] The subsequent growth of new public and private local outlets began to eat into audience figures of the national radio services, especially France-Inter. By mid-1982, more than 150 radio stations had sprung up around metropolitan Paris alone, with program formats ranging from English-language rock to those espousing homosexuality and eroticism. In an effort to prevent chaos, the new Socialist government of Francois Mitterand moved, in July 1982, to limit the number of private radio stations in Paris. Those offering religious, educational, and classical music programming were favored in the licensing process.[12]

President Mitterand wasted little time in applying to broadcasting his campaign promise to decentralize government in France. One of his first actions upon taking office in mid-1981 was to appoint a commission to make proposals on how best to reorganize the telecommunication media system so as to promote the French language and culture within a framework of public and private ownership.[13] This culminated in the Moinot Report, named after the group's chairman, whose recommendation provided the foundation for the broadcasting reform act of July 29, 1982.[14]

Organizational Policy and Structure

The new law, effective January 1, 1983, has adopted four principles for French broadcasting: (a) public access to a variety of informational and programming services over the air or by cable is guaranteed; (b) gatekeepers and producers shall have operational autonomy from government and from private financial interests; (c) a decentralization of broadcasting is to be achieved through development of local radio and regional TV stations and programming; and (d) the state shall have continued responsibility for licensing the use of the spectrum and the transmission infrastructure used by all broadcasters.[15]

The 1982 reform law modified the traditional French broadcasting system in a number of ways. Foremost among these innovations is an end to the state's monopoly of programming services. This has been achieved through creation of an independent regulatory body and through separate companies responsible for production and programming services on national, regional, and local levels. Another major change entailed the formation of a national advisory board whose members represent a wide range of professions and interests. Furthermore, all French citizens are guaranteed opportunities for access to the telecommunication media, including the legal right of reply to broadcasts affecting them adversely. Finally, no film may be broadcast or sold in cassette or disc form during its first 6 to 18 months of exhibition in public movie theaters.

Control

The government has commissioned four institutions to implement telecommunication policy and to provide mechanisms for public participation in the workings of broadcasting and cable. The Parliamentary Delegation for Audiovisual Communications is a committee of "rapporteurs," including representatives from the Commissions of Finance and Culture, Audiovisual Affairs, and the Senate. They will permanently monitor the public service functions of all broadcasters and offer advice through an annual report to parliament.

Perhaps the most important new institution is *The Audiovisual Communications Authority,* France's first independent regulatory agency for broadcasting. Referred to as the Haute Authorité, or simply the Authority, its main responsibility is "to guarantee the independence of the public radio and television services" by ensuring that they respect pluralism, balance, and human dignity in programming, safeguard the French language, promote regional languages and culture, and adopt technologies to serve the hearing impaired. The Authority also appoints the Presidents and Administrative councils of the production companies, regulates political and electoral broadcasts, administers the right of reply procedures, monitors broadcasters' public service obligations, licenses local cable radio and TV services, supervises advertising, organizes French participation in international nongovernmental organizations, and submits an annual report to the President of the Republic. The Authority's nine members serve non-renewable 9-year terms and are not subject to dismissal. The first appointments were made in August 1982.[16]

The *National Audiovisual Communications Council* (whose French abbreviation is CNA) is a 56-member pluralistic advisement board that comments to the Authority on virtually all forms of public telecommunications operations. The Council's membership, appointed for 3 years, is comprised of seven representatives from the following eight domains: the regions, professional organizations, popular culture and education, family and consumers, the broadcasting unions, journalism and the communications industry, the cultural and scientific worlds, and the major religions and philosophical communities.

Lastly, the *Regional Audiovisual Communications Committee* advises on ways of developing telecommunications for the purposes of preserving the heritages, identities, languages, and cultural traditions of the various regions.

Services

The current public radio and television system of France contains ten elements, having assimilated the previous seven organizations created by the 1975 Act. Each operates according to specified regulations issued jointly by the Ministers of Telecommunications (relay networks) and Communications (mass media), in consultation with the Authority (regulator) and the Parliamentary Delegation (performance monitor). The ten units are:

1. *The Public Transmission Establishment* (Telediffusion de France, or TDF) is responsible for all modes of transmission and has financial and administrative autonomy from the program companies which use its facilities and networks. It is run by a 16-member council, each with 3-year terms, and is financed by payments from its national and regional broadcasting clients and from a share of the license fee income. TDF operates under joint authority of the Minister of Telecommunications and the Minister of Communications.

2. *Radio France* is the national company responsible for the three networks (*France-Inter, France-Culture,* and *France-Musique*) and manages two national symphonic orchestras, a chorus, and a choir. It also helps finance the 12 regional radio companies that together manage roughly 100 local stations. Like all of the following companies, Radio France is run by a 12-member Administrative Council, each having three year appointments.

3. *Radio France International* (RFI) is the official external shortwave broadcasting service. The company is co-owned by Radio France and the state, the former being the majority stockholder. Besides French, it also broadcasts in English, German, Spanish, and Portuguese in Europe, Africa, and the Americas.

4. *Television Francaise* (TF1) is one of two national TV companies provid-

ing a network service using the 819 line system for monochrome and 625 lines for SECAM color transmissions. TF1 operates about 37 hours weekly.

5. *Antenne 2 France* (A2F) is the other national TV program company whose network operates on the 625 line SECAM color system about 36 hours a week.

6. *France Regions 3* (FR3) has been a noncommercial national TV service supplying three regions (Lorraine, Dijon, and Limoges) with programming via a 625 line/SECAM network. Its mission under the 1982 reorganization act is to implement the decentralization plan by loaning money to, and coordinating the programming for, the 12 regional TV companies now being developed. FR3's future as of 1983 was somewhat uncertain in that it may be replaced by the dozen regional stations. Each new TV outlet will have its own Regional Audiovisual Communications Committee to help it achieve programming autonomy by 1987 and to reflect its indigenous cultural characteristics. FR3 also offers radio programs.

7. *The National Overseas Broadcasting Company* is in charge of programming radio and TV stations of the Overseas Department and Territories of France. It is a common subsidiary of Radio France and France Regions 3. FR3 formerly had responsibility for programming the overseas stations, RFI, and France-Inter-Paris et France-Inter 12 Provinces (FiP & Cie). The new company is called RFO (Rtv Francoise d'Outre-Mer).[17]

8. SFP, standing for the former private production company, *Societé Francaise de Production*, has been retained as the designation for the new national production firm, the majority of whose stock is held by the state, with the TV network companies also having a share. SFP makes programs for other French TV companies under contract and for the international market.

9. *The Marketing Company* receives the rights to programs produced by other French companies and markets them abroad. It is administered by a nine-member board and is owned by the state, the program companies, and various public agencies.

10. *The National Audiovisual Communications Institute* (INA) is a national agency responsible for conducting research, training personnel, and marketing archival programming (over 5 years old) to domestic and foreign broadcasters. Like SOFIRAD, it is "a public state establishment of an industrial and commercial character." INA has financial autonomy from the program companies and is run by a council of 16 appointees with 3-year terms.

In addition to the 10 autonomous bodies comprising the public broadcasting system in France, a Local Radio Commission has been established to provide consultation to the Authority on the licensing and development of private local stations. The task will be aided by a support fund for local radio, with money being raised through a monthly levy on the government's advertising agencies to be collected by the INA. The Authority had licensed 22 local radio stations in Paris and 46 elsewhere in the country by mid-1983.[18]

Financing

The public radio and television complex is financed by revenues from the annual license fees on television receivers, and by advertising, the latter having been authorized by the 1974 law. Some income is also realized through the international marketing of French productions. However, advertising may not account for more than 25% of a program company's annual income, and is limited to no more than 24 minutes per day on television.[19] Fees in 1983 were $40 for a black and white receiver and $60 per color set.

Cable, Teletext, and Satellites

The French government announced plans in early 1983 for a massive national cable network using optic fibres and to be run as a public monopoly by the PTT, which will have no involvement in content. Local public and private groups may bid on franchises to operate and program community cable systems. France has moved quickly to head off competition in cable technology from the UK, U.S., and Germany.

The system will be tied in with the national telephone service and to Teletel, the PTT's interactive videotex service. A number of locations were being wired throughout the nation by 1984, with several million households to be connected by 1985. France already has a large number of MATV and CATV systems that relay terrestrial services. France also has operationalized an advanced teletext system called ANTIOPE. The developing cable network will also be able to receive programming from the joint French-German DBS, scheduled for launching in 1986. The satellite will offer three channels at the start and five by 1990.[20]

Problems and Prospects

The most persistent problem in French broadcasting has been government interference in programming. This has deprived French audiences of objective newscasts and a choice in appealing entertainment programming on radio (especially pop music) and television (escapist series). The 1982 Act has set in place a less centralized system in which competing program companies and the introduction of private local radio should redress this chronic deficiency.

Traditional broadcasting is being reinforced in other ways in the 1980s. A fourth TV network, *Canal Plus,* has been developed under the leadership of the chairman of the government-backed advertising agency, Havas.[21] Following its activation in 1984, the fourth channel is a free over-the-air service by day and converts to a pay-per-view operation during the evening hours.[22]

External SW broadcasting by RFI has been among the least active in the Western world, due in part to the French government's reliance on SOFIRAD's activities to make its influence felt in other nations. Under reorganization, however, RFI's operating hours have been expanded from 125 a week in 1981 to 421 in 1983, with a target of over 1000 hours per week by 1987. Its current annual budget likewise will be tripled to roughly $85 million by decade's end. The

French government also imposed a $60 annual license fee on home video record-
ers in November 1982 in an attempt to exploit its popularity as a means of
subsidizing traditional public broadcasting services in France.[23]

The release of two official reports during 1985 signalled that private television
may be on the way in France. The Bredin Report in May recommended that two
national commercial networks be authorized provided that they not transmit
during the day, that each—like the public TV channels (TF1, A2F and FR3)—
devote 60% of its airtime to French or other European programming, and that
their programs not be interrupted by advertising spots. The report also envisioned
a boom in private TV, with 62 regional stations supplying daytime programming
and perhaps as many as 133 affiliates and 40 independent outlets coming on the
air within a decade. Two neighboring broadcasters, RTL and Europe 1, are
interested in investing in any new French TV networks.

A second report was issued in July by Prime Minister Laurent Fabius. It
proposed that four private networks be started, with three to be run by large radio
stations in close cooperation with SOFIRAD and the fourth serving as a non-pay
version of Canal Plus. As France's first pay-TV service, Canal Plus attracted
many subscribers when it began in late 1984 but had lost many customers by
mid-1985 due to its disappointing schedule of old movies and American reruns.
The government is expected to make a decision before the 1986 elections and, no
matter which plan prevails, France almost certainly will have private TV by the
late 1980s.[24]

ITALY

There is a bitter irony in the fact that the father of radio, Guglielmo Marconi, had
his brilliant invention shunned by the authorities of his native Italy. He was
forced to take his wireless transmitter to England, where the conditions were
better suited for technological innovation and entreprenurial enterprise. This, in
retrospect, may have been a blessing in disguise, since the 1920s, the decade of
radio's infancy, saw the coming to power in Italy of Benito Mussolini and his
doctrine of totalitarian Fascism.[25]

Although radio developed as a monopoly, reform laws during the 1970s
unleashed a torrent of private local radio and television stations throughout the
Italian Republic. Today, Italy has one of the richest assortments of broadcasting
and cable programming available anywhere in the world.

RAI-Radiotelevisione Italiana is currently defined as a state broadcasting
monopoly jointly owned by public and private capital stockholders, with legal
and administrative headquarters in Rome. It is licensed by the PTT to operate all
transmission facilities. RAI had a monopoly on Italian broadcasting from 1952
until the 1970s, when the idea of private television began to germinate. A 1975
Reform Law and 1976 Constitutional Court ruling extended RAI's monopoly of
national network broadcasting, but implicitly permitted private TV stations to

exist. Public broadcasting in Italy continues to be based on the principles of independence, objectivity, and sensitivity in reporting on, and programming for, the nation's various political segments and cultures.[26]

Control

RAI is regulated by a 10-member Parliamentary Commission which oversees programming, budgetary and planning activities, and also sponsors audience and content research. The RAI company is administered by a 16-member Board of Directors, elected by Parliament for 3-year terms, and having responsibility for all aspects of its operations. A Director-General is appointed by the Board to hire a staff and act as the chief executive of the company.[27]

Programming and Services

RAI maintains regional radio and television centers in Milan, Naples, and Turin—each of which produces programming for, and supplies news to, the national networks and local outlets in their regions.

Currently, the public RAI provides the following radio and TV services:

Radio:
Radiouno (Radio One)—a popular music and news network via AM;
Radiodue (Radio Two)—variety, quiz shows, and news network via AM;
Radiotre (Radio Three)—a literary, scientific, and classical music FM chain for listeners with cultivated tastes;
TV:
National Programme (RAI-1)—schools programming during morning hours, children's shows afternoons, and general interest evenings;
Second Programme (RAI-2)—films, opera, and theatre during evenings only;
Third Programme (RAI-3)—minority interest programming, 5:30–9 pm daily, formed in 1976. RAI-3's programming is carried by the nation's 20 regional channels, along with their own productions.

In addition, RAI operates an external broadcasting service on shortwave in eight foreign languages, 20 regional radio stations in Italy, and domestic programming services in German for Bolzano Province, in Slovene for Trieste, and in French for the Aosta Valley. A special German-language service, *Rundfunkanstalt Sudtirol* (RAS), relays radio and TV programs from Germany, Austria, and Switzerland to the German-speaking population in the autonomous Province of Southern Tirol.[28]

Most of the 13% of foreign programming imported by RAI-TV comes from Yugoslavia, Switzerland, and France.[29] However, Italian law allows foreign TV signals, like *Tele Monte Carlo* (TMC) from Monaco, to be relayed throughout the country via a network of TV repeater transmitters. In fact, TMC contracted with RAI in the spring of 1982 to offer a joint service to both Monaco and northern Italy. RAI further promised to invest $5 million in financially-troubled TMC and provide it with 4 hours of programming daily.[30]

Commercial broadcasting competition in Italy has opened many new avenues of political, social, and cultural involvement at the community level. Another possible effect has been suggested by a study which showed that private TV stations rely heavily upon entertainment, averaging 80 to 85% of their total airtime, while the public RAI's averages were 35% entertainment, 25% news, and 40% cultural, educational, and sports programming.[31]

Private broadcasting in Italy was still in a state of flux in the early 1980s due to the vagueness of its legal and regulatory status. By 1986, there were hundreds of private radio stations, mostly FM, and 13 major MW stations with regular schedules. However, if those stations broadcasting at irregular times are counted, the total is closer to 2000. In terms of television, there are over 350 private local stations.

Although private TV networks are not explicitly authorized to transmit nationally, several commercial stations have taken advantage of the vagueness of Italian broadcast law. The first of these, *Canale 5*, has now established some 60 repeater stations throughout Italy, and sends them cassettes of its programming daily for simultaneous airing. Since these stations are not interconnected by a transmission network, they operate legally as independent transmitters, but in fact constitute a nationwide service of identical programming.

The practice in turn had inspired other stations—*Rete A, Rete 4, Italia Uno, Euro TV,* and *Video Music*—to form networks having from 14 to 100 affiliates each by 1986.[32] Private stations receive no part of the license fee revenue, but also have no advertising limits as does RAI. Hence, they now rival RAI in total income. They also rival RAI's networks in popular support. The May 1983 Neilsen figures showed that the private TV stations had a combined audience share of 53.5%, beating RAI for the first time. By contrast, the RAI channels attracted 86% of the viewers in November 1977, while the commercial stations' shared total was a paltry 7.7%, the balance tuning to foreign spillover channels.[33]

The official policy response to the private competition has been to let them continue as long as they don't interfere with RAI operations.[34] The popularity of the private TV networks seems to assure them of a bonafide legal future when RAI's statutory monopoly on national networking expires in 1987. The intensity of the ratings race, especially that between *RAI-1* and *Canale 5*, is being run with massive amounts of imported programming. To illustrate the scope, nearly all of the series aired on Italian TV in 1983 were American, and 80% of the films telecast were foreign productions.[35] From a viewer's perspective, of course, the competition has brought about an Italian renaissance in television programming in which quantity is also being matched with quality.

Finances

RAI's main source of income is derived from the annual license fees for radio and TV receivers and cable connections. The second income source comes from advertising proceeds. Commercials may not exceed 5% of the total airtime for radio and television. RAI can sell time directly or indirectly through an advertising subsidiary, SIPRA, that acquires sponsors and writes contracts with advertisers. RAI's actual income level from advertising is established by the Parliamentary Commission. A third source of revenue is paid to RAI by the government for services of social utility which are beyond its charter obligation. These include minority language broadcasts, educational programs to the schools, and the shortwave overseas service.[36]

Problems and Prospects

Italy is experiencing a rapid transition from limited-broadcast channels controlled exclusively by the state to a multi-channel marketplace of ever-increasing private radio, television, and cable outlets. This situation, like the one in France, indicates a trend away from spectrum scarcity and state monopoly toward a technological proliferation and commercialization of programming options. One problem is that this growth has happened with the tacit rather than explicit approval of government, raising questions as to how well the spectrum and cable channels are being managed, the amount of programming Italian society can absorb, and the collective impact that the commercial competition is having on the audience and programming of the public RAI. And while private local broadcasting may enhance local control and access, the emphasis on mass appeal entertainment could dilute popular support for RAI's more serious programming mission.

In addition to the expansion of local cable systems, Italy joined the European Space Agency (ESA) in 1977, a consortium of 11 European nations. It was one of four countries to propose a Large Telecommunications Satellite (L-SAT) project to ESA's Board of Directors, calling for a two-channel DBS to be launched in 1985. One of the TV channels would be used by Italy experimentally in the 20–30 GHz band, although RAI had not formulated plans for its use. The project is seen by Italy as giving a boost to its telecommunications industry, nevertheless.[37]

WEST GERMANY

Nowhere do the First and Second Worlds of broadcasting confront one another more starkly than in Germany. What was a single nation became divided into the Federal Republic of (West) Germany and the (East) German Democratic Republic at the end of World War II. Contemporary German broadcasting is therefore a tale of two countries, which, despite a common heritage, have necessarily devised two media systems as divergent as their respective governments.

The distinguishing characteristic of West German broadcasting can be traced to the nation's post-War political structure, a decentralized federal arrangement in which governmental power and responsibility is shared among its ten states (called Länder). The rationale for regionalized institutions in the new West Germany stemmed from the bitter legacy of abused central authority under Hitler. Thus, under federalism, the responsibility for broadcasting also resides with the individual Länder. Each broadcasting corporation therefore is established by state law as a public corporation or, literally, an Institution of Public Rights (Anstalt des Offenlichen Rechts). The legislatures of the Länder have the authority to license broadcasters and set their license fees.[38] Besides being free of private ownership and influence, steps have also been taken to guarantee that West German broadcasting is independent of government influence and responsive to the public. For example, Article 5 of the Federal Republic's Constitutional Law, which pledges the nation to freedom of thought and information, effectively prevents official control of programming. Further, representatives of various population segments within the Länder are selected to sit as advising counsellors on the boards of all broadcasting organizations in order to ensure that each broadcaster fulfills its chartered obligations to serve the collective public interest.[39]

Organizations

The present broadcasting arrangement in West Germany may legitimately be described as an oligopoly of regional public corporations that operate autonomously under charters awarded to them by their individual provinces or through interstate agreements. Nonetheless, it became clear early that some national broadcasting services would be necessary in order to unify the citizenry and effectively project West Germany's national interests abroad. In 1950, the regional broadcasters thus formed a cooperative union, known as Arbeitsgemeinschaft der öffentlichrechtlichen Rundfunkanstaltern der Bundesrepublik Deutschland (ARD). In English, this means "an organization of federated public-legal radio corporations of the Federal Republic of Germany." The German title is precisely meant to indicate that these public broadcasting corporations, through sovereign organizations, are better able to pursue their common objective of providing programming that is free of commercial and political influence by working together as a group than by operating independently of one another.[40] The ARD also enabled them to coordinate their programming and to initiate a national television network in 1954 called Deutsche Fernsehen (DFS), which thus depends upon program contributions from its regional members in a fashion similar to Britain's ITV.

Subsequently, three other national broadcasting entities were authorized. A 1960 law established Deutsche Welle (DW), a worldwide shortwave service, and Deutschlandfunk (DLF), a powerful longwave station covering all of Europe and directed especially at East Germany.[41] During the following year, another national TV network was created by inter-Länd agreement to compete with the ARD channel, DFS. This public corporation, *Zweites Deutsches Fernsehen* (ZDF), or Second German Television, established administrative headquarters in Mainz, constructed a landline network parallel to ARD's, and activated studios in Berlin, Hamburg, and Munich. Its first programs were broadcast in April 1963.[42] ZDF's interstate treaty calls for it to be financed by license fees, to acquire any programming it cannot produce itself from freelance producers or third parties, and to exchange production services and resources with ARD in the interest of cost efficiency.[43]

ARD and ZDF remain the nation's two principal broadcasters, the latter being an autonomous body. ARD is currently a confederation of nine regional broadcasting corporations and the two state-run radio services. These are:[44]

BR—*Bayerischer Rundfunk* (Bavarian Broadcasting Corporation, Munich)

HR—*Hessischer Rundfunk* (Hessen Broadcasting Corp., Frankfurt-am-Main)

NDR—*Norddeutscher Rundfunk* (North German Broadcasting Corp., Hamburg)

RB—*Radio Bremen*

SDR—*Süddeutscher Rundfunk* (South German Broadcasting Corp., Stuttgart)

SFB—*Sender Freies Berlin* (Radio Free Berlin, West Berlin)

SWF—*Südwestfunk* (South-West Broadcasting Corp., Baden-Baden)

SR—*Saarlandischer Rundfunk* (Broadcasting Corp. of the Saar, Saarbrucken)

WDR—*Westdeutscher Rundfunk* (West German Broadcasting Corp., Cologne)

DLF—*Deutschlandfunk* (Radio Germany, a longwave service for Europe)

DW—*Deutsche Welle* (Voice of Germany, a shortwave worldwide service).

Each regional member operates three radio services and two television channels within their respective Länder. Two of the radio services counterprogram a schedule of popular and traditional music, light entertainment, and news. The third offers intellectual and cultural programming and classical music. Most provide regular programs for foreign workers in their native languages as a part of these services. In terms of geographical jurisdiction, all but three of the regional corporations serve a single state. Specifically, NDR covers three Länder, SWF broadcasts to one and part of another, and SDR serves only a segment of one.[45] The regional broadcasters also take turns serving a term as ARD manager. For instance, BR was chosen for 1982 and 1983; NDR became manager in 1984.[46]

Control

Statutory responsibility for the regulation of broadcasting in West Germany is divided between the individual Länder, who license a single corporation to offer radio and TV programming services within their respective regions, and the national government's PTT (Deutsche Bundespost), which provides transmitters and distribution services. Each chartered broadcasting organization has a Board of Governors, Administrative Council, and Director General (Intendant) to make policy and manage day-to-day operations. A 1974 law placed cable within the domain of broadcasting. No private ownership of radio and TV stations had been allowed as of 1983, and advertising time is greatly restricted. The public nature of broadcasting's proprietorship insulates programmers from direct influence by government or commercial interests, yet the power of political parties to make appointments to broadcasting boards has been used at times as a kind of leverage on the system.[47]

Financing

All public broadcasting services in West Germany are supported by a monthly fee paid on television receivers, and by limited advertising proceeds. Educational broadcasting, however, is financed directly from the public treasury by taxes. The fee, which is the same in all Länder, was raised in 1983 to $6.25 a month through 1986. Most of the fee revenue is divided between the radio (29%) and television (65%) services, with the balance (6%) being allocated among *Deutschlandfunk* (DLF), four pilot cable projects, a fund to develop satellite technology, and an expansion of terrestrial broadcasting relays into remote mountainous regions of the country.[48] ARD receives 70% of all license proceeds, which are divided among its members using a formula based on their respective production quotas and coverage areas. The remainder (30%) goes to the national ZDF television network.[49] Currently, ARD receives 68% of its annual income from license fees and 32% from advertising, while the respective figures for ZDF are 62% and 38%.[50]

Services and Programming

Residents of West Germany typically receive three radio stations (*Program 1, 2, and 3*) from the ARD corporation enfranchised to serve their specific region, plus the following three TV options:

> *Channel 1*—Regional programs from the Land broadcaster in the daytime; and the ARD's cooperative service, DFS, during prime time.
> *Channel 2*—ZDF, the separate national network.
> *Channel 3*—The noncommercial educational service produced by five groups.

During evening (peak viewing) hours, the national services, DFS and ZDF, are required to offer viewers a choice between different types of programs. In reality, however, they tend to compete with, rather than to complement, one another, while the Third Channel offers the only genuine alternative.[51]

Specifically, each of ARD's nine regional organizations has three programming missions to carry out via its two TV channels. On one (*Channel 1*), it must broadcast its own productions to its regional viewers several hours daily and also contribute productions to ARD's national TV network, DFS, which it carries evenings during prime time. Its other outlet (*Channel 3*) is devoted to noncommercial educational and cultural programming, currently produced by five groups—BR, HR, WDR, NDR (with assistance from SFB and RB), and a joint production team involving SR, SWF, and SDR.[52]

ARD's constitution requires each regional broadcaster to produce some TV programming for the cooperative pool that schedules DFS, the national distribution network. Their individual production loads are proportionate to their financial resources and populations served. Present quotas are: WDR (25%), NDR (20%), BR (17%), NR, SFB, SDR, and SWF (8% each), and RB and SR (3% each.[53] The strength of ARD's federal structure lies in its pluralism, given that the majority of programming is regionally produced and includes local news, some entertainment, and commercials.

A breakdown of TV programming into categories shows the following averages for the combined national channels, DFS and ZDF: Entertainment (29%), Public Affairs (26%), Feature Films (13%), News (11%), Sports (9%), Children (7%), and other (5%).[54] There is no legal restriction on the amount of foreign programming that can be aired on West German television. Recent figures indicate that ARD imports about a quarter of its program schedule (23%), ZDF nearly a third (30%).[55]

Other Services

A number of other broadcasters, mostly foreign supported, operate from West German soil. Their uniqueness and variety bear mentioning. For example, a commercial radio station, *Europe No. 1,* operates from bordering Saarland under West German jurisdiction, although its signal is directed to cover most of France with a pop music format in French. Another unique station is RIAS—Radio in the American Sector of Berlin—established by the Allies in February 1946 as a wired service for Germans living in the city's U.S. zone. It has since become an important international broadcasting voice, targeted mainly at East Germany and financed jointly by the U.S. and West German governments. At the present time, RIAS is controlled and supported principally by the Federal Republic. Like the aforementioned *Deutschlandfunk,* RIAS programs Western news and music and extensive coverage of East German affairs.[56]

A highly popular broadcasting presence throughout West Germany is AFN, the American Armed Forces Network. Its AM and FM stations fill the airwaves with virtually every type of American music, plus stateside news and entertainment fare. AFN is particularly popular with West German youth. Other military stations can also be found in various parts of the country, operated by Britain, Canada, and France. In addition, *Radio Free Europe/Radio Liberty* maintain their chief base of operations in Munich, a city that also hosts a Voice of America station.[57]

Problems and Prospects

West German broadcasting has been criticized at home for its lacklustre programming, but is universally praised for its technical achievements. Specifically, radio and television programming have been plagued with complaints about political bias, unimaginative production techniques, and insufficient choice. The public-federal structure also presents problems. Although one of the best financed broadcasting systems in the world, future license fee increases, no matter how unpopular, will be necessary to pay for program expansion and new delivery systems like cable, DBS, and teletext.[58]

The election of a new conservative government in 1982 signalled a number of changes for West German broadcasting in the decade ahead, especially in terms of cable and private broadcasting. The ruling Christian Democrats quickly doubled the funding for cable development to nearly $400 million, and went on record as favoring private involvement in the construction and operation of cable systems, as well as the licensing of commercial broadcasting companies.[59]

Four cable projects have been scheduled for construction during the 1980s. Two, in Dortmund and Munich, will be run in cooperation with their existing public broadcasters. The one in Berlin will be operated by a public corporation and SFB. Another, in Ludwigshafen, has been established solely as a public organization with no broadcaster involvement. The Munich system will eventually provide about 30,000 households with 50 to 60 channels, including films, minority-interest offerings, and educational programming.[60] A teletext system has also been tested by the government. The three parties most interested in using teletext are the public broadcasters, the PTT, and the domestic publishing industry.[61]

The governments of West Germany and France contracted in 1979 to produce a pair of direct broadcast satellites for launching in 1985 or 1986. Each country will be served by three channels initially and five by 1987. Details as to who will program the DBS channels are being worked out, but the present public broadcasters in West Germany intend to be included.[62]

The policy issues facing West Germany's postal and telecommunications administration, the Deutsche Bundespost (DBP), are inextricably tied to broadcasting and cable to a greater degree than is found in most other countries. This is due in large measure to the reliance of the various state broadcasting corporations on the transmission facilities of the national DBP monopoly.

A series of official reports between 1979 and 1981, especially those issued by the so-called Monopoly Commission, struggled to define the proper roles to be played by the DBP and by competing private enterprises in providing West

Germans with their future telecommunication hardware and services. The consensus in the early 1980s was that the DBP should retain its monopoly position over the transmission networks, but that terminal equipment for cable TV and teletext be provided by competing private firms. Other concerns in the ongoing policy debate include the influence of foreign commercial interests on national telecommunication industries (from the U.S. and Japan) and on domestic television content (from the U.S. and Luxembourg), not to mention the effect that proposed private radio and television stations would have on the present public broadcasting system.[63]

Private broadcasting is almost certain to develop in the FRG. In June 1981, the nation's supreme Federal Constitutional Court (BVG) struck down the section of the Saar's 1967 broadcasting law that prohibited private licensees. This landmark decision made it clear that the framework for introducing private broadcasting should be left to the individual Länder. The BVG did, however, set minimum requirements for licensing private radio and television stations—such as banning print media from owning broadcast outlets, and restricting advertising.

The Monopoly Commission's November 1981 report, "Anti-Trust Problems in the Introduction of Private Radio and Television," agreed in principle that private ownership would bring badly needed economic competition and program diversity to German broadcasting. A 1983 report by the governing Christian Democratic Union will hasten that party's commitment to a new marketplace of broadcast and cable programming services. Private radio stations will mark the first stage of change, followed by a private TV network.

Finally, two developments in January 1984 set the privatization trend in motion. Radio-Tele-Luxembourg began a new channel in German, with coverage to 1.7 million viewers in the Saar, part ownership by German interests, local news from two regional newspapers, and unlimited advertising. It broadcasts 5 hours daily and runs one film each night and several on weekends. This RTL station, plus a private TV station licensed to start up in Lower Saxony in mid-1985, means that more Länder will authorize additional private TV operations forthwith.[64]

THE NETHERLANDS

Holland has perhaps the world's most open, diversified, and truly democratic broadcasting arrangement. Programming for the system is provided by a complex aggregate of pluralistic religious and secular groups representing virtually every segment of Dutch society. These formal associations are each licensed to program freely through the publicly-operated radio and television service. The size of each organization's membership in turn determines the amount of airtime it will be alloted, as well as its share of total license fee revenue. Dutch broadcasting historically has been noncommercial, but limited advertising has been authorized in recent years. Local stations also are being phased in.

Organizations

To qualify for a broadcasting license, an organization must demonstrate a sufficient number of dues paying members to meet one of three categories (A, B, or C). Specifically, at least 60,000 members are needed to qualify for temporary Candidate status, limited to 2 years. A minimum of 150,000 members is required for Category C, 300,000 members for B, and 450,000 for Category A.[65]

There are currently nine broadcasting organizations in Holland, eight chartered membership groups, and an umbrella agency—NOS (Nederlandse Omroep Stichting), the Netherlands Broadcasting Foundation—which coordinates their programming schedules and provides them with production and transmission facilities. NOS has the largest share of airtime and fills it with programming of national interest from its hugh production center outside of Hilversum. The eight franchised broadcasters comprising the NOS cooperative, as rank-ordered by size and membership affiliation, are:[66]

Category A:	AVRO	(independent)
	TROS	(independent)
	KRO	(Catholic)
	NCRV	(Protestant)
	VARA	(socialist)
Category B:	none	
Category C:	VPRO	(social criticism)
	EO	(Evangelical)
	VOO	(mass entertainment)

The tasks of NOS include: (a) coordinating program transmission times for all member broadcasting organizations; (b) producing general interest programming, like news and sports; (c) exporting programs; (d) providing and operating all radio and television studios for member groups; (e) supervising all personnel contracts and budgetary matters; and (f) representing Dutch broadcasting's interests abroad. NOS is governed by the Executive, a decision-making body made up of individuals appointed by the Crown, the member organizations, and various cultural groups selected by the Minister. The NOS Board of Management carries out Executive Decisions and is in charge of daily operations. Each NOS member has a board and is responsible for its own business, technical, personnel, and programming affairs.

Educational broadcasting is provided by two other agencies. NOT, an educational foundation, was created separately in the early 1960s to produce instructional programming for the schools. This was augmented subsequently by TELEAC (the Television Academy), which is chartered to provide adult education programs for home viewing through the facilities of NOS.[67]

Experiments in local radio, TV, and cable were authorized during the 1970s. Several regional radio stations were also activated. These had to be financed by the local communities, since advertising was originally banned.[68] However, the

Broadcasting Advertising Foundation, STER (Stichting Ether Reclame), was licensed by the government in 1967 as a monopoly in charge of producing all commercials and scheduling them for air play through NOS. Today, advertising messages from STER occupy over 4 hours of radio airtime weekly, and 3 ½ hours on television.[69]

Services and Programming

The transmission system used by all Dutch broadcasters is owned by the Nederlandse Omroep Zender Maatschappij (NOZEMA), located in Flevoland, but NOS controls the use of the national radio and TV studios in Hilversum. Holland's current broadcasting services are structured as follows.[70]

National Radio Networks:

Hilversum I—General interest programming 24 hours a day, AM & FM
Hilversum II—Daily general interest and evening cultural fare on AM & FM;
Hilversum III—Popular music 24 hours a day on AM & FM Stereo;
Hilversum IV—Serious music, 6 am–10 pm via FM Stereo.

Regional Radio Stations:

ROZ—Regional Omroep Zuid—serves the southern portion of the country;
Radio Noord—covers the northern region;
Radio Oost—broadcasts to the eastern region.

Local Radio Stations:

STAD—Stichting Amsterdamse Draadloze Omroep—serves Amsterdam;
SROB—Stichting Regionale Omroep Brabant—in Eindhoven;
Radio Fryslan—located in Leeuwarden.

External Shortwave Service:

Radio Nederland Wereldomroep—broadcasts in seven languages from Hilversum.

National Television Networks:

Nederland 1—telecasts a full range of programs approximately 40 hours weekly;
Nederland 2—telecasts complementary programs approximately 40 hours per week;

Cable

By 1984, cable television had penetrated 70% of the nation's households.[71] These are nonprofit operations funded by municipal and regional governments and sponsoring organizations.[72] NOS also has a highly developed teletext service in place.[73] VCRs were being used in 16% of Holland's homes by 1984.[74]

Control

Under the operative Broadcasting Act of 1980, the Minister of Culture, Recreation, and Social Work is responsible for NOS's general policy, revenues, and administration. A Crown-appointed Commissioner for Broadcasting sees that NOS correctly implements the Act and supervises its budget. A 12-member Broadcasting Council meets 15 to 20 times annually to advise NOS on matters of policy and legislation affecting broadcasting.[75] The Act further limits advertising to 30 minutes daily for TV, and 45 minutes on the radio networks. No advertising is allowed on Sundays.[76] Cable also falls under the statute's jurisdiction, but the importation of foreign channels and advertising have been embargoed by the government.[77]

Finances

The 1980 Act stipulates that all expenses incurred by the PTT, NOS, the Broadcasting Council, and Government Commissioner be covered by total license revenues and the net advertising proceeds of STER. The annual license fee is determined by Parliament, levied per household rather than on receivers, collected by the PTT, and disbursed by the Minister. After collection, administrative and transmission costs are deducted, funds are allocated to the broadcasting organizations of NOS and the World Broadcasting Service, based on size and need, respectively. Regional radio stations operate independent of NOS and are entitled to only marginal financing. Local TV and cable operations must be locally financed, since advertising on cable has been prohibited. Discussions have ensued on the possibility of commercializing cable. All network broadcasting is financed by an annual fee per each household with a TV set and through limited advertising. The network broadcasters presently rely on national advertising for 25% of their income.

Problems and Prospects

Public demand and private pressures for mass television entertainment, pop music radio, and broadcast advertising have in recent years resulted in fierce competition among licensed groups for members. In the context of an increasing youthful and less religious society, some newer organizations (notably, AVRO, TROS and VOO) are drawing members away from the older broadcast licensees based on formal religions. This, in the opinion of many, has led to less program diversity. It also has led to more imported programming, which occupied 40% of Holland's TV airtime by 1983.[78] In fact, only EO, NCRV, KRO, and VARA continue to interpret the broadcasting code's spirit by representing a specific religious or political view. The other broadcasting groups seem more interested in viewing ratings.[79]

A survey by NOS revealed that listenership for pirate radio increased from 28% to 42% in 1982, due largely to the prevalence of songs with Dutch lyrics in their programs. This type of pirate station caters to local audiences and also honors requests. Ironically, the official NOS pop music service, *Hilversum 3*, airs mostly songs in English. A second category of pirate broadcaster is the commercial radio station that competes with *Hilversum 3* as a source of Anglo-American music, only with more advertisements and deejay chit chat. A third type of illegal station is the highly mobile clandestine transmitter often affiliated with and run by an activist group, like the peace movement or an esoteric youth cult.[80]

A 1982 report by the Dutch Scientific Council for Government Policy focussed attention on a future media strategy for the Netherlands. It has recommended the widest possible adoption of new services, especially commercial cable, with locally-originated programming, and subscription TV. Other print and broadcast media organizations would also be allowed to apply for cable licenses. Regional and local radio companies could be established, providing their communities are prepared to finance them. Existing broadcasters fear, however, that cable could siphon off some of their commercial revenue.[81]

The government followed the report by issuing a White Paper in the fall of 1983 that proposed sweeping changes for both broadcasting and cable in Holland. The first of these would introduce Pay-TV as an exclusively private and commercial enterprise; the second would divide NOS into three separate organizations and essentially end its life as the "umbrella" for private broadcasting groups in the Netherlands.

The fate of NOS was not clear at the end of 1984, but it appears that the future NOS will be responsible only for a joint program mission of news and cultural events of national importance. Its former Facilities Department, owner of the Hilversum studios and remote broadcasting equipment used by all licensed foundations, would become an independent company whose stock would be held by the state (75%) and the broadcasting organizations (25%). The General Secretariat of NOS would become the administrative arm of a new regulatory body, the Commission of the Media, comprised of five commissioners who would be appointed by the Minister of Culture. The new Media Commission would have autonomy and distance from the sitting government of the day, enabling it to regulate broadcasting and cable activities and to decide programming issues that might come before it.[82]

SWEDEN

The level of media consumption and saturation in contemporary Sweden is among the highest of any nation in the world. Swedish radio and television programming enjoy an enviable reputation for quality and seriousness throughout the world of broadcasting. The affluence and cooperative spirit that characterize Swedish society have been directly translated into a broadcasting service devoted to producing quality programming for an enlightened audience.

No doubt the most unique trait of Sweden's broadcasting system is the fact that it is privately owned, yet noncommercial. In fact, Sweden is the only Western nation that allows no advertising on its airways. After nearly six decades of highly centralized radio and television services, the Swedish Parliament brought about sweeping reforms with the passage of the Broadcasting Act of 1979. The new legislation reorganized and decentralized the structure of Swedish broadcasting while retaining the system as a noncommercial public service. Quality, cultural integrity, and diversity are the keynotes of its current programming mandate.

Organization and Services

Sveriges Radio A.B. (the Swedish Broadcasting Corporation) is an integral organization whose stock is owned by three categories of shareholders: a spectrum of social forces like trade unions, churches, and popular movements (60%); industry and commerce (20%); and the Swedish press (20%). SR-SBC is supervised by a 13-member Board of Governors—six of whom (including the chair) are appointed by the government, five by the shareholders, and two representing the employee unions.[83]

As restructured, SR is the parent corporation of four wholly-owned subsidiary companies. Each is a noncommercial public entity with its own Board of Managers and autonomous programming responsibility for its broadcasting services. These are:[84]

1. *Sveriges Television A.B.* (Swedish Television Company) operates two national television channels—SVT-1 and SVT-2—each offering a full range of programming approximately 12 hours daily.

2. *Sveriges Riksradio A.B.* (Swedish Radio Company) administers three national FM radio networks—First Programme (news and light music, 15 hours per day), Second Programme (serious music, some news, and educational programming, 19 hours daily), and Third Programme (light music and entertainment service to the local stations, 24 hours a day). It also operates Radio Sweden International, an external shortwave service with regulary broadcasts in English, French, German, Russian, Portuguese, Spanish, and, of course, Swedish.

3. *Sveriges Lokalradio A.B.* (Swedish Local Radio Corporation) is comprised of 24 noncommercial, local FM stations carrying the Third Programme, except for roughly 8 hours each week when they opt out for their own local newscasts during breakfast hours, noontime, and evening. These breaks average 195 minutes on weekdays, 2 hours on Saturdays, and 150 minutes on Sundays. There is no local TV.

4. *Sveriges Utbildingsradio* (Swedish Educational Broadcasting Company) provides instructional programming for the schools and educational broadcasts for adults, mostly within the schedule of the second radio network. This service is financed separately by the treasury rather than through the annual license fee like the other companies.

Financing

All general programming services in Sweden are supported entirely by an annual TV license fee levied on each household with a receiver. The government, however, pays for all educational broadcasts. The 1983 fee structure was $84 for black and white sets and $110 for color.[85] Radio, which has no fee, is financed from TV's proceeds. *Televerket* (The Swedish Telecommunications Administration) collects all license fees and has responsibility for operating all transmission facilities used for program distribution. The license fee is set by Parliament. SR-SBC files an annual budget request to the government, which then appropriates the funds, disbursed on the basis of need, from fee revenues. Hence, while government has no direct control over SR's content, it can apply fiscal pressure to influence programming volume and growth.[86]

Control

The Swedish Broadcasting Corporation (Sveriges Radio A.B) now functions under the legal auspices of Parliament, which grants its charter to operate according to the mandates of the 1979 Broadcasting Act. A Parliamentary Media Committee oversees the interests and needs of all mass media in Sweden, recommending the amount of funding the SR-SBC shall receive annually from the Broadcasting Fund of license fee revenues collected by the Swedish Telecommunications Administration (Televerket).[87]

While programming policy and production are controlled by SR's four subsidiary companies, the Radio Responsibility Act confines programming legalities on radio and television largely to libel and slander.[88] The Radio Council (Radionamnden), a standing state committee, maintains an ombudsman position over content by receiving and reviewing complaints from any source about programs after they have been broadcast, and makes an adjudication based on the tenets of the 1979 Act. The government has no prior control over programs.

Aside from budget appropriation and programming legalities, most administrative influence over Swedish broadcasting is performed internally by SR's Board of Governors, which appoints the Director-General of the parent company as well as the Boards and managers of the four programming units.[89] Specifically, *Sveriges Radio A.B.* is responsible for (a) ensuring the programming independence of its four subsidiary companies, (b) negotiating with the government and distributing license fee revenues, (c) gathering information for policy-making, and (d) representing Sweden in the international broadcasting arena.[90] The Telecommunications Administration (Televerket) owns and operates all transmission facilities and networks.

Programming

Swedish radio and television have a reputation for seriousness, integrity, and quality. The three national radio services provide 85% of all radio programming, the 24 local stations the remainder. Television plays an influential role in domestic politics and national culture. Entertainment fare is popular with viewers, but occupies only a fifth of the total schedule of both channels. Despite a decentralization of production, almost all (97%) TV programming is distributed nationally from SR's Stockholm studios—although a third of it is now produced at various regional centers. Another nod toward pluralism is evident in the gradual introduction of regional TV newscasts.

About one quarter of SR's total TV schedule is foreign, with imports coming from the United Kingdom (28%), the USA (24%), France (10%), West Germany (7%), Canada (4%), and from other Scandanavian countries (27%). Violence as a mode of entertainment is considered unacceptable by Swedish television executives, but sexual themes and nudity are generally tolerated.

Radio and television services are scrupulous in addressing the needs of minority, immigrant, and special audiences. For example, subtitles are provided for viewers with hearing impairments, and low ratings do not result in the cancellation of cultural programs of merit simply because they are enjoyed by very small audiences. Nearly 10% of Sweden's population is foreign-born; hence 4 hours of TV and ten of radio are programmed each week in Finnish, Greek, Turkish, and Serbo-Croation. The Lapps of the North have their own regional radio service.[91]

Cable and Satellites
Although cable TV is available only in a few urban pockets, roughly half of the households in Sweden are connected. The PTT is prohibited by law from relaying foreign programming signals into the country, however. Pressure groups and some politicians are demanding an increase in regional TV stations from the current 7 to 11, a move that would require transferring nearly 40% of license funds from the networks to the provinces.

Construction was begun on Sweden's first cable TV network during 1983 in the southern city of Lund, with 4,000 households being connected. The service will carry 20 television and 20 radio channels, including TV programs from East and West Germany, Denmark, and SVT's two national networks.[92]

Relatedly, VCRs are selling fast in affluent Sweden, especially among the young male population in urban areas.[93] Approximately half a million VCR units were in use by 1983 in about 17% of the nation's households.[94] Another common practice is the weekend rental of home video machines. Feature films and foreign crime dramas are the most popular software items, but music video and some SBC programs were becoming available to VCR users in the mid-1980s.[95]

Teletext is also gaining strength. In 1983, SVT's second channel began signing on with 10 minutes of teletext information. The system further provides a superb subtitle service for the deaf, considered by experts to be the best in Europe besides Holland's.[96]

Original satellite plans called for a cooperative DBS service, NORDSAT, having a five-channel capacity. This was scaled down to two channels in 1981, due to cost projections.[97] Three Scandanavian countries signed an agreement in April 1983 to share the cost of the new Tele-X communications satellite. Sweden will finance 80% of the project, Norway and Finland 15% and 4%, respectively. The $167-million satellite will offer various telecommunication services, including two new television channels.[98]

Problems and Prospects

The emergence of cable, VCRs, and the promise of DBS has caused the proprietors of the public service Sveriges Radio to worry about foreign program competition and increasing expenses. Proponents of NORDSAT cite the freedom of programming choice and offerings to cultural minorities, especially Scandanavians living in other Nordic countries, as DBS benefits. Opponents argue that the Scandanavian cultures would be further diluted due to the quantum increases of Anglo-American programming in English, since so much already exists on Nordic TV channels. Such concerns are understandable in Sweden, since English-language imports are merely subtitled rather than dubbed into Swedish.

A 1982 poll by the Stockholm School of Economics found that, while most Swedes were not very well informed about the license fee mechanism, 70% did not want television supported directly by the government through taxes. Surprisingly, the vast majority would accept a maximum of 12 minutes of advertising daily, adjacent to the evening newscasts, if more money would result in a continuation of high program standards. This could provide a future rationalization for limited commercial participation in Swedish broadcasting, although the competition for advertising budgets would hurt the already ailing domestic newspaper industry.[99]

Following a 1984 report, "Advertising in the Electronic Media," Swedish broadcasting officials and the major ownership group of SR began considering TV advertising as a means of bringing in badly needed revenue. One idea is to set up an independent advertising agency with no involvement in programming. SR was ordered to take austerity measures through 1987—including a 2% annual budget cut, laying off 500 personnel, and sustaining the cost of running its educational service (Sveriges Utbildningsradio).

A government commission issued a report in 1985, *Via Satellite and Cable,* proposing that a Cable Authority be established to license and regulate originating programming services (as opposed to CATV systems which simply retransmit terrestrial or DBS signals from domestic or foreign channels) and that cable operations be allowed to develop in a free market. Each system, however, will have a monopoly on cable in its particular area. The report, which is the basis of future legislation, suggested certain conditions on cable operations. These include: (a) non-transferable, 3-year licenses, (b) open public service channels, (c) no mixing of local and satellite programming on the same channel,

(d) no inter-community cable networking, (e) no advertising or sponsorship, (f) no discrimination against ethnic groups, and (g) no sales of exclusive rights to hard news reporting.[100]

SVT faces three options when its current state contract expires in June of 1986: (a) continuing with its two-channel system; (b) modeling the two channels after the BBC, with one popular network and a smaller cultural service; or (c) creating a two-channel arrangement in which one is produced in Stockholm and the second is programmed cooperatively by 11 regional TV stations. Pay TV is also a real prospect, since the cable industry is under development.[101]

JAPAN

The present broadcasting duopoly in Japan finds a national public corporation in competition with a healthy private sector of local radio stations and television networks. The Japanese Broadcasting Corporation, NHK (Nippon Hoso Kyaki), originally formed in 1926, became the centerpiece of the present broadcasting structure with the passage of three pieces of legislation in 1950. These statutes— the Radio Wave Law, Broadcast Law, and Radio Regulatory Commission Establishment Law—formulated spectrum and ownership guidelines, restructured NHK as a public corporation independent of government control, authorized the introduction of commercial broadcasting, and created a regulatory agency similar to the American FCC.[102] The duopoly became a reality in 1951 with the issuance of the first licenses to private stations and the formation of the National Association of Commercial Broadcasters (NACB).[103]

The NHK is administered by a Board of Governors and an Executive Organ comprised of people representative of all Japanese society. They are appointed by the Prime Minister and approved by Parliament. The Board makes all business and programming policy for NHK; it also appoints a President for the purpose of hiring an executive staff, choosing department directors, and managing the day to day operations of all services. The NHK Board, in consultation with the staff, determines the license fee and financial needs for the coming year. The NHK's budget recommendation and program schedules are then sent to the National Diet (parliament) for deliberations and final approval or rejection, as is the annual report.

NHK is organized around four major departments—general broadcasting administration, technical administration and instruction, audience service administration, and staff administration. The headquarters is located in its Broadcasting Center in Tokyo, but seven regional offices and 62 local stations are maintained throughout the country. In addition, NHK has research institutes for studying popular culture and public opinion, as well as laboratories for technical and scientific research.[104]

Control and Financing

Public and private broadcasters in Japan are licensed and regulated by the Radio Regulatory Bureau of the Ministry of Posts and Telecommunications in accordance with the laws of 1950. Each broadcasting company is responsible for its own legal and operational administration. The Broadcast Law, in particular, guaranteed: (a) the availability of radio and TV signals to the whole nation; (b) freedom of expression and program autonomy from official or commercial interests; and (c) broadcaster accountability to the public, in keeping with the principles of democratic societies.[105]

The public NHK, as a noncommercial and autonomous corporation, is supported exclusively by the revenues it collects from annual license fees levied on TV receivers. All of the private radio and television companies rely entirely on advertising for their support.[106]

Services

On a nationwide basis, the average resident of Japan has access to between four and eight TV channels, three to six MW radio signals, several FM stations, and a domestic shortwave service.[107] By 1986, private broadcasters operated 48 local AM, 15 FM, and nearly 100 TV stations (divided about evenly between VHF and UHF), as well as Radio Tanpa, the national SW service of Nihon Broadcasting Company, Limited.[108] Four commercial television companies have formed regional networks around their flagship stations—NTV, TBS, Fuji, and ANB. TV Tokyo Channel 12 is a fifth major commercial force in terms of viewership.[109]

NHK operates 122 AM, 58 FM, and 98 TV stations throughout Japan. These are affiliated with its four national networks. NHK's two nationwide TV channels, *General Programming* (GTV), and *Educational Programming* (ETV), both broadcast 18 hours daily in full color. On the radio side, NHK runs two national AM chains, the general *Radio 1* and educational *Radio 2,* as well as a VHF stereo service offering classical music, jazz, and cultural programs. NHK also has responsibility for *Radio Japan,* the official overseas SW service.[110].

Programming

Broadcast Programme Consultative Committees were established in 1959 for both NHK and the commercial operators by way of an amendment to the 1950 Broadcasting Law. Their purpose is to set programming standards, to ensure a harmonious balance between news, culture, and entertainment in broadcast schedules, and to prohibit the formation of nationwide commercial networks.[111] Further, NHK has its own programming council and boards which set and review guidelines for meeting the public's needs and expectations—a highly sensitive function, since NHK depends solely on receiver license fees for its income.

The competition from the commercial TV stations, which generally attract more viewers except for news, makes NHK's obligation to the public all the more challenging. Generally speaking, NHK's programming is highly regarded for its quality and for its facility in promoting traditional Japanese culture through prime time dramas, political forums, cultural presentations, and newcasts.

NHK airs approximately 13,000 hours of television programming annually, which comes to about 250 hours a week on each network. GTV's program schedule is comprised of news and sports (35%), entertainment (25%), cultural presentations (25%), and educational productions (15%). NHK was importing 4% of the programming shown on its general channel and only 1% of ETV's schedule by 1983, but plans to double its imports before 1990. Foreign content, which seldom airs during prime time, comes from the U.S. (40%), Western Europe (35%) and various other nations (25%). The highest rated domestic programs (attracting 60% to 70% audience shares) on the GTV service are the morning news, sports events, and the daily 15-minute serial dramas.[112]

The commercial television networks, on the other hand, emphasize mass entertainment, feature many "sumurai" dramas (akin to the American "western"), and are generally considered to be both more exciting and more vulgar than NHK.[113] By 1983, the private stations were importing an aggregate average of nearly 10% of their total air product.[114]

Given the Japanese fascination with America, it is ironic that U.S. television shows, including "Dallas," are typically less popular in Japan than elsewhere in the world.[115] This is particularly interesting in that the Japanese are now the world's heaviest TV viewers. A 1982 Nielsen study indicated that a typical *family* in Tokyo watched 8 hours and 12 minutes of television daily;[116] but, since many households have several sets, the average viewing time *per person* was closer to 3 hours.[117]

NHK's ETV service is devoted mainly to instructional and adult education content, but also presents some cultural programs (18%) and a bit of news (2%).[118] The two AM services are similarly programmed: *Radio 1* features news, popular music, entertainment, and some culture; *Radio 2* offers instruction to the schools and educational programs to the general audience at home. The *NHK FM* network programs high quality music in stereo. In fact, NHK maintains a 120-member symphony orchestra and a 4,000 seat auditorium at its Broadcast Center in Tokyo.[119]

But news is perhaps NHK's strongest suit. While the commercial stations depend largely upon newspapers and wire services for their copy, NHK has its own extensive news-gathering facilities—including 14,000 reporters in Japan alone and over 40 correspondents in 21 of the world's major cities. The result is a popular, highly credible, and excellent news product, compiled by professional broadcast journalists and presented by news "readers," not anchor personalities.[120] GTV offers 11 newscasts daily—with major ones at 7 am, noon, and 7 pm—and *Radio 1* broadcasts news every hour. NHK's local affiliates opt-out several times a day for local newscasts, traffic reports, and brief musical interludes.[121] NHK functions under a social responsibility mandate, enjoying journalistic freedom and a minimum of government interference.[122]

NHK's commitment to educational broadcasting to the general public and to the schools goes back to the 1930s. Few nations have established national educational radio and TV services that are backed by resources equal to those used for general broadcasting. For example, language lessons in basic and conversational English, French, German, Spanish, and Chinese are a regular feature of *Radio 2*. These are augmented by the English language services of the American Forces Far East Network, which operates stations in Japan and Okinawa.[123] So, too, has broadcasting promoted a common Japanese idiom. While this has helped standardize language usage, it also has been blamed for weakening local dialects and minority cultures.[124]

Cable and Satellites

In the late 1970s, experimentations went forward in the areas of stereo TV sound, teletext, direct satellite broadcasts, and video cassettes (called "video packages" in Japan). Private broadcasters collaborated with NHK in developing CATV operations in the largest cities. By decade's end, they had established a joint Japan Satellite News Pool.[125]

Japan has been in the forefront of videotex hardware development. Its system, CAPTAIN (Character and Pattern Telephone Access Information Network), began in Tokyo on an experimental basis in 1979. This was done in cooperation with the Posts and Telecommunications Ministry and with NTT, the national telephone and telegraph corporation. CAPTAIN inaugurated national service in 1983, and optical fiber cable systems with digital switching were being extended to all population centers by 1984.[126]

A medium scale Broadcast Satellite for Experimental Purposes (BSE), nicknamed "Yuri," operated from 1978 until mid-1980. This Broadcast Series (BS) grew out of the early Communication Series (CS) satellites, which were used for international telecommunication transmission. The government recommended in 1982 that Japan put a four-channel DBS in orbit by 1989. Two of the four transponders are earmarked for NHK, one for the commercial broadcasters, and the fourth for a "university of the air" service similar to Britain's Open University. The satellite report, prepared by a panel of advisors to the PTT's Radio Regulatory Bureau, called for scheduled launches of BS-2a and BS-2b (a spare) broadcast satellites in the mid-1980s.[127]

Problems and Prospects

Japanese broadcasting faces relatively few problems at the present time. It is well financed, generally popular with the public, and, in the instance of NHK, fulfills a vital national cultural mission. Some pockets of the population are still not covered by television but will be shortly. The density of commercial stations per geography and demographics has resulted in a vast array of channels in most urban areas. CATV will continue to develop, and DBS will supply international channels by the end of the 1980s.

In preparation for direct satellite broadcasting, NHK has developed an advanced HDTV system which was demonstrated in the U.S. and Europe during 1982. A 1983 Research and Study Council on the Diversification of Broadcasting found the most common public complaint to be a lack of variety in programming. Most viewers surveyed wanted more music, cinema, and news programs, as well as more information on health subjects and hobbies. The Council subsequently recommended that NHK direct more of its programming to smaller audiences having specific needs and interests, since the commercial channels are already mainly preoccupied with mass entertainment.[128]

By the end of 1984, 12% of Japan's TV households had cable, VCR penetration was 21%, and the BS-2 and 3 (SAKURA) series of satellites were aloft.

COMPARISONS, CONTRASTS, AND TRENDS

This chapter began by comparing vital national characteristics and identifying some salient broadcasting issues common to six representative Western nations. The foregoing case studies have illustrated a number of similarities and differences among the broadcasting systems of Western Europe and Japan. Closer analysis reveals these points of *agreement:*

1.   All, except for Japan, have gone through several reorganizations since World War II and have enacted new broadcasting laws since the mid-1970s.

2.   All share the philosophy that broadcasting is too important a sociocultural resource to be left largely to market forces and private enterprise; thus each has developed a national institution to provide radio and television programming that (a) preserves its national cultural heritage, (b) formally and informally educates its citizens, (c) facilitates the free flow of information, and (d) offers popular diversion for the mass audience as well as special language broadcasts for indigenous and immigrant minorities.

3.   All have imposed receiver license fees as the principal source of financing their public broadcasting services and, except for Sweden, have also allowed a limited amount of advertising to generate supplemental income.

4.   The broadcasting monopolies of Western Europe have decentralized their policy-making, production, and services in recent years; hence, programming has become more pluralistic, typically distributed via regional TV and new local radio stations.

But the six Western broadcasting models also differ from one another in ways that are both minor and significant. For example, the market arrangements for broadcasting in France and Sweden remain monopolies. Italy and Japan, on the other hand, each operate as a duopoly, with private stations and networks permitted to compete with the national public services. And the diversified broadcasting groups that constitute Holland's public corporation actually function more like the oligopolistic West German confederation of broadcasting companies than the monopoly that NOS technically considers itself.

Slight regulatory variations also exist among West European broadcasting systems. Two major sources of control seem to apply—*parliamentary* and *executive*. France's new Haute Authorite, for instance, is a creature of the National Assembly. In West Germany, the Länder parliaments charter their own broadcasting organizations, while the federal post office licenses all transmission facilities. Italy, likewise, relies on a Parliamentary Committee for legal guidance and its PTT for technical oversight. But separate executive bodies have jurisdiction over broadcasting in the other three nations. The Swedish Telecommunications Administration (Televerket) regulates both the programming mission and transmission facilities of SR. Similarly, Japan's PTT has its Radio Regulatory Bureau to oversee all broadcasting activities. The Netherlands places control in the hands of the Minister of Culture, Recreation, and Social Work. Of course, all of these broadcasting organizations are administered by their own executive boards and are run with relative autonomy by professional staffs.

The amount of foreign programming aired on domestic television channels offers another element of contrast. Sweden, West Germany, and the Netherlands have relatively high levels of imported programming, while Japan, France, and Italy buy much less content from abroad.

An inventory of vital criteria which help to define these six national broadcasting arrangements is offered in Table 4-2.[129] While the specific numbers will undoubtedly change from year to year, the data serve as a ready reference by which to compare and contrast the telling ingredients of these major broadcasting models. The following survey will round out the West European broadcasting picture as of the early 1980s, and further demonstrates the diversity of systems and policies extant in the First World.

A WEST EUROPEAN OVERVIEW

The pattern of privatization, localization, and commercialization in broadcasting evidenced in the foregoing case studies also can be clearly seen elsewhere on the continent. A general survey reveals that broadcasting authorities throughout the region have made both structural and policy adjustments in their systems in hopes of enhancing public accountability, addressing economic realities, and accommodating the new technologies of mass telecommunication.[130]

Austria
In *Austria,* for example, the national broadcasting organization, ORF (Österreichischer Rundfunk), operates national MW, FM, and TV networks with pro-

Table 4-2 A Comparative Summary of Broadcasting Criteria in Selected Western Nations

Criteria	France	Italy	West Germany	The Netherlands	Sweden	Japan
Market Model	Decentralized Monopoly	Public Monopoly Private Stations	Public Oligopoly	Pluralistic Monopoly	Noncommercial Monopoly	Public-Private Duopoly
Major Broadcasting Organization(s)	TF1, A2F, FR3, Radio France, SFP, TDF, INA	RAI-Radiotelevisione Italiana	ARD (9 Regional Brdcstng. Cos. ZDF (nat'l TV net)	NOS (8 Public Brdcstng. Orgs. Rep. of Society)	Sveriges Radio AB (Swedish Brdcstng. Corp)	NHK-Nippon Hoso Kyokai & NACB in Japan
Sources of Income	License Fee Advertising Gov't (Ed. R-TV)	License Fee Advertising Gov't (Ed. R-TV)	License Fee Advertising Gov't (Ed. R-TV)	License Fee Advertising (special Gov't services)	License Fee NO Advertising Gov't (Ed. R-TV)	License Fee (NHK) Advertising (on commercial stations only)
Regulatory Body	Haute Authorite	Parliamentary Committee & License by PTT	ARD & ZDF Brds. of Governors & Post Office	Min. of culture, Recreation & SW Com. for Brdcst.	Televerket & SR-SBC Boards	PTT's Radio Regulation Bureau
Operative Legislation	Act of 1983	1975 Reform Law & 1976 Constitutional Court Rul.	Act of 1974	Broadcasting Act of 1980	1979 Broadcasting Act	Laws of 1950

Programming Priorities	French	Italian	German	Dutch	Swedish	Japanese
Programming Priorities	Culture & Educ. Information Entertainment	Entertainment Information Culture-Educ.	Information Entertainment Education-Cul.	Information Entertainment Culture-Educ.	Culture Information-Ed. Entertainment	Information Culture-Educ. Entertainment
% of Imported Programming	9%	13%	ARD = 23% ZDF = 30%	40%	33%	NHK = 1%E/4%G Private AVE = 10%
Principal Lang(s)	French	Italian	German	Dutch	Swedish	Japanese
Minority Lang(s)	Ital, Port, Serbo-Croat, Arabic, Sp.	English, French German & Slovene	Italian, Turkish Serbo-Croat, Sp.	Arabic, Turkish Portugese, Grk.	Lapp Finnish	Lessons: Eng., Chinese, Ger., Russian, Sp.
Fee/Year: Radio	None	$ 2.65		$15.54	None	None
B & W TV	$40 per HH	$31.25 per HH	$75 per HH	$52.50 per HH	$ 84 per HH	$25 per HH
Color TV	$60.00 per HH	$57.75	$75	$52.50	$110	$42
No. of Sets: TV	17.6 million	13.5 million	21.5 million	4.2 million	3.2 million	29.7 million
(% in Color)	(53%)	(38%)	(71%)	(70%)	(74%)	(99%)
Radio	18.3 million	13.9 million	23.6 million	4.3 million	3.3 million	120 million
TV Systems: Lines	809 and 625	625	625	625	625	525
Color	SECAM	PAL	PAL	PAL	PAL	NTSC

gramming supplied from independent radio and television studios located in each of the country's nine Länder. This arrangement is similar to West Germany's ARD. In the case of TV, the regional outlets account for about 1 of 19 hours of programming daily on ORF's two national channels.[131]

Belgium

Officials in *Belgium* have felt public pressure to end the state's broadcasting monopoly. One plan under consideration in 1983 would introduce private competition to the nation's Dutch and French language TV networks in the form of a consortium of regional television companies operating together like Britain's ITV.[132] Local radio is also a possibility.[133] Belgium has the distinction of being the world's most cabled nation, with 85% of its households connected as of 1983.[134]

Switzerland

Broadcasting in *Switzerland* is provided by a nonprofit monopoly service, SSR (The Societé Swisse de Radiodiffusion et Telèvision), which is licensed by the government and chartered to operate through the PTT under provisions of the confederation's constitution. All broadcasting is financed by annual license fees on radio and TV receivers, and by television advertising revenues.

Switzerland also has a number of privately owned or community cable systems which mostly distribute programming signals from neighboring countries, particularly France, Austria, Germany, and Italy. In 1982, the Federal Council authorized the issuance of experimental (3- to 5-year) licenses for local radio and TV stations, providing they operate on a nonprofit basis and that advertising be allowed on radio but not on television.[135] Switzerland's regulatory body, the Department of Transport, Communications, and Energy, approved 30 of over 250 applications to start radio operations in 1983. The commercial stations will supplement SSR's radio services by concentrating on local news and affairs, but may also compete head to head with SSR programming at times. SSR has offered to cooperate with the local broadcasters by training their personnel, by giving technical assistance and by representing them in dealings with foreign and international organizations. Direct economic competition will be avoided, since SSR allows some TV advertising but none on radio. Seven local TV stations were also issued 5-year licenses in 1983.[136]

Several government commissions in recent years have recommended that an overall national policy and law be instituted for broadcasting so that the federal parliament would have more authority over the development of local stations, cable systems, and satellites. The latter, however, have low priority. Pay-cable and subscription TV were approved in late 1983.[137]

Greece

The broadcasting system in *Greece* has been overhauled and liberalized following historic changes in its political order. Prior to the election of its first socialist government in 1982, one of Greece's two television channels was run by the Hellenic Armed Forces Information Service (YENED), and the other by Greek National Television—ERT (Elliniki Radiophonia Tileorassi)—the state-run monopoly. The new government's reform policies included a restructuring of Greek broadcasting. One of the first changes was the conversion of YENED into a second national TV network, ERT-2, thus bringing it under the civilian management of the national broadcasting organization. Another change to take place during the 1980s will be in the amount and source of home-produced programming. Before 1982, nearly all of Greece's nonnews TV schedule was foreign, and the domestic programming was made by independent producers rather than by ERT. Under the new arrangement, home-production will be increased and is to originate from the stations themselves.[138]

Although the original home content target for ERT-1 was 70%, two-thirds of its 1983 schedule was imported—with 80% coming from America. Greek broadcasters still hope to reduce foreign content to about 40% by 1990, and will rely more on programming from the Soviet Union, Romania, and Bulgaria. ERT-2 also will change its importation policy away from American program sources.[139]

The restructured ERT plans further channel expansions in the coming decade. ERT-1 wants to rent a channel on the new DBS being placed in orbit over the Aegean in the mid-1980s by Italy's RAI. A cable TV service was proposed in 1983, along with new local TV stations in the five main provinces of Greece. The five regional channels will be linked to ERT-1 but will produce much of their own programming around local interests.[140] Strict new controls are also being imposed on TV advertising, which is currently limited to 30 minutes a day. Most notable is the ban on all tabacco and alcohol commercials from Greece's airwaves.[141]

Spain
After decades of heavy-handed censorship under the Franco regime, broadcasting in Spain finally has the opportunity to get in step with and enjoy the democratic principles practiced elsewhere in the West. The national system, RTVE (Radiotelevision Espanola), was restructured by a new Broadcasting Charter of 1980. The new law places management and administration under the Public Establishment wing of government, while radio and television services will be run by three state companies: Television Espanola (TVE), Radio Nacional de Espana (RNE), and Radiocadena Espanola (RCE).[142] TVE is the national television service, and operates two channels. RNE is responsible for national radio services, including those to the nation's Autonomous Communities, which have special cultural needs. RNE's main network, Radio 1, emphasizes information, opinion, music, and cultural programming. RCE oversees all local and regional stations, whose programming is geared to their specific service areas. These stations do not compete with RNE's national programs, especially news, but may contribute to national unity by bringing the regions and Autonomous Commu-

nities together while also reinforcing their own cultural and provincial interests. A third TV channel has been assigned to the independent regions.

The programming goals under Spain's 1980 Broadcasting Charter are explicit and complementary. Information must be presented in an objective, impartial, and truthful manner, yet free expression must be balanced with a respect for privacy. Broadcasters also must disseminate and promote Spanish culture, both national and regional. An attempt should be made to tie sports broadcasts to the goals of physical education in the nation's schools. RTVE is mandated to provide and produce entertainment in Spanish as a means of increasing both the proportion of domestic TV content and the export sales of programming. It is also expected to produce programs for children of all ages, stressing pro-social educational themes rather than permissiveness and violence.[143]

Spain's Constitutional Court ruled in 1982 that private broadcasting was legal. As in Italy a decade earlier, many parties began applying for private broadcasting licenses. The national TVE company objected, but has garnered little support from either the government or a dissatisfied viewing public. The Court's decision led to a draft proposal which could create a government agency to license broadcasters, monitor programming performance, regulate advertising, and set legal and technical guidelines of operation.[144]

A 1982 poll indicated that 70% of the public favored private competition in broadcasting. A number of small private TV stations emerged in various parts of the country during the following year. The Spanish government announced in 1984 that it would introduce a bill in late 1986 authorizing a national private television network modelled after Britain's IBA structure. Several groups have applied for the unassigned fourth TV channel.[145] Private cable and satellite services will also be licensed, as VCR growth continues.[146]

Portugal

In neighboring *Portugal*, Radiotelevisao Portuguesa increased its home-produced content to levels of 80% on Channel 1 and 60% on Channel 2 by late 1982. New domestic programs include quiz shows, detective series, comedies, concerts, and various cultural events.[147] Both national networks now operate about 15 hours daily.[148]

Norway

In Scandanavia, Sweden is not the only country undergoing important changes. *Norway's* noncommercial Norsk Rikskringkasting (NRK) operated for years as an independent state monopoly, until a new conservative government came to power in 1981 and opened the airwaves to private groups wanting to run radio stations and cable systems. Their transmitters, however, would be built and operated by the national PTT.[149]

Finland

The *Finnish* Broadcasting Company (Yleisradio), in cooperation with its national PTT, began constructing local cable networks in 1982 to carry its radio services and subscription or pay TV programming. The private Helsinki Television also operates a subscription cable service in the capital. The PTT further authorized several hours of commercial TV programming from the CTS Satellite in the evenings.[150]

Yleisradio's Board of Governors expended the experimental news broadcasts of Mainos-Televisio, a commercial TV channel, through 1984.[151] Finland's new TV transmitters have been a recent antagonism to Soviet officials, since Yleisradio's programming now carries further into neighboring USSR, causing protests as to the ideological intentions of the Finnish broadcaster.[152]

Cable, teletext, and shortwave services are also being expanded in Finland. HTV, the newspaper-owned private cable system in Helsinki, began providing teletext news on an experimental basis weekdays to over 80,000 viewers in 1983. Newspapers in three other cities also have pilot news services on cable TV. These augment Yleisradio's national teletext service, which started in late 1981.[153] YLE's external shortwave service, Radio Finland, began broadcasting eight half-hour programs daily in English in 1983, but a new $20 million transmitter site will enable the service to expand to other languages when it become operational in 1987.[154]

Denmark

In 1982, *Denmark's* Radio Council authorized the national broadcasting system, Danmarks Radio (DR), to grant its nine local radio stations financial, administrative, and programming independence. These stations had been part of DR's separate regional service.[155] Danmark Radio also launched a teletext news service to 30,000 viewers in May of 1983,[156] and began a 2-year experiment in local TV broadcasts featuring topical magazine programs. If successful, private TV stations could be licensed after 1985.[157]

The unique language obligations facing broadcasters in Belgium, Finland, Luxembourg, Spain's Basque region, Switzerland, and among West Germany's immigrant populations will be looked at in their cultural contexts in Chapter 7.

CONCLUSION

Broadcasting has undergone structural reorganization during the past decade in France, Greece, Italy, Spain, and Sweden. These changes have led in nearly all cases to a decentralization of programming services, greater public accountability and access, more contemporary programming formats (such as rock music on radio and diversionary TV entertainment), and a general effort to depoliticize broadcasting—with the possible exception of West Germany. Private broadcasting competition and further commercialization have either taken place or are under serious considerations in all Western countries but Portugal and Sweden. These trends lead to the inescapable conclusion that Western broadcasting has become Americanized. And as the coming chapters show, broadcasting elsewhere in the world is becoming increasingly Westernized.

CHAPTER 4 NOTES

[1] Don R. Le Duc, "West European Broadcasting Policy: Implications of New Technology," *Journal of Broadcasting* 23(2) Spring 1979, pp. 237–244.

[2] Roland S. Homet, Jr., "Communications Policy Making in Western Europe," *Journal of Communication* 29(2), Spring 1979, pp. 31–38.

[3] Roberto Grandi, "Western European Broadcasting in Transition," *Journal of Communication* 28(3), Summer 1978, pp. 48–51.

[4] Data used in Table 4-1 came from the following sources: *Information Please Almanac, Atlas and Yearbook 1982*, 36th. Edition (New York: Simon and Schuster, 1981); Raymond D. Gastil, ed., *Freedom in the World: Political Rights and Civil Liberties 1980* (New York: Freedom House, 1980); and *The World Almanac and Book Of Facts 1981* (New York: Newspaper Enterprise Association, Inc., 1980).

[5] Walter B. Emery, *National and International Systems Of Broadcasting: Their History, Operation And Control* (East Lansing, MI: Michigan State University Press, 1969), pp. 238–245.

[6] Burton Paulu, "Public and Private Corporations: France, the Netherlands, Italy, and Sweden," in Alan Wells, ed., *Mass Communications: A World View* (Palo Alto, CA: Mayfield, 1974), pp. 21–23.

[7] Emery, pp. 250–254.

[8] Patrice Flichy, "France: 'Parallel' Radios and Program Revitalization," *Journal of Commication* 28(3), Summer 1978, pp. 70 and 72.

[9] Douglas A. Boyd and John Y. Benzies, "SOFIRAD: France's International Commercial Media Empire," *Journal of Communication* 33(2), Spring 1983, pp. 57–69.

[10] Jean Rocchi, "France: Decentralization and Dissension," *Journal of Communication* 28(3), Summer 1978, pp. 73 and 74.

[11] *World Radio TV Handbook* (New York: Billboard Publications, vol. 36, 1982), pp. 83 and 390–391 (hereinafter cited as WRTH 1982). See also: Antoine de Tarle, "France: The End of the Monopoly, InterMedia 19(3), May 1982, p. 22.

[12] "Government to Pull Plug on Offbeat Paris Radio," AP wire story in the Buffalo (NY) *Courier-Express*, July 27, 1982, p. B-9.

[13] "France: New Broadcasting Law," *InterMedia* 10(3), May 1982, p. 8.

[14] Georges Ridoux, "Audiovisual Communications in France: From One Reform to the Next," *EBU Review* XXXIII(2), March 1982, pp. 28 and 31.

[15] George Ridoux, "Audiovisual Communications in France—Stage Two: the Act of 29 July 1982. Compromise and Transition," *EBU Review* XXXIII(6), November 1982, pp. 6ff. (Note: All information on the current organization of French broadcasting, except where otherwise notated, is taken from this source).

[16] "Plans for a Mixed Network," *InterMedia* 10(6), November 1982, p. 6.

[17] WRTH 1983, pp. 85–87 and 396–397.

[18] "France: Developments and Prospects," *EBU Review* XXXIV(2), March 1983, p. 50.

[19] InterMedia 10(3), May 1982, p. 8. (cf, Note 13).

[20] "France: Yes to Optical Fibre," *InterMedia* 11(1), January 1983, pp. 4–5.

[21] "Fourth French Channel Plans," *TV World*, May/June 1983, p. 30.

[22] *InterMedia* 11(1), January 1983, pp. 4–5. (cf, Note 20).

[23] "France: Developments and Prospects," *EBU Review* XXXIV(1), January 1983, p. 45.

[24] Pierre Braillard, "France: Going Commercial," *InterMedia* 13 (4/5), July/September 1985, p. 3. See also: "Roger M. Williams, "France: A Revolution in the Making," *Channels*, September/October 1985, pp. 60–61.

[25] Emery, pp. 260–261.

[26] Guiseppe Richeri, "Italy: Public Service and Private Interests," *Journal of Communication* 28(3), Summer 1978, pp. 75–77.

27 RAI, "Broadcasting in Italy," in William E. McCavitt, ed., *Broadcasting Around the World* (Blue Ridge Summit, PA: TAB Books, 1981), pp. 275–282.

28 WRTH 1982, pp. 101–103 and 395.

29 Kaarle Nordenstreng and Tapio Varis, *Television Traffic—A One-Way Street? A Survey and Analysis of the International Flow of Television Programme Material*, UNESCO Reports and Papers on Mass Communication, No. 70. (Paris: UNESCO, 1974), p. 14.

30 "Monaco: TMC Joins Italy's RAI," *InterMedia* 10(3), May 1982, pp. 5–6.

31 Richieri, p. 78.

32 WRTH 1986, pp. 108–110 and 407–408

33 Stephen Dembner, "RAI and Private Stations Jostle for Advantage," *TV World*, October 1983, pp. 11–12.

34 Roberto Grandi, "Policy Response in Italy and France," a paper presented at the World Communications: Decisions for the Eighties conference, The Annenberg School of Communications, University of Pennsylvania, Philadelphia, PA, Tuesday, May 13, 1980.

35 Stephen Dembner, "Ratings Conflicts But Berlusconi Advances," *TV World*, August 1983, pp. 36–37.

36 RAI, in McCavitt, pp. 282–286. (cf. Note 27).

37 Roberto Grandi and Giuseppe Richeri, "Western Europe: The Development of DBS Systems," *Journal of Communication* 30(2), Spring 1980, pp. 172–173.

38 Emery, pp. 295–298.

39 Richard Dill, "Broadcasting in the Federal Republic of Germany," in William E. McCavitt, *Broadcasting Around the World.* (cf, Note 27).

40 Arthur Williams, *Broadcasting and Democracy in West Germany* (Philadelphia, PA: Temple University Press, 1976), pp. 13–16.

41 *Ibid.*, p. 23.

42 *Ibid.*, pp. 24–34.

43 Alois Schardt, "Television Production at ZDF: A Central Organization, Federal in Structure," *EBU Review* XXXII(6), November 1981, pp. 11–13.

44 Williams, pp. xix–xx.

45 *Ibid.*, pp. 13–24.

46 "West Germany: More Money for TV," *InterMedia* 11(1), January 1983, p. 6.

47 Alex Toogood, "West Germany: Federal Structure, Political Influence," *Journal of Communication* 28(3), Summer 1978, pp. 86–89.

48 *InterMedia,* January 1983, p. 6.

49 Williams, pp. 49–54.

50 Dill, in McCavitt, pp. 225–226. (cf, Note 39).

51 Williams, pp. 43–46.

52 *Ibid.*, p. 41; and WRTH 1982, pp. 87–95.

53 Dill, in McCavitt, p. 227.

54 Nordenstreng and Varis, p. 22; and, *Ibid,* p. 229.

55 Nordenstreng and Varis, p. 14.

56 Donald R. Browne, *International Radio Broadcasting: The Limits of the Limitless Medium* (New York: Praeger, 1982), pp. 132–135.

57 WRTH 1982, pp. 93–94.

58 Toogood, p. 83.

59 "West Germany: A New Team," *InterMedia* 10(6), November 1982, p. 3.

60 "German Cable," *TV World*, September 1982, p. 8. See also: "More Cable Bids," *InterMedia* 10(4/5), July/September 1982, p. 4.

61 Richard W. Dill, "The Future of Public Broadcasting," *EBU Review* XXXII(1), January 1981, pp. 29–30. (For a legal account, see "Legal Notebook," *EBU Review* XXXII(5), September 1981, pp. 43–44).

[62] "Satellite Pact: Construction Plans are Finalised," *TV World,* August 1982, p. 8.

[63] Marcellus S. Snow, "Telecommunications and Media Policy in West Germany: Recent Developments," *Journal of Communication* 32(3), Summer 1982, pp. 10–32.

[64] "Kabel +: Germany Gets More Channels," *InterMedia,* 12(2), March 1984, p. 3; and, "West German Private TV," *TV World,* March 1984, p. 8.

[65] Hans H. J. Van Den Heuvel, "Broadcasting in the Netherlands," in McCavitt, p. 296. (cf., Note 27).

[66] Kees Van Der Haak and Joanna Spicer, *Broadcasting in the Netherlands* (London: Routledge and Kegan Paul, 1977), pp. 79–80.

[67] *Ibid.,* pp. 17–19, 36–38 and 79. See also Emery, *op. cit.* p. 151.

[68] Kees Brants and Walther Kok, "The Netherlands: An End to Openness?" *Journal of Communication* 28(3), Summer 1978, pp. 94–95.

[69] Van Der Haak and Spicer, pp. 19–21.

[70] WRTH 1982, pp. 105–108 and 396.

[71] *TV World,* May/June 1983, p. 6.

[72] Van Der Haak and Spicer, pp. 58–59.

[73] Colin McIntyre, "Teletext in Europe: Today, Tomorrow," *EBU Review* XXXIV(2), March 1983, pp. 12–13.

[74] Kees Van Haak, "Extending the Visual Media," *InterMedia* 11(4/5), July/September, 1983, p. 63.

[75] Van Den Heuvel, in McCavitt, pp. 288–296. (cf., Note 64).

[76] Van Der Haak and Spicer, p. 29.

[77] "Dutch Ban on Cable Ads," *InterMedia* 8(3), May 1980, p. 4.

[78] "A Broadcasting Octopus?" *TV World,* February 1983, p. 14.

[79] Bill Third, "Entertainment Winning Through," *TV World,* February 1985, pp. 24–25.

[80] "Growing Audience for Pirate Radio Stations in the Netherlands," *EBU Review* XXXIII(1), January 1982, p. 49.

[81] "The Netherlands: A Proposed Overall Media Policy," *EBU Review* XXXIV(2), March 1983, pp. 53–54.

[82] Piet te Nuyl, "Sowing the Seeds for Pay-TV," *InterMedia,* 12(1), January 1984, pp. 9–11.

[83] Olof Hulten and Ivar Ivre, "Sweden: Small but Foreboding Changes," *Journal of Communication* 28(3), Summer 1978, pp. 96 and 97.

[84] WRTH 1982, pp. 118–122 and 397–398.

[85] "Radio and Television License Fees 1983," *EBU Review* XXXIV(2), March 1983, p. 63.

[86] Hulten and Ivre, p. 97.

[87] Noble Wilson, "Concerto and Compromise: An Outsider's View of Broadcasting in Sweden," *EBU Review* XXXIII(2), March 1982, p. 36.

[88] Herbert Soderstrom, "Broadcasting in Sweden," in McCavitt, p. 308.

[89] Hulten and Ivre, p. 96.

[90] Wilson, P. 36.

[91] Soderstrom, p. 306.

[92] "Swedish Cable TV," *TV World,* July 1983, p. 28.

[93] Olof Hulten, "Using Video in Sweden," *InterMedia* 11(1), January 1983, pp. 42–44.

[94] *InterMedia* 11(4/5), September 1983, p. 69.

[95] Wilson, pp. 35–36.

[96] McIntyre, p. 11. (cf, Note 73).

[97] Hulten and Ivre, p. 104.

[98] "Nordic Satellite," *TV World,* May/June 1983, p. 30.

[99] Orjan Wallquist, "The Media Structure in Sweden in the Years to Come," *EBU REview* XXXIII(3), May 1982, pp. 8–10.

[100] Olof Hulten, "Sweden: Preparing Legislation for Cable," *InterMedia* 12(6), November 1984, p. 7.

101 "Swedish TV: Under Pressure," *TV World*, May/June 1984, pp. 52–54.

102 Emery, pp. 480–483.

103 Izumi Tadokoro, "Japan," in John A. Lent, ed., *Broadcasting in Asia and the Pacific: A Continental Survey of Radio and Television* (Philadelphia, PA: Temple University Press, 1978), pp. 65–66. Note: the NACB is known in Japan by the abbreviation MINPOREN.

104 NHK, "Broadcasting in Japan," in McCavitt, pp. 78ff.

105 *Ibid.*, p. 97.

106 *Ibid.*, p. 78.

107 Mikio Momiyama, "The Broadcasting Mix," *InterMedia* 11(1), January 1983, pp. 20–21.

108 WRTH 1983, pp. 215–218 and 418–420.

109 Ian De Stains, "Complex Broadcasting Structure," *TV World*, August 1983, p. 16.

110 WRTH 1983, pp. 215–218 and 418–420.

111 Tadokoro, in Lent, p. 66.

112 "Public Service NHK," *TV World*, October 1983, p. 20.

113 Bernard Krisher, "What Public Television Can Be: Japan's NHK," in Wells, p. 36. (cf, Note 6).

114 Nordenstreng and Varis, p. 14.

115 *TV World*, October 1983, p. 20.

116 "Unrivalled for Eager Viewing," *TV World*, August 1982, p. 24.

117 Momiyama, p. 20.

118 Krisher, p. 35.

119 NHK, in McCavitt, pp. 80–82.

120 Krisher, pp. 37–38.

121 NHK, pp. 82–83.

122 Tadokoro, pp. 68–69.

123 WRTV 1982, pp. 212–215.

124 Tadokoro, p. 68.

125 NHK, pp. 96–97; and, *Ibid.*, pp. 72–73.

126 Shiro Ito, "Towards the Information Network System," *InterMedia* 11(1), January 1983, pp. 22–25.

127 "Japan: Satellite Broadcasting," *InterMedia* 10(3), May 1982, p. 5.

128 Momiyama, p. 21.

129 Data used in Table 4-2 came from the following sources: *Broadcasting/Cable Yearbook* 1981 (Washington, DC: Broadcasting Publications, Inc., 1981), pp. F-62–F-67; European Broadcasting Union, "Radio and Television License Fees 1983," *EBU Review* XXXIV(2), March 1983, pp. 62–63; Nordenstreng and Varis, p. 14 (see note 29); and, WRTH 1982 or 1983, pages as per country.

130 Carol M. Thurston, "Accountability in Broadcasting," *Journal of Communication*, 28/3, Summer 1978, pp. 112–117.

131 "Regional Studios Make a Decisive Contribution to ORF Programming," *EBU Review* XXXIII(3), May 1982, p. 46.

132 "Advice for Belgium," *TV World*, August 1982, p. 8.

133 "Recognition for Local Radio," *EBU Review* XXXII(5), September 1981, pp. 49–50.

134 *TV World*, May/June 1983, p. 6.

135 "Switzerland: Bits of a New Policy," *InterMedia* 10(6), November 1982, pp. 8–9.

136 "The SSR Defining Its Position on Local Broadcasting Trials," *EBU Review* XXXIII(6), November 1982, p. 48.

137 "Newsreel," *EBU Review*, XXXV(1), January 1984, pp. 37–38.

138 Lucia Rikaki, "ERT Transformed," *TV World*, September 1982, pp. 18–19.

139 _____, "Broadening Horizons, *TV World*, April 1983, p. 118.

140 "New Greek Channel," *TV World*, October 1983, p. 8.

141 "Greece Tightens TV Advertising Controls," *TV World*, July 1983, p. 8.

142 "Reorganization of Services," *EBU Review* XXXII(2), March 1981, pp. 64–65.

[143] "Basic Programming Principles Adopted by RTVE," *EBU Review* XXXII(6), November 1981, pp. 40–42.

[144] "Spain: Private TV Wins Support," *InterMedia* 10(3), May 1982, pp. 3–4.

[145] Esteban Lopez-Escobar, "Spain Waits for Private TV," *InterMedia* 11(6), November 1983, pp. 40–44; "Private TV Likely," *TV World,* May/June 1984, p. 9.

[146]"Fighting Back Against the Pirates," *TV World,* February 1983, p. 12.

[147] "RTP's Programming at a Turning Point," *EBU Review* XXXIII(1), January 1982, p. 51.

[148] "Innovations at RTP," *EBU Review* XXXIV(1), January 1983, p. 45.

[149] "Private Local Broadcasting to be Introduced," *EBU Review* XXXIII(1), January 1982, p. 50.

[150] "YTV Cable Bid," *TV World,* July 1982, p. 9.

[151] "Independent News Extension," *TV World,* December 1982/January 1983, p. 8.

[152] "Finnish TV to USSR," *TV World,* February 1983, p. 10.

[153] "Cabletext Debut," *TV World,* May/June 1983, p. 28.

[154] "New Transmitter for External Services," *EBU Review* XXXIV(3), May 1983, p. 42.

[155] "Decentralization Projects at DR," *EBU Review* XXXIII(4), July 1982, p. 45.

[156] "Teletext Launched," *EBU Review* XXXIV(3), May 1983, p. 42.

[157] "Denmark Tries Local TV," *TV World,* September 1983, p. 6.

Chapter 5

The Second World: Broadcasting in the Soviet Union and the Communist Bloc Countries of the East

Broadcasting in communist societies is a direct manifestation of the Marxist-Leninist principles that govern all of their political, economic, and social activities. Second World nations, as classified by Freedom House, are those having Communist, one-party polities and generally Socialist inclusive economies. They include Albania, Bulgaria, the People's Republic of China, Cuba, Czechoslovakia, East Germany, Hungary, Kampuchea (formerly Cambodia), North Korea, Mongolia, Poland, Romania, the USSR, Vietnam, and Yugoslavia.[1]

This book uses the term "communist" rather than "socialist" in referring to these nations since the two words differ as to kind and degree of social control exercised. Socialism, for instance, may designate a political as well as an economic system, yet a nation with some form of planned economy may also have competing political parties, free elections, and many civil liberties. Such is the case, in fact, with most of the West's social democracies and with a number of Third World states. Communism, on the other hand, applies to sovereignties whose entire economies are under total government control and whose political systems allow only one party to exist legally. This universal lack of freedom and competition in both political and economic realms thus makes communism a totalitarian arrangement that places all of a society's institutions and activities under centralized state authority. In other words, ideational institutions—like education, broadcasting, and the arts—exist along side manufacturing, transportation, health care, and the military as coequal segments of one huge national infrastructure, managed by a contralized bureaucracy and financed as parts of the government's overall budget.[2] Knowledge and ideas therefore are produced and distributed in much the same fashion as are society's other goods and services.

Nevertheless, although the East European nations are contiguous to and under the resolute domination of the USSR, each has its own history, national pride, indigenous culture, ethnic and linguistic pluralism, and separate international relationships. National variations thus can be found among communist broadcasters, whose facilities and programs necessarily have been tailored to meet the unique needs and circumstances of their respective countries. Still, as a group they typically conform to Marxist-Leninist doctrine and the Soviet model of broadcasting.

As stated in the opening chapter, the Communist philosophy of mass communication is rooted in the authoritarian notion that the Communist Party is the source of all information and knowledge. This means that mass media in the Second World are organized hiarchically as state monopolies that function principally as official instruments of party ideology and government policy. The task of describing and analyzing communist broadcasting systems, therefore, is simplified by the fact that, unlike the organizational diversity found in the First World, all are based upon the USSR's archetype.

This chapter closely examines broadcasting in the Soviet Union and offers some generalizations about the common and unique features of radio and television operations in communist settings elsewhere in the world. The methodological schema presented in Chapter 1 is followed in studying Soviet broadcasting, while the other Second World examples are treated in broader terms and profiled in tabular form.

THE NATIONAL CONTEXT OF THE SOVIET UNION

The Union of Soviet Socialist Republics, as the name denotes, is a political amalgam of 15 union republics, 20 autonomous (ethnic) republics, 120 oblasts (provinces), eight autonomous oblasts (ethnic regions), and myriad raions (districts), krays (precincts), and cities. Each of the Union Republics is named after its dominant nationality. These are: Russian, Ukrainian, Belorussian, Latvian, Estonian, Lithuanian, Moldavian, Georgian, Armenian, Azerbaidzhani, Turkmenian, Kirgiz, Tadzhik, Uzbek, and Kazakh.

The Soviet Union is the world's largest nation in land mass and has an ethnically diverse population of nearly 268 million people. Russians comprise the largest nationality (52%), followed by the Ukrainians (17%), Uzbeks (5%), Belorussians (4%), and 150 others. The official language of the USSR is Russian, but 16 principal languages are spoken in the major regions, and nearly 200 distinct dialects continue to flourish in the various ethnic enclaves. Literacy within this multicultural environment is almost universal (99%). Seven of every ten Soviet citizens profess to be atheists, the remainder claiming religious affiliation with the Russian Orthodox church (18%), the Moslems (9%), or some other denomination (Jewish, Protestant, Buddhists, et al.).

The USSR is rich in natural resources and second only to the United States in heavy industry. Just over half of its exports are to other communist nations; one-third go to the West. Its socialist industrial economy had a Gross National Product of $1,082 billion by 1980, and per capita income was pegged at nearly $4,000.[3] While this may seem low by American standards, it represents a continual improvement in the lives of most Soviet citizens.

Government and Party
The Soviet Union is ruled by parallel governmental and party organizations, the latter being the dominant force. The national (All Union) government has three

components—legislative, executive, and judicial. The bicameral Supreme Soviet of the USSR is the highest legislative authority, comprised of the Soviet of the Union (with 767 deputies) and the Soviet of Nationalities (having 750 members). The Supreme Soviet elects the 37-member Presidium to deal with state matters on a continuing basis, and its President also serves as Head of State. The Supreme Soviet appoints the 90 Party Officials who head the major departments of the central government, including broadcasting. These department commissars serve on the Council of Ministers, the chief executive body in the Soviet Union. The Council's chairman also holds the title of Premier, the nation's second highest office. Judicial authority resides in the Supreme Court of the USSR, whose officers and members are elected by the Supreme Soviet. On the regional level, each of the 15 Union Republics and 20 Autonomous Republics has its own Supreme Soviet, Presidium, Council of Ministers, and Supreme Court.

But the country's sole political force is the Communist Party of the Soviet Union (CPSU), an organization of 17.5 million individuals, responsible for all policy-making and the important positions in the society. Only 9% of the adult population are party members, and admission to the CPSU is a highly selective process. A person first must be recommended for membership by a veteran member, then must serve a 1-year probationary period as a candidate member and, finally, must be approved for admission by two-thirds of the local party organization. Besides these regular members, there is an elite cadre of full-time party professionals. These highly educated party executives make and implement policy and hold top positions of authority in all Soviet institutions.[4]

The organization of the CPSU parallels that of the government. Its supreme organ is the All Party Congress, whose nearly 500 members meet every 4 to 5 years to elect the party's Central Committee, which, in turn, chooses the Politburo (Political Bureau) and the Secretariat. The Politburo makes all Party policy, and its chief, the General Secretary, heads both the government and the Communist Party.[5] It is within this framework that Soviet broadcasting operates.

THE IDEOLOGICAL BASIS OF SOVIET MEDIA

Karl Marx interpreted world history as being a class struggle between the owners of property (Capitalists) and the workers who produce the wealth (Proletarians). He further believed that life's tangible conditions influence a person's thinking and a society's culture (Material Determinism), meaning that the rich control not only their own lives but everyone else's as well. Owning the mass media is, of course, one method of such control. His answer to this basic conflict and inequity is that the workers should own the means of production (A Dictatorship of the Proletariat) through their surrogate, the government, with the Communist Party as its proprietor and ideological mentor. This, Marx felt, would create a classless society based upon economic justice.[6] A Marxist analysis of broadcasting therefore suggests that those who own the channels also decide the programming, and do so with their own best interests at heart.

The Soviet Communist theory of mass communication, as introduced in the first chapter, holds that all mass media must be government-owned and serve as instruments of state and party leadership, policy, ideology, information, propaganda, agitation, and organization. This yields an effective censorship apparatus for keeping all forms of public expression in line with the party line.

The father of the Soviet state, Vladimir Ilyich Lenin, regarded the newspaper as an essential tool in marshalling a political movement and in maintaining power once it had been achieved. Besides its ability to disseminate ideas, serve as a means of political education, and enlist allies to the revolutionary cause, Lenin saw the newspaper, and later radio, as a collective propagandist, agitator, and organizer.[7] The USSR's first leader also supplied the rationale for media censorship: "Why should a government which is doing what it believes to be right allow itself to be criticized? It would not allow opposition by lethal weapons, and ideas are much more fatal than guns."[8]

Official policy on free expression was later codified in a 1936 law which nominally insured the freedoms of speech, press, assembly, and public protest. The Soviet meaning of freedom, of course, is qualified in the sense that citizens are free to express only those ideas which figuratively bear the stamp "government approved." This was made explicit 2 years later in the *Law of the Soviet State* by Andrei Vishinsky, who wrote: "In our state, naturally, there is and can be no place for freedom of speech, press and so on for the foes of socialism."[9] To express opposition to government policies and party ideology is thus regarded as "irresponsible" at the very least and as a counterrevolutionary crime in the extreme. Criticisms of poor performance by state services like broadcasting, however, are tolerated.

Contemporary communist views on media freedom and personal expression are spelled out in law and dutifully practiced by a variety of organizations. Consider Article 50 of the 1977 Constitution of the USSR:[10]

> In accordance with the interest of the people and in order to strengthen and develop the socialist system, citizens of the USSR are guaranteed freedom of speech, of the press, and of assembly, meeting, street processions and demonstrations.
>
> Exercise of these political freedoms is ensured by putting public buildings, streets and squares at the disposal of the working people and their organizations, by broad dissemination of information, and by the opportunity to use the press, television and radio.

The first two lines contain the operative meaning, for political rights like candidacy and voting are carefully controlled by the CPSU. So, too, are civil liberties such as domestic and foreign travel, religious worship, and public dissent. Private entreprenurial activity and independent labor organizations are illegal. Relative to other Second World nations, Freedom House rates the USSR as being as free as Cuba, freer than East Germany, but less free than Hungary.[11]

Information control and dissemination is of paramount importance in such an environment. One agency historically involved in keeping public communication doctrinarily correct is GLAVIT, devoted since Czarist times to literary and publishing censorship. Today it functions largely as a security arm of the Ministry of Information, concerned more with aiding the military and internal police in keeping state secrets than in censoring domestic media.[12]

In fact, censorship effectively has become a self-perpetuating process, due to the careful placement of party loyalists into gatekeeping positions and to a surfeit of practical guidelines from officialdom. One set of rules is provided by the Central Committee's Department of Propaganda and Agitation, AGITPROP for short, a policy-making agency that issues secret directives to those having editorial authority.[13] Members of the journalism profession came up with a list of responsibilities and duties. These included: (a) acceptance of the Communist Party's philosophy and goals, (b) maintaining a high level of ideology within news content, (c) transmission of information truthfully, (d) keeping an orientation and responsiveness to the public, (e) being with rather than above the people, and (f) engaging in self-criticism and criticism of the "faults and failures" of the state and party, but not of party ideology.[14]

The national news organization is TASS (Telegraph Agency of the Soviet Union). It, like the state broadcasting system, operates under the direction of the governmental Council of Ministers of the USSR. TASS gathers and distributes news and photographs to the central press bureaus in Moscow, to all regional media networks, and to foreign news media the world over. The Union of Journalists and Writers operates its own agency, NOVOSTI, which serves as a conduit for sending articles and essays to over 100 international publishers.[15]

The Soviet Union has nearly 8,000 daily and weekly newspapers, with sales totalling 170 million copies annually. The major national newspapers are *Pravda* (Truth), the official organ of the Communist Party, having a yearly circulation of 10.5 million; *Izvestia* (News), the central government's paper, reaching 8 million readers; *Komsomolskaya Pravada*, the journal of the Communist Youth League, circulation 10 million; and *Trud*, the organ of the trade unions, with sales of 8.5 million copies a year.[16]

In sum, communist ideology sees the media as extensions of the state, free to operate in the knowledge that they are not free. It is against this backdrop that we examine the Soviet model of broadcasting.

BROADCASTING IN THE SOVIET UNION

The government has always owned, controlled, and managed all broadcasting activities in the Soviet Union. The State Television and Radio Committee of the USSR Council of Ministers is the centralized agency responsible for administering all broadcasting services. The Committee has a chairman, five vice-chairmen, and a 12-member board of management to oversee all operations of the central broadcasting organization, *Gosteleradio*. It has five major departments—Domestic Radio, Domestic Television, External Broadcasting, Engineering Operations, and Financial Services—each headed by a deputy chairman.

The State Television and Radio Committee reports to the Council of Ministers, the central government's main executive body. The Chairman of the Committee sits on the Council of Ministers, and, as such, is both a government official and party member. In addition to its national (All Union) responsibilities, the State TVR Committee is also the regulatory body for broadcasting in the Russian Soviet Federated Socialist Republic (RSFSR). Each of the other Union and Autonomous Republics has its own broadcasting committee, and hundreds more such committees oversee broadcasting in the various regions, oblasts, districts, and cities throughout the Soviet Union.[17]

Financing

The State Television and Radio Committee receives an annual subsidy from the tax-generated government budget to cover most of the costs associated with operating and maintaining its domestic and external broadcasting services. Additional income comes from state-run advertising, a sales tax on new TV sets, the sale of radio and television programs, and public concert proceeds. Annual receiver license fees ended in 1962.[18]

Advertising, being a state monopoly in the USSR, is rationalized by officials as serving the government's commerce and production goals, rather than existing as a means of exploitation for profit. In practice, it therefore strives to be cautiously informational in order to avoid the promotional hard sell of the bourgeois media. American-style sponsorship of programming is forbidden on Soviet airwaves. Instead, short advertising spots are clustered into 10- or 15-minute blocks of time in between programs, as is the case in most West European systems.[19]

Services: Their Development and Diffusion

The broadcasting infrastructure of the USSR is the product of interacting geographic, demographic, and political conditions. It is easy for the outside observer to conclude that Soviet broadcasters are faced with a conspiracy of natural and man-made constraints. First, a land mass that spans two continents and 11 time zones has made electrification costly and program scheduling a nightmare. Next, a diverse and dispersed population, rugged terrain, and inhospitable climate have conspired to make universal radio and television coverage a difficult task to achieve. For instance, two-thirds of the population is clustered in the Central European section of the Soviet Union, the rest scattered throughout more remote areas. And the multicultural nature of the national populace further complicates broadcasting's programming mission, since over 100 languages and dialects are still in use. This, in turn, has kept alive a spirit of separatism within the various atuonomous republics, a circumstance that exacerbates the central government's quest for a genuine national unity. Finally, broadcasting takes place within an authoritarian political environment in which opinion and behavior are manipulated and dissent is not easily tolerated.[20]

To accommodate this situation, the Soviet Union has devised a complex interlacing of radio and TV services that is vertically structured (central–regional–local), makes skillful use of satellites and ground station relays to transmit and time shift programs, broadcasts in Russian and 15 other principal languages, employs a sophisticated wired radio network to control and target program exposure, and generates the most extensive output of international shortwave propaganda of any nation on earth.

From the 1917 Revolution until the mid-1950s, the Soviets effectively shut out all foreign media. Mass communications planning and development were given low priority during Stalin's reign, a period in which the media existed more for the pleasure of the political elite than for the masses. Following his death in 1953, the new leadership initiated a build up of national and regional radio and television stations.[21] Table 5-1 indicates the scale of this expansion over the two succeeding decades, in terms of tranmission and reception facilities.[22]

Radio

Of the estimated 130 million radios currently in use in the USSR, roughly half are wired—interconnected to some 33,000 distribution networks that crisscross the nation. There were about 60 longwave, 300 medium wave, 90 shortwave, and scores of VHF (FM) stereo stations on the air in 1982—the latter found only in densely populated areas.[23]

Table 5-1   Growth of Soviet Transmission and Reception Facilities: 1962–1982

Year	Program Originating Stations		(Relay Transmitters)	National Networks		Receivers (in Millions)		Coverage of Population	
	Radio	TV	(Relays)	Radio	TV	Radio	TV	Radio	TV
1962	407	100	(175)	1	1	66	8.3	85%	10%
1972	430	285	(1466)	3	1	105	45	95%	70%
1982	450[a]	478	(3000)	4[b]	2	125[c]	80	99%	87%

Sources: See Note 22.

[a]This figure does not include the smaller local stations.

[b]Although there are technically seven radio networks by the Central Radio Service, one (Program V) is an international SW service and two others (Programs VI and VII) are time-shifted repeats of the four national networks (Programs I-IV).

[c]Approximately half of these are wired. With the proliferation of transistor radios, the total number of receivers is no doubt larger.

Radio programming services are organized into Central, Regional, and External sections. The Central Radio Service from Moscow provides a total of seven programs, all in Russian. Four of these are national network services for all domestic listeners, a fifth is for Soviet citizens living abroad (especially seamen and military personnel), and two others are designed specifically to reach distant regions of the country. Their programming formats and hours of operation are as follows:[24]

> *Program I*—A general programming service of information, literature, drama, and children's shows, broadcast 20 hours daily on a time-shifted schedule to five European regions, although it is available to all republics and to some local stations.
>
> *Program II*—Called ''Mayak'' (beacon or lighthouse), this is a 24-hour service to seven regions, featuring all kinds of music, 5- to 10-minute newscasts twice each hour, plus light entertainment and sports. Parts are carried locally.
>
> *Program III*—A cultural and educational format of mostly literary readings, dramas, and musical concerts, daily from 6 am to 10 pm, for Central European sections of the USSR.
>
> *Program IV*—Offers primarily classical music via MW and VHF stereo on weekday afternoons and evenings for 8 hours, and all day Saturdays and Sundays for 13 hours.
>
> *Program V*—An around-the-clock music, news, and sociopolitical shortwave service for Soviet citizens living abroad, with special transmissions beamed to merchants and fishermen at sea.
>
> *Program VI and VII*—These include mainly repeats of Program I that are time-shifted to reach listeners in different time zones of the eastern regions—specifically, the Soviet Far East, Siberia, Central Asia, and the Urals (Kazakhstan).

The institution of broadcasting, like the government and the Communist Party, is organized as a tiered hiarchy in which each regional and local entity has a radio and television committee that is responsible for its own programming services. Besides the State Radio and TV Committee, which oversees broadcasting nationwide and in the Russian Republic (RSFSR), separate broadcasting committees exist in the other 14 union republics, as well as in 20 autonomous republics, 112 regions and oblasts, seven districts, and 153 cities and localities.[25]

The main purpose of the regional and local radio stations is to provide indigenous news and cultural programming in the ethnic language of each area. In addition to the Central services in Russian, regional stations broadcast in 15 principal dialects—viz., Ukrainian, Belorussian, Uzbek, Tatar, Kazakh, Azerbaijanian, Armenian, Georgian, Lithuanian, Moldavian, German, Estonian, Latvian, Chuvash, and Tadzhik. Local broadcasting is even more pluralistic; 68 separate vernaculars occupy the airwaves. Collectively, radio programming totalled nearly 1100 hours daily in the Soviet Union by 1980.[26]

The Soviet government sponsors the world's most ambitious external broadcasting service, Radio Moscow. It presently broadcasts 24 hours a day in 64 foreign languages to listeners in Europe, Africa, the Middle East, Asia, the Far East, Latin America, Australia, New Zealand, and North America via a vast global network of shortwave transmitters. In addition, ten republican SW stations and another one run by a consortium of public organizations transmit regularly in several dozen languages to foreign audiences in specific locations around the world.[27] The subject of international broadcasting and propaganda is examined more thoroughly from a world perspective in Chapter 8.

Television

Television, like radio, is operated by broadcasting committees at the central, regional, and local levels. By the early 1980s, most Soviet viewers could receive two national TV services from Moscow and at least one regional station, with even more options available to those living in or near major urban centers. Moscow, for example, is served by four channels, Leningrad has three, and 81 other cities have two channels each. Outside of the Russian Republic, stations in the 14 Union Republic capitals produce TV programming in their respective national languages, as well as in Russian. And colorcasting is common in some 120 cities across the USSR.[28]

The Ministry of Communications is in charge of maintaining all technical facilities used for telecommunication, and also performs other PTT-type functions, like assigning broadcasting frequencies and coordinating radio, TV, satellite and cable transmission. At present, television programming is distributed nationwide through a complex network of six different kinds of satellites, nearly 500 high-power terrestrial transmitters, and over 3,000 relay stations. The 625-line standard and SECAM color system are employed throughout the Soviet Union. The manufacture and sale of TV sets continues to increase at a dramatic rate. An estimated 75 to 80 million receivers are in use, and over 6% were color-capable in 1983.[29]

The seat of Soviet broadcasting is the All-Union Television Center in Ostankino, a Moscow suburb. Its strategically-timed opening in October 1967 presented state officialdom with the doctrinaire occasion to christen it "The 50th Anniversary of the October Revolution Television Center." The facility, now referred to as the Ostankino Center, has 21 fully-equipped TV studios, supplemental technical and production areas, and an 800-seat auditorium. A 12-story office complex for administrative and programming personnel is located next door.[30]

The Central Television Service in Moscow, operating under authority of the

State Committee for TV and Radio, is responsible for programming the four channels that serve Moscow and the RSFSR. Two of these are also All-Union channels, distributed nationwide via satellites, relay stations, and cable.

Central TV's four channels provide the following program services and schedules:[31]

> *The First Program* (Moscow, Ch. 1)—This is a national network service of news, sociopolitical, cultural (concerts and literary dramas), and entertainment for all European Republics and parts of central Asia and Siberia. The schedule typically runs from 7 to 10 am and 2 to 10 pm weekdays, and from 6 am to 10 or 11 pm on Saturdays and Sundays. Known as the First All Union Channel, it covers 87% of the population in 1982, with 95% the goal by decade's end.
>
> *The Second Program* (Moscow, Ch. 6)—This local channel offers cultural and informational programming to Moscow and vicinity only, and is on the air from late afternoon through early evening, approximately 40 hours weekly.
>
> *The Third Program* (Moscow, Ch. 8)—This Moscow-based service is devoted entirely to instructional and educational purposes. It operates on a split schedule about 6 hours daily, Tuesday through Saturday, broadcasting to schools in the morning, providing professional training programs in the afternoon, and offering the public university-level courses in science and the arts via "The People's University" during evening hours. Through relays, it covers the entire Russian Republic and is being made available to many localities. Approximately one quarter of the Soviet population receives its broadcasts.
>
> *The Fourth Program* (Moscow, Ch. 11)—This, the Second All-Union Channel, carries sociopolitical, artistic, and sports programming an average of seven hours a day to 40% of the population in seven union republics. Coverage is being expanded to 60% of the public as new satellites become operational throughout the 1980s.

Besides Central TV's two networks from Moscow, each republic has an additional channel which broadcasts mostly in its respective local language but includes some Central programming in Russian. Provincial capitals and larger cities have regionally-controlled TV studios which produce programs in their indigenous dialects. The major regional production studios are located in Leningrad (RSFSR), Minsk (Belorussian), Riga (Latvia), Tallinn (Estonia), Baku (Azerbaijan), Tashkent (Uzbekistan), Yerovan (Armenia), Tblilisi (Georgia), Vilnius (Lithuania), Alma-Ata (Kazakhstan), and Kishinev (Moldavia).[32] By 1980, there were over 130 satellite-linked telecenters throughout the Soviet Union, providing evidence of a trend toward decentralization and localism in television programming as in radio.[33]

The USSR occupies one-sixth of the earth's land surface, over 8.6 million square miles stretching from Eastern Europe across North Asia to the Pacific Ocean. Its pioneer status in the use of satellites was born of the necessity to reach audiences spread over such vast distances. The first generation of satellites, the solar-powered Molniya series, has brought television signals to increasing numbers of people in remote regions since 1965. These satellites transmit to an elaborate system of 90 ground stations known as Orbita, a network that distributes and repeats national programming to three large areas spanning various time zones. Specifically, Orbita 1 is targeted to audiences in Tchukotka, Kamchatka, Sakhalin, and Magadansky. Orbita 2 covers the districts of eastern Siberia and Primoria in the far east. Orbita 3, referred to as Vostox, is directed to western Siberia, the middle east and Kazakhstan, the Urals, and the far north.

A second system of satellites, named Ekran, was introduced during the 1970s to distribute Central TV's two All Union programs to Siberia and to the country's middle time zones, those 4 to 7 hours ahead of Moscow time. Ekran uses the UHF band and a network of 1,500 ground stations, a system of inexpensive collective (i.e., community) antennas designed for placement in smaller cities and rural population centers. Another type of satellite, Moskya, has begun transmitting in the 3/4 GHz band to a network of 50 ground stations as a supplement to the Ekran system in the western and, eventually, eastern reaches of the Soviet Union.[34]

This combination of satellites, ground stations, powerful terrestrial transmitters, relays, and cable thus distributes two All Union TV services to most Soviet citizens. Together with regional and local stations, the average viewer in the 1980s can receive at least three television channels, more in certain sections and in larger urban areas. But these are only the technological means for delivering broadcasting's end product—programming.

Programming and Audiences

Soviet broadcasting has no need for a detailed programming policy since it is state-owned and party-operated. Marxist-Leninist ideology, as discussed earlier, is inherent in all radio and television programming, irrespective of type. The broadcaster's task is simply "to promote communist awareness." In general terms, broadcast messages aim to stimulate, to educate, to further the public's intellectual and cultural interests, to inform and to mould public opinion. The desired outcome is to instill a spirit of patriotism and help the individual feel a sense of solidarity with the government's policy goals.[35] In essence, the programming priorities of the State Committee for TV and Radio are: (a) *political education* (propaganda, in-school and adult instruction, and children's shows); (b) *information* (news and documentaries); (c) *culture* (music, drama, and folk arts); and (d) *entertainment* (sports, variety, and feature films).[36] Achieving these programming targets is eased by the centralized nature of Soviet broadcasting's decision-making, production, and distribution.

In practice, radio and TV content is inherently "educational" in the sense that virtually all domestic shows contain storylines and object lessons designed to indoctrinate, socialize, or instruct audiences in the proper norms of conduct and thinking. Good working habits and pride in one's occupation are common themes in game shows and light drama. There is very little sex, violence, or material greed. One popular police series, "The Experts Investigate," features three young detectives (two males and a female) who solve crimes based on actual cases. However, the show emphasizes the social origins of criminal deviance rather than action and force. Classical and pop concerts, cultural events, and science documentaries are also prevalent program types. Among the most popular offerings are variety shows and feature films, both domestic and from other communist nations.[37]

As in America, sports are valued very highly in the Soviet Union by officialdom and public alike. The airwaves are crowded with live coverage of ice hockey, soccer, gymnastics, water polo, volleyball, swimming, basketball, and chess. Newscasts, too, routinely include sports summaries, but news is defined differently by the First and Second Worlds.[38]

In totalitarian societies like the USSR, news is the central activity of the mass media; it is through the news media that the goal of political indoctrination can be most easily pursued.[39] Of course, the Anglo-American concept of news is essentially market-based in that it flourishes in an atomosphere of competition (among media and between them and the government), strives for objectivity (or a balance of views), and often resorts to sensationalism to attract audiences and thus maximize profits.[40] By contrast, the Soviet State RTV Committee has defined news as "the purposeful, directed selection of those facts and events, which graphically, convincingly propagandize the policies of our Party and mobilize the people for the successful construction of the Communist Society."[41] Although this view has journalists serving as the government's watchdogs of the media, Soviet newsmaking rivals the West's in volume if not in veracity.

Central Radio and Television Services depend upon a number of domestic news sources and also exchange information with scores of foreign news services, including Reuters, AP, UPI, Agence France Presse (AFP), Intervision, and Eurovision. The three main national sources are TASS, Agentstvo Pechati Novosti (APN), and a reciprocal network which links together the chief regional news organizations in the 15 Union Republics. Although newspapers are the primary source of news for most people in the USSR, the information services of radio and television are highly developed and popular.

The primary national TV network offers 5-minute newscasts at mid-day, at five and six o'clock in the afternoon, and at sign-off. But the major TV newscast, *Vremya* (Time), airs nightly from 9 to 9:30 pm. *Vremya* begins each broadcast with a musical theme, "Time, Go Forth." Co-anchors read the news, which is watched by nearly 100 million viewers every evening. The format and production being used in 1984 were very similar to American network newscasts except that all the bad news has happened in other countries and all the good news occurred at home. *Vremya* features mostly government economic news, followed by national and regional affairs, an international news segment, and a 5-minute block of sports. It closes with a weather report and forecast. This, ironically, is the segment that is watched most carefully by Western diplomats and journalists, since it carries the only bad Soviet news likely to be aired—extreme natural conditions capable of affecting the all-important agricultural industry. Regularly scheduled newscasts also occur in the indigenous languages via the local radio stations and each region's own television channel.[42]

During the 1960s, Soviet officials became anxious over the growing popularity of foreign media within their borders, despite attempts to selectively jam Western radio broadcasts and to systematically screen out films and print materials from both the East and the West. Rather than continue with expensive jamming operations and largely ineffectual media interdictions, the authorities adopted some of the production formats of the Western media and began to expand all forms of Soviet mass communication. This required that radio and TV become more entertainment oriented, which in turn called for the ruling elite to revise their thinking about mass appeal content. The result has been a shift toward more entertainment products in order simultaneously to satisfy audience demands and blunt the interest in ideologically-tainted Western programs.[43]

Entertainment programming, nevertheless, presents Party gatekeepers with a dilemma. On the one hand, they know it is wanted by, and good for, the contentment of their citizens; yet broadcasters must operate under a mandate to include communist ideology in mediated messages. This is further complicated by the traditional Marxist view that mass appeal entertainment is necessarily imbued with bourgeois elements like decadent music, cheap eroticism, commercialism, violence, banal plots, vulgar language, and low aesthetic qualities. Soviet policy-makers have tried several strategies to resolve their programming quandary over the years. In the 1960s, Central Radio had an Editorial Office on Satire and Humor to guide program producers through the ideological obstacle course.[44] Today's programmers are more practical: coat the ideological pill with diversionary sugar and call it something besides entertainment.

Surveys of Central TV's program schedule over the past two decades reveal that Party gatekeepers have been more responsive to audience desires for entertainment than either vague statistics or official euphemisms suggest. Program categories in 1962 were listed as follows: Feature Films (22%), Drama (19%), Music and Variety (18%), News and Information (17%), Youth Programs (14%), Political and Economic Content (8%), and miscellaneous (2%).[45] Ten years later showed a more detailed distribution of programming:[46]

15.9%—Music
13.2%—Feature Films
 9.5%—New Information

9.4%—Educational
9.2%—Drama
8.9%—Children
8.5%—Sports
6.6%—Documentary
6.3%—Political and Economic
4.3%—Cultural
3.8%—Youth
2.3%—Folk Themes
2.1%—Miscellaneous (including ads)

Despite studious attempts to avoid the word, clearly half of the above content fits the universal criteria of "entertainment." And the deliberate distortion continues in the 1980s. For instance, a broadcast scholar at Moscow State University has described the air schedule of the nation's most popular channel, Central TV's First Program, as being 40% "literary and musical shows" and 60% "informational, socio-political, scientific and popular" shows.[47] This tactic of lumping types of programming together into broad categories is intended to camouflage specific amounts and relative popularity of entertainment fare from the more "purposeful" programs favored by the state. Still, it has been impossible to hide the fact that the Soviet public prefers escapism to dogmatism when watching television and listening to the radio. This mass appetite for diversion has been ascertained repeatedly through audience surveys and opinion polls; research of a kind engaged in reluctantly and belatedly in the USSR.

Soviet policymakers have come to realize in recent years that the official channels of feedback, heretofore controlled by the Communist Party, have been both unrepresentative and unreliable measures of genuine public opinion. This finding can be traced back to two traditional Marxist notions about the nature of audiences and the mass communication process itself. The first misconception was that transmitting the message and understanding it were one and the same process. A second assumption was that the mass audience is undifferentiated, meaning that everyone has an equal capacity to correctly interpret all mediated messages. In other words, if a broadcast is received, then it is also comprehended by every member of the audience in exactly the way the sender intended.

Research since the late 1960s has convinced Soviet leaders that neither of the preceding notions is correct; that attention and comprehension are separate communication functions; that the mass audience is highly differentiated as to message selection, interest, and the ability to understand content. Accordingly, media practitioners in the Soviet Union have reassessed their attitudes toward audiences, the need for new and better feedback channels, and alternative approaches to programming policies and audience measurement methodologies.[48] This has resulted in a less doctrinaire and more scientific approach to mass communication and audience research; it also has yielded a wealth of significant data about TV viewing patterns inside the USSR. These findings are particularly interesting when compared to similar studies in the U.S.

Russian and American Audiences Compared

Current Roper surveys indicate that the television set is on over 6 ½ hours each day in the average American household, and is watched nearly 3 hours daily by the typical viewer. In the Soviet Union, by comparison, urban men average 10 to 12 hours weekly in front of the tube and urban women about 6 to 7 hours. These figures are nearly double for viewers in rural areas. As in the United States, peak viewing time is between 7:30 and 11 pm. The daytime TV audience in both societies is dominated by housewives, although a higher proportion of Soviet women (85%) are employed outside the home, and spend more time housekeeping and shopping than their U.S. counterparts.

A large 1975 audience survey in Moscow found that entertainment programs (movies and variety, especially) occupied the top seven positions in viewer preference (60% or higher), with sports placing eighth. The least popular broadcasts (20% viewership or less) were programs devoted to adult education, "high" culture (poetry readings and symphonic concerts), and some children's shows. Therefore, as in America, entertainment and sports have greater appeal than do education and culture.

Viewing patterns between the sexes in the two countries differ somewhat. In the USSR, men watch more sports events and follow political coverage more attentively, while women prefer the arts and cultural events like plays. In the U.S., however, viewing distinctions by sex are much more subtle, with men having a slight edge in sports broadcasts, women ahead in sitcoms, and the two virtually even in news and public affairs programs.

It is noteworthy that Soviet viewers tell pollsters they want educational, cultural, and sociopolitical programs but actually watch them very little. This discrepancy stems in part from respondents not wanting to risk the displeasure of the officials by revealing their true feelings, or, it could also be due to a form of hypocrisy often associated with personal revelations of taste—as similarly occurs in American polls on such matters.

The better-educated people in both nations are less enthusiastic and more critical of television than less-educated viewers, who tend to watch more TV and find it more satisfying. But, in terms of media consumption, the well-educated Soviet citizens spend far less time watching TV, and depend upon it less for entertainment, than do college-educated Americans.[49]

Trends and Prospects

Like its neighbors in Western Europe, the USSR is experiencing an increase in channels and a decentralization of production, insofar as regional stations are allowed to make programs in their ethnic languages. So, too, are the new technologies making their way into Soviet society.

By 1984, Central TV's First Program was reaching 87% of the public, with 40% able to receive the Second All Union service. Coverage by the two networks is expected to have reached 97% and 87%, respectively, by 1990. This expansion is possible by virtue of the ongoing development of the Ekran system, which uses UHF repeaters, satellites, and cable to link the country's distant regions.[50] The current plan is to provide 95% of the people with increased channels and hours of TV programming by 1990.[51]

The State Radio and Television Committee's goals for the decade of the nineties are: (a) to initiate a multicultural TV service for all regions, (b) to expand the hours of programming via the present First and Second All Union channels to 16 hours a day each and add a Third All Union educational service for 12 hours daily, and (c) to construct additional regional and municipal stations. These changes would provide each Soviet citizen with at least five TV program options by the year 2000—three national networks, a republican channel, and the multicultural service. Urban dwellers will have an additional two or three viewing choices,[52] but there is no official commitment to cable.

Cable television is most likely to develop in the major cities and other densely concentrated pockets of population. Cable-satellite interconnections will allow for program exchanges between regional and central broadcasters. The implications of two-way cable, video cassettes, and video disks are also under active consideration by broadcasting's policymakers. The Institute for Electro-Technical Communication in Leningrad demonstrated a 3-D color TV system in early 1983 that can be used with existing receivers if colored glasses are worn by viewers.[53]

Direct satellite telecasts also are being planned for the late 1980s, but Soviet officials are quick to point out "that it opens the way to an unimpeded penetration of TV programs into the territories of other countries, which would (sic) prevent the development of domestic television."[54] It would, of course, also expose Soviet citizens to information and ideas of popular cultures unacceptable to and outside the control of Communist Party authorities. Not surprisingly, the USSR supports a "balanced" rather that "free" flow of information in the international communications arena, and also favors the rights of receiving nations to be able to accept or reject programs via DBS. The Second World's stance on the New World Information Order debate is explored further in the next chapter.

AN OVERVIEW OF SECOND WORLD BROADCASTING

In communist broadcasting systems, the political rulers influence (a) the degree of radio and television diffusion, (b) the extent of government control over programming, (c) the ways in which programming serves the individual and the whole society, and (d) the physical characteristics of broadcasting organization. But these four factors may differ somewhat from one communist country to another, depending on each nation's wealth, resources, geography, ethnic composition, and level of compliance with the Soviet Union's policies.[55]

Table 5-2 provides a starting point for comparing and contrasting selected vital statistics on the socioeconomic contexts and technological diffusion of radio and television in 15 Communist Bloc nations.[56]

Analysis of the data in Table 5-2 invites a number of insights. The pressures of colonialism and trade are apparent in the types of TV systems found within the Second World. The American presence in Southeast Asia is no doubt responsible for Kampuchea and Vietnam having the only 525-line picture systems, just as Cuba's NTSC color standard stems from its development of TV in pre-Castro days and its proximity to the U.S. The independent course charted by Yugoslavia under Tito, and the autonomous trade policies of North Korea and China, likewise led them to adopt the West German PAL color technology while the other communist broadcasters chose SECAM.

Advertising and receiver license fees are employed as income supplements in seven East European nations; the USSR and China have ads but no fees; and Mongolia levies license fees but allows no commercials. The rest rely solely on government funding, being nations both more hard-line and less industrialized.

Culturally, most have relatively homogeneous populations. China, Romania, the Soviet Union, and Vietnam are ethnic states with various subnationalities. Czechoslovakia is officially a binational state with two large language groups, and Yugoslavia is a multinational society possessing three official languages and eight significant subcultures.

East Germany leads all Second World countries in color TV set saturation, having double that of second place Poland and nearly three times the proportion found in Hungary or the USSR. All but Kampuchea have nationwide TV service, with 10 of the 15 nations having at least two national networks. National radio diffusion ranges from a single service in Albania, North Korea, and Vietnam to nine central stations in Yugoslavia.

In terms of reliance on foreign TV programming, Bulgaria imports nearly half of its schedule, with Hungary a close second. East Germany buys a third of its programs abroad, Romania and Yugoslavia over a quarter each, and Poland almost one fifth. The USSR and China import the least among Second World systems.

Having looked at these quantitative profiles, a brief survey of national broadcasting organizations throughout the communist world will demonstrate further similarities and differences which exist among them in terms of program controls, services, and diversity.[57] Given the indigenous cultural complexities in Czechoslovakia and Yugoslavia, radio and TV services are offered in separate languages. Discussion of these multicultural broadcasting situations is deferred to Chapter 7.

Obviously, all communist broadcasting systems resemble the Soviet model in governance (by state committee) and structure (central, regional, and external

Table 5-2 An Index of Socioeconomic and Broadcasting Data Among Communist Countries

Descriptors	Albania	Bulgaria	China	Cuba	Czechoslovakia	East Germany
Population in Millions	2.8	8.9	980	9.9	15.4	16.7
Literacy Rate	75%	95%	70%	94%	99%	99%
GNP in Billions (US $)	2.2	32.7	517	13.9	80.5	107.6
Per Capita Income ($)	400	2100	390	840	3985	4120
Deaths per 1000 Births	N/A	21.8	26	24.8	18.7	13.2
Life Span: Male	64.9	68.7	60.7	68.5	66.9	68.8
Female	67	73.9	64.4	71.8	74	74.4
TV Sets (in Millions)	.02	2	2+	.725	4.1	5.84
(% of Color Receivers)	(NA)	(NA)	(1)	(NA)	(1)	(26)
Radios (in Millions)	.20	2.75	20	2.1	4.4	6.5
License Fee (Yes/No)	No	Yes	No	No	Yes	Yes
Advertising (Yes/No)	No	Yes	Yes	No	Yes	Yes
No. of Languages Aired	1	1	11	1	4	1
Scanning System Used	625	625	625	625	625	625
Color Standard Used	N/A	SECAM	PAL	NTSC	SECAM	SECAM
No. Nat'l Networks: TV	1	2	2	2	2	2
Radio	1	3	2	5	5	4
% TV Programs Imported	N/A	45%	1%+	N/A	N/A	32%

services). In keeping with the Marxist-Leninist philosophy of media, program gatekeepers give priority to political content and censored information, although minority languages and cultures are promoted and entertainment is increasing in all but the poorest or most doctrinaire settings. And since communist regimes attach great importance to domestic and international propaganda, each Second World broadcasting system maintains an active and well-financed external short-wave service.

Nevertheless, each Communist Bloc nation has tended to adapt nationalist rather than purely Soviet approaches in designing broadcasting policies and services best suited to their unique cultural and physical circumstances.[58] In Eastern Europe, for example, national broadcasters have had to choose or compromise between three programming policy options: (a) dependence on communist allies, (b) heavy reliance on Western producers, or (c) self-sufficiency. In fact, most Warsaw Pact countries, excluding the USSR, had media systems based on the Anglo-American model prior to becoming Marxist states. Czechoslovakia's mass media were more highly developed than Russia's prior to 1948. History also shows that radio, along with the newspaper, has been the most nationalistically independent of all media. Feature films, for exhibition on TV as well as in theatres, have been imported in significant numbers from both the East

Table 5-2   (continued)

Hungary	Kampuchea	North Korea	Mongolia	Poland	Romania	USSR	Vietnam	Yugoslavia
10.7	9	18.7	1.7	35.9	22.5	268	53.5	22.5
98%	48%	85%	95%	98%	98%	99%	75%	85%
41.3	.5	19.7	1.3	135.5	41.8	1082	8.9	53.8
2750	N/A	590	N/A	2740	2360	3990	140	2210
24.3	N/A	N/A	N/A	22.4	31.2	27.7	N/A	33.6
66.5	44	58.8	59.1	66.9	67.4	64	43.2	65.4
72.4	47	62.5	62.3	74.5	72	74	46	70.2
2.8	N/A	N/A	.005	8	3.8	80	.525	3.9
(11)	"	"	(N/A)	(13)	(0)	(10)	(N/A)	(10)
2.7	"	"	.166	8.4	3.6	125	3	4.3
Yes	No	No	Yes	Yes	Yes	No	No	Yes
Yes	No	No	No	Yes	Yes	Yes	No	Yes
1	1	1	1	1	5	68	1	8
625	525	625	625	625	625	625	525	625
SECAM	N/A	PAL	SECAM	SECAM	N/A	SECAM	N/A	PAL
2	0	1	2	2	2	2	1	3
3	1	6	2	4	3	7	1	9
40%	N/A	N/A	N/A	17%	27%	5%	N/A	27%

and the West. But the most conspicuous foreign presence in Eastern European media can be seen in the pattern of television program imports.

The amount and sources of imported airproduct can provide clues to a nation's broadcasting policy and practices. In the case of communist systems, the proportion imported from Western TV producers can serve as a telling index of programming liberalness. Bulgaria and East Germany, for instance, have been most dependent on Soviet programming, while Poland, Hungary, Czechoslovakia, and Romania have drawn from Western and Eastern sources alike. Yugoslavia's bold autonomy from the Soviet Union was signified by its steady dependence on the West for news as well as entertainment during the 1960s. By 1970, 84% of that country's TV imports was coming from capitalist broadcasters.

The East's chief motive for importing Western television productions may be more ironic than dogmatic: i.e., to syphon the attention of their domestic audiences away from West European radio and TV stations whose pop music, news, and mass entertainment penetrate the Iron Curtain. Less ironic is the fact that Second World media products are no match for the West's in the international marketplace.[59]

Although it is tempting for outside observers to paint all communist societies with the same red brush, the hues and tones of governmental tolerance for

Table 5-3   Relative Freedom of the Principal Second World
States

Most Controlled		Least Controlled	
Group I	Group II	Group III	Group IV
Albania	Czechoslovakia	China	Hungary
Bulgaria	East Germany	Cuba	Yugoslavia
Kampuchea	Romania	USSR	Poland
North Korea			
Mongolia			
Vietnam			

personal expression and media freedom are shaded by each nation's leadership. The degree and nature of official control over broadcast content vary discernibly from one communist country to another. To clarify these relative increments of freedom, the 15 principal Second World states may be classified into four categories of control and arranged along the continuum shown in Table 5-3.

The nations in Group I exercise the most rigid controls over their people and their channels of communication. They also are the least industrially developed of the communist countries.

Albania
Albania's Radiotelevisione SHQIPTAR is perhaps the most primitive broadcasting system in Europe, having a closer resemblance to those found in Southeast Asia. Its facilities number less than 20 radio and only nine TV stations, none color capable. Albania's leadership also ranks near the top in authoritarianism and ideological rigidity. Domestic programming is incessantly propagandistic, open expression of personal opinion is rare, religion is banned by law, and communication from the outside world is minimal. Radio Tirana is the fourth most active SW propaganda station in the Communist Bloc.

Bulgaria
Bulgarian Radio offers national services in MW, SW, and FM stereo, while the twin networks of Bulgarska Televisia transmit in color an average of 4 hours daily each. All broadcasts are closely monitored by the government and, in the case of TV, heavily dependent on East European imports.

Kampuchea
The Voice of the People of Kampuchea is one of the most underdeveloped broadcasting systems in the world. Its home radio service consists of two MW and five SW stations. An external outlet, Thini Phnon Penh, transmits spo-

radically in five languages. The country's only two TV stations air limited schedules in monochrome from studios in Phnom Pehn and Bokor.

North Korea

The (North) Korean Central Broadcasting Station (Choson Chungan Pangsong) operates six national and ten regional radio stations. The external station, Radio Pyongyang, is the communist alliance's third most active SW propaganda, KCBS runs the nation's only television station from Pyongyang, the capital.

Mongolia

The Mongolian People's Republic is served by Ulan Bator Radio's two networks and by the nationwide channel of the Mongolian TV Centre. Some of the content on all four services is programming relayed from Radio Moscow and from the USSR's First Central TV via Orbita. Its foreign SW service, "This is Bator Calling," maintains a modest broadcast schedule in five languages.

Vietnam

The Vietnam Radio and Television Commission is in the process of building a national broadcasting system to link the previously partitioned North and South regions. At present, radio stations total 15 MW, 26 SW, and one FM (in Ho Chi Minh City, formerly Saigon). Television of Vietnam programs the single national service to five urban TV stations. The Voice of Vietnam broadcasts in shortwave, mostly to Southeast Asia in 11 foreign languages from Hanoi.

The Group II nations share a penchant for wielding a sophisticated brand of totalitarian control over all means of information. Although satellite states of the Soviet Union, their authoritarian methods are harsher and more efficient than the communist superpower.

East Germany

Responsibility for broadcasting in the German Democratic Republic (GDR) is divided between two state committees, one for radio (Staatliches Komitee für Rundfunk beim Ministerrat) and another for television (Staatliches Komitee für Fernsehen der DDR). Each body's officials are appointed by and report to the CP's Council of Ministers. All transmission facilities are tended by the Ministry of Postal Services and Telecommunications.

East Germany has four national radio networks (Radio DDR 1, Radio DDR 2, Stimme der DDR, and Berliner Rundfunk) and 10 regional stations. These are augmented by the multilingual Radio DDR Ferienwelle (in German, Slovak, Czech, and Polish) and by the seasonal service, Radio DDR Messewelle, heard 18 hours a day during the Leipzig Fairs each fall and spring. Radio Berlin International, The Voice of the GDR, transmits abroad via SW in 14 languages. The entire country also is covered by two TV networks from Fernsehen der DDR.

Romania

The Socialist Republic of Romania is a culturally pluralistic state with territorial subnationalities. Besides Romanians, the country's major ethnic groups are German, Hungarian, and Serbian. These four languages, plus some French, are commonly heard on the regional radio stations. The national broadcasting organization, Radioteleviziunea Romana, runs three central and six regional radio stations, two national TV channels, and Radio Bucharest, the international shortwave service in a dozen foreign languages.

Group III countries allow a large measure of freedom in nonpolitical and cultural activities, including broadcasts.

China

The People's Republic of China (PRC) is composed of several ethnic subnationalities, chiefly the Tibetans, Uighurs, and Mongols. Popular opinion and peer pressure play a bigger role in social conduct than in other Second World cultures. The media are tightly controlled but have enjoyed expanded freedoms in cultural programming in recent years. Eleven languages now fill the PRC's airwaves. These are Standard Chinese (Mandarin), Amoy, Cantonese, Fuzhou, Hakka, Kazaky, Korean, Mongolean, Tai, Tibetan, and Uighur.

Broadcasting is administered on three levels by committees in the provinces, in the 29 autonomous regions and in many municipalities. All regulatory authority over radio and television resides in the Central Broadcasting Administration (CBA), which reports to the Propaganda Committee of the Chinese Communist Party's Central Committee. The Directorate General of Telecommunications functions as the PTT minister and has charge of all transmission links and facilities.

National services are provided by the China Central Television Station (CCTV) via its two channels and by the Central People's Broadcasting Station (CPBS), which operates two radio networks. Regional and local RTV committees run their stations under the guidance of the CBA, the Minister of Culture, and local Party officials. These services are called the Provincial People's Broadcasting Station (PPBS), the Autonomous Municipality Broadcasting Station (AMBS), and the Local People's Broadcasting Station (LPBS). The external operation, Radio Peking, is the second largest SW broadcaster in the communist world.[60]

The Beijing (Peking) Municipal Station operates four radio and two TV channels. Several large cities originate two local TV channels, and other cities have one apiece. The First Central China TV network is on the air about 5 hours each day and reaches 40% of the population. Interest in increasing the amount of imported entertainment programming has been evidenced by CCTV's recent purchases or rentals of Western TV programs and series from NBC, CBS, and BBC.[61] There are currently over 300 MW, SW, and FM stations in China, and about 100 million loudspeakers (wired receivers) in homes and public places. At least 36 TV stations were on the air with studio originated programs in the early 1980s.

By 1985, China was using INTELSAT's satellite above the Indian Ocean to stretch CCTV's coverage to 62% of the nation. This is only a temporary measure until the PRC can build 50 new ground stations and launch its own bird, enabling CCTV to reach the remote territories of Tibet, Inner Mongolia and Xinjiang with its signals. There were 67.5 million TV sets in Chinese homes at the end of 1985, an average of 30 per every 100 households.[62]

Cuba

Broadcasting in the Republic of Cuba is the responsibility of the Instituto Cubano de Radio y Television (Radiodifusion), which, like all mass media, operates under the authority of the Minister of Communications. Regulatory oversight is exercised by the Director General of Telecommunications, and program policy is formulated by the National Radio Directing Board.

Radiodifusion offers five central radio networks: Radio Station CMBF/Radio Musical Nacional (classical music), Radio Progressor (drama, music, and children's programs), Radio Rebelde (education, information, humor, and sports), Radio Liberacion (political education), and Radio Reloi (24-hour time checks).[63] In addition, there are seven provincial and 40 regional or local stations. The government also operates two external facilities: The Voice of Cuba (La Voz de Cuba), transmitting evenings in English to North America on MW frequencies, and Radio Havana, an around the clock SW service in eight languages. The island nation receives its television programming from two services, each having 26 regional transmitters. These are Tele Rebelde, with studios in Santiago, Holguin, and Havana, and Television Cubana from Havana.

The Group IV states have the most flexible controls and liberal programming policies, as long as personal and media expression remains within clearly defined norms.

Hungary

Hungary's broadcasting authority, Allami Radio Es Televizio, has programming and operational jurisdiction over all broadcasting. Magyar Radio offers three central networks (Kossuth Radio, Petofi Radio, and the FM Program) and a program service to five regional stations. Radio Budapest broadcasts daily in seven languages to international audiences via shortwave. Hungarians at home receive two national TV channels from Magyar Televizio. The first service is on the air 76 hours weekly and the second for 23 hours. By the early 1970s, Hungary was importing 40% of its television content, nearly half of it in the form of Western entertainment and the remainder being informational and educational programs from the Third World and Eastern Bloc. Only Yugoslavia has imported more TV productions from the West than from its communist neighbors.[64]

The nightly news in Hungary is relatively free of ideological controls. A typical newscast is full of hard news from Europe, North America, and the Middle East. Although there is no real criticism of the Soviet Union, neither is the news slanted to fit the Party line. The top Hungarian TV journalist, Andras Sugar, travels all over the world and claims he is free to say what he wants to 99% of the time.[65]

Poland

Polskie Radio I Televizja, Poland's broadcasting organization, has authority over four national radio networks, all regional radio stations, two central TV services, and Radio Polonia, the external SW operation in eight languages. Poland was the freest of the communist states until marshal law was declared in early 1982 following the formation and rising power of the trade union, Solidarity.

Television in Poland practiced the "propaganda of success" during the 1970s by telling the people how well the economy was doing and satisfying their normal demands for entertainment and information. But the national strike by the 10 million members of Solidarity changed all that. It speaks for itself that the third of the 21 conditions contained in Solidarity's Gdansk agreement of August 1980 was a demand for "freedom of expression and publication," and access to state television (televizja). The government found the latter to be politically unacceptable and, by way of reaction, proceeded to shift control of Poland's broadcast media from the regions to a body of national functionaries. The State Committee on Radio and Television also slipped further into the grasp of officialdom during 1981 as program gatekeepers and editorial decision-makers in news fell under the direct-line control of the Propaganda Secretary.

An illustration of how communist broadcasters can turn Western TV programs to their own ideological advantage can be seen in the case of *Kojak*. The American detective series, the most popular import on Poland's airwaves, is gratuitously scheduled on Sunday mornings in hopes of discouraging church attendance.[66]

REVIEW

Broadcasting in the USSR, as in every nation, has been shaped by its own distinct set of conditions, needs and problems. These may be summarized as follows:

* Radio and television policy making and services are completely in the hands of the Communist Party and a tiered government hiarchy of central, regional, and local broadcasting committees. All facilities are government owned, operated, and financed, although some state approved advertising is allowed.
* Broadcasting is run by politically appointed operatives of the Party rather than by communication professionals; hence, free expression and creativity in

programming are subservient to state doctrine. The result is content that is replete with manifest and latent ideological symbols intended for political education, information, and instruction, in lieu of diversion and escapism. Another result is programs lacking in marketability abroad.

• Soviet broadcasting, unlike its communist counterparts, was not fashioned after nor materially influenced by Western Models. In recent years, however, Western influence can be seen in the expansion of entertainment programs, produced in an attempt to satisfy home audience desires and to lessen the attractiveness of foreign media.

• The huge area and multicultural population comprising the Soviet Union's 15 national republics require the judicious use of microwave relays, wired diffusion networks, cable, and communication satellites in order to achieve nationwide coverage in Russian and scores of territorial languages while also maintaining firm control over the dissemination of ideas. One constant challenge has been to foster a sense of national unity in the face of intransigent ethnic separatism, a sentiment fueled by language loyalty and regional pride. Although some of Central Television's national programming in Russian is translated into over 60 local dialects, the finished message is often culturally irrelevant to these diverse ethnic audiences.[67]

With this review of the Soviet model of broadcasting, the mold from which all communist radio and TV systems have been cast, we conclude by identifying the common features, national variations, and general trends that characterize broadcasting in the Second World.

Common Features

1. Broadcasting is but one of many government-owned and party-operated monopolies that must be managed by a centralized bureaucracy and financed primarily by state funds, with receiver license fees and/or advertising sometimes providing supplementary income.

2. Program policy making and the on going gatekeeping functions are performed by Communist Party officials, who run the RTV committees on central, regional, and local levels. Such an arrangement helps maintain radio and television as instruments of state power and party leadership, and guarantees that programming objectives and priorities conform to Marxist/Leninist principles.

3. The national news agency is central to broadcasting's programming mission, since news is regarded as an extension of government intended to advance state policies as opposed to the Free World notion of being an independent public service which monitors government and operates by the rules of the marketplace.

4. Entertainment is publicly denounced by party officials, yet is exploited by them as a means of pandering to popular tastes and diverting mass attention from the generally more appealing Western programming.
5. In addition to controlling program policy and scheduling, communist broadcasters continue to utilize elaborate networks of wired radio receivers in order to regulate and target transmissions, to reach some locations cheaply, and to minimize audience exposure to foreign broadcasts.
6. Most communist societies are composed of relatively homogeneous populations, but 6 of the 15 observed have significant ethnic subnationalities living within their borders, thus requiring broadcasting services in a variety of languages.
7. The Second World stands united in favoring a "balanced" rather than "free" flow of international information via mass media, meaning support for the licensing of foreign journalists by host governments and for sovereign states having the authority to approve or reject transmissions of foreign TV programs into their territories from DBS.
8. Information and statistics on national broadcasting in communist countries are never uniform, seldom reliable, and always difficult for outside agencies (including the UN) and individuals to obtain. As a result, their data lacks credibility and their organizational reputations lose prestige in official international circles.

National Variations

1. While the broadcasting systems of the East have copied the Soviet model of governance and organization, each nation has fashioned policies and services that meet their own historical conditions. This is most obvious in addressing cultural pluralism and in programming matters.
2. Second World broadcasters vary in the amounts and sources of TV programs they import and air. Several nations are largely self-sufficient program producers, some import mostly communist made TV shows, and still others rely heavily on imports from Western as well as Eastern TV production centers.
3. Domestic programming also differs in diversity and freedom among communist nations depending on the type and degree of controls levied on their broadcasting organizations. These range from highly rigid strictures on all forms of expression to official tolerance for artistic and cultural content that is ideologically nonthreatening. Another manifestation of the level of freedom is the relative presence or absence of entertainment programming aired.

Trends and Patterns

1. The number of radio and TV transmitting stations and receivers are increasing throughout the Second World, particularly in Eastern Europe.

2. Program production and origination is in the process of decentralization in most communist countries, as evidenced by the proliferation of regional and local stations, mostly radio.

3. Channel multiplication is being accompanied by expanded radio and TV coverage and set saturation, making national and regional program options available to more people and hence promoting pluralism.

4. The amount of mass appeal entertainment programming is growing as a proportion of total air schedules. More communist nation are acquiring television series from the West, and some are adopting Anglo-American production formats.

5. Advertising continues to gain official and public acceptance, both as a source of income for broadcasters and as an aid to consumers.

6. The impact of the new technologies is being felt in the USSR, Eastern Europe, and China as broadcasters develop cable systems and initiate DBS, and as transistorized receivers and home video become available to the public.

7. The leadership throughout the Communist Bloc is showing signs of frustration as attempts to control the diffusion of high technology and the dissemination of information become increasingly futile in the wake of satellite broadcasting and transnational data flows.

8. Opinion and audience research methodologies, traditionally unsophisticated by Western standards, are becoming more scientific as party officials and gatekeepers recognize the need for improved polling techniques and surveys in order to obtain accurate feedback as to popular tastes and public opinion.

CHAPTER 5 NOTES

[1] Raymond D. Gastil, ed., *Freedom in the World 1980: Political Rights and Civil Liberties* (New York: Freedom House, 1980), pp. 40–45.

[2] Mark Hopkins, "Media, Party and Society in Russia," in Alan Wells (ed.), *Mass Communications: A World View* (Palo Alto, CA: Mayfield, 1974), p. 50.

[3] Information on the national context of the Soviet Union is from *The Europa Year Book 1981: A World Survey,* Vol. I (London: Europa Publications, 1981); and *Information Please Almanac* 1982 (New York: Simon and Schuster, 1981), pp. 245ff.

[4] Ellen Propper Mickiewicz, *Media and the Russian Public* (New York: Praeger, 1981), pp. 118–120.

[5] Burton Paulu, *Broadcasting in Eastern Europe* (Minneapolis, MN: The University of Minnesota Press, 1974), pp. 28ff. (Cf. Note 3).

[6] Fred S. Siebert, Theodore Peterson, and Wilbur Schramm, *Four Theories of the Press* (Urbana, IL: University of Illinois Press, 1956 and 1963).

[7] Paulu, p. 40.

[8] *Ibid.,* p. 39.

[9] *Ibid.,* p. 44.

[10] *The Europa Year Book 1981: A World Survey* (London: Europe Publications, 1981), p. 1243.

[11] Gastil.

[12] Paulu, pp. 46–47.

13 *Ibid.*, pp. 49–50.

14 Hopkins, p. 55.

15 Unesco, *World Communications: A 200-Country Survey of Press, Radio, Television and Film* (Paris: UNESCO Press, 1975), pp. 14 and 508–510.

16 Mickiewicz, pp. 51ff. (Cf., pp. 118–120).

17 Paulu, pp. 53–55. For a brief but current summary, see: "What Do You Know About Russian TV?" *TV World,* May/June 1983, pp. 31–32.

18 Unesco, p. 510.

19 Paulu, p. 57.

20 Hopkins, pp. 49ff.

21 Jeremy Tunstall, *The Media are American: The Role of Anglo-American Media in the World* (New York: Columbia University Press, 1977), pp. 187–188. See also: W. Phillips Davison, "The Media Kaleidoscope: General Trends in the Channels," in Harold D. Lasswell, Daniel Lerner and Hans Speier (eds.), *Propaganda and Communication in World History,* Vol. III: *A Pluralizing World in Formation* (Honolulu, HI: University Press of Hawaii, 1980), p. 226.

22 Sources of the data in Table 4-1 are: *The Europa Year Book,* p. 1269; Hopkins, pp. 59–67; *InterMedia* 10(3), May 1982, p. 6; Paulu, pp. 66–82; UNESCO, pp. 507–513; *World Radio TV Handbook* 1983 (London: Billboard, 1983), pp. 136ff and 407ff; Vladimir Yaroshenko, "Broadcasting in Russia, in William E. McCavitt (ed.), *Broadcasting Around the World* (Blue Ridge Summit, PA: TAB Books, 1981), pp. 64–75.

23 Data concerning communist broadcasting systems are notoriously inconsistent, unreliable, and difficult to obtain. These figures are culled from the following sources: *Broadcasting Yearbook 1981* (Washington, DC: Broadcasting Publications, Inc., 1981), p. D-67; and, *Ibid.*

24 WRTH 1983, pp. 136–145; and, *Ibid.*

25 Paulu, p. 54.

26 *Ibid.,* pp. 24, 75, 87, 200 and 206–207. See also: WRTH 1983, p. 136 and *The Europa Year Book,* p. 1269.

27 UNESCO, P. 511 and WRTH 1983, p. 145.

28 *The Europa Year Book,* p. 1269.

29 "USSR: More Satellites," *InterMedia,* 10(3), May 1982, p. 6. For receiver estimates, see: *Broadcasting Yearbook, WRTH 1983,* p. 407, and Yaroshenko, p. 68.

30 Paulu, pp. 75–76.

31 Same as Note 22. See also: Mickiewicz, pp. 18–19.

32 WRTH 1983, p. 407.

33 Yaroshenko, pp. 69–70.

34 *Ibid.,* pp. 68–75; and *InterMedia,* p. 6.

35 Kaarle Nordenstreng, "Broadcasting in the Soviet Union," *EBU Review,* 117(6), November 1969, pp. 19ff.

36 Paulu, pp. 94–100 and 125–130.

37 Mickiewicz, pp. 20–21.

38 Paulu, pp. 174–179.

39 Tunstall, p. 185.

40 *Ibid.,* p. 199.

41 Paulu, p. 100.

42 *Ibid.,* pp. 104–105; Mickiewicz, p. 21; and, John Iams, "Soviets Broadcast Only Their 'Good News'," *Buffalo (NY) News,* September 6, 1983, p. B-8.

43 Tunstall, p. 198.

44 Paulu, pp. 174–175.

45 Hopkins, p. 58.

46 Paulu, p. 88.

47 Yaroshenko, p. 69.

48 Ellen Mickiewicz, "Feedback, Surveys, and Soviet Communication Theory," *Journal of Communication* 33(2), Spring 1983, pp. 103–109.

49 All of the foregoing comparative information came from: Mickiewicz, *Media and the Russian Public*, Chapter 2. (Cf., Note 4).

50 *InterMedia*, p. 6. See: "Update for Soviet TV," *TV World*, November 1984, p. 7.

51 Yaroshenko, p. 72.

52 *Ibid.*, pp. 74–75.

53 *TV World*, December 82/January 83, p. 8.

54 Yaroshenko, p. 73.

55 Davison, p. 220. (Cf. Note 21).

56 All data used in Table 4-2 is drawn from the following sources: *Broadcasting Yearbook* 1981, pp. F62–7; *Information Please Almanac 1982; Freedom in the World 1980*; WRTH 1983; and, Kaarle Nordenstrng and Tapio Varis, *Television Traffic—A One-Way Street? A Survey and Analysis of the International Flow of Television Programme Material*. Reports and Papers on Mass Communication, No. 70 (Paris: UNESCO, 1974), p. 16.

57 *Ibid.* (Except where otherwise cited, all information used in sketching the following 12 national broadcasting systems came from the above sources. For a less current but fully treatment of China, Kampuchea, North Korea, Mongolia, and Vietnam, see: John A. Lent (ed.), *Broadcasting in Asia and the Pacific: A Continental Survey of Radio and Television* (Philadelphia, PA: Temple University Press, 1978), pp. 11, 21–41, 55–60 and 93–120.

58 Tunstall, p. 185.

59 *Ibid.*, pp. 185–187 and 189–192.

60 John Howkins, *Mass Communication in China* (New York: Longman, 1982), Chapter 3.

61 "CBS Television Plays in Peking," *Newsweek* June 13, 1983, p. 66. See also: Howkins, pp. 45–46.

62 "China: Satellite Television Now," *InterMedia* 13(4/5), July/September 1985, p. 10.

63 International Organization of Journalists, *Mass Media in CMEA Countries* (Prague: Council of Mutual Economic Assistance, 1976), pp. 165–166.

64 Tunstall, pp. 189–192.

65 R. W. Apple, Jr., "A Reporter's Notebook: Consumerism in Hungary," *New York Times*, December 27, 1981, p. 14.

66 Rob Steiner, "The Struggle for Poland's Airwaves," *Channels*, October/November 1981, pp. 24ff.

67 Hopkins, pp. 48–49.

Chapter 6

The Third World: Broadcasting, Nation-Building, and Media Imperialism in the Developing Countries

The Third World is a geopolitical label for an aggregate of nations in various stages of transition from largely agrarian economies under Colonial rule into sovereign states with industrial economies. These developing nations are found in five geographic regions of the globe—Africa, Asia, the Middle East, Latin (Central and South) America and the Caribbean, and the Pacific Islands of Oceania. In purely demographic terms, a majority of the earth's peoples and countries belong to the Third World.

A closer look reveals important political, economic, and sociocultural differences among the emerging nations. Many have won their independence in recent years, while some have enjoyed sovereignty for decades. A few are democratic societies, but most are ruled in an authoritarian fashion by leftists, right wingers, Marxists, monarchs, or the military. And they range in development from rapidly industrializing Brazil and oil-rich Saudi Arabia to so-called Less Developed Countries (LDC) like Ethiopia. Nevertheless, the common keynote of all Third World nations is *development*. Each is involved in a nation-building mission centered on political, economic, and sociocultural development. This theme permeates all institutional activity throughout the Third World, especially broadcasting.

THE NON-ALIGNED MOVEMENT AND THE THIRD WORLD

The Non-Aligned Movement (NAM) was born in the post-war years out of a desire by the emerging nations to steer a third geopolitical course between capitalism and communism. This nominal "third world" of newly-founded states shared a past marked by colonialism and a future buoyed by the promise of change and national development. These common experiences and interests formed the basis of discussions during the early 1950s, and eventually led to a formal organization (NAM) in 1955 when representatives from 29 developing Asian and African nations met in Bandung, Indonesia to discuss their common interest in national independence through liberation from political colonialism and economic imperialism. It was agreed that a neutral policy toward the two superpowers was the best way to address the problems of poverty, illiteracy, and disease.[1] Gradually, Latin America and a few Marxist states like Cuba and Yugoslavia were attracted to the non-aligned cause.

160

Their collective efforts were to crystalize in 1961 at the First Non-Aligned Summit in Belgrade, Yugoslavia. The strategy to emerge from this historic occasion was to tie their common political and economic goals to the world's information systems and resources.[2] The theme of linking economic development with information equity on a worldwide basis was refined at subsequent Non-Aligned Summits in Lusaka (1970), Algiers (1973), Colombo (1976), and Havana (1979), as well as in numerous international and regional meetings sponsored mainly by the United Nations and UNESCO.[3]

For example, at the first UN Conference on Trade and Development in 1964, a fraternity of nations calling themselves the Group of 77 emerged as a critical force in the fight to achieve a just balance in economic and informational relations between the developing and developed worlds. By 1980, this group had swelled to 122 countries and had become the Third World's major voice in UN affairs.[4] Today, roughly half of the nations in the Non-Aligned Movement are truly *independent* of the two superpowers, while the remainder are about evenly divided into *radical* (Eastern) and *conservative* (Western) camps.[5]

This chapter examines a range of Western influences on the structure and function of Third World broadcasting in terms of ownership, control, financing, technical infrastructure, and programming policies and issues. The focus is on regional rather than national broadcasting systems and features in Africa, Asia, The Middle East, Latin America and the Caribbean, and Pacific Oceania. This global assessment is followed by a discussion of the New World Information and Communication Order debate within the context of media imperialism and current patterns of TV programming flow worldwide.

TRANSFER MODES OF WESTERN INFLUENCE ON THIRD WORLD BROADCASTING

Radio, above all forms of mass communication, is the most important tool in helping formative countries to educate, inform, and unite their citizens, yet it is inexpensive and portable enough to serve local cultures, interests, and needs. Television, on the other hand, is confined mostly to the major urban areas, where it serves as an elite symbol of modernity rather than as an aid in genuine national development. TV is often used by Third World rulers as a means of projecting an image of effective leadership to their populations. In truth, most TV programming is imported entertainment designed to divert public attention away from governmental failures and corruption, while at the same time turning a profit for the state through foreign and domestic advertising.

In their classic study, *Broadcasting in the Third World*, Katz and Wedell demonstrate the ways in which broadcasting has been transferred from the developed nations to the developing world. This transfer process can be seen most clearly in the adoption of Western broadcasting *models, technology, policies,* and *attitudes* by Third World broadcasters.

Models

The structure of broadcasting organizations and systems throughout the Third World has been patterned primarily after the American, British, and French models, depending on each colonial power's sphere of geopolitical influence. For example, the American concept of privately-owned commercial stations has taken root largely in Latin America, the Caribbean, and much of Pacific Oceania. Britain's noncommercial public service model prevails in Anglophone Africa and parts of Asia. And the unitary French system of state-controlled broadcasting can be found in Francophone Africa, Indo-China, and areas of the Middle East. Other European broadcasting models were similarly transplanted, such as the pluralist Dutch scheme in Indonesia, Belgium's public agency to the Congo states like Zaire, and the state-run Spanish system to Equitorial Guinea. Various hybrid arrangements were also adopted by countries based on their local circumstances.[6]

Technology

Transfers of Western technology have shaped the infrastructures and purposes of national broadcasting systems in the Third World in terms of the transmission, production, and reception equipment they employ. These transactions have tended to emphasize the building of studio hardware and transmitters over providing radio and TV receivers to the people. The major Western manufacturers to distribute broadcast production equipment to the Third World have been American (RCA and Ampex), British (EMI and Marconi), French (TRT and Thomson-CSF), German (Fernseh and Siemens Telefunken), Dutch (Philips), and Japanese (Nippon Electric). Generally speaking, developing countries have tended to favor the companies of their former colonizer, although the marketplace has offered them many alternative suppliers in recent years.

Both wireless and wired transmission facilities have been installed in developing nations, though over-the-air broadcasting is more prevalent than cable (rediffusion) services, thanks in large part to the advent of the transistor radio. Distribution patterns of transmission equipment are determined by the type of broadcasting system favored throughout the region. For example, shortwave (SW) radio is utilized more in Africa than in Asia and Latin America. Overall, however, two-thirds of all radio stations in the Third World operate on medium wave (MW) frequencies. In the case of television, South America has more than twice as many stations as does Africa, Asia, or Central America. And the quality and availability of the VHF band have made it the preferred means of transmission for both radio and TV services in most developing nations, with FM stereo becoming especially popular.

A breakdown of the proportionate types of radio systems utilized throughout the five regions in the late 1970s showed that MW was most prevalent (65%), then SW (26%) and FM (9%). The diffusion of television has been greatest in Latin America, followed by Asia, The Middle East, Africa, and Oceania. Another measure of technological transfer is the adoption pattern of color TV systems by Third World nations. Again, the territorial and trade imperatives of three Western powers can be seen at work. The German PAL system is used by 42 Third World nations (mostly in Asia, The Middle East, and Africa); the American NTSC method is in 38 countries (predominantly in Latin America and Oceania); and France's SECAM technology is utilized by 25 national systems, mainly in Franco-phone Africa, the Mid East, and a handful of island nations in the Carribbean and the South Pacific.[7]

Attitudes and Policy

Accompanying the transfer of Western models and technology to the Third World has been a similar transference of programming policies and attitudes about broadcasting. Attitudes have often gotten in the way of sound policymaking. Reliance on the West to train so many Third World broadcasters has resulted in many returning to their homelands with a kind of commercial and entertainment ethos about broadcasting. They also have become imbued with notions of having to offer a full schedule of TV programming, going beyond what is feasible or compatible with nation building. As a result, broadcast policies have not been well integrated into national development policies in many Third World nations.

Broadcasting has been most instrumental in serving the larger goals of national integration, socioeconomic growth, and cultural survival. The task of achieving national integration has been served through universal coverage of the population with national news. This has helped to unite people and give them a sense of identity and patriotism. Broadcasting in a national language has also aided national integration in those nations that are less culturally diverse.[8] As vehicles of modernization, radio and television also contribute to symbolic and real socioeconomic growth in formative societies by disseminating information and knowledge, stimulating the marketplace through advertising, and acting as agents of change by fostering new attitudes and modifying social behavior.

Britain's Jeremy Tunstall has suggested that Western (and especially American) media have impacted on foreign countries in terms of politics, commerce, and ideas. The fact that Western broadcasters operate relatively free of governmental control invests them with a kind of independent power over public opinion, political coverage, and cultural expression. The use of radio and television for advertising also makes them the tools of private interests and commercialism. The worldwide sale of programs and broadcasting equipment by multinational corporations is an extension of their commercial values and goals. As a result: foreign countries are markets to be developed; audiences are consumers to be exploited; information and entertainment are commodities to be sold. In short, these notions are irrelevant to the Third World's concerns with national development and cultural survival.[9]

Outside aid can also influence programming policies and operational attitudes. The Western-trained cadres of professional broadcasters often find it difficult to implement their talents and expertise when they return home to highly bureaucratized broadcasting organizations. Since most Third World countries lack the industries and universities to develop broadcast policymakers, managers, program producers, and technicians, many young people are sent abroad to acquire broadcasting competence, usually in the West. Some never return home, having found life too comfortable. The ones who do return are often imbued with show business values and "ratings" mentalities. But things are improving. Through the efforts of UNESCO and various foreign industrial and educational institutions, training centers have been established throughout the developing world, as cited in Chapter 2.

Further tangible aid, both technical and material, has been sent to the Third World and put to good use in broadcasting. But this has also created problems. Aid packages from Western countries sometimes have come with strings attached, such conditions as requiring the recipient to purchase all future equipment from the lending nation and to formulate its broadcasting system along ideological lines favored by the donor.[10]

The influence of Western attitudes can also be seen in the way television has been developed in many Third World countries. Policymakers and proprietors alike often exhibit a kind of "capital city" elitism which causes them to be aloof from the public in general and regional interests in particular. For example, all too many Third World broadcasters have apparently forgotten the simple fact that people in the Northern Hemisphere tend to lead *indoor* lives, while the prevailing lifestyle in the Southern Hemisphere is *outdoor*-oriented.

The Dutch scholar Cees Hamelink points out that Western standards of professionalism, organizational structure, and cultural attitudes accompany international shipments of equipment from the industrialized countries to the Third World, largely through Westerners who are sent in to train personnel in the receiving nations in the correct use of the technology. This process reinforces the contention that technology is not neutral or "value free."[11]

Furthermore, the mere presence of modern technology in traditional cultures becomes a potent force in shaping national communication policies in the Third World. This is particularly applicable in the case of broadcasting, since the requisite technology dictates the physical design and organizational structure of the system, defines its operational functions and programming objectives, shapes the broadcaster's material inventory and human resource needs, and ultimately decides the rules and mechanisms by which radio and television will be controlled.[12]

A REGIONAL OVERVIEW OF THIRD WORLD BROADCASTING SYSTEMS

Institutions of modern mass communication are not native to the Third World, but rather have been transplanted there from developed countries. This accounts in large part for a lack of public respect and government protection for news media in many emerging nations.[13] The existence of hundreds of different languages throughout the Third World has made the goals of nationalism and broadcasting more difficult than in Europe and the Americas. Some African and Asian states do not have a uniform national language; hence, many societies are fragmented along ethnic and tribal lines to such a degree that cross-cultural and transnational communication are impeded if not impossible. This special relationship between multilingualism and national broadcasting policy is looked at more closely in the following chapter.

Africa

A number of endemic factors have affected the development of broadcasting on the continent of Africa. The most salient of these are the region's polylingual oral traditions, low literacy rates, lack of power plants needed for extensive electrification and affordable energy, and the relative inexpense and portability of radio vis-a-vis other media. As a result of these circumstances, radio is the most pragmatic and valuable mass medium in Africa. Print media are used mainly by the educated elite, and are limited to a handful of languages, including English and French. Television, on the other hand, is found almost exclusively in the major cities, where only a middle class minority can afford receivers.

In his book, *Broadcasting in Africa,* Sydney Head has summarized some of the problems that have plagued broadcast policymakers on the continent. For a start, more resources and official attention have been paid to developing the technical infrastructure of Africa's broadcasting systems than to distributing receiving equipment to the public and making programming. The scarcity and expense of appropriate radio and especially TV receivers have impeded many well-intended policies of national broadcasters.

Another obstacle to success in building audiences has been the receiver license fee, a method of raising income that has priced many citizens out of the broadcast audience or else resulted in widespread fee evasion. These problems have been overcome in many nations during the past decade by removing high import duties on receivers, eliminating license fees, extending credit toward the purchase of radio and TV sets, developing inexpensive wired distribution services in populated areas, and establishing public listening and viewing facilities.[14]

By 1984, seven out of 10 national broadcasting systems in Africa were government owned and operated, excluding the northern Arabic states and the smaller island republics. Lesotho, Madagascar, Mozambique, Swaziland, and Tanzania have created state-run commercial companies. Broadcasting in Ghana, Malawi, Mauritius, Nigeria, and Zimbabwe is the responsibility of public statutory authorities, with the latter two heavily dependent on advertising. All told, about half of Africa's broadcasting systems rely on some mixture of advertising, license fees, and government subsidies for their financial support; just over one-quarter depend on taxes only; and the rest have some combination of state funding with either advertising or fee income. The only national broadcaster that offers a purely commercial service on the continent is the Liberian Broadcasting System.[15]

Asia

Asia is the world's most populous continent, claiming over two-thirds of the earth's people. Like Africa, it is characterized by a high degree of polylingualism, with some countries supporting several hundred dialects. Radio is therefore the region's most highly valued mass medium, since it is generally localized, is able to cover remote areas, and does not require literacy. By contrast, television is confined mostly to urban centers, although satellites are making it a more pervasive medium. TV sets are still considered a luxury in most Asian countries; thus, radio, especially shortwave, is the main medium.

Asian broadcasting systems are primarily national, government-controlled, and financed through some combination of taxes, license fees, and, increasingly, advertising. While four-fifths of the countries in the region boast some level of TV service, nearly a third were still not color capable in the mid-1980s. The PAL standard has been adopted by over half of Asia's television operations. The prevailing Western influence on Asian broadcasting structure has been the British public service model, although the number of private stations is growing. Most nations on the continent have designed broadcasting systems to meet the specific needs of their people and the developmental objectives of their governments.

Asia also seems to have emphasized the construction of studios and transmission infrastructures over the diffusion of radio and television receiving equipment. The transistor is quickly rectifying this imbalance by making portable radios affordable and, therefore, available to most people. Today, Asia has the largest proportion of radio receivers among the five Third World regions and is second only to Latin America in its share of TV sets.

Entertainment programming dominated Asia's airwaves in the formative years of broadcasting and, while still significant, has given way to the more serious developmental mission during the past two decades by offering increasing amounts of education, cultural, and news programs. Much of the home-production is devoted to instructing the public in matters of hygiene, child care, farming methods, literacy lessons, and technical skills.

Training centers have been established throughout Asia by UNESCO and the Asian Broadcasting Union for the purpose of developing professional staffs to program and operate radio and TV stations. Nevertheless, the financial and creative burdens of attempting to offer full program schedules on television have required most national systems to import significant amounts of foreign programs. America and Britain are the major sources of imports, but Japan provides many children's shows, documentaries, and movies.[16] Another effort in rural development is being studied by the Asian Mass Communication Research Center in Singapore, which proposes to use audio cassettes as a viable and inexpensive way to communicate with people in rural communities.[17]

The government of India committed $68 million in 1984 to expand AIR's national TV system and convert it to color. The money will increase the number of transmitters from 43 to 180, thus extending coverage to 70% of the population. The move has been as controversial as it is costly, since only 15% of the population has color TV receivers. However, the government has lowered its excise tax on all receivers, so that color sets cost about $500 instead of the previous $900, and black and white receivers are only $100.[18]

Across the border, Bangladesh Television put four new regional TV transmitters on the air between 1982 and 1984 at a cost of $2.6 million, and also upgraded its central station in Dhaka to a fulltime color operation. These improvements have expanded its coverage, increased the share of domestic production to 70% of the air schedule, and enhanced the service's earnings from advertising, license fees, and program exports. Bangladesh had 260,000 TV sets by 1984, 12% of them color capable.[19]

The Middle East

The Middle East is a vital geopolitical entity of 22 nations stretching across North Africa and South Asia from the Atlantic to the Indian Ocean, and bounded by four seas (the Mediterranean, Black, Caspian, and Red) and three strategic waterways—the Persian Gulf and the Gulfs of Oman and Adan. To avoid misinterpretation, the following countries are considered to be part of the Middle East: Egypt, The Sudan, Lebanon, Syria, Jordan, the Peoples Democratic Republic of (North) Yemen, the (South) Yemen Arab Republic, Iraq, Iran, Kuwait, Saudi Arabia, Bahrain, Qatar, the United Arab Emerates, Oman, Algeria, Libya, Morocco, Tunisia, Turkey, Cyprus, and Israel. Except for Iran and Israel, all countries in the region are Arab-speaking Islamic cultures dominated by the Sunni Moslem faith. Most Iranians, however, are Persian-speaking Aryans whose communal language is Farsi. The majority are Shiite Moslems, a minority sect within the Islam religion. By contrast, Judaism is the state religion of Israel and its predominantly Jewish population speaks the official vernacular, Hebrew. Despite the deep religious differences throughout the area, Arabs and Israelis share a common ethnic bond as Semitic peoples.[20]

Broadcasting in the Middle East is largely a government-owned operation, but six countries—Egypt, Algeria, Morocco, Turkey, Cyprus, and Israel—have systems run by public authorities. Private broadcasting is present in Saudi Arabia and is being allowed to develop in several other oil-rich states. Over a third have government-financed systems, and one-half draw their incomes from some combination of state subsidization, advertising, and receiver license fees. Only Algeria and Israel rely entirely upon license fees to support their radio and television activities.

Generally speaking, television development in the Middle East has lagged behind that in Asia and Latin America. The French and British models are the only Western structures to have been successfully transplanted in the region; thus, the PAL and SECAM color standards prevail. TV signals cross borders easily in the proximal Persian Gulf states, due to the flat terrain and shared Arab language, factors that have enhanced viewing choice. Program exchanges are also common among members of the Arab States Broadcasting Union, and via satellite with Eurovision and Intervision.[21]

Douglas A. Boyd has provided a definitive overview of the region in his study, *Broadcasting in the Arab World*. Typical of the Third World, radio is the most important mass medium in the Middle East, due to the oral tradition of Arab culture and the transnational fluency of the Arabic language. The development of high-powered AM transmitters in the 1950s by Egypt, Syria, and Iraq also gave medium wave radio the international coverage usually attributed to shortwave. Accordingly, radio broadcasting in the Middle East has been a powerful political tool of established governments, which often resort to propaganda. Moreover, the availability of transistor radios among Arabs of all nationalities has made the region a popular target for international shortwave broadcasters.[22]

The historic conflict between Arabs and Jews in the region has intensified the use of "clandestine" radio stations since the 1948 Palestine War. These stations operate unofficially, meaning that they are not legally licensed, but their locations and political affiliations are public knowledge. Many factions within the Arab world also rely on clandestine broadcasts to enervate religious and political minorities and to promote revolution. In the past two decades, various militant groups have operated major clandestine stations to foment popular unrest in Syria, Egypt, Tunisia, Saudi Arabia, Iraq, South Yemen, Oman, and Iran. One of the most active political outlets in the Middle East has been the Voice of Palestine, the radio service of the Palestine Liberation Organization (PLO).[23]

Television is a fact of life throughout the Middle East, in poor countries as well as in the affluent oil-producing nations. TV is both a useful development resource and a status symbol in Arab societies large and small. Oman and the Sudan, which are big and poor, have managed to scrape up the money to install expensive satellite ground stations to distribute signals domestically, while the richer nations in the Arabian Gulf area have extensive state-of-the-art TV facilities.

Nevertheless, Arab TV is more western than Arabic, due to the adoption of French and British models, the acquisition of American and West European equipment, and the training of managers and production talent in the West. Boyd further points out three interlocking problems endemic to Arab broadcasting: a lack of effects research, a lack of mechanisms for citizen input into operational decision-making, and a lack of central planning and policy goals for informational and entertainment programming.[24]

Although the Arab countries share a regional language, religion, and culture, the various national differences have made so-called Arab unity a myth. Broadcasters in the region must be credited nonetheless with having forged a degree of cooperation between competing nations through the Arab League and the Arab States Broadcasting Union (ASBU). Besides assisting inter-state exchanges of programs, audience research, and professional expertise, the ASBU has become a vital news source for regional events and for Western TV news reports, via satellite links with the European Broadcasting Union and national networks in North America.

Shortages in professional personnel, trained and educated in contemporary broadcasting, continue to plague the Middle East. Other than Europe and America, the only effective places of instruction in the area are several Egyptian universities and the ASBU Training Center in Damascus, Syria. Another chronic weakness among most Middle East broadcasters is finding adequate financing to keep pace with programming costs and technical advances. One unique means of income used in Egypt, Jordan, and Tunisia is a surcharge on citizen's electric bills, given that everyone uses and benefits from broadcasting. On the technical front, Arab broadcasters have engaged in a kind of wattage war by escalating transmitter power in an attempt to outdo one another. Such competition is partially caused by (yet also exacerbates) a scarity of medium wave frequencies assigned to the region, and has also stimulated interest in FM development and home stereo systems.[25] The status of satellite broadcasting in the Middle East is detailed in Chapter 8.

Egypt plays a leadership role in the Middle East as a major source of Arab-language programming, as a broadcasting pioneer, and as a training ground. It is the center of broadcasting education and professional training in the region and, through cooperative efforts with the ASBU, has produced and facilitated exchanges of dramatic TV programs with its Arab neighbors. The Egyptian Middle East News Agency (MENA) has also provided media training to hundreds of Third World journalists since its formation in 1956.[26]

Cairo has been described as "the Hollywood of the Arab World" because of the volume and popularity of the films and TV shows, mostly soap operas in Arabic, that it sends throughout the Middle East. Egypt's TV system has been on the air since the early 1950s, longer than any other Arab broadcaster. This accounts in part for its virtual monopoly of Arab-language television. Another factor derives from the influence of its European colonizers, dating back to Napoleon's 1798 invasion and through its occupation by Britain in the nineteenth century, events that turned Egypt's upper class toward the West. Today, Egyptian television has a number of "off shore" production companies in Jordan, Tunisia, Dubain, Abu Dhabi, Greece, West Germany, and Britain—so named because they have been bank-rolled by wealthy oil titans. These studios sprang up in the late 1970s, after many Arab governments boycotted productions by Egypt's government TV organization in order to punish Sadat for making peace with Israel; but their foreign locations also were convenient for avoiding taxes and program regulations.

Egyptian state TV tailors its programs to the tastes of local audiences and traditional Arab culture, adhering closely to their codes of modest dress, little overt sexuality, and no controversial political themes. Things began to liberalize in the 1980s, and several co-productions with French and Spanish TV companies were being planned. Egypt's richest export markets are the Gulf states and Saudi Arabia; therefore, Egyptian TV producers take care not to offend Islamic values. At the same time, their TV programs consciously promote Egyptian culture. Domestic broadcast policy, however, sets rigorous air-time quotas on TV programming from the West.[27]

Israel is commonly perceived as a First World nation in the heart of the Arab Third World. Although settled by immigrant European Jews after World War II, Israel is still in the process of forging a new state within a Middle Eastern context, and television is one of its chief instruments of development. Originally under the authority of the Prime Minister, the government created the Israel Broadcasting Authority (IBA) in 1965 and modelled it after the BBC. Its policy is set by a 31-member plenary and its daily operation is the responsibility of a seven-member board of directors and the director general's staff. Revenue comes from a TV receiver license fee, which is augmented by an annual government allocation.

IBA's single TV channel concentrates on news and entertainment, but became highly politicized under Begin's rule. This politicalization affected IBA's journalism to the point where all foreign TV news reports were subject to clearance by an Israeli government censor before being transmitted beyond its borders—a practice which still occurs during military episodes.[28] This policy was apparently overlooked by the director of Israel's Government Press Office, Zev Chafets, when he criticized ABC News and the BBC in 1982 for allowing their reporters in Beirut to allegedly be intimidated by death threats from the PLO and Syria.[29]

Today, there is an on-going struggle between the observant orthodox camp and the secular Jews over broadcasting. The former want all TV broadcasting ceased on the Sabbath (Shabbat); the latter demand that programs be aired every day of the week. The appointment of Micha Yinon as chairman of the IBA in the Spring of 1984 was a kind of compromise, in that he is an orthodox Jew who favors daily broadcasts. Yinon also favors introducing commercial advertising on Israeli TV as a means of generating badly needed operating revenue, but he vows that it will be carefully regulated.[30]

Latin America and the Caribbean

Broadcasting in this region, the world's second most populous after Asia, is patterned after the American model predominantly, with some vestiges of the British and French models in the West Indies. Two-thirds of Latin America's radio and TV services are commercial enterprises, owned either privately or by the state. The remaining stations are noncommercial government or public operations. Advertising is the major source of income for broadcasters in the region, although taxes contribute to the upkeep of network infrastructures and operations. Four-fifths of Latin/Caribbean countries have TV systems, the highest saturation of any Third World region save the Middle East. The American NTSC color standard is used by nearly eight of every 10 TV stations in the area. Television, though not as available to everyone as radio, is quite common. Over half of the Third World's TV receivers are in Latin America, nearly twice that of second-ranking Asia, though the two regions are virtually equal in ownership of radios.

More than a quarter of the region's airtime is taken up by advertising, a level that rivals the most commercially-cluttered North American stations. Entertainment programs dominate the rest of the schedule, most of it from the U.S. On average, about a third of the TV shows aired on Latin American TV are foreign made, with the American share of the market ranging from 80% in Argentina to two-thirds in Mexico.[31] Spain is also a major exporter to the region.

Spain's RTVE has a separate department for marketing its programming to Spanish-language broadcasters around the world. Its principal clients are Colombia, Chile, Argentina, and the Hispanic stations in North America. Productions have also been sold to Bolivia, Costa Rica, Cuba, Ecuador, El Salvador, Guatemala, Honduras, Mexico, Nicaragua, Panama, Paraguay, Peru, Dominican Republic, Uruguay, and Venezuela. Sales totalled $2 million a year by 1984, and include properties such as dramatic series, documentaries, children's programs, and musical shows. Spain's Castillian accent has proved to be somewhat of a problem to Latin American viewers, but is acclimated to easily. Productions are made in both 625 PAL and 525 NTSC formats, so that virtually all Latin countries can be served.[32]

Brazil is the largest TV market in Latin America, with 70 million viewers, five commercial networks, and one educational broadcasting service, and with over one billion dollars in annual TV advertising receipts as of 1984. The country's newest TV network, *Manchete* (meaning ''Headlines''), went on the air in June 1983. Its format features extended newscasts, cultural and arts programs, and American TV series and first-run films. Brazil's biggest TV network, *Globo*, attracts nearly two-thirds of the audience nightly by airing soap operas, variety programs, and talk shows. Unlike the new Manchete channel, Globo airs almost no American shows.[33]

In Argentina, the Federal Broadcasting Committee drafted a legislative proposal and sent it to the government for approval in July 1984. The new law will allow print media interests to apply for TV channels, but a watchful legal eye will prevent news media monopolies from developing. Regional radio and TV interests and cultural concerns will also be better served under the new structure.[34]

Cable television was approved by the government of Uruguay in 1984 and will operate under the control of the national PTT, Antel, and the National Directorate of Public Relations, DINARP. No advertising will be allowed via the system, and it must produce or acquire its own material, since no programs from either domestic or foreign TV stations may be rebroadcast.[35]

In Nicaragua, the government-run Sandinista Television System (SSTV) of the People's Broadcasting Corporation fills its two TV channels with an unlikely video goulash of programs from East Germany ("Marx y Engels"), Mexico ("Telenovela"), Britain ("Civilization"), and America ("Lou Grant"), plus many hours of its own productions. This provides the country's 2.7 million people with a choice of programs, except in the case of news, where "Noticiero Sandinista" is aired on both channels simultaneously.

Still, such a choice of diverse offerings is exciting in a country where per capita income is less than $1,000 a year and TV is the people's passport to both fantasyland and the outside world. Viewers in border regions have the bonus of watching TV shows spilling over from Costa Rica, Honduras, and El Salvador. Virtually everyone is able to receive AM signals from Mexico and the U.S., as well as shortwave broadcasts from many nations.

After years of superficial TV programming and irrelevant news under the Samoza regime, it is ironic that the public has more and freer newscasts under its new communist leadership. But what makes Nicaragua singularly different from other communist states is a lack of blatant propaganda and a genuine interest in foreign news reports. Domestic TV news does not criticize the government, but that is true throughout the Third World, including U.S.-backed countries like El Salvador and Guatemala. The news is slanted against the U.S. government, but is not anti-American, since so much U.S. popular culture is in demand. One writer has captured the uniqueness of Nicaraguan TV by calling it "a medium that really is incomprehensible in either American or communist terms."[36]

The Pacific Islands of Oceania

The string of islands that dot the central, southern, and western Pacific Ocean make up the region known as Oceania. Most of these islands are independent nations, but some continue to have colonial ties as protectorates of America, Britain, and France. Australia and New Zealand, although geographically a part of the region, are not included in the following assessment, since they are not Third World nations.

Broadcasting is controlled by the government in approximately two-fifths of the islands of Oceania, with more commercial than public systems operating in the remaining islands. All are financed either by advertising or state revenues or both. Radio did not come to most of these Pacific nations until after World War II. Television arrived even later, or not at all. In fact, only about a third of the region's states had TV in the mid-1980s. This will change as direct broadcast satellites cast their footprints across the South Pacific. Those having television systems have been conspicuously influenced by their colonial mentors. Correspondingly, about eight out of 10 TV systems in the Pacific region have adopted the American NTSC color standard, and the rest use the French SECAM.[37]

Fiji's experience is interesting. The Fiji Broadcasting Commission is an independent statutory body whose service is half commercial and half cultural. Television only came to the island in 1982. Prior to that, it had been one of the few societies in the world untouched by TV. The government created a unique service that is essentially a videotape production and distribution center which makes local programs for public viewing via receivers located at community centers. Actually, affluent viewers have been importing tapes of foreign shows for home viewing in recent years. Now everyone on Fiji has some access to television. This is seen as a first step in approving local TV stations on the island, but the $20 million price tag to develop a full TV network makes that option unlikely at present.[38]

By way of summary, Table 6-1 compares vital broadcasting statistics in these five regions of the Third World. What follows is an in-depth look at the North-to-South flow of entertainment and news as interlocking forces in the juggernaut of media imperialism that menaces Third World broadcasters.

MEDIA IMPERIALISM VERSUS NATIONAL AND CULTURAL SOVEREIGNTY

Media imperialism exists when one (dominant) culture imposes its values, beliefs, assumptions, and language upon another (dependent) culture through the process of communicating via the mass media. It is, in fact, a power relationship that lends itself to various levels of conflict between senders and receivers, since mediated products reflect the cultures that produce them and today's telecommunication message systems can transmit them so easily across national frontiers. It is also understandable that poor developing societies, tied to traditional cultures and pre-industrial life styles, feel threatened by the electronic deluge of news and entertainment emanating from a handful of affluent high-tech democracies.

By contrast, *cultural autonomy,* as defined by Holland's Cees Hamelink, means that a society is able to decide for itself how to allocate its own communication resources in order to adapt to its unique historical environment. When a nation's cultural decisions are made by outside forces like foreign media and transnational corporations, then its own cultural sovereignty gives way and becomes moulded into an imitation of the alien culture. Hamelink calls this process *cultural synchronization,* meaning that the receiving culture takes on the shape of, or becomes synchronous with, the outside culture.[39]

Cultural synchronization can occur in two ways: when one culture is *imposed* upon another, either accidentally or intentionally; and when cultural products of a foreign nation are *invited* into another country's media systems. In broadcasting, the former takes place when the radio and TV signals of a dominant culture spill over the border or are beamed (via shortwave or satellite) into another sovereign culture; the latter happens when one nation buys foreign programming to rebroadcast over its own stations.

The fact that Western media imperialism and cultural synchronization are

Table 6-1 A Comparison of Broadcasting Descriptors in Five Third World Regions, 1984

Criteria	Africa	Asia	The Middle East	Latin America and The Caribbean	Pacific Islands of Oceania
No. of Nations	52[a]	25	22	44	26[b]
Population/Millions	330[c]	1400[d]	249.5	350	6
Type of Ownership					
Government	71%	64%	59%	23%	42%
Public	10%	16%	27%	11%	23%
Private	6%	0	0	36%	27%
State Commercial	11%	12%	14%	0	4%
Public Commercial	2%	8%	0		4%
Type of Financing					
Fees Only	0	0	5%	0	0
Ads Only		0	0	30%	27%
Taxes Only	17%	8%	36%	2%	23%
Fees/Ads/Taxes	47%	40%	27%	4%	0
Ads/Taxes	27%	24%	23%	64%	50%
Fees/Taxes	7%	8%	9%	0	0
Other Hybrids	2%	20%	0	0	0
Service Diffusion					
Radio	100%	100%	100%	100%	100%
Television	63%	80%	100%	82%	35%
Color: None	24%	30%	0	3%	0
NTSC	0	10%	5%	78%	78%
PAL	42%	55%	54%	11%	0
SECAM	34%	5%	32%	8%	22%
Combo	0	0	9%[e]	0	0
Western Models					
American	0	4%	0	57%	48%
British	40%	35%	14%	16%	8%
French	43%	13%	17%	11%	11%
Other[f]	5%	4%	0	2%	22%
N/A	12%	44%	69%	14%	11%
Radio Sets: Total	26.2M	108.4M	41.M	102.8M	2.5M
Third World Share	9%	38.6%	14.7%	36.6%	1.1%
TV Sets: Total	2.4M	19.9M	11.8M	39M	.4M
Third World Share	3%	27%	16%	53%	1%

[a]Does not include six Arabic nations of North Africa.
[b]Does not include Australia and New Zealand.
[c]Does not include 112 million people in six Arabic nations of the North.
[d]Does not include populations of PRC (970M), Japan (118M), and Taiwan (18M).
[e]Cyprus and Saudi Arabia use both PAL and SECAM.
[f]Primarily Belgium, Spain and Holland.
Sources: *World Radio TV Handbook 1984.*
  Katz and Wedell, *Broadcasting in the Third World,* pp. 47, 50, 59, and 62.

regarded as threats to the cultural autonomy of Third World countries has made this aspect of international communication a contentious worldwide issue, especially in the age of satellite broadcasting. The issue as it applies to world broadcasting is perhaps best analyzed in terms of two separate but interrelated concerns: (a) the debate over old versus new international information and economic orders; and (b) global patterns of television programming flow.

GLOBAL PATTERNS OF TELEVISION PROGRAMMING FLOW

UNESCO commissioned two Finnish communication scholars, Kaarle Nordenstreng and Tapio Varis, to survey and analyze the international flow of TV program material during 1972 and 1973. Their study concluded that: (a) the flow of TV programming was *one-way*, from the big Western exporting countries to the rest of the world; and (b) that entertainment material dominated the flow.[40] Varis repeated the study a decade later and found few changes in the overall flow or dominance of TV program traffic worldwide, but he did find evidence that more regional program exchanges were taking place.[41] And, of course, there were changes in the diffusion of television technology in the interim. In early 1973, for example, a worldwide TV audience, estimated at 884 million viewers, was watching approximately 273 million receivers. The figures 10 years later found 1.5 billion viewers and about 550 million TV sets in use.[42]

Research centers in Latin America, North America, Asia, The Middle East, Africa, and Eastern and Western Europe collected and evaluated programming flow data for a 2-week period in early 1983, using the same sampling procedures and method of analysis. Their goal was to measure the dimension of TV flow within eight major program categories, and to identify general program flow patterns worldwide. The eight content categories were: (a) Information, (b) Education, (c) Culture, (d) Religion, (e) Children's, (f) Entertainment, (g) Unclassified, and (h) Advertisements. The results of the 1983 follow-up study are presented in Table 6-2, which compares the 1973 data on imported TV programming to total and prime time data for 1983 in seven continental regions of the globe.

The following trends and conclusions can be gleaned from the data in Table 6-2:

- Imports account for roughly one-third of the world's total TV airtime.
- In all regions, there are countries that are heavily dependent on imported programs and also those only slightly dependent.
- Imports, as a proportion of total versus prime time, are fairly close in all regions in 1983, except in Latin America, where prime time is dominated by foreign shows.

In sum, the worldwide pattern of TV programming flow is much the same in 1983 as it was in 1973, yet specific differences and changes are apparent both within and between regions.

Table 6-2 A Comparison of Imported TV Programming Worldwide in 1973 and 1983

Country and broadcasting institution	% of programming imported in		1983, prime time
	1973	1983	
North America			
Canada/CBC	34	32	24
Canada/RC	46	38	31
United States/comm.	1	2	2
United States/educ.	2		
Latin American and Caribbean			
Argentina/Canal 9	10	49	53
Brazil	—	30	23
Chile	55	—	—
Colombia	34	—	—
Cuba	—	24	9
Dominican Republic	50	—	—
Ecuador	—	66	70
Guatemala	84	—	—
Mexico	39	34	44
Uruguay	62	—	—
Venezuela	—	38	42
Western Europe			
Austria	—	43	61
Belgium/BRT	—	28	33
Belgium/RTBF	—	29	28
Denmark	—	46	32
Fed. Rep. of Germany/ARD	23	13	7
Fed. Rep. of Germany/ZDF	30	23	23
Fed. Rep. of Germany/Regional	—	24	—
Finland	40	37	37
France	9	17	17
Greece	—	39	—
Iceland	67	66	66
Ireland	54	57	58
Italy	13	18	19
Netherlands	23	25	24
Norway	39	30	28
Portugal	35	39	—
Spain	—	33	35
Spain/EIT.B Regional	—	74	—
Sweden	33	35	28
Turkey	—	36	49
United Kingdom/BBC	12	15	21
United Kingdom/ITV	13	14	20
United Kingdom/Channel 4	—	26	15

Table 6-2   (continued)

Country and broadcasting institution	% of programming imported in		1983, prime ti me
	1973	1983	
Eastern Europe/Soviet Union			
Bulgaria	45	27	21
German Dem. Rep.	26	30	39
Czechoslovakia	—	24	25
Hungary	24	26	35
Poland	17	—	—
Romania	27	—	—
Soviet Union	5	8	18
Yugoslavia	27	29	22
Asia and the Pacific			
Australia	57	44	46
Brunei	—	60	28
People's Rep. of China	1	8	—
Hong Kong/Asia TV Chinese	31	24	16
Hong Kong/Asia TV English	40	64	72
Hong Kong/Asia TV Ltd.	—	27	9
India/Calcutta	—	3	6
India/Delhi	—	11	10
Japan/NHK educ.	1	—	—
Japan/comm.	10	—	—
Republic of Korea/Tong-yang	31	—	—
Republic of Korea/Munhwa TV	—	16	0
Malaysia	71	54	31
New Zealand/one	75	72	64
New Zealand/two	75	75	66
Pakistan	35	16	12
Philippines	29	12	20
Philippines/Metro Manila	—	40	—
Singapore/Channel 8	78	55	70
Singapore/Channel 5	78	70	66
Sri Lanka	—	24	22
Thailand	18	—	—
Vietnam	—	34	—
Near East and Arab Countries			
Algeria	—	55	55
Egypt	41	35	41
Israel	55	—	—
Kuwait	56	—	—
Lebanon	40	—	—
Saudi-Arabia/Riyadh TV	31	—	—
Saudi-Arabia/Aramcu TV	100	—	—

(*continued*)

Table 6-2   (continued)

Country and broadcasting institution	% of programming imported in		1983, prime time
	1973	1983	
Syria	—	33	35
Tunisia	—	55	35
People's Rep. of Yemen	57	47	—
Africa			
Ghana	27	—	—
Kenya	—	37	60
Nigeria	63	40	—
Republic of South Africa	—	29	31
Uganda	19	38	38
Zambia	64	—	—
Zimbabwe	—	61	—

Source: Reprinted from "The International Flow of Television Programs" by Tapio Varis in the *Journal of Communication,* 34 (1), Winter 1984, pp. 146–147, copyright © 1984.

In *North America,* for example, the U.S. imports only 2% of its TV programs, most of it from Britain by Public Television and the rest from Latin America for the growing Hispanic TV market. The picture in Canada, as discussed in Chapter 3, shows little change in imports by the CBC English network, and only a slight decrease in the Radio Canada French channel. Private telecasters still rely heavily on outside (U.S.) productions, especially during prime time. The national TV services in *Latin America* devote approximately half of their schedules to entertainment programming, three-quarters of which comes from the U.S.

The *West European* countries show the greatest variation in import program policies and practices of any region in the world. Thirty percent of their collective airtime is comprised of foreign content. This comes from America (44%), the United Kingdom (16%), West Germany and France (5–10% each), and other West European (18%) and Eastern Bloc (3%) countries. Finland imports the most programming from the East, with France, Britain, and West Germany buying lesser amounts. *East European* broadcasters and the USSR import mostly entertainment shows, followed by cultural programs. Over half (57%) of these are acquired from noncommunist countries.

The vast geographic differences among the *Asian* and *Pacific* nations make analysis of their TV import policies difficult. The regional average for foreign programming is just over a third (36%), almost all of it devoted to news and entertainment. In fact, roughly half of all children's programs and entertainment shows on Asia's airwaves are imported, while informational, educational, cultural, and religious programming is mostly home-produced.

The Middle East buys 42% of its TV programming abroad, a third of it from other Arab states. The largest non-Arabic sources are the U.S. (32%), France (13%), Britain (7%), Japan (6%), West Germany (5%), and the Soviet Union (3%). Egypt, at one time the largest exporter of Arab-language content to the region, is now second (with 6%) behind the United Arab Emirates (10%) in the 1983 sampling. This slippage is due in part to an Arab boycott in retaliation for Egypt's peace treaty with Israel, although private broadcasters in the Middle East buy many productions from "off shore" Egyptian studios located outside of the country. Saudi Arabia and Kuwait are tied at 4% each as sources of imported TV.

In Africa, where television is still in its infancy and largely confined to major urban areas, four out of every 10 programs aired are foreign. Most imports are entertainment and, again, America is the leading source, followed by several West European countries. Zimbabwe imports the largest share of its TV schedule (61%), while the Republic of South Africa, which started TV in 1976, purchases the smallest amount (29%).

Table 6-3 breaks down the distribution of seven types of programming by region.

Latin America, the Arab region, and Africa all import over 70% of their entertainment fare, followed by the Western and Eastern European countries and Asia, which import about half of theirs. Asia and Latin America lead in informational imports, whereas Africa buys the largest share of children's programs. Canada's entertainment imports are mainly in the form of movies and sitcoms; Asia and Pacific Oceania rely most heavily on the children's shows; the Arab states mainly acquire TV plays and documentaries; and Africa imports films, TV dramas, and educational programs. The European nations, East and West, exchange a great deal of programming directly through the EBU's Eurovision and OIRT's Intervision networks.

Several conclusions of particular significance to the Third World can be drawn from the data presented in Tables 6-2 and 6-3. One is that the U.S. is the source of most TV programming imported by Third World broadcasters, with the West Europeans and Japanese active secondary suppliers. Next is the fact that from one third to one half of all programming is exchanged between countries and within regions. Third, the global flow of TV programming is overwhelmingly North to South and West to East. Furthermore, entertainment programs still dominate the traffic, followed by sports and children's programs, while informational and educational programs were the types most likely to be produced domestically.

Katz and Wedell found that action-adventure and situation comedies were the

Table 6-3 Distribution and Proportion of Imported TV Programming by Region and Category in 1983

Program category	U.S. all %	U.S. imp. %	Canada all %	Canada imp. %	Latin America all %	Latin America imp. %	W. Europe all %	W. Europe imp. %	U.S.S.R. all %	U.S.S.R. imp. %	E. Europe all %	E. Europe imp. %	Asia all %	Asia imp. %	Arab Region all %	Arab Region imp. %	Africa all %	Africa imp. %
Informative	19	1	35	—	16	20	29	5	30	2	20	7	15	30	22	12	39	8
Educational	7	0	8	—	7	13	9	10	14	—	13	9	7	13	6	1	9	27
Cultural	6	9	8	24	2	14	6	12	15	4	12	21	3	6	6	2	3	29
Religious	3	—	2	28	1	18	1	11	—	—	—	—	2	9	5	1	1	—
Entertainment	40	2	36	72	44	71	35	53	27	14	36	49	48	53	42	72	30	73
Sports	4	2	3	—	5	18	8	36	9	32	10	43	10	28	6	2	6	60
Other (ads, children's, unclassified)	25	0	8	35	25	37	12	30	5	5	9	21	15	41	13	50	12	40
Total %	100		100		100		100		100		100		100		100		100	
Minutes	17,344,100		84,166		670,088		236,207		22,080		60,097		152,978		48,689		30,524	

Note: The figures are indicative to the regions as a whole as represented by the countries included in the study. The Republic of South Africa is not included in the figures. Yugoslavia, as a member of the European Broadcasting Union, is included in Western Europe.

Source: Reprinted from "The International Flow of Television Programs" by Tapio Varis in the *Journal of Communication*, 34 (1), Winter 1984, pp. 150–151, copyright © 1984.

most popular genres of TV imports throughout the Third World, and that countries with competitive channels tended toward program duplication instead of diversity in their head-to-head scheduling.[43] And finally, the global trend in both direction and volume of TV programming flow has not changed significantly in the past decade and does not seem likely to change in the future, since the same few sources continue to monopolize the burgeoning home video market worldwide. It has been in the realm of news flows, however, where the emotions of broadcasters all over the world have run the highest.

GLOBAL PATTERNS OF INFORMATION FLOW

To fully appreciate the geopolitical dynamics of the global flow of information and culture, begin by considering the simple fact that the number of nations has nearly quadrupled since World War II. This single statistic has transformed the Non-Aligned Third World into a power bloc inside international forums like the United Nations (UN), the United Nations Educational, Scientific and Cultural Organization (UNESCO), and the International Telecommunication Union (ITU). In the two decades following World War II, Western interests expanded their dominance over the sources and channels of mass communication worldwide; but the shear quantity of emerging nations imbued them with the electoral muscle and the will to begin asserting some control over the information flowing so freely across their national frontiers. Since most Third World nations have underdeveloped economies unable to support mass marketing or to generate private capital, the presence of Western news, popular culture, and high technology is seen by them as being inappropriate to their people's needs, hostile to their best national interests, and threatening to the survival of their authentic cultures.

The International Debate Over Free Versus
Balanced Flows of Information

The idea that information should be allowed to flow freely between nations is as old as the UN itself. In the 1970s, however, it began being challenged in UNESCO and elsewhere by Third World and Soviet bloc nations. The challenge has been cast in terms of a debate between a "free" versus "balanced" international flow of information.

The *free flow* side is supported by the Western nations of the First World, which adhere to democratic principles and the market imperatives of capitalism. The *balanced flow* side is favored primarily by the Third World countries out of concerns that their national images are being distorted by the news media of the developed world and that their national cultures are being dominated by information and entertainment from the West, especially Anglo-American media. The Second World also advocates a balanced flow of information since government would do the balancing. The forces prefering a more balanced (two-way) flow of information have used the forum of UNESCO to propose a New World Information Order (NWIO) as a means of correcting the imbalances and inequities created by the free (one-way) flow of the existing information order.

As the controversy unfolded, the First World and a handful of free developing nations with colonial ties to the West were pitted against UNESCO's majority membership from the Second and Third Worlds. Virtually all of the emerging states realized by 1970 that they had become critically dependent upon information reaching them via a one-way flow from media systems in the West.[44] Out of this awareness, they linked the NWIO concept to the formulation of their own national communication policies. In short, most Third World governments felt that the balanced flow of information proposal was better suited to their developmental needs than the existing, market-dominated free flow arrangement. The communist bloc, seeing this as an opportunity to put the West on the defensive and exploit the conflict for its own gain, encouraged and supported the developing nations in their pursuit of changing the patterns of world communication.[45]

The tactic taken by the Soviet Union to put controls on the free flow of international information has been to sponsor a series of resolutions at UNESCO and UN meetings during the 1970s. The first of these, a Declaration of Guiding Principles on the Use of Satellite Broadcasting, was proposed at UNESCO's 1972 General Conference and subsequently passed by the UN General Assembly.[46] The U.S. and six Western allies objected to Article 9 of the measure, which stipulated that a DBS could not transmit into other countries without the prior consent of their governments.[47]

A second Soviet resolution, also introduced in 1972, called for the world's mass media to be used only for peaceful and humanitarian purposes. The measure was raised and tabled at the 1974 and 1976 biennials, and finally adopted in somewhat sanitized form at UNESCO's 1978 General Conference as the Declaration on the Mass Media Principles Favoring Peace and International Understanding and Combatting War, Propaganda, Racialism and Apartheid.[48] The USSR further courted the Third World by sponsoring a resolution requiring future UNESCO meetings on national communication policies to be held outside of the Western world.[49]

The Third World's position is that the free flow concept had little meaning to developing nations, since they lack the means to communicate on an equal footing with the developed countries. Furthermore, they are very sensitive about the distorted coverage of the Third World by the major foreign news media from the East and West. Cultural imperialism is a third chronic problem facing them. A concensus thus formed among Non-Aligned Third World nations that the free flow of information is an ideal that in practice will never serve its best interests until both economic inequities and information imbalances are adjusted on a worldwide scale.

The New International Economic Order Proposal

The Third World coalesced behind a strategy to link information with economics as parallel issues to be addressed in the international arena. The international economic order following World War II was authored largely by the U.S., with no Third World involvement. A host of global institutions (such as the World Bank, the International Monetary Fund, and the General Agreement on Trade and Tariffs) forged a development model for the Third World in the post-war years based on the pre-existing structure of colonialism and economic imperialism. While this arrangement helped the developing countries to industrialize, their growth and economies were vitally dependent on the industrialized First World.[50]

The UN General Assembly formally addressed this issue in a May 1974 Special Session which produced a Declaration and Action Program on the Establishment of a New International Economic Order (NIEO). Most of the new order's principles were proposed by Third World nations, but subsequently were to be approved by a majority of the world's governments.

A Dutch scholar, Cees Hamelink, has provided a cogent outline of the principles and assumptions underlying a "new" versus "old" economic order in his book, *Cultural Autonomy in Global Communications*. In support of the NIEO proposal, the claim is made that the present order has failed the developing world.

Most Third World governments feel that the world's economic inequities could be remedied under international law through a NIEO. Its key principles would grant all nations the right:[51]

- to participate fully and effectively in all international decision-making;
- to adopt appropriate economic, political, and cultural systems;
- to full and permanent sovereignty over their national resources;
- to regulate the activities of foreign entities, such as transnational corporations, in concurrence with national goals and priorities;
- to formulate a model of autonomous development geared toward the basic needs of the population;
- to pursue progressive social transformation that enables the full participation of the population in the development process.

Concurrent with the Third World's calls for a new economic order was a corollary demand for a similar change in the information order. Concerns over the essentially one-way flow of media messages from North to South became the centerpiece of deliberations at virtually all subsequent meetings held by the Non-Aligned Movement and UNESCO.

The Non-Aligned News Agencies Pool

Most Third World leaders had been mobilized into a united front by 1973 when the Fourth Non-Aligned Summit convened in Algiers. The 75 member nations pledged themselves to an Action Program for Economic Cooperation in which mass communication figured prominently. From this came the idea to establish a Non-Aligned News Agencies Pool (NANAP), a cooperative venture allowing for the exchange of news items among the press agencies of the developing countries. The Pool began operations in January 1975 under the direction of Tanjug, the Yugoslavian news service, relaying some 3500 items from 26 national news agencies in English, French, and Spanish during its first year.[52]

Today, the Non-Aligned News Agency has grown to 85 members, but it still faces many problems. Being a pool instead of a news agency, it has no correspondents and therefore must rely solely on dispatches from a very limited number of contributors. Specifically, only about 30 countries participate on a regular basis, with 60% of the Pool's annual volume supplied by only seven nations. This level of participation has translated into financial burdens and a relatively small impact on prevailing patterns of information flow from the West.[53]

A number of other cooperative regional news pools are facilitating news coverage and exchanges in the interest of development throughout the Third World. Some of the most successful ones are the Inter Press Service (IPS), the Pan-African News Agency (PANA), Egypt's MENA, the Association of South East Asian Nations (ASEAN) agencies, Reuters-affiliated LATIN agency and Action of National Information Systems (ASIN) in Latin America, the Caribbean News Agency (CANA), and the Asian-Pacific News Network (ANN).[54]

ANN, for example, is being assisted by the Asia-Pacific Institute for Broadcast Development in Kuala Lumpur, an intergovernmental organization that was created in 1977 to serve countries in the region (from Iran to Western Samoa) in training, professional consultation, technical cooperation, and prototype research projects. ANN became operational in 1981.[55]

Despite such "bootstrap" efforts, the Third World needs more technology, money, and institutional development. But it also needs an elimination of protectionism, and the open and unconditional sharing of knowledge, if efforts to reduce disparities and restore cultural dignity are to succeed. It is for these reasons that the Non-Aligned Movement has consolidated its resources within UNESCO to fight so assiduously for making the New World Information Order a reality.

The NWIO became the centerpiece of the so-called MacBride Commission, a nongovernmental body formed by UNESCO to study the problems of global information flow. It also provided the incentive for the Non-Aligned Movement to create its own news pool. But the antecedent to all North–South communication conflicts can be found in their divergent views of news.

Western Objectivity Vis-a-Vis Development News

The First and Third Worlds have had difficulty in agreeing upon what constitutes news. Any definition of news must take into account the selection criteria, sources, content, and the fundamental role of journalism in given societies. A delineation of Western versus Third World news values clearly shows why such a conflict exists and why it will not easily be resolved—especially in the age of direct satellite broadcasting.

By one definition, news in the Western sense of the word "is an accurate, fair, balanced, and objective report that must have certain news values based on such criteria as impact, prominence, proximity, timeliness, human interest, conflict, and oddity."[56] Westerners also conceive of news as a commercial product that is sold to them by information brokers—the news media—for profit.[57] Audience tastes and the profit motive therefore influence the criteria for selecting news in most Western media. Accordingly, the Western news model doesn't suit the needs or cultural traditions of most Third World countries. To illustrate, crime and punishment are dramatically different notions in the Middle East than in North America. In many Arab countries, thieves are punished by having their hands chopped off, and adultery is a capital offense. In the U.S., by contrast, sex is routinely exploited, criminals are treated as celebrities by the media, and crime itself is often indistinguishable from "business as usual."[58]

Journalists throughout the Third World tend to value press freedom, but generally must place a higher premium on national development than on their own professional privilege. For them, news must be regarded more as a positive social force, like education, in order to marshal public opinion behind official policies aimed at instilling a sense of national cohesion and identity in societies often marked by ethnic, cultural, and religious diversity. This means that media in the Third World accept the rationale that government has a legitimate role in "guiding" the press toward national objectives, in much the same way that parents, teachers, and clergy guide the development of children until such time that they are ready to think for themselves and take responsibility for their actions.

Government guidance of the media in the Third World is done in the name of *developmental journalism,* a term given to the practice of mobilizing available media in support of specific nation-building programs, like a health or literacy campaign.[59] The product of this type of journalism has been called *development news,* which, like all communication technology, is regarded as a scarce public resource to be strategically allocated by the state in the interests of nationhood and modernization.[60]

So great is the cause of sovereignty within the developing nations that they also demand the right to control the flow of foreign information and programming crossing their borders. These views run contrary to Western principles of press freedom, and thus form the core of the classic debate between "balanced" versus "free" flows of international information.[61] And this was the debate that UNESCO's MacBride Commission hoped to resolve.

The MacBride Commission Report

The most important outcome of the 1976 General Conference was the formation of the International Commission for the Study of Communication Problems. This 16-member board was appointed by the Director General of UNESCO, Amadou Mahtar M'Bow.[62] Headed by Ireland's Sean MacBride, founder of Amnesty

International and recipient of both the Nobel and Lenin Peace Prizes, it was comprised of media experts from five Western countries (Canada, France, Japan, the Netherlands, and the U.S.), two communist nations (Yugoslavia and the USSR), and eight Third World states (Chile, Colombia, Egypt, India, Indonesia, Nigeria, Tunisia, and Zaire).[63] Known as the MacBride Commission, its mandate was to investigate: (a) the current state of world communications; (b) the problems surrounding a free and balanced flow of information, and how the needs of the developing countries link with the flow; (c) how, in light of the NIEO, a New World Information Order may be created; and (d) how mass media can become vehicles for enhancing public opinion on world issues.[64]

The Commission solicited information and various points of view during 42 days of formal hearing in France, Sweden, Yugoslavia, India, and Mexico. Its work culminated 3 years later in the 300-page MacBride Report—published as *Many Voices, One World*—containing 82 recommendations and identifying a dozen items requiring further study. The document was presented to UNESCO for final adjudication at its 1980 General Conference in Belgrade, Yugoslavia, although an interim report was discussed at the 1978 biennial in Paris.[65]

Reaction to the MacBride Report was mixed. Like so many other UNESCO undertakings, it gave every side something and no side everything. Cees Hamelink and 10 colleagues criticized the report for not going far enough to meet the Third World's demands. Specifically, they faulted it for not articulating the basic features of the New World Information and Communication Order and how it would serve humankind, and for not giving more attention to communication research and training in developing countries. They also opined that the new telecommunication technologies are inherently dangerous to most of the world's people, since they are produced and controlled by Western businesses interested mainly in turning the planet into a "corporate village" and establishing a kind of "world order of the transnational corporation."[66]

The Soviet faction in UNESCO rejoiced at the MacBride Report's anti-business slant, and emphasized all negative references to the commercial and market aspects of world communications. They cited specific instances of alleged American transgressions in media activities, such as monopolizing international news flow, practicing imperialist propaganda, and using journalists as covers for espionage.[67]

The American strategy was to offer a concrete aid package to the Third World rather than engage in polemics over the MacBride Report. It did respond in due course, however, to both the NWICO proposal and the Right to Communicate concept it advanced.

The New World Information Order Proposal

Mustapha Masmoudi, Tunisia's information minister and UNESCO representative, became the Third World's public spokesman for a new information order. He articulated seven specific forms of imbalance in the international flow of information:[68]

1. A flagrant quantitative imbalance exists in the volume and direction of news flow between the developed North and developing South. For example, nearly 80% of world news flows from four major Western agencies (AP, Reuters, Agence France Presse, and UPI) to the Third World, yet only about one-quarter of their news coverage is devoted to developing countries.

2. A significant inequality in information services can be seen in the monopoly of transnational information flow by the above four Western wire services and the Soviet Union's news agency, TASS, while almost a third of the developing nations have no national news agency. So, too, do the First and Second Worlds control 90% of the electromagnetic spectrum, leaving the Third World as largely passive and defenseless audiences of foreign broadcasts.

3. Western communication institutions in fact dominate and are indifferent to Third World media problems, concerns, and aspirations; the developing countries are treated as mere consumers to be sold information as they would other commodities.

4. The developed world lacks complete and accurate information on the developing nations. News about the Third World is reported by the giant transnational media to nations all over the world, including the developing countries themselves; but the information processed for coverage is generally an unfavorable and distorted account of events (like terrorism, political coups, civil war, strikes, street demonstrations, and natural disasters). Such items are selected more to meet the expectations of audiences in the industrialized countries than to show positive Third World achievements in an objective light.

5. The established information systems of the developed world seem to be captives of their own colonialism. This is evidenced by their inability or unwillingness to reflect the moral, cultural, and political values of the Third World rather than to sensationalize and trivialize events so as to perpetrate negative stereotypes in order to suit their own interests.

6. Foreign media have an alienating influence on the economic, social, and cultural life of emerging societies through their direct investments in Third World media, monopoly on advertising, opposition to social evolution, and cultural domination and acculturation of developing nations.

7. The messages disseminated by developed media are often ill-suited to the needs of the Third World. News coverage, for instance, is designed to meet the needs of the sending nations rather than those of the receiving nations.

UNESCO and the Non-Aligned Movement have alleged that the preceding imbalances could be redressed through a formal New World Information Order that would require:[69]

1. Regulation of the right to information by preventing abusive use of the right to access of information;

2. Definitions of appropriate criteria to govern truly objective news selections;

3. Regulation of the collection, processing, and transmission of news and data across national frontiers;
4. Enforcement through domestic legislation and a new supranational agency of a proposed international journalistic code and penalities;
5. A formal procedure whereby a state could request of another government that its news media publish a communique rectifying and supplementing the false or incomplete information already disseminated.

The Right to Communicate

The New World Information *and* Communication Order (NWICO) that emerged from the MacBride Commission is predicated on a compromise proposal that synthesizes "a free *and* balanced flow of information" with a Third World edict termed the "right to communicate."[70] Proponents of this principle equate it with the right of all nations to have equal access to the world's presses, airwaves, and orbital satellite slots in space; in other words, the right to talk back to the transnational media giants and tell their own story to the world directly;[71] the right to send as well as receive; and the right to reply to, and have corrected, erroneous media reports. However, opponents of the Right to Communicate see it as a euphemism for governments to limit their people's access to information, and to thwart their rights to inform and be informed.[72]

Western criticism came from the World Press Freedom Committee and the International Federation of Journalists. Both groups indicated that any new information order should come from communication professionals in the media, not from government. The WPFC cited several negative aspects of the MacBride Report, including its apparent bias against private media ownership and advertising, and also its willingness to let government set the goals for and monitor the world's media.[73] But the First World's strongest criticism came from a convention of Western media leaders in Talloires, France.

The Talloires Conference

In May of 1981, news media representatives from 20 Western countries met in Talloires, France to organize a counterattack against the NWICO and its apparent approval of a licensing system for journalists working in foreign countries. Such a scheme, these representatives argued, would obstruct the free flow of information, a basic human right, and would involve governments in the gatekeeping process so that official policies in Third World nations purportedly would be covered "fairly." The licensing would be done by a Commission for the Protection of Journalists, which would issue ID cards to foreign reporters and revoke them at the request of home governments. The Soviet Bloc would, in effect, be imposing its will on the world's media.[74]

The Tallories Conference was co-sponsored by Tufts University's Edward R. Murrow Center of Public Diplomacy and the U.S.-based World Press Freedom Committee. Its closing declaration stated that censorship should be eliminated, and that access to information should be unrestricted. It also asserted that journalistic codes are impossible in a pluralistic world and, if adopted, should only be decided by journalists, not government officials. The group went on to chide the notion that journalists need this kind of "protection," since national and international laws already protect them. Licensing journalists is tantamount to licensing the right to knowledge and information of all people in all countries. The conferees concluded that UNESCO should seek practical ways to make information flow both free and fair, such as through improved training, reduced tariffs, and more technology transfers.[75]

In response to the Talloires meeting, the U.S. Senate let the State Department know that it did not like the idea of American dollars supporting UNESCO's efforts to license journalists and control transnational communication.[76] By year's end, UNESCO had begun backing away from its earlier commitment to the NWICO. Its second thoughts were triggered in large part by U.S. threats to cut back or terminate its funding of UNESCO and its sponsored activities, including the new International Program of Development Communications.

The International Program for Development of Communications (IPDC)

If the MacBride Commission Report was the most notorious item to emerge from UNESCO's 1980 General Conference in Belgrade, then the International Program for Development of Communications was the most tangible and useful outcome. The IPDC is "an international clearinghouse for communications development needs, resources, and priorities that will permit public and private sectors in both developing and developed countries to cooperate more effectively in this field."[77] Its projects are to be voluntarily funded by 35 member governments and outside foundations, international agencies, private corporations, and other sources, but will be administered on a bilateral basis within the framework of UNESCO.[78] Some Westerners are skeptical of having the IPDC tied in any way to UNESCO's bureaucracy, which has not demonstrated much managerial competence nor sympathy for free market economies, multinational corporations, or free press practices.[79]

The IPDC will serve three areas of communications needs within the Third World. One will involve the development of infrastructures such as information systems, postal and telephone services, production facilities for newsprint and broadcasting equipment, news-gathering agencies, rural and community radio, and program exchange mechanisms. Another will provide a variety of professional training programs, materials and centers for production, technical, and management personnel, plus scholarships and learning opportunities for study and acquiring skills at home and abroad. A third area is assistance in transfering appropriate equipment and technology to specific countries and adapting them to fit local conditions and needs.[80]

Despite the fact that UNESCO had benefitted the developing world with hundreds of programs and millions of dollars during its four decades of existence, its Western members had grown weary of the agency's retreat from its original commitment to democratic ideals, and of its fiscal irresponsibility. By the early 1980s, UNESCO had become an overpaid bureaucracy whose budget growth outpaced all other UN departments and whose high-living Paris-based officials showed little will to control expenses.[81] This disenchantment reached a peak during 1983, and culminated with a surprise from Washington.

The U.S. Withdraws From UNESCO

In early December of 1983, America's Secretary of State, George Shultz, announced that the U.S. would withdraw from UNESCO at the end of 1984. A year's notice is necessary under UN rules. The pullout was approved at month's end by President Reagan. The decision, which sent shock waves through UNESCO's leadership, received widespread support within the U.S. government and among the American public. Even liberal papers like the *Washington Post* and the *New York Times* applauded the move.[82]

The U.S. gave several reasons for its action, the major ones being that UNESCO had become politicized and insolvent. The Reagan Administration further charged that UNESCO was dominated by Third World and Communist nations that consistently have opposed democratic and free market principles with programs and proposals that have no place in an organization devoted to education, science, and culture. The two chief examples cited were the calls for new *economic* and *information* orders for the world.[83]

Fifty African nations were quick to appeal to the American government to reconsider its decision. Many Asian, Arab, and Latin American nations followed suit. All feared that America's absence might undermine the agency's future—especially the absence of nearly 50 million American dollars a year. Canada, Japan, and West Germany indicated that they would remain members of UNESCO, but shared U.S. concerns about its politicalization and left open their options to follow America's example. Predictably, the Soviet news agency TASS said the U.S. had demonstrated an "imperial haughtiness" toward the UN and toward world cooperation.[84]

What are the implications of America leaving UNESCO? The organization that most people and governments around the world think is the UN's best and most humanitarian enterprise will almost certainly survive. Some have speculated that the U.S. left as a means of dramatizing the need for change in UNESCO, that the action could be a catalyst to improve the agency by applying the leverage necessary for wholesale reform.[85]

SOME CONCLUSIONS AND A SUMMARY OF TRENDS

The developing nations of the Third World, as the word "developing" denotes, are in a state of flux—of becoming. None of their social institutions better represents this melieu of change than does broadcasting. Add sociocultural diversity to this developmental dynamism and one is faced with a situation much like trying to photograph a fast-moving object—difficult but not impossible.

Certain trends can be gleaned from the foregoing descriptive analysis of broadcasting systems, policies, and issues in the Third World. To begin, the structure of national broadcasting is still dominated by government ownership and semi-commercial financing through taxes and advertising rather than license fees, but privatization and commercialism are on the ascendancy.

Radio is universally available and therefore the most salient local and national medium in the Third World. Television, by contrast, remains a Western-influenced urban phenomenon that is heavily dependent on imported programming, with the US being the principal source. In fact, while about one-third of all TV programming aired worldwide is imported, the Third World's share is the highest—averaging just over 40% throughout its five regions. Most home-production in the Third World is informational and instructional programming. Roughly half of the televised news feeds are of foreign origin, but most (70%) come from other developing countries.[86]

This predominant one-way flow of information and entertainment—from North to South—is encumbering the Third World's development mission by wreaking havoc with broadcasting's attempts to promote national unity and pride, to achieve social and economic goals, and to assist in the survival of authentic cultures and indigenous languages. Of course, much of this external influence can be attributed to the Western training of many Third World broadcasters, to the fact that it is cheaper to buy foreign programming than to produce one's own, and to policies that consciously pander to popular tastes.

To redress these imbalances and other inequities in the allocation of wealth, spectrum frequencies and orbital space, nearly all Third World governments favor a New World Information and Communication Order. Some advocate even stronger measures, such as licensing foreign journalists and requiring legal guarantees of access to international channels and a sovereign Right To Communicate.[87] And the 1984 U.S. withdrawal from UNESCO has only heightened such concerns.

But America does not plan to turn her back completely on the Third World's communication needs. The U.S. State Department has promoted plans for bringing together the private and public sectors in order to channel an amount of money roughly equal to America's former contribution to UNESCO into alternative Third World programs in science, education, communication, and culture which it deems acceptable. Under discussion in late 1984 were:[88]

- $47.6 million for nearly 20 projects developed by the State Department's Bureau of International Organization Affairs, with $3 to $5 million earmarked for communication programs;
- A $1.5 million for A-V instructional materials for Arabic children;

- A $1 million "electronic Peace Corps" using satellite communication between experts in America and the Third World;
- $2 million is slated for videotaped engineering courses;
- $2.5 million for technical language training programs to be broadcast via radio and television;
- $1.4 million for bilateral training projects in cooperation with UNESCO's International Program for Development Communications;
- $1 million more to the U.S. Telecommunication Training Institute;
- $600,000 to Third World recipients for communications training through the UN Development Program;
- $2.5 million for low cost earth stations for satellite demonstration projects;
- $5 million for training journalists and rural broadcasters through a new U.S. Center for Microcomputers and the Third World;
- $20 million for undefined programs to strengthen development communications and the transfer of technology and information to unspecified Third World countries.

Efforts to generate contributions from the private sector have been largely insincere and unproductive, but this may change after the Maitland Commission finishes analyzing Third World communication needs and formulates a collective response from the industrialized nations.

Under the stewardship of Britain's Sir Donald Maitland, a 17-member group of communication experts established the Independent Commission for Worldwide Telecommunications Development in 1984 as an advisory service to the ITU. The Maitland Commission consulted with government officials and business executives in Western and developing countries with the objective of finding ways to correct the technical and administration problems in Third World communication systems and reporting its findings and recommendations back to the ITU at year's end. The idea behind the Maitland Commission is to stimulate Western investment and trade with the Third World as a means of promoting open markets and improving the management of telecommunication systems in developing nations.[89]

Autonomous measures like the Maitland Commission and the aid programs announced by the U.S. government may provide a future model for assisting the Third World outside of UNESCO. Such a notion gained credibility in late 1984, when the British government gave UNESCO a year's notice that it too would pull out if the agency didn't put its financial and ideological house in order.[90] Although the Foreign Office was not successful in getting other European Common Market countries to join the U.K. and America in the exodus, the future may witness the defection of other Western nations from UNESCO.[91]

CHAPTER 6 NOTES

[1] Kuldip R. Rampal, ". . . In The Third World," in L. John Martin and Anju Grover Chaudhary (Eds.), *Comparative Mass Media Systems* (New York: Longman, 1983), pp. 147ff.

[2] Tran van Dinh, "Nonalignment and Cultural Imperialism," in Kaarle Nordenstreng and Herbert I. Schiller (Eds.), *National Sovereignty and International Communication: A Reader* (Norwood, NJ: Ablex, 1979), p. 265.

[3] Karl P. Sauvant, "Sociocultural Emancipation," in Nordenstreng and Shiller, *op. cit.*, pp. 10–11.

[4] Cees J. Hamelink, *Cultural Autonomy in Global Communication: Planning National Information Policy* (New York: Longman, 1983), p. 125.

[5] Thomas L. McPhail, *Electronic Colonialism: The Future of International Broadcasting and Communication* (Beverly Hills, CA: Sage, 1981), p. 251.

[6] Elihu Katz and George Wedell, *Broadcasting in the Third World: Promise and Performance* (Cambridge, MA: Harvard University Press, 1977), Chapter 3.

[7] *Ibid.*, pp. 53–64.

[8] *Ibid.*, pp. 239ff.

[9] Jeremy Tunstall, *The Media are American: Anglo-American Media in the World* (New York: Columbia University Press, 1977), pp. 262–270.

[10] Sydney W. Head (Ed.), *Broadcasting in Africa: A Continental Survey of Radio and Television* (Philadelphia, PA: Temple University Press, 1974), pp. 359–367.

[11] Hamelink, p. 16.

[12] *Ibid.*, p. 101.

[13] Ande-Michael Habte, "The Mass Media Role in the Third World," in Martin and Chaudhary, *op. cit.*, pp. 95–109. (Cf. Note #1).

[14] Head, pp. 347–350.

[15] *World Radio Television Handbook* 1984 (New York: Billboard Publications, 1984, volume 38), pp. 155–178. (Hereinafter referred to as WRTH).

[16] Sir Charles Moses, "Asian Broadcasting: Problems, Challengers, and Prospects," in John A. Lent (Ed.), *Broadcasting in Asia and the Pacific: A Continental Survey of Radio and Television* (Philadelphia: Temple University Press, 1978), pp. 3–7.

[17] *Journal of Communication,* 34(2), Spring 1984, p. 3.

[18] James Traub, "Beaming the World to Andhra Pradesh," *Channels,* May/June 1984, pp. 41–43.

[19] "Bangladesh TV Expanding Fast," *TV World,* May/June 1984, p. 7.

[20] Paul S. Underwood, "Europe and the Middle East," in John C. Merrill (Ed.), *Global Journalism* (New York: Longman, 1983), p. 105.

[21] *Ibid.*, pp. 110–111.

[22] Douglas A. Boyd, *Broadcasting in the Arab World* (Philadelphia: Temple University Press, 1982), pp. 3–5.

[23] *Ibid.*, pp. 263–269.

[24] *Ibid.*, pp. 6–9.

[25] *Ibid.*, pp. 273–278.

[26] Karen Finlon Dajani, "Egypt's Role As A Communications and Media Training Center in the Arab World," *Mass Comm Review,* 8(1), Winter 1980–81, pp. 1520.

[27] Milton Viorst, "The Television That Rules the Arab World," *Channels,* January/February 1983, pp. 35–37.

[28] Milton Viorst, "The Tug of War in Israeli Television," *Channels,* December/January 1982–1983, pp. 40–42.

[29] David K. Shipler, "Israeli Criticizes Mideast Reporting," *New York Times,* February 14, 1982, p. 9.

[30] "Yinon to Head IBA," *TV World,* May/June 1984, p. 6.

[31] Kaarle Nordenstreng and Tapio Varis, *Television Traffic—A One-Way Street? A Survey and Analysis of the International Flow of Television Programme Material* (Paris: UNESCO, 1974), pp. 19–21.

[32] "Common Culture and Language Aid Sales," *TV World,* April 1984, pp. 76–78.

[33] "Brazilian TV Uses US Shows," *The Buffalo (NY) News,* August 6, 1983, p. B-9.

[34] "New TV Law in Argentina," *TV World*, April 1984, p. 20.

[35] "Cable Laws Passed," *TV World*, May/June 1984, p. 9.

[36] T. D. Allman, "Television, Sandinista Style," *Channels*, September/October 1983, pp. 49–51.

[37] Ralph D. Barney, "Pacific Island," pp. 298ff; and Ian A. Johnstone, "South Pacific Commission," pp. 374–378, in Lent, *op. cit.* (Cf. Note 16).

[38] "Land Without TV," *The New York Times*, October 10, 1982, p. 53.

[39] Hamelink, pp. 3–23.

[40] Nordenstreng and Varis, Reports and Papers on Mass Communication, No. 70. *op. cit.* (Cf. Note 31).

[41] Tapio Varis, "The International Flow of Television Programs," *Journal of Communication*, 34 (1), Winter 1984, pp. 143–152. All of the following information on imports comes from this source unless otherwise notated.

[42] *BBC Annual Report and Handbook 1982* (London: British Broadcasting Corporation, 1982), p. 50. Note: See Chapter One, Table 1-7.

[43] Katz and Wedell, *op. cit.*, pp. 157ff. (Cf. Note 6).

[44] McPhail, pp. 93–94.

[45] Leonard R. Sussman, "Freedom of the Press: Problems in Restructuring the Flow of International News," in Raymound D. Gastil (Ed.), *Freedom in the World: Political Rights and Civil Liberties* 1980 (New York: Freedom House, 1980), p. 54.

[46] Hilding Eek, "Principles Governing the Use of the Mass Media as Defined by the United Nations and UNESCO," in Nordenstreng and Schiller, *op. cit.*, pp. 192ff.

[47] William A. Hachten, *The World News Prism: Changing Media, Clashing Ideologies* (Ames, Iowa: Iowa State University Press, 1981), p. 99.

[48] George Gerbner and Marsha Siefert (Eds.), *World Communications: A Handbook* (New York: Longman, 1984), p. 506.

[49] McPhail, p. 94.

[50] Hamelink, p. 90.

[51] *Ibid.*, pp. 91–92.

[52] USICA, *The United States and the Debate on the World "Information Order"* (Washington: Academy for Educational Development, Inc., 1979), p. 27.

[53] Hachten, pp. 107–108.

[54] Munir K. Nasser, "New Values Versus Ideology: A Third World Perspective," in Martin and Chaudhary, *op. cit.*, pp. 56–57. (Cf. Note 1).

[55] Ling Liong Sik, "Is There a Third World View of Communications?" *InterMedia*, 10 (6), November 1982, pp. 44–45.

[56] Masser, p. 46.

[57] Kuldip R. Rampal, "Development Journalism: Another Perspective," *World Media Report*, 1 (2), May 1983, p. 2.

[58] Nasser, pp. 45–50.

[59] Rampal, *World Media Report*, p. 2.

[60] Glen Fisher, *American Communication in a Global Society* (Norwood, NJ: Ablex, 1979), pp. 66–67.

[61] Hachten, pp. 72–73.

[62] Jonathan Fenby, "The Politics of UNESCO," *World Press Review*, November 1981, pp. 32–36.

[63] Robert L. Stevenson, "The Politics of Information," *Communication Research*, 8 (4), October 1981, pp. 499–509.

[64] McPhail, p. 209.

[65] Report by the International Commission for the Study of Communication Problems, *Many Voices, One World* (New York: Unipub, 1980), pp. 253–275. (Hereinafter referred to as the MacBride Report).

66 Kusum Singh and Bertram Gross, "The MacBride Report: The Results and Response," in Gerbner and Siefert, *op. cit.*, pp. 451–452.

67 Yassen Zassoursky and Sergei Losev, "The MacBride Report: A Soviet Analysis," in Gerbner and Siefert, *op. cit.*, pp. 457–460.

68 Mustapha Masmoudi, "The NWIO," in Gerbner and Siefert, *op. cit.*, pp. 14–27.

69 Hachten, p. 107.

70 Singh and Gross, pp. 448–449.

71 Hachten, p. 106.

72 "Whose Right to Communicate?" *InterMedia*, 11 (6), November 1983, p. 3.

73 McPhail, p. 231.

74 "The Press Vs. UNESCO," *Newsweek*, June 1, 1981, p. 79.

75 "UNESCO Asked to End Its Bid to Curb News," AP wire story, *Buffalo* (NY) *Courier-Express*, May 18, 1981, p. 8.

76 "Senate Wants Cutback of UNESCO Funds," *Broadcasting*, June 22, 1981, p. 24.

77 William G. Harley, "The US Stake in the IPDC," *Journal of Communication*, 31 (4), Autumn 1981, p. 150.

78 *Ibid.*, pp. 151ff.

79 McPhail, pp. 142–144.

80 Harley, p. 155.

81 "Politics, Bureaucracy Obscure High Hopes of Agency's Founders," *The Buffalo* (NY) *News*, December 30, 1983, p. A-4.

82 Don Oberdcreer, "Shultz To Propose Pullout From UNESCO," *The Buffalo* (NY) *News*, December 24, 1983, p. A-4.

83 "US Unlikely to Reverse Decision to Pull Out of UNESCO," *The Buffalo* (NY) *News*, December 30, 1983, p. A-4.

84 "50 Nations of Africa Issue Plea," *The Buffalo News*, December 30, 1983, p. A-4.

85 Aline Mosby, "UNESCO Reform Eyed as a Benefit of Pullout by US," *The Buffalo News*, January 1, 1984, p. A-5.

86 Robert L. Stevenson, "Pseudo Debate," *Journal of Communication*, 34 (1), Winter 1984, pp. 134–138.

87 Annabelle Sreberny-Mohammadi, "The 'World of the News' Study," *Journal of Communication*, 34 (1), Winter 1984, pp. 121–134.

88 "Curtain Calls For Charadesmanship," *Chronicle of International Communication*, V(7), September 1984, pp. 3–4.

89 "Global Telecommunication Advisory Services Wanted," *Chronicle of International Communication*, V(7), September 1984, pp. 1–4.

90 "British Add To Problems of UNESCO," AP wire story, *Buffalo* (NY) *News*, November 23, 1984, p. A-6.

91 "Britain Reported Set To Follow US Suit and Quit UNESCO," *The Christian Science Monitor*, November 19, 1984, p. 2.

The Fourth World: Broadcasting in Culturally Pluralistic Societies

Language is the primary symbolic code upon which all media of mass communication are dependent. This statement is no less true of the telecommunication media, despite their capacity to also transmit pictorial, graphic, aural, and musical symbols. The underlying truth remains that language, written and spoken, is the essential ingredient in the scripting and presentation of all messages mediated via the mass telecommunication channels of radio, television, satellite, and cable. And an even more basic truth is that a language has intrinsic value as the primary source of ethnic identity and cultural expression for groups and individuals alike. As will be shown in the following pages, more and more cultural proprietors and national policy-makers have come to recognize that telecommunication technology can be an ally rather than an enemy in the task of saving minority languages and authentic cultures from extinction.

In today's world, it is not difficult to understand why access to the airwaves and cable systems is seen by cultural minorities virtually everywhere as a practical and effective means of survival for their beleaguered native tongues. Yet two chronic problems frequently accompany pluralistic broadcasting efforts around the world. These are:[1]

1. a lack of adequate money to construct and operate radio and TV stations for minority populations living in the peripheral regions of a country without also weakening the national broadcasting systems which favor transmissions in the official language(s);
2. the harsh reality that differing cultural groups within a nation-state often do not particularly like one another, yet must compete among themselves and with the majority culture for the nation's finite resources.

This chapter examines broadcasting policies and practices in various culturally diverse settings where competing language groups co-exist. These languages may enjoy equal status as official languages of the state, or they may languish within minority cultures which are "linguistically handicapped" and often stigmatized for using a dialect other than the society's dominant one.[2] A language may achieve dominance because the majority of people speak it out of cultural tradition or because it is the language of a colonial or imperial ruling elite—a minority which controls the nation's government, economy, and sociocultural institutions like education, religion, and the mass media.

Any language will eventually die out if it is not used by common people on a daily basis. But popular usage in and of itself will not guarantee a language's survival within a technological society unless it also has access to the major channels of public communication. No matter how diligent the attempts by parents and teachers to speak an ethnic dialect within the home and school, living languages have become critically dependent upon broadcasting for their continued vitality. The reasons for this are several:

- Radio and television are the most powerful conduits for transmitting national and popular cultures from one generation to another.
- Languages used on the air gain credibility and legitimacy in the minds of audiences, especially children and minorities.

Access to modern channels of public communication has proved to be an especially emotional problem for the so-called "stateless nations of the Fourth World," minority cultures which exist within countries but whose ancestral languages are threatened with extinction by the dominant culture of the national majority population.[3]

Pluralistic Fourth World cultures can be found within many First, Second, and Third World nations where national broadcasting systems have responded to indigenous linguistic needs in various ways and degrees. Following an introductory survey of the situation as it exists in the United States and worldwide, we examine nine case models of pluralistic broadcasting policies as implemented in the *minority cultures* of Wales, Ireland, and the Basque Region of Spain; in *bilingual* Canada, Belgium, and Czechoslovakia; in *multilingual* Switzerland and Yugoslavia; and in *polylingual* Africa. The chapter concludes by citing common problems, making comparisons and contrasts, and summarizing trends in the relationship of broadcasting to ethnic identity, cultural pluralism, national unity, and the survival of minority languages in today's volatile world.

BROADCASTING AND EMERGING BICULTURALISM
IN AMERICA

The United States is not a bilingual society officially but is rapidly becoming one in practice. Our second language is, in fact, Spanish. Although the 1983 Census counted nearly 16 million persons of "Spanish origin" living within the 50 states, a more realistic estimate, taking illegal residents into account, places the figure at 19.8 million.[4] Regardless of the specific head count, it is generally agreed that the Hispanic population will be the largest minority in the nation by 1990.

American Hispanics are concentrated by nationality in three regions of the U.S.: Mexicans in the Southwestern states, Puerto Ricans in the metropolitan New York City area, and Cubans in South Florida. For example, 4.5 million Hispanics live in California, comprising 20% of the state's population. One in every four residents of Texas is of Mexican heritage, a total of almost 3 million. Nearly a million Cubans now live in the Miami area, and over two million Puerto Ricans make their home in New York City and northern New Jersey.[5]

But despite differences in national origin, America's Hispanics share a common language and fierce cultural pride. Most feel that retaining fluency in Spanish separates them from the country's other immigrants, who, they argue, have succumbed to "cultural and linguistic colonization by the Anglo majority."[6] These demographic patterns, together with the proximity of their respective homelands, have helped all Hispanics to retain their language and maintain contact with their native cultures easier than other newcomers to America. And much of the credit for their cultural continuity must go to broadcasting.

At the beginning of the 1980s, there were 23 Spanish language television stations in seven states, ten in California and six in Texas. Eight more were licensed for Puerto Rico, and two experimental Spanish outlets existed in Denver and Washington, D.C. In addition, 26 Mexican TV stations were operating within 200 miles of the US border, serving significant numbers of American Hispanics. Spanish language radio, too, was popular. By 1981, 118 stations were on the air in 18 states. Texas led the nation with 42, and California was second with 30. Many Hispanic station executives belong to the National Association of Spanish Broadcasters (NASB), a professional lobby group located in Washington.[7]

The largest force in Spanish language broadcasting in America, however, is the Spanish International Network (SIN). Begun in 1961 by the Spanish International Communications Corporation, SIN currently reaches an audience of over 12 million Hispanics via satellite-linked cable and TV stations in 62 American cities. SIN's operations center is KWEX-TV, Channel 41 in San Antonio, Texas. The station takes programming from Mexico, Spain, and Latin America directly off the Westar satellite, and retransmits it via domestic satellite to SIN affiliates across the nation. The most popular programs among American Hispanics are the *novellas,* highly emotional soap operas made in Mexico and starring that nation's top movie stars.[8] Also popular are variety shows, soccer games, boxing matches, and the daily news hour from Mexico.

SIN has proved that Spanish language television in the U.S. can be profitable. It has been estimated that Hispanics earn nearly $52 billion annually in the U.S. and spend roughly 60% of it on consumer goods. Major American ad agencies like Young and Rubicam and J. Walter Thompson have established Hispanic departments based on evidence that Spanish language advertising yields product loyalty and enthusiastic response from Hispanic viewers. SIN also operates a national Spanish language pay-cable service called "Galavision," which offers subscribers first-run Spanish and Mexican movies, sports, and specials similar to those of HBO and Showtime.[9]

But SIN has been criticized for relying too much on foreign programming at the expense of covering issues of interest to American Hispanics. One reason for this is that production is cheaper in Latin America than in the U.S., as is the rental of foreign material. It is interesting to note, however, that two independent Spanish language TV stations in San Francisco and New York beat the SIN affiliates in head-to-head competition, using some bilingual and some all-English programming.[10] By 1982, there was only one Spanish-controlled Public TV station in America, KZLN-TV in Harlingen, Texas, airing mostly bilingual programming to the predominately Hispanic audience living near the Mexican border.[11]

Bicultural broadcasting is still in the formative stages in the United States, although Spanish is clearly becoming a second language of considerable cultural, economic, and political significance. In fact, some Americans fear that a sizeable class of Spanish-speaking residents could lead to the kind of fractionalism that plagues our northern neighbor. Whether or not such a concern is warranted, the status of the Spanish language and its relationship to broadcasting in the U.S. provides a relevant backdrop to the following examination of pluralistic broadcasting in various other nations.

AN OVERVIEW OF MULTILINGUAL BROADCASTING AROUND THE WORLD

The broadcasting systems of Europe were developed to be instruments of nationalism and public service, but the proximity of nationalities and the technical proclivities of broadcasting made signal spillover common. The flow of TV programs across national frontiers has been less of a problem, due to the medium's inability to transcend natural barriers (like mountains), technical restrictions (like incompatible color systems), and legal considerations (like copyright laws and channel allocations).

Cable and satellite technology, however, have eroded national boundaries in the case of television as well as radio. West Germany, France, and the Benelux countries have received each other's TV signals for years, but cable now enables viewers in Belgium to receive two Dutch channels, three from France and West Germany, and one from Luxembourg. Direct broadcast satellites will make the airwaves even more internationalized in the coming decade.

The European Institute for the Media, together with the European Cultural Foundation, is studying the complex issues arising from transnational and transcultural broadcasting. For example, Dutch, Danish, and Greek TV programs compete in the marketplace against the larger outputs of programming in English, French, and German. What is at stake are the national identities and cultures of smaller countries who may be flooded by low-cost foreign language programming from the United States and Britain.[12]

The influx of significant numbers of foreign guest workers into West Germany over the past several decades has resulted in increasing hours of native language broadcasts being targeted to Greek, Italian, Yugoslavian, Spanish, and Turkish immigrants.[13]

It is no doubt a little known fact outside Scandinavia that Finland has two official languages—Finnish and Swedish—the latter having been the dominant tongue until Finnish was granted equal footing in 1863. Today, Swedish is spoken by only 6% of Finland's population, while Finnish is almost universally (90%) used. Many people in the south of the country speak English, with German the next most common foreign language.[14] Accordingly, Finland's broadcasting organization (YLE) has been debating the possibility of starting a Swedish-language TV channel to serve its coastal region across the Baltic Sea from Sweden. At present, money problems have put the project in doubt, though official commitment is firm.[15]

In 1983, Hungary's second TV channel began broadcasting programs once a month in the mother tongues of the nation's four ethnic minorities—Serbo-Croatian, German, Rumanian, and Slovak.[16] Languages pose an even greater challenge in other Second World societies, as will be shown subsequently in the cases of Czechoslovakia and Yugoslavia, and as was previously mentioned in Chapter 5, where China airs programs in 11 domestic languages and the USSR in 84.

It will be interesting to see what the future holds for Hong Kong's bilingual broadcasting arrangement after Britain's lease on the colony expires in 1997 and the city-state is repatriated by the Peoples' Republic of China. Since 1968, Television Broadcasts Limited (TVB) has offered two TV channels—Jade (in Chinese) and Pearl (in English)—for its major language groups. These have operated along side dual language public and commercial radio services.[17]

In India, 16 major languages are spoken by over 40 million people in the nation's 23 states. In addition, another 51 dialects and 87 tribal tongues are in use. The national broadcasting agency, All India Radio (AIR), tries to meet the challenge of providing their diverse and mostly (80%) rural population with programming via single radio and television networks, and nearly 90 local radio stations. These services cover three-quarters of India's territory and nine of ten citizens, yet only 15% of urban dwellers can receive TVI's programs, and a mere 20% of the population has access to regular radio reception.[18] AIR currently transmits in the following 18 languages: Assamese, Bengali, Dogri, English, Gujarati, Hindi, Kannada, Kashmiri, Marathi, Malayalan, Nepali, Oriya, Punjabi, Sanskrit, Sindhi, Tamil, Telugu, and Urdu.[19]

While most countries in the Middle East are dominated by Arab-speaking populations, most also have significant minorities who speak their own language or a European language like English, French, or Dutch—depending on which nation colonized them. Thus, Middle Eastern media may be found in Arabic, indigenous dialects, and one or more Western language(s).[20]

The TV networks of the Arabian Gulf region—Saudi Arabia, Kuwait, Qatar, United Arab Emirates, Bahrain, and Oman—are dominated by programs in English as well as Arabic, due to the presence of large immigrant and expatriot populations from various parts of Asia, Europe, and the Americas. These oil-rich nations have the money to buy expensive foreign programs from the U.S.,

Britain, France, and Egypt, as well as to build state-of-the-art studios for their own productions. While this menu of quality imports is favored over local TV programming by the immigrant communities, the Arabs tend to remain faithful to broadcasts in their own language. Bahrain and Dubai each has an English-language channel for the benefit of their expatriot viewers, yet the other Gulf states also intersperse significant amounts of foreign imports into their predominantly Arabic air schedules.[21]

Just as opportunity and freedom have lured settlers to America, Canada, and West Germany, so has Australia opened her shores to peoples of various nationalities looking for a better life. In order to accommodate the informational, cultural, and entertainment needs of the newcomers, Australia established the multi-cultural Special Broadcasting Service (SBS) in 1980. SBS's Channel 0-28 offers English lessons and programs from Holland, Hungary, Brazil, France, Sweden, Italy, and several other homelands.

Although the new service has met many cultural needs of Australia's immigrant populations, it also attracted criticism. The SBS has been faulted for its weak transmissions, exhorbitant costs to the public, and what is seen as elitist programming decisions. For instance, Francophones make up less than 1% of Australia's ethnic population, yet 15% of Channel 0-28's programming is in French—including films by rather esoteric directors like Truffaut and Resnais. By comparison, Greeks comprise nearly 13% of the urban populace, but less than 9% of Channel 0-28's programs are in Greek. Italian programming is proportionate to its audience size, but the Scandinavians and Portuguese receive far more airtime in their mother tongues than their numbers justify. Furthermore, since all foreign-language programming on Channel 0-28 is subtitled in English, native Anglophones have the added advantage of being able to see classic French and Swedish films that have more cultural relevance to them than to their intended audience of working class immigrants.[22] Despite such defects, SBS's multicultural TV will be expanded beyond Sydney and Melbourne to ten new cities and regional centers by the late 1980s.[23]

These are but a few examples of how national broadcasters have devoted airtime and resources to indigenous and immigrant audiences through programming services in their native languages in order to reinforce their authentic culture and bolster pride in their ethnic heritages.

BILINGUAL BROADCASTING POLICY AND PRACTICES IN CANADA

Canadian society is a multicultural mosaic comprised of eight significant language groups, the largest being English (68.2%) and French (24.5%).[24] Even though English and French have always been spoken in Canada, they did not become equal and official languages until passage of the 1969 Official Languages Act. Today, 80% of French-speaking Canadians reside in Quebec

Province, while the Anglophone population is more widely dispersed throughout the nation.[25] Regardless of historic attempts to forge a sense of "national unity and identity,"[26] English and French Canada remain, in the words of a CBC president, "the two solitudes."[27] The presence of two proud and vital cultures has both complicated and necessitated the development of bilingual broadcasting in Canada.

In the early days of radio, stations in Montreal and Ottawa mixed programs in English and French together in their broadcast schedules. This practice, however, drew much public criticism. Over a period of time, broadcasting in each language was done only over separate facilities. Bilingual broadcasting in Canada, in practice and in law, is therefore defined as occuring through stations licensed in either English or French. A few exceptions have been made where stations are licensed in both (bilingual) or other (multilingual) languages.[28]

A review of the major royal commissions and legislative acts pertinent to broadcasting in Canada indicates that bilingual policy and services evolved through five stages of development.

Stage 1. The first public policy emerged from the 1928 Royal (Aird) Commission on Broadcasting, whose report a year later led to passage of the Canadian Radio Broadcasting Act of 1932 and formation of the first national radio service. The language issue also surfaced in the Aird Report, charging that the French-speaking population was not being adequately served by broadcasting.[29] Hence, the 1932 Act prescribed that autonomous programming services be established in English and French.[30] This initiative was intended to assist the disadvantaged Francophones with broadcasts aimed at meeting their unique needs.[31]

Stage 2. New legislation, the Canadian Broadcasting Act of 1936, created the CBC and gave it a mandate to develop bilingual services in order "to improve French-English relations."[32] However, there were growing objections by the Anglophone majority in the late 1930s over the use of French on the national radio system. Since French was "not an official language of the whole of Canada," they argued that it constituted a violation of the British North America Act, which governed Canada at the time. Others felt that the CBC's separate language broadcasts prevented rather than promoted the goal of national unity.[33] Further, bilingualism became tied to the question of how the CBC should be financed—by advertising or by public funding? The former option was opposed by most Quebecois, who feared that private marketplace forces might lead to the cultural dilution of French-language programming. The latter scheme, however, would seem to discriminate against English Canadians, who, as the taxpaying majority, would shoulder the lion's share of the expenses for both CBC operations.[34]

Although the ultimate purpose of the CBC's new language policy was "to help make the whole of Canada bilingual," practical problems arose in applying the same policies and standards to each service equally.[35] And how could dual services help the two language groups to experience each other's culture via the airwaves? Related to these concerns was the English network's heavy dependence on U.S. programming while the French system was nearly self reliant.

Stage 3. The CBC began its television network in 1952 with an English flagship station in Toronto (CBLT) and a bilingual station in Montreal (CBFT).[36] The policy decision to fund CBC-TV with public money, as recommended by the Massey Commission (1949–1951), proved problematic in the face of declining government interest. Accordingly, the CBC permitted advertising to help finance the new service since most viewers already received American television. Besides, commercials were well established on CBC radio by then.[37] By the mid-1950s, Montreal had separate TV outlets in each language, 80% of Quebec was covered by the French network, and the CBC was reaching half of English Canada. Television's impact proved to be greater on French Canada than on the Anglophone audience, since U.S. programming never competed significantly with French productions within Quebec. As a result, French Canadian culture was given a boost while the dominant culture was overwhelmed by American television.[38]

Stage 4. The growing presence of American TV throughout English Canada called into question the basic assumptions underlying bilingual broadcasting policy. In 1955, the Royal (Fowler) Commission on Broadcasting launched a review of CBC-TV activities. The Fowler Report of 1957 praised the broadcaster's penetration of both language segments, but recommended some fundamental changes in Canadian broadcasting. These formed the basis of the Broadcasting Act of 1958, which established an autonomous Board of Broadcast Governors (BBG) to regulate and license both CBC and private stations. Second, the CBC was to be funded jointly by annual appropriations from Parliament and by advertising. And all stations were to be operated and principally owned by Canadians.[39] The Act also mandated that one-third of all programming aired be Canadian produced by the 1960 season, and increased to 55% within 2 years.

Implementation of the new Act subsequently required another official review by a second Fowler Committee on Broadcasting. The 1965 Fowler II Report criticized the CBC for failing to "foster understanding between the two main groups," but concluded that the French operation (i.e., Radio Canada) was "more profitable" and culturally important to Quebec than the English CBC was to the rest of Canada. At that time, 92% of the English population was being served through 47 CBC-TV affiliates, and 71% by 11 CTV stations, while 89% of Quebec's households were reached by 13 CBC French outlets.[40]

Stage 5. The second Fowler study was followed by 2 years of parliamentary debate on a bill that addressed a wide range of telecommunication activities. The resulting Canadian Broadcasting Act of 1968 set forth the nation's current language policy and formed the Canadian Radio-Television (now Telecommunications) Commission (CRTC) to implement it. Among the objectives stated in

Section 2 of the Act are several aimed at keeping the ownership, content, and purpose of broadcasting "predominantly Canadian" so as to serve and express the interest of national unity and identity.[41]

In its first decade, the CRTC advanced bold initiatives to extend CBC coverage in both languages to all communities with populations over 500, enforce and increase Canadian content levels, license new commercial stations in English and French, and enfranchise many cable systems.[42] Specifically, the first private TV network in French, Les Tele-Diffuseurs (TVA), was authorized in 1971 to serve Quebec Province; a second commercial network in English, Global Communication, was certified a year later for southern Ontario Province.

A review of radio and TV services offered in both languages at the beginning of the 1980s will provide some indication of how effective the implementation of bilingual policy has been in terms of reaching and satisfying Anglophone and Francophone audiences.

The number of *private radio stations* licensed in English, by type, were 212 AM and 125 FM, as compared to 43 AM and 26 FM in French. There are no private radio networks in Canada. *Public radio's* saturation is national yet somewhat uneven. The CBC's AM networks provide universal coverage (99%) to both language audiences via 80 stations in English and 41 in French. Eleven FM affiliates serve 74% of the nation's Anglophones, and nine French FM outlets reach three-quarters of French Canada.

Private TV independents tallied 11 in English and one in French. In terms of *private TV networks,* the CRTC estimated in 1980 that 96.4% of the English-speaking population was being covered by 26 CTV affiliates, and a third by Global's six transmitters in Ontario only. Six TVA outlets penetrated 98% of Quebec's households.[43]

CRTC efforts in television have increased the number of Canadian stations, productions, and cable operations since 1968, yet overall viewership of domestic programs has actually decreased as larger audiences in both languages have opted for foreign (i.e., American and French) content.[44] One survey suggests that French language stations, both public and private, have been more successful in attracting adult viewers to Canadian programs than have their English counterparts. Also, children from each language group increasingly choose foreign shows over Canadian ones. Another interesting trend shows that Francophones are gradually selecting more U.S. programming as cable and dubbing practices make it more accessible to them in their own tongue. In fact, TVA's share of the Quebecois audience recently surpassed that of its public rival, Radio Canada.[45]

A 1980 analysis of the CBC's television services in English and French revealed several significant findings. For example, while two-thirds of each network's total program schedule was Canadian content, both imported over half of their entertainment programs. In the case of the English CBC, 53.1% of its light entertainment schedule came from the U.S. and another 12% from Britain.

Similarly, Radio Canada bought nearly a third (31.8%) of its mass appeal programming from France and a fifth from America.

It is also noteworthy that the English TV operation brings in more advertising revenue than does Radio Canada, yet the latter spends 40% of the CBC's annual budget to reach less than a third of Canada's population. In other words, the French network is in large part subsidized by the English-language service. Finally, each network attracted only about half of the adult audience to its domestic programs in 1980 and both TV services are facing a serious erosion of viewership by Canadian children.[46]

By way of summarizing bilingual broadcasting in Canada, it seems clear that more flaws can be detected in the developmental design of language policy than in the execution of it by the broadcasters. For example, why wasn't the 1936 Act's charge to offer separate services in English and French accompanied by federal legislation making the two vernaculars co-equal and official languages of Canada? Instead, Parliament let the CBC be its language stalking horse for 33 years before making the nation legally bilingual. And a case can be made that separate language broadcasts have only helped to divide the attention of the two cultures—creating, in the words of a CBC president, "two monologues and not a real French-English dialogue."[47]

Finally, Canada's bilingualism has been further complicated by its proximity to the United States. The availability of American radio and TV programming to most Canadians has been a problem to Canada's bilingual broadcasting efforts. Historically, the U.S. presence has been felt in English Canada almost exclusively, but the increased dubbing of American material into French promises to extend the problem to Francophone audiences. It remains to be seen if the Canadian Content quotas offer a realistic solution. Audiences tend to respond to quality rather than quantity when expressing preferences in television programming.

On the other side of the Atlantic Ocean lie two societies faced with cultural and geographic circumstances similar yet distinct from Canada's. Both Belgium and Czechoslovakia have employed similar broadcasting strategies to address their respective bicultural imperatives, yet neither is quite like those chosen by Canada. A closer look will invite further comparisons and contrasts.

BILINGUAL BROADCASTING IN BELGIUM

Belgium has been compared to Canada in kind, if not in degree of biculturalism. While over 90% of its nearly 9.9 million people are Roman Catholic, they are sharply divided into two ethnic cultures that are fiercely autonomous and speak different languages. The Dutch-speaking Flemish of the north account for 56% of the population, while the French-speaking Walloons comprise 32% and live mainly in the southern region of the country. Another 11%, mostly Walloons, are considered bilingual. The fact that Belgium borders France, West Germany,

Holland, Luxembourg, and the North Sea has helped keep the two cultures separate, but the establishment of Dutch and French as equal official languages has aided the cause of political and economic nationhood.[48]

National broadcasting in Belgium began with a 1930 law that created a monopoly *Institut* having French (INR) and Dutch (NIR) operations. This consortium was replaced in 1960 by a new organization with separate French (RTB) and Dutch (BRT) services.[49] Since 1979, each language community has its own independent broadcasting monopoly: *BRT,* Belgian Radio and Television-Dutch Transmission (Belgische Radio en Televisie-Nederlandse Uitzendingen); and *RTBF,* Belgian Radio and Television-French Transmission (Radio et Television Belge-Emissions Francaises).

The Dutch BRT and French RTBF are both statutory bodies mandated to provide news, entertainment, education, and a spectrum of opinion on public issues. Since advertising is banned on Belgium's airwaves, their annual budgets are allocated by the national parliament, with two-thirds of that money coming from radio and TV taxes. This revenue is administered to BRT and RTBF through grants from the Flemish Council and the French Language Council, respectively.

Both broadcasters operate two television and three radio networks in their respective languages, as well as separate international shortwave services to foreign audiences. The First Channel of BRT and RTBF offers a full range of programming to their Flemish and Walloon viewers, while their Second Channel, both begun in 1977, provides entertainment and education but no news. Their radio networks are centralized operations as well, but some local or regional programming is scheduled.[50]

BRT's shortwave service transmits to five continents in Dutch, English, and Spanish, while RTBF's smaller international station mostly relays its home services in French and German to listeners in Africa and Europe. In addition, two domestic FM stations have formed a nominal German Language Network called BRF (Belgisches Rundfunk-Und-Fernsehzentrum für Deutschesprächige Sendungen), which carries RTBF's shortwave service in German to Belgium's small German-speaking population living along its border with West Germany.[51]

RTBF and BRT each have separate news bureaus and air their main newscasts daily at 7:30 pm and 7:45 pm, respectively. Both strive for objectivity and cover issues of national import while also addressing specific cultural matters for their own language groups. Perhaps the most unique feature of Belgium's bilingual broadcasting situation is that the BRT and RTBF each subtitle their newscasts in the other's language, so that the two communities can watch and understand. Thus TV is used to transcend the language barrier and foster better understanding and contact between the two cultures.[52] But the two broadcasters do reflect different foreign perspectives. RTBF's news, for instance, tends to cover events in France, Quebec, and the French-speaking world, while the BRT focuses more on Dutch, German, and British affairs.[53]

Cable TV, which was started in 1960 by private companies, spread rapidly during the 1970s from the south into the central and northern regions of Belgium. Nearly 85% of Belgian households are now connected to some 200 cable systems—half private, a third public, and the rest having mixed ownership—making it the most cabled country in the world. These cable companies offer up to 17 channels, including the four domestic networks in both languages of the Dutch BRT and French RTBF, three each from France (TF1, A2, and FR3) and Germany (ARD 1 and 3, and ZDF), two from Holland (NOS 1 and 2), one commercial station from Luxembourg (RTL), and up to four British channels (BBC 1 and 2, ITV, and Channel Four) along the North Sea coast.

Cable companies are regulated by a 1966 Royal Decree which forbids them to produce their own programs or to purchase and transmit special productions. They tend to ignore the ban on carrying advertising from foreign channels, however, mainly because it is too expensive and difficult to delete. The Belgian networks in both Dutch and French have lost many viewers to neighboring stations carried on cable, but the audience remains loyal to their newscasts and better entertainment programs.[54] As in Canada, Francophones in Belgium are increasingly being attracted to the more commercial offerings from adjacent Luxembourg.[55]

Cable practices vary slightly in different parts of Belgium. Interactive cable has been authorized on an experimental basis in the southern Francophone region, while, in the northern area of Flanders, community local cable and local radio are illegal. Flemish broadcast policy seems generally to favor centralization over localism, while the Walloon community is more willing to experiment with local radio and cable.[56]

A new tower was completed and activated in 1983 at the Broadcasting Center in Brussels, and will be used by both the RTBF and BRT. It will also have international uses by linking Belgium's broadcasters to the Eurovision network and to London, Paris, Frankfurt, and Hilversum, and by receiving satellite transmissions from various earth stations.[57]

BILINGUALISM AND BROADCASTING IN CZECHOSLOVAKIA

Czechoslovakia was formed in 1918 when the territories of Bohemia, Moravia, and Slovakia merged following the collapse of the Habsburg Empire, which had ruled Austria-Hungary for 300 years. It prospered as an industrial democracy until the 1938 Munich Agreement and the aftermath of World War II transformed it into a communist satellite state of the USSR in 1948. But the nation experienced its most traumatic year two decades later, when Czechoslovakia was transformed from the freest of the Communist Bloc countries under the reign of Alexander Dubcek into one of its most totalitarian societies during an 8-month period known as the "Prague Spring," a popular revolt that ended with an invasion and occupation by the Soviet Union in August of 1968. From that point forward, the nation's mass media have been tightly controlled and ideologically rigid.

The Czechoslovakia of today is actually two nations in one. This binational arrangement is officially described in its 1969 Constitution as "a unitary State," comprised of the Czech Socialist Republic and the Slovak Socialist Republic, having co-equal rights and separate governments. Prague is the national capital, but Bratislava, the third largest city, serves as the capital of Slovakia.

Their respective cultural tongues, *Czech* and *Slovak,* are also recognized as equal and official languages, but citizens of Hungarian, Ukrainian, and Polish nationality are also ensured of "every opportunity and all means of education in their mother tongue and for their cultural development." Czech is the dominant language, since it is spoken by 65% of the national population of 15.5 million, which reside largely in Bohemia and Moravia. The Slovak-speaking group accounts for another 30%, and the balance claim Hungarian, German, Ruthenian, or Polish as their native vernacular. The Constitution regards radio and television as "national property" and guarantees them "freedom of expression" in the conditional Soviet sense of the phrase.[58]

Czechoslovakia's radio and television services have been separately managed and operated since 1959, with transmission facilities coming under the authority of the PTT ministry. Both receive funding directly from government, but this is supplemented by annual receiver fees of approximately $10 for radio and $30 for TV, plus revenues from state-run advertising.

The radio division, called *Ceskoslovensky Rozhlas,* has five national networks—two in Czech ("Praha" and "Vitava"), two in Slovak ("Bratislova" and "Devin"), and one bilingual ("Hvezda"). In addition, there are ten regional stations divided between the two national republics, and two minority-language radio services in Hungarian and German. Nearly two-thirds of radio's content is music, the remainder being news, education, drama, and children's programs.[59] Radio Prague transmits daily to Europe, the Americas, Asia, and the Pacific region in eight foreign languages via shortwave, and in both Czech and Slovak as well.[60]

Two nationwide TV services are provided by *Ceskoslovenska Televize.* The first channel operates about 76 hours a week in Czech, and the second nearly 40 hours in Slovak.[61] Roughly half of all TV programming is information and sports, a third features entertainment and culture, and the rest is educational or children's fare.[62]

While all programming serves the interests of the state, distinctions can be made between program types. News and public affairs broadcasts are the most blatantly ideological. Children's programs range from purely educational to agents of socialization. Sports is perhaps the best produced of all TV programming in Czechoslovakia, bolstering nationalistic pride more than Marxist-Leninist doctrine. A number of foreign films and dramatic series, although carefully selected, add balance and enhance air schedules by providing programs of genuine entertainment appeal and cultural value. Besides sports, classical music is perhaps the greatest source of pride in the nation's cultural heritage, again serving the ends of nationalism more than communism. Films and dramatic series are most popular; news and cultural broadcasts are the least.[63]

BROADCASTING TO A MINORITY CULTURE IN WALES

The Principality of Wales, although a political component of the United Kingdom, nevertheless regards itself as a nation in cultural and geographic terms. While all of the 2.7 million people of Wales are able to speak English, 20% prefer to use Welsh as their first language. This means that 80% of the population are English monoglots and the remaining fifth are bilingualists. The Welsh-speaking population is known as the *Cymry Cymraeg*.

Welsh belongs to the Brythonic group of Celtic languages, and is the oldest vernacular spoken on a daily basis in Europe. This ancient language was nurtured through the centuries by the Welsh culture's rich oral tradition, replete with its indigenous storytellers. Today, a uniform Welsh idiom is used, having been maintained and disseminated from the pulpit since the Bible was translated into Welsh in the 16th century. The role of the storyteller and preacher, as purveyors of the ancestral language, has now been replaced by Welsh language broadcasting services.[64]

Guardians of the Welsh language have fought to gain access to the airwaves from the earliest days of radio broadcasting in Britain.[65] The BBC began broadcasting major cultural events in Welsh in 1929 and initiated the Welsh Home Service in 1934.[66] When television arrived, the BBC's 1952 charter established National Broadcasting Councils for Wales and Scotland to supervise regional programming.[67] Twelve years later, a BBC Wales regional TV service commenced and was augmented with Radio 4 Wales,[68] a bilingual operation which split into two separate stations in 1977—Radio Wales in English, and Radio Cymru in Welsh.[69]

With the coming of commercial TV, ITV assigned Television West and Wales (TWW) to be its Welsh franchise in 1958.[70] Another ITV company, Wales West and North (WWN), started a somewhat redundant service to sparsely populated areas in 1962 and soon failed.[71] The Television Act of 1964 established an ITV Welsh Committee to see that its programming met ''the particular needs and wishes of Wales.'' TWW eventually lost its franchise due to persistent protests from viewers wanting more Welsh language programming. It was replaced in 1968 by Harlech Television (HTV), the present ITV licensee for Wales.[72]

Welsh language broadcasts increased during the 1970s. By the end of the decade, the BBC Wales was airing a weekly average of 7 hours of TV programming in Welsh and 6 in English.[73] The BBC's Radio Wales and Radio Cymru were each on the air 65 hours per week in English and Welsh, respectively.[74] HTV had increased its weekly output to 7½ hours in Welsh and 4 in English. Wales also benefits from two Independent Local Radio Stations, in Cardiff and Swansea,[75] the latter contributing nearly 3 hours of daily programming in Welsh.[76]

But another controversy was brewing in Wales. This centered on the question of a Welsh programming policy for Britain's fourth TV channel, which eventually was to come under the control of the Channel Four Television Company, a subsidiary of the Independent Broadcasting Authority. In Wales, the debate was between having all Welsh language programming placed on the new Channel Four, the side favored by Welsh-speaking nationalists, or continuing to spread it over several channels, mixed with English, as was supported by HTV and most English monoglots. The former "Welsh on Four" position was held by the Conservative Party prior to the 1979 general elections, but was abandoned after its victory. This turnabout by the Tories infuriated Welsh nationalists, galvanized public opinion in Wales, and led to acts of violence, civil disobedience, a TV license fee boycott, and a hunger strike threat from a prominent political leader. These events forced the Government to recapitulate.[77]

Channel Four began operations throughout the UK in the Fall of 1982. In Wales, however, the new service is called Sianel Pedwar Cymru (S4C), which is Welsh for Channel Four Wales. S4C is run by a separate Welsh Fourth Channel Authority, which reports directly to the Home Secretary instead of IBA, the owner of the national Channel Four Television Company. From the beginning, S4C has reached 90% of the households in Wales, with 22 hours of the 75-hour weekly programming total being in the Welsh language. Ten hours of the Welsh total is produced by the BBC Wales, 9 by HTV, and the remaining airtime by independent producers.[78] Its English language programming is supplied free from the national Channel Four.

S4C is uniquely financed in that the programming it gets from the BBC and Channel Four is free, paid for by the license fee and advertising, respectively. Further, IBA gives S4C a grant from the proceeds it collects from its 15 independent companies for the operation of Channel Four UK-wide. S4C then buys programming from independent producers at negotiated prices. It also pays for the programs from HTV Wales, which in turn keeps the advertising proceeds.[79]

Several questions await answers in the 1980s, however. One is whether or not the 22 hours preempted from the Channel Four nationwide service in English will become a source of resentment by the non-Welsh-speaking majority in Wales. Such preemptions in the past have caused many monoglots to turn their TV antennas toward transmitters in England to avoid unwanted programming in Welsh and still catch the more popular shows in English seen elsewhere in Britain on the BBC and ITV national networks. Other unanswered questions relate to governance of and cooperation between the new channel's program suppliers (BBC and HTV), the availability of sufficient home-grown talent to produce over 3 hours of airproduct daily in Welsh, the level of Welsh program quality vis-a-vis that in English, and the feasibility of making TV ads in Welsh for a maximum audience of about 600,000 viewers, all of whom understand English.[80]

In summary, Channel Four has increased television programming in Welsh from 14 to 22 hours by 1983, nearly half of the service's output. And with a regional authority controlling its operation in Wales, the prospects seem good for a significant and expanding Welsh language TV presence sure to please even the most vocal critics. In addition, the BBC is increasing the airtime of Radio Wales and Radio Cymru to 90 hours each per week within the decade.[81] These developments seem to augur well for the survival and enhancement of the ancient language of Wales in the near term.

BROADCASTING TO IRELAND'S MINORITY CULTURE

Ireland, like Canada and Wales, is a bilingual nation by law. Article 8 of the Irish Constitution recognizes Irish as "the national . . . and first official language." English is cited as "a second official language."[82] Irish, an ancient Gaelic dialect, is rooted in the Goidelic branch of the Celtic language group. Its use as a first language has dwindled over the years, like the Irish population itself. This is due in part to centuries of social subjugation by the British and, in this century, to gradual modernization.

Today, only about 5% of the Republic's nearly 3.5 million inhabitants speak Irish exclusively. Most of these Irish monoglots (the *Gaeltachti*) live in the western counties of Donegal, Galway, and Kerry—a region known as the Gaeltacht. However, nearly two-thirds of the total population speaks English almost entirely, knowing only a few words in Irish. The remaining residents, about 30%, are relatively fluent bilingualists—using Irish mainly in the home and pub, and English, typically, for business and more formal occasions.[83]

Irish language broadcasting and discussions about a Gaeltacht station can be traced back to 1926, when Ireland put its first service, Radio Eireann, on the air.[84] Programs in Irish have always been interspersed into the English-dominated schedule of the national radio system. These attempts, however, have provoked chronic controversy from Gaelic groups who want more and better programs, and from the English-speaking majority who want less.[85] Nevertheless, the programs in English have always been more popular and better supported than have Irish language broadcasts.[86]

The Irish government formed two committees in 1958 to study different aspects of the language issue. The Commission on the Restoration of the Irish Language deliberated until 1964, but its recommendations ironically never considered the possibility of starting an all-Irish radio station to encourage the use of Irish.[87] The Television Commission, convened to plan Ireland's first domestic TV system, advised in its 1959 report that the nation's radio and television services should "provide for the use of the Irish language and for the adequate reflection of the national outlook and culture."[88] The Irish Parliament codified this recommendation in Section 17 of its 1960 Broadcasting Act, requiring the national broadcaster to address "the national aims of restoring the Irish language and preserving and developing the national culture."[89] The resulting national broadcasting organization, Radio Telefis Eireann (RTE), translated this statutory mandate into a self-imposed goal of producing at least 10% of its television programming in Irish.

During the 1970s, a number of important events helped to advance the cause of bilingual broadcasting. First, RTE inaugurated *Raidio na Gaeltachta* in 1972, an exclusively Irish language service aimed at reaching the three principle Gaeltachti strongholds along the western seaboard with 4 hours of culture-specific programming each evening.[90]

Next, the most complete articulation of an official language policy for RTE was set forth in 1974 by a government-appointed Broadcasting Review Committee, whose report identified the following objectives:[91]

> 1) To present programmes in Irish over the full range of output; 2) to present programmes, in English and Irish, aimed at creating an awareness in the public mind of the philosophy and significance of the Irish language; 3) to encourage in the broadcasting staff an appreciation of the vital contribution they can make towards the national objective of language restoration, and 4) to seek to implement this policy by providing (a) programmes in Irish for those competent in the language, (b) bilingual programmes for those with a limited knowledge of Irish, (c) programmes aimed at helping those learning the language, and (d) programmes, in English and Irish, analysing and explaining the philosophy of Irish language, culture and tradition.

Finally, passage of the Broadcasting Authority (Amendment) Act of 1976 replaced the 1960 law and strengthened the cultural thrust of Section 17 by requiring that "special regard" be given to the distinguishing elements of the "whole island of Ireland," particularly the Irish language.[92]

Raidio na Gaeltachta subsequently expanded to nationwide coverage in 1979, and increased its daily schedule by 90 minutes to include morning and mid-day broadcasts. Within a year of these improvements, RTE added second television and radio networks, in 1978 and 1979 respectively.[93] While these new services multiplied program options and coverage nationwide, their effect was less than helpful to the cause of Irish language broadcasting. Radio 2, for example, broadcasts in English only and RTE-2 was allowed by the Irish government to import up to 80% of its programming, mostly from Britain and therefore in English.

By 1980, it was clear that the launching of a second television channel had affected RTE's bilingual programming performance several ways. First, while the number of hours of programming produced and aired by RTE-TV in both languages increased, imports (in English only) had jumped by two-thirds. Second, the proportion of English-language TV programming, home-produced and imported, remained constant at nearly 90% of RTE's total broadcast schedule over the two channels—despite the fact that programs in Irish had increased more than 1 hour a week on average.[94]

We can therefore conclude that the public received more program options and hours in both languages, but at the expense of doubling imports, further reducing domestic production as a proportion of the total broadcast schedule, and with no appreciable gain in Irish language programming vis-a-vis English.

A 15-year analysis of RTE television programming trends, as shown in Table 7-1, confirms that the advent of a second TV channel has contributed to a growing dependency on foreign programming imports while only marginally aiding Irish language content.

By the end of 1981, for instance, 62% of all TV programming aired by RTE's two channels together was imported, and only 4.2% of their combined airtime was in the Irish language. However, 11% of the nearly 1900 hours of television programming produced by RTE during the 1980–81 season was in Irish.[95]

But the 1980s should prove to be a healthier decade for bilingual broadcasting in Ireland. Raidio na Gaeltachta, with its national coverage, currently averages 40 hours of folk music and information weekly in Irish, over 2000 hours per year.[96] Surveys conducted in 1980 showed that the listenership to Irish language

Table 7-1 Breakdown of RTE TV Programming Schedules by Language and Source: 1965–1980

	1965 %	1970 %	1975 %	1980[a] %
Home-produced in Irish	4.2	6.5	2.8	3.3
Home-produced in English	54.3	40.0	38.2	29.2
Home-produced, bilingual[b]	2.9	1.1	0.8	n.a.[c]
Imported (in English only)	38.6	52.4	58.2[d]	67.5
Annual total	100.0	100.0	100.0	100.0

Note: Content analyses of RTE television programming were conducted during two-week periods of Novermber 1965, 1970, and 1975 by a public interest research group, Citizens for Better Broadcasting (see 6), using social scientists and graduate students from University College, Dublin, as coders. Data from 1980 come from (30).

[a]RTE operated only one channel until 1978; hence 1980 data are averages of two services.

[b]Bilingual programming is defined by RTE as programs predominately in English, with some Irish words or phrases interjected (6, p. 86). These programs ceased being tabulated separately in 1978.

[c]By 1980, only one bilingual series was produced and included in the Irish language total.

[d]1975 imported programming breaks down as follows: U.S., 64.1 percent; U.K., 32.5 percent; Canada, 0.7 percent; Australia, 2.7 percent (6).

Source: W. J. Howell, Jr., "Bilingual Broadcasting and the Survival of Authentic Culture in Wales and Ireland," *Journal of Communication* 32(4), Autumn 1982, p. 46.

programming was growing in all regions of the country.[97] At present, bilingual discussion programs are also being included on the general service Radio 1, and Radio 2's output in the Irish language is rising.[98]

Perhaps the best omen of all for the future of Irish language broadcasting came in March of 1980 when the RTE Authority unveiled a plan to substantially upgrade TV programming in Irish during the decade. Guidelines were proposed calling for 20% of all future home-production to be in Irish, a goal that must be achieved by all programming departments. In addition to the current nightly newscast (Nuacht, in Irish), one other program in the native language will be aired each evening on one of the RTE channels during prime time. Another strategy designed to generate more and better programs in Irish involves the preferential hiring by RTE of writers and producers conversant in the native tongue.[99] The campaign also provides for reinstating instructional features on radio and television to teach adult audiences the Irish language.[100]

MINORITY CULTURE BROADCASTING IN THE BASQUE REGION OF SPAIN

The Basques of Spain number about 2 million and reside in the northern region of the country adjacent to the French border, west of the Pyrenees, in an area blessed with good soil and many natural harbors along its coast on the Bay of Biscay. Basque cultural pride is fierce, and they have fought the Spanish government for autonomy since losing it centuries ago. Spain's new socialist leadership in Madrid has recognized that the only solution to the historic conflict with Basque nationalists, separatists, and the militant ETA terrorists is to grant more independence to the provinces of Vizcaya, Guipuzoa, and Alava—the region's main enclaves. A vital part of the new scheme is to encourage the use of broadcasting as a means of helping the authentic Basque culture and language to survive.[101]

The Basque language is called "Euskera"; the people who speak it are "Euskaldun"; the region is known as "Euskal Herria." Euskera is a highly unique language, one unrelated to the other languages of Europe. For years it was repressed and, under Franco's reign, could not even be spoken legally. But things have improved dramatically for the Basques since the death of Franco in 1975. Under King Juan Carlos and the new social democratic leadership, the Basque and Spanish governments signed a statute of autonomy at Guernica in 1979. The act gave the Basques the right to own, regulate, and maintain their own mass media, and to establish a regional government in their regional capital of Vitoria.

While Spanish is considered the nation's official language, the new-found political freedom legally recognizes the Basque language as well as those of other Autonous Regions—namely, Catalan, Castilian, Valencian, and Andalusian.[102] Another regional station, TV-3, went on the air in January 1984 to serve

Catalonia in Catalan. Basque is now spoken by about 700,000 people, a third of the Basque population, with 300,000 using it as a first language. As in Wales, the young people are studying it in school again and, thanks to broadcasting, are beginning to use it daily. Radio and television are well suited to the oral tradition of Basque culture—a culture which has no literature but is rich in folklore, dances and other rural customs appropriate to their families, churches, and villages.

A 1982 law created the Ente Publico Radio Television Vasca, known in Basque as Herri Erakundea Irrati Telebista. It has two subsidiaries—a radio company, *Euskal Irrati,* and a TV company, *Euskal Telebista* (ETB). The Basque parliament regulates ETB through a 15-member committee, and provides it with an annual appropriation of 9 million dollars, but advertising is being considered as an additional source of future revenue. ETB's offices and two TV studios are located in Durango. The station's objectives are to present objective, accurate, and impartial news; to keep commentary clearly separate from factual reporting; and to promote the Basque culture and language.

ETB began operations in the spring of 1983 with 3 hours of programming in Basque each evening. A 30-minute Basque-language newscast preempts the national news at 7 pm from Spain's RTVE weekday evenings. Much of ETB's schedule is imported from major Western broadcasters and from S4C in Wales. Some cartoons are also purchased from Eastern Europe. All foreign productions are dubbed into Basque, but also carry Spanish sub-titles. In addition, Basque radio stations are currently being established in the provincial capitals of Vitoria, San Sebastian, and Bilbao.

ETB now employs about 90 people and maintains separate transmission facilities from RTVE's national services, although the two broadcasters cooperate on the use of microwave links and frequencies. ETB's technical, financial, regulatory, and programming autonomy are being further augmented by inexpensive portable equipment and a mobile van which increase opportunities for public access and localism. Television exposure, especially, lends credibility and prestige to the Basque language, allowing ETB to present news from a Basque perspective and reflect the unique needs and interests of the region.

MULTICULTURAL BROADCASTING IN TRILINGUAL SWITZERLAND

Switzerland's mountainous plateaus are surrounded by the Alps and bordered by France, West Germany, Austria, Liechtenstein and Italy. Nearly six and a half million people are spread among three official language groups and 26 autonomous cantons (provinces) that comprise the Swiss Confederation. The German-speaking population (65%) resides in the central and northern regions, the Francophones (18%) inhabit the west, and the Swiss who speak Italian (12%) are concentrated in the south.[103]

Each language community has its own radio and television society with exclusive rights to broadcast in either German, French, or Italian. The programming of all three is coordinated and scheduled by the national Swiss Broadcasting Corporation (SBC)—or Societe Swisse de Radiodiffusion et Television (SSR)—a nonprofit body that is chartered by the Federal Council and financed by radio and TV license fees and limited amounts of advertising. Roughly 70% of the license proceeds is divided among the three broadcasters while the remaining 30% goes to the PTT for operating its landline networks. The three broadcasting societies are:[104]

Radio-und Fernsehgesellschaft der Deutschen und der Raeto Romanischen Schweiz, which is centered in Zurich, operates three radio networks (Schweizer Radio DRS-1, DRS-2, and DRS-3), three local radio stations, and one TV network service in German.

Société de Radiodiffusion et de Télévision de la Suisse Romande, with studios in Lausanne and Geneva, programs three radio networks (Radio Swisse Romande) and a TV network in French.

Società Cooperativa per la Radiotelevisione nella Svizzera Italiana (CORSI), runs two radio networks (Radio nella Svizzera Italiana) and a TV program service from its Lugano studios.

Journalists of all three languages had to work out of SSR's only News Department in Zurich until 1982. This centralization of news operations, which produced newscasts in all three vernaculars but used common film footage, was done in the interests of cost efficiency and national unity of coverage. Opponents of the universal system claimed, however, that it was impossible to meet the specific interests and cultural needs of all three language communities under such a rigid arrangement. Further, journalists representing the French and Italian regions were isolated from their own people and felt like exiles in German Zurich. As a result, SSR's news-gathering process and presentation format appeared inferior to Swiss viewers, compared to newscasts they are able to receive from neighboring countries.

SSR responded to these criticisms by regionalizing the News Department into three separate branches—*Tagesschau* (in German), *Téléjournal* (in French), and *Telejiornale* (in Italian)—which went on the air in January of 1982. Under decentralization, SSR's three news operations are still not completely autonomous, since national unity would suffer and costs would triple. Thus, two new agencies—the Chief Editors' Conference and the News Coordination Department—were created to ensure that important domestic and foreign news is disseminated equally to all three language groups, and that each ethnic community is kept abreast of happenings in the other regions.

To avoid duplication, newsworthy events around the country are assigned to only one film or ENG crew, but all three news departments are sent the visuals to use and script as they see fit. Reporters from all ethnic regions cover some major events simultaneously, and there are some correspondents from each language working in the others' territories. So far, the regionalization of television news in Switzerland has actually strengthened national unity.[105]

Switzerland has a number of cable TV systems at present, and several dozen private radio stations were given the go ahead in 1983 to begin operations. A teletext proposal also was approved in late 1983. The service is to be run jointly by SSR and the Swiss Newspaper and Magazine Association (ASEJ). The company hopes to receive a small portion of the TV license fee on a monthly basis, and to also sell advertising.[106]

An experimental English-language VHF stereo station, *Radio X-tra,* began serving the Geneva area 12 hours daily in the spring of 1983 with a program format of news, community information, documentaries, features, and music. The latter is aimed at the Anglo-American audience and includes classical, country and western, jazz, and the current hit records from the U.S. The station is operated by Swiss Radio International and Radio Swisse Romande. Its programming is targeted at the international community that lives and works in Geneva, the home of many world service organizations.[107]

MULTILINGUAL BROADCASTING IN YUGOSLAVIA

Yugoslavia was once described as "a state with six republics, five South Slav peoples, four languages, three religions, two alphabets and one political party."[108] The clever symmetry of this statement provides a quick though somewhat superficial sketch of the very complicated multicultural nature of this East European nation. Today's Socialist Federal Republic of Yugoslavia is comprised of six national territories (Serbia, Croatia, Macedonia, Slovenia, Montenegro, and Bosnia-Hercegovina) and two autonomous regions (Vojvodina and Kosovo). This multinational amalgam totaling 23 million persons consists of Serbs (40%), Croats (22%), Bosnian Muslims (8%), Macedonians (6%), Albanians (6%), Montenegrins (2%), Hungarians (2%), Turks (1%), and various other ethnic strains (5%).

Historically, a major internal split has existed between the two Slavic cultures: Serbia, having an Orthodox religion and a language based on the Cyrillic alphabet; and Croatia, which is mostly Catholic and has a Roman-based language. Their two languages, formerly separate, have since been combined into one—Serbo-Croatian—which the Serbs write in Cyrillic and the Croats in the Latin alphabet. Yugoslavia now recognizes three official languages—*Serbo-Croatian, Slovenian,* and *Macedonian.*[109]

Credit for keeping Yugoslavia's various ethnic groups culturally autonomous yet politically united must go to the man who ruled the nation for over three decades. Josip Broz, known as Marshall Tito, became head of state in 1946 and remained President of Yugoslavia until his death in 1980. Under his leadership, Yugoslavia prospered with a socialist-market economy, developed regional rather than national mass media, and remained free from direct Soviet control.[110]

In fact, Yugoslavia is the only East European nation which is not a member of the Warsaw Pact.[111]

Such extensive cultural pluralism has necessitated highly decentralized governmental and broadcasting structures. In fact, a complex arrangement of multilingual national, regional, and local broadcasting services may be regarded as the connective tissue which holds these cultural parts together and thus makes nationhood possible. Like West Germany, broadcasting in Yugoslavia is federalized, meaning that each republic and both autonomous areas has its own radio and TV services. These eight broadcasting organizations are headquartered in their respective capital cities and each operates two or three radio and television services. Programming is aired in the three national languages as well as in Albanian, Hungarian, Rumanian, Ruthenian, Slovakian, Turkish, and Italian. In addition, special summer broadcasts for tourists can be heard in English, French, German, and Russian.[112] This federalized structure is shown in Table 7-2.

Media content in Yugoslavia is determined by regional ethnicity and, in addition to the three official tongues, is disseminated in well over a dozen local dialects.[113] As Table 7-2 illustrates, five of the eight broadcasting systems use Serbian and/or Croatian, while Macedonian, Slovenian, and Albanian dominate one region each. Most of the nation's TV production is in the three official languages, although programs are offered occasionally in a minority tongue. Two regional channels—Koper TV and Pristina TV—broadcast in Italian and Albanian, respectively. The television networks in each region transmit approximately 12 hours daily on Program 1 and 6 hours via Program 2.

One of the radio networks in the eight regions is on the air 24 hours a day, while the remaining one or two offer regular schedules ranging from 12 to less than 6 hours, depending on program format. The 144 local radio stations operate between 3 and 6 hours daily, with music dominating spoken word content by roughly a two-to-one ratio.[114]

But the eight major broadcasters do not have complete autonomy. All radio outlets are coordinated by *Jugoslavenska Radiotelevizija* (JRT), a government institution which formulates programming policy, regulates technical operations, and collects national license fee revenues on radio and TV receivers and disburses funds to the eight regional broadcasters using a population formula. JRT is also responsible for the international shortwave service, *Radio Yugoslavia*, which transmits daily in ten foreign languages. All local radio stations, however, are independent of JRT.

The body of law by which Yugoslavia's broadcasters operate is derived from the national constitution and various statutes pertaining to the press, information media, telecommunication carriers, and the charters of the various broadcasting organizations. Three-quarters of all domestic broadcasting is supported by the annual license fees, and the remainder comes mostly from advertising.[115]

JRT's programming policy supports the ethnic identity and cultural sovereignty of the regions by calling for "the full development of national cultures

Table 7-2   Broadcasting Organizations, Services, and Languages Used in Yugoslavia: 1984

National Republics	Radio Networks	Local Stations MW & FM		TV Program Services
SERBIA (Serbian) Radiotelevizija Beograd	3	27	8	2
CROATIA (Croatian) Radiotelevizija Zagreb	3	37	9	2
SLOVENIA (Slovene) Radiotelevizija Ljublijana	3	4	8	2 Koper TV[a]
BOSNIA/HERCEGOVINA (Serbo-Croatian) Radiotelevizija Sarajevo	3	19	3	2
MACEDONIA (Macedonian) Radiotelevizija Skopje	3	10	1	2
MONTENEGRO (Serbian) Radiotelevizija Titograd	2	5	2	2
Autonomous Republics				
VOJVODINA (Serbian) Radiotelevizija Novi Sad	2	4	7	Novi Sad TV[b] Beograd 1 relay Beograd 2 relay
KOSOVO (Albanian) Radiotelevizija Pristina	2			Pristina TV[c] Beograd relay

[a]Foreign relay in Italian
[b]Regional channel
[c]Regional channel
Source: World Radio TV Handbook 1984, pp. 151–153 and 410–411.

and the use of national languages as well as a more thorough coverage of political, economic and cultural events in individual republics and autonomous provinces.''

Yugoslavia's relative independence from Moscow has meant a greater degree of freedom than is customary in communist societies. News reporting, though not free to attack communist ideology, may offer various points of view and criticize government performance without fear of precensorship. The national news agency, *Tanjug,* supplements JRT's domestic and foreign coverage with international news and program exchanges from print and broadcast services abroad, such as Reuters, Agence France Presse, UPI, VISNEWS, UPITN, Eurovision, and Intervision.

TV was penetrating nearly two-thirds of the nation's households by late 1985, with feature films, entertainment series, and news attracting the largest audiences. Yugoslavia began providing a teletext service in 1984 but in the future will rely more on its two planned domestic satellites than on cable systems to achieve nationwide coverage via as many as eight channels.[116]

But Yugoslavian broadcasters face hard times ahead. Belgrade Radio and Television was experiencing a financial crisis by 1984 as advertising revenues fell and inflation climbed. Even a 24% increase in the TV license fee was not enough to solve its money problems. This means that Yugoslav viewers will pay more for less in the future, as fees are hiked and as cutbacks in imported programming lead to further reruns.[117]

AN OVERVIEW OF BROADCASTING IN POLYLINGUAL AFRICA

The existence of hundreds of languages and local dialects poses a greater challenge to broadcasters in Africa than anywhere else in the world. Many of Africa's vernaculars have no written alphabet, having evolved from completely oral cultures. Since these forms of expression do not exist in print media, radio is therefore the most important mass medium to national leaders, who use it to educate and inform, and to the people, who rely on it as a source of enlightment and regard it as a vital means of keeping their ancestral languages alive.

Minorities demand that their languages be broadcast out of reasons ranging from ethnic pride and status to outright fear that their mother tongues may become extinct. But the goals of national unity and cultural pluralism often are in conflict, if not mutually exclusive. Governments sometimes must agonize over whether to broadcast only in the dominant language(s) and thus risk separatist unrest and the possible demise of minority cultures and ancestral languages, or to allow many traditional dialects to share the airwaves while lessening broadcasting's role as a unifying force and nation-building resource. Faced with limited economic resources, technology, frequencies, and talent, most African countries tend to want to develop national broadcasting services that are both cost efficient and able to offer a full range of programs.[118]

The number and variety of vernaculars found within some African nations make it difficult to keep track of which, when, and where local tongues are broadcast. Most national broadcasters specify only the primary languages and the most commonly used local dialects; others give the number rather than names of vernaculars aired; some list only the principle languages, and add the words "vernacular" or "local languages." All told, some 200 different languages and dialects are currently being broadcast by 63 sovereign countries in Africa.[119] Table 7-3 identifies 67 languages by name that were being used in broadcasting throughout Africa as of 1984.

A third of these nations listed numbers of unspecified *local* languages (58), *vernaculars* (53), *national* languages (16), and *Indian* languages (6). In addition,

18 nations cited French, 22 English, and another 20 air both. Arabic is the next most common language on the airwaves of Africa, used by 11 nations, five of which are located in north Africa but aligned with the Middle East: Algeria, Egypt, Libya, Morocco, and Sudan.[120]

The typical African now learns two or more local dialects in order to communicate with neighboring tribes, yet the lingua franca of the better-educated urban dwellers is commonly a European language like English or French. Although a native vernacular is usually an African's first language, the ability to speak an English or French dialect makes intercultural communication possible within and between nations.[121] The historical presence of Western colonial powers left a legacy of several European languages having been adopted as national lingua franca if not official languages throughout the continent, as well as the delineation of African states into Anglophone and Francophone regions.

Anglophone West Africa includes Nigeria, Ghana, Liberia, and Sierra Leone. The Francophone nations are found mainly in West and Equitorial Africa. Chief among these are the Central African Republic, Chad, The (formerly Belgian) Congo, Djibouti, Gabon, Guinea, Ivory Coast, Mali, Mauritania, Niger, Senegal, Togo, Upper Volta, and Zaire.

As discussed in the last chapter, Western broadcasting systems were transferred to Africa where, besides cultural and linguistic manifestations, their national philosophies also were reflected in the structure of programming services. The French, for example, instituted highly centralized broadcasting systems which attempted to disseminate French culture; to teach Africans to master classical French and become, in effect, black Frenchmen; and to impose a uniform ideology nationwide rather than cultivate local languages, culture, and governance. By contrast, the British favored a more decentralized approach to colonial rule in which regions were granted autonomy to administer their own affairs and to use broadcasting to inform, train, and entertain their people as well as to promote and preserve local languages and cultures.[122] A brief look at several African systems illustrates the continent's broadcasting diversity.

Nigeria is perhaps the strongest example of the British tradition of federal regionalism. English, although a minority language, has the unusual status of being Nigeria's official lingua franca, since it is the only vernacular understood nationwide.[123] The Federal Radio Corporation of Nigeria (FRCN) offers two national radio networks in English and a variety of vernaculars, and 32 state radio stations that broadcast in English, Yoruba, Hausa, Ibo, and a dozen local tongues. The Nigerian Television Authority coordinates programming that is provided to it by six Zonal Boards and transmitted over NTA's 19 state TV stations.[124]

A similar situation exists in *Uganda*, where English is the official language and is thus used by its national broadcasting services, Radio Uganda and Uganda Television.[125] In addition, 19 local dialects are aired at various times in different parts of the country as follows: Ateso, Lusoga, Kupsbiny, Lusania-Lunyole-

Table 7-3 Principal Languages of Broadcasting in Africa: 1984

Country	Language(s)
Algeria	French, Arabic, Kabyl
Angola	Portuguese + 10 vernaculars
Ascension Island	English
Benin	French, English + 18 local languages
Botswana	English SeTawana
Burundi	Kirundi, Swahili, French
Cameroon	French, English + vernaculars
Canary Island	Spanish
Cape Verde	Portuguese, Creole
Central African Rep	Sango, French
Chad	French, Arabic + 8 local languages
Comoros	French, Comorian
Congo	French, Lingala, Kikongo
Djibouti	French, Somali, Afar, Arabic
Egypt	Arabic
Equatorial Guinea	Spanish + Vernaculars
Ethiopia	Amhoric, Somali, English, French, Arabic, Afar, Tigre, Tigrigna, Oromigna
Gabon	French
Gambia	English, French + 7 local languages
Ghana	Akan, Ewe, Dagbani, Ga, Hausa, Nzema, English
Guinea	French + Vernaculars
Guinea Bissau	Portuguese
Ivory Coast	French + 13 Vernaculars
Kenya	English, Swahili, Hindustani + 11 Vernaculars.
Lesotho	Sesotho, English
Liberia	English, Liberian + 15 Vernaculars
Libya	Arabic
Jamahiriya	Arabic
Madagascar	Malagasy, French
Madeira	Portugese
Malawi	Chichewa, English
Mali	French + 7 local languages
Mauritania	Arabic, French + Vernaculars
Mauritius	English, French + 6 Indian languages
Mayotte	French, Mahorian
Morocco	Arabic, French, Spanish, English, Berber, Hassania
Mozambique	Portuguese + Vernaculars
Niger	French, English + 7 Vernaculars
Nigeria	English, Yoruba, Hausa, Ibo + 12 local languages
Reunion	French
Rwanda	Kinyarwanda, Swahili, French, English
Sao Tome E Principe	Portuguese
Senegal	French, Arabic, English, Portuguese + 6 local languages
Seychelles	Creole, English, French
Sierra Leone	English, Mende, Temne, Krio, Limba
Somalia	Somali

Table 7-3   (continued)

Country	Language(s)
South Africa	English, Afrikaans, North Sotho, South Sotho, Zulu, Tswana, Xhosa, Venda, Tsonga
Bophuthatswana	SeTwana, English, Afrikaans
Ciskei	Xhosa, English, Afrikaans
Namibia	Tswana, Damara, Nama, Kwangali, Mbukushu, Gciriku
Tanskei	Xhosa, English
Venda	Venda, Afrikaans, English
St. Helena	English
Sudan	Arabic
Swaziland	English, Siswati
Tanzania	Swahili, English
Togo	French + Vernaculars
Tristan Da Cunha	English
Tunisia	Arabic
Uganda	English + 19 Vernaculars
Upper Volta	French + 16 national languages
Zaire	French, Lingola, Kikongo, Tshiluba, Swahili
Zambia	English + 7 vernaculars
Zimbabwe	English, Shona, Ndebele, Chewa

Sources: WRTH 1984, pp. 155–179
            Sydney W. Head, *Broadcasting in Africa*, pp. 406–411.

Lugwe, and Lumasaba in the East; Alur, Kakwa, Karamojong, Kuman, Lugbara, and Luwo in the North; Rukonjo, Runyakole-Rugiga, and Runyoro-Rutoro in the Western region. Luganda is the language of Uganda's largest tribe, the Boganda, which occupies the nation's midlands. Ironically, the most popular African language among most Ugandan tribes is Swahili, but its use is confined to Radio Uganda's external service, along with French and Arabic. Nevertheless, broadcasts in Swahili are heard in Uganda from stations in neighboring Zaire, Tanzania, Kenya, and Rwanda, and can also be picked up via Radio Uganda's shortwave station.[126]

Ghana claims to have the oldest independent broadcasting service in Africa.[127] The present-day Ghana Broadcasting Corporation runs two radio networks, the first programming in English and six vernaculars and the second being a commercial service in English only. Its TV service is limited to about 6 hours of operation daily via five stations and four repeaters.[128]

The first French-language broadcasting system in Africa was founded in *Senegal*.[129] Today, the government-run Office De Radiodiffusion-Television Du Senegal operates one national radio service in French and vernaculars, and five regional stations in local languages. Radio Dakar, its international shortwave service, broadcasts in French, Portuguese, Arabic, and English. Senegal Television provides only 35 hours of mostly educational programming each week via the nation's only TV station in Dakar.[130]

Egypt is a leader in broadcasting among Arab nations and a major exporter of mediated products to Middle Eastern countries. Its language situation is also of particular interest. The first Egyptian radio service used English and French mostly.[131] Today, the official language, Arabic, dominates domestic broadcasting, although some 36 local dialects are spoken by Egypt's 41 million people.[132] Besides Arabic, the Egyptian Radio and Television Federation broadcasts in many of the local tongues, plus Hebrew and Russian, on its regional radio stations. It also maintains a foreign language radio service for the various expatriate populations by scheduling 15-minute blocks of airtime throughout the broadcast day in Armenian, Greek, Italian, German, French, and English—with regular newscasts aired in the latter three.[133]

Tunisia put a second national TV channel on the air in 1983 with considerable financial help from France. The new service broadcasts mainly in French, but some programs in English and German will also be carried.[134]

The Republic of *South Africa* is a racist regime in which the minority white population (17.5%) dominates all of the country's political, economic, and social life. The races are separated through apartheid policies that extend to the South African Broadcasting Corporation, a state-subsidized monopoly which broadcasts primarily in English and Afrikaans.[135] The two-thirds black majority receives most of its programming in 14 local vernaculars via regional radio stations. Two newly independent republics, Bophuthatswana and Namibia (formerly South West Africa) also have initiated modest TV operations—the former having begun its own TV service in 1984, transmitting in Setwana, Afrikaans, and English to the Odi region.[136]

A REVIEW OF TRENDS AND ISSUES

Multicultural societies face an uncomfortable dilemma when forced to decide between broadcasting nationwide in one official language or providing regional radio and TV services in the native tongues of their principal minority cultures. Each decision has its trade-offs.

Choosing *one* language offers the advantages of developing a comprehensive national broadcasting organization with a standardized means of universal expression and identity that contributes to the cause of nationhood. Such a unitary structure is more cost-efficient than running a highly decentralized system of regional stations which fragments airtime and spectrum space and also requires separate staffs to produce specialized programs in a multitude of tongues. A pluralistic broadcasting arrangement creates costly and wasteful duplications of services and personnel, and often yields amateurish programming of poor production quality.

On the other hand, failure to reach and serve various ethnic segments of a nation's population with broadcasts reflecting their cultural identities is often a prescription for alienation and political separatism. The case for *multicultural* and *polylingual* broadcasting is therefore based on the rationale that the ethnic pride and status of minority groups is bolstered; that native languages and traditional customs are preserved; that a larger aggregate audience is reached because programs of relevance are extended to all cultural segments; and that the loyalty diverse minority cultures feel toward their nation and government is strengthened by this official show of sensitivity to their needs and interests.

Ironically, these very arguments for broadcast pluralism can also backfire by unwittingly encouraging if not facilitating tribalism, separatism, and even terrorism. Incentives to learn a national language are effectively lessened as it becomes easier to live and work in an isolated cultural ghetto. Naturally, a compromise can be struck by offering national broadcasting services in the official language(s), while also serving subcultural needs through LPTV, local radio stations, and special cable channels.

Another emergent pattern is recognition by national broadcasting organizations of their capabilities to target specialized programming to narrowly-defined audiences without depriving the larger audience of its general interest broadcasts. This also implies that language guardians and policy-makers have accepted telecommunication technology as an ally rather than enemy in their mission to save authentic cultures and celebrate ethnic pride. Future claims for access to the multiplying channels of mass telecommunication will no doubt increase. At the same time, direct broadcast satellites will be competing for the attention of millions of people in hundreds of countries by offering mass appeal programming in dozens of languages.

Authentic folk cultures like those of the Cymry Cymraeg, the Gaeltachti, and the Euskaldun do not adapt as well to television as to radio because they are essentially rural and community-based civilizations with rich oral rather than visual traditions. But this does not mean that TV, an urban technology and symbol of modernity, cannot be adapted to folkloric cultures. Since these ancient cultures continue to endure amid technologized societies, television is seen by them as the most effective storytelling medium for keeping their heritages alive, for legitimizing past folkways to their children, and for satisfying normal appetites for news and diversion in their native tongues.

This is a value that the speakers of Welsh, Irish, and Basque share with Belgium's Walloons, Canada's Francophones, the Slovenes of Yugoslavia, the Italian-speaking Swiss, and myriad tribal members throughout the continent of Africa. In short, to live in today's world is to want relevant entertainment and credible news in one's own language via state-of-the-art telecommunications media, irrespective of whether one belongs to a minority or dominant culture.

The foregoing examples of pluralism in world broadcasting demonstrate that interest in preserving and promoting ancestral languages, cultural heritage, and ethnic identity is alive and well in virtually all multicultural societies, no matter what type of political or economic philosophy governs them. It has in effect become an accepted birthright of human kind regardless of national citizenship.

CHAPTER 7 NOTES

[1] John Howkins, "Basques Use TV To Speak Their Own Language," *InterMedia* 11(3), May 1983, pp. 20–25.

[2] Michael H. Prosser, *The Cultural Dialogue: An Introduction to Intercultural Communication* (Boston: Houghton Mifflin, 1978), pp. 104–105.

[3] William F. Mackey, "Language Policy and Language Planning," *Journal of Communication* 29(2), Spring 1979, p. 50.

[4] *Ibid.* See also: Jefferey Mills, "Hispanic Population On Upswing in US," *Buffalo News* (NY), April 25, 1984, p. A-7.

[5] Jan Jarboe, "The Special Case of Spanish-Language Television," *Washington Journalism Review,* November 1980, p. 21.

[6] *Ibid.*

[7] *Broadcasting/Cable Yearbook 1981* (Washington, DC: Broadcasting Publications, Inc., 1981), pp. B-149 and D-91 & 92.

[8] Jarboe, p. 21.

[9] *Ibid.,* p. 22.

[10] *Ibid.,* p. 23.

[11] *Ibid.,* p. 25.

[12] George Wedell, "The End of Media Nationalism in Europe," *InterMedia* 11(4/5), July/September 1983, pp. 80–81.

[13] Michael Darkow and Josef Eckhardt, "Hardly Different from the Germans Themselves," *EBU Review* XXXIV(1), January 1983, pp. 26–31.

[14] John Howkins, "Communications in Finland," *InterMedia* 10(4/5), July/September 1982, p. 43.

[15] *TV World,* May/June 1983, p. 33; and November 1983, p. 7.

[16] "Hungary Now Broadcasting for All Ethnic Minorities," *TV World,* November 1983, p. 7.

[17] Sheri Tillman, "TVB's Jade and Pearl Channels: 15 Years On," *TV World,* May/June 1983, pp. 8–9.

[18] Mehra Masani, "Broadcasting in India," in William E. McCavitt (ed.), *Broadcasting Around the World* (Blue Ridge Summit, PA: TAB Books, 1981), pp. 9–24.

[19] *World Radio Television Handbook 1984* (New York: Billboard Publications), p. 204. (Hereinafter referred to as WRTH).

[20] Jeremy Tunstall, *The Media Are American* (New York: Columbia University Press, 1977), p. 235.

[21] Ralph Shaw, "Gulf Broadcasters Building Independence," *TV World,* March 1984, pp. 13–14.

[22] Christopher Day, "Ethnic Diversity," *TV World,* November 1982, pp. 10–11.

[23] "Multi-Cultural TV," *TV World,* August 1982, p. 8.

[24] *CBC Annual Report, 1979–1980* (Ottawa: CBC, 1980), p. 25. N.B. The other six languages, in order of use, are: Italian, German, Ukranian, Native Indian, Greek, and Chinese.

[25] W. S. Hallman, with H. Hindley, *Broadcasting in Canada* (London: Routledge & Kegan Paul, 1977), pp. 2–3.

[26] W. J. Howell, Jr., "Broadcast Spillover and National Culture: Shared Concerns of the Republic of Ireland and Canada," *Journal of Broadcasting* 24(2), Spring 1980, p. 228.

[27] A. W. Johnson, *Touchstone for the CBC* (Ottawa: CBC, 1977), p. 10.

28 W. Brian Stewart, "The Canadian Social System and the Canadian Broadcast Audience," in Benjamin D. Singer (ed.), *Communications in Canadian Society* (Toronto: Copp Clark, 1975), p. 44.

29 Frank W. Peers, *The Politics of Canadian Broadcasting, 1920–1951* (Toronto: University of Toronto Press, 1969), pp. 49–51.

30 Frank W. Peers, *The Public Eye: Television and the Politics of Canadian Broadcasting, 1952–1968* (Toronto: University of Toronto Press, 1979), pp. 414–415.

31 *Ibid.*, pp. 417–419.

32 *CBC—A Brief History and Background* (Ottawa: CBC, 1972), p. 10.

33 Peers, *The Politics of . . .* , pp. 138–145.

34 *Ibid.*, pp. 121–122.

35 *Ibid.*, p. 250.

36 *CBC—A Brief History . . .* , p. 21.

37 Peers, *The Public Eye,* p. 422.

38 *Ibid.*, pp. 52–60.

39 *Ibid.*, pp. 154–156.

40 *Ibid.*, pp. 284–292.

41 *Broadcasting Act of 1968* (Ottawa: Queen's Printer, 1970), Part I, S 3(a).

42 *Regulations Respecting Radio (TV) Broadcasting* (Ottawa: CRTC, 1972), pp. 6–7.

43 *CRTC Annual Report, 1979–80* (Ottawa: CRTC, 1980), p. 9.

44 *The CBC—A Perspective* (Ottawa: CBC, 1978), p. 20.

45 *Ibid.*, pp. 277–281.

46 W. J. Howell, Jr., "Language Policy and Television Efficacy in Canada," *Mass Comm Review,* 10(1/2), Winter 1982/Spring 1983, pp. 6–7.

47 Johnson, p. 6.

48 *Information Please Almanac, Atlas and Yearbook, 1982* (New York: Simon and Schuster, 1981), pp. 139–140.

49 Walter B. Emery, *National and International Systems of Broadcasting: Their History, Operation and Control* (East Lansing, MI: Michigan State University Press, 1969), pp. 124–137.

50 Guido Fauconnier, "Serving Two Cultures: Local Media in Belgium," in George Gerbner and Marsha Siefert (eds.), *World Communications: A Handbook* (New York: Longman, 1984), pp. 322–323.

51 WRTH 1984, pp. 78–79.

52 Karel Hemmerecht, "News as a Factor in National Cohesion: the BRT Experience," *EBU Review* XXXIII(4), July 1982, pp. 8–11.

53 Pierre DeVos, "News and Current Affairs at RTBF: the Pros and Cons of Pluralism," *EBU Review* XXXIII(4), July 1982, p. 11.

54 Fauconnier, pp. 323–325.

55 A. Kooyman, "The New Television Culture," *EBU Review* XXXII(1), January 1981, p. 33.

56 Fauconnier, pp. 326–327.

57 "BRT/RTBF's Telecommunications Tower Optional," *EBU Review* XXXIV(3), May 1983, p. 41.

58 Burton Paulu, *Radio and Television Broadcasting in Eastern Europe* (Minneapolis, MN: The University of Minnesota Press, 1974), pp. 313–317.

59 *Ibid.*, p. 325.

60 WRTH 1984, pp. 82–83.

61 *Ibid.*, p. 399.

62 Paulu, p. 328.

63 *Ibid.*, pp. 352–353.

64 W. J. Howell, Jr., "Bilingual Broadcasting and the Survival of Authentic Culture in Wales and Ireland," *Journal of Communication* 32(4), Autumn 1982, p. 42.

65 Harri Pritchard Jones, "Wales Gets Its Own TV," *Irish Broadcasting Review,* No. 13, Spring 1982, p. 26.

[66] Asa Briggs, *The Golden Age of Wireless* (London: Oxford University Press, 1965), pp. 322ff.

[67] *BBC Handbook 1980* (London: British Broadcasting Corporation, 1980), p. 258.

[68] Broadcasting Council for Wales, *The Committee on the Future of Broadcasting 1974: Memorandum from the Broadcasting Council for Wales* (Cardiff: BBC, 1975), p. 4.

[69] *BBC Handbook 1980*, pp. 81–82.

[70] *ITV: A Comprehensive Guide to Independent Television* (London: ITV, 1966), pp. 14–15.

[71] Cymdeithas Yr Iaith Gymraig, *A Welsh Fourth Channel: The Only Answer* (Cardiff: The Welsh Language Society, 1979).

[72] HTV Wales, *The Fourth Channel in Wales* (Cardiff: HTV Wales, 1979), p. 8.

[73] *BBC Annual Report and Handbook 1981* (London: BBC, 1981), p. 84.

[74] *BBC Handbook 1980*, p. 82.

[75] *Television & Radio 1981* (London: Independent Broadcasting Authority, 1980), pp. 118 and 132.

[76] Interview, author with Wyn Thomas, Head of Welsh Programming, Swansea Sound, Ltd., in Swansea, Wales, 27 May 1980.

[77] For a complete account, see: W. J. Howell, Jr., "Britain's Fourth Television Channel and the Welsh Language Controversy," *Journal of Broadcasting* 25(2), Spring 1981.

[78] Jones, p. 30. (Cf. Note 65).

[79] Patrick Campbell, "SuperTed Champions the New Welsh Broadcaster," *TV World*, May/June 1983, p. 10.

[80] Howell, "Britain's Fourth Television Channel . . .", pp. 135–137.

[81] *BBC Handbook 1980*, p. 82.

[82] Howell, "Bilingual Broadcasting . . . ," p. 40. (Cf. Note 64).

[83] *Ibid.*, pp. 40–42.

[84] Maurice Gorham, *Forty Years of Irish Broadcasting* (Dublin: RTE/The Talbot Press, Ltd., 1967), p. 35.

[85] *Ibid.*, p. 58.

[86] *Ibid.*, p. 311.

[87] Le Nollaig O'Gadhra, "Broadcasting in Irish: Problem or Opportunity?" *Irish Broadcasting Review*, No. 1, Spring 1978, pp. 33–34.

[88] *Report of the Television Commission, 1959* (Dublin: The Stationery Office, 1959), pp. 5–6.

[89] *Broadcasting Authority Act, 1960*, Section 17, No. 10 (Dublin: The Stationery Office, 1976).

[90] Brian MacAongusa, "The Development of Raidio na Gaeltachta," *Irish Broadcasting Review*, No. 8, Summer 1980, p. 35.

[91] Broadcasting Review Committee, *Report 1974* (Dublin: The Stationery Office, 1974), p. 86.

[92] *Broadcasting Authority (Amendment) Act, 1976*, Section 17 (Dublin: The Stationery Office, 1976).

[93] Louis McRedmond, "Growth and Growing Pains in Irish Broadcasting," *EBU Review* III(4), July 1979, pp. 21–24.

[94] Howell, "Bilingual Broadcasting . . . ," p. 46.

[95] *RTE Annual Report 1981* (Dublin: Radio Telefis Eireann, 1981).

[96] *RTE Annual Report 1980* (Dublin: Radio Telefis Eireann, 1980).

[97] P. J. Moriarty, Chairman, RTE, "Broadcasting in the Eighties," an address to the Public Relations Institute of Ireland, in Dublin, 2 December 1980.

[98] McRedmond, p. 21.

[99] "Irish-Language Content on Television to be Increased," *EBU Review* XXXI(2), March 1980, pp. 37–38.

[100] Moriarty speech.

[101] Howkins (Cf. Note 1). All information on Basque broadcasting was taken from this source.

[102] *The World Almanac and Book of Facts 1981* (New York: Newspaper Enterprise Association, Inc., 1980), p. 577.

[103] Jorge Wolodarsky and Jose Maria Villagrossa, "New Channels Shaping Up," *TV World*, May/June 1984, pp. 42–43.

[104] WRTH 1984, pp. 124–126 and 409.

[105] Heinz Schollenberger, "The Regionalization of Television News in Switzerland," *EBU Review* XXXIV(2), March 1983, pp. 33–35.

[106] "Project for the Definitive Introduction of a Teletext Service," *EBU Review* XXXIV(3), May 1983, p. 46.

[107] "An Experimental English-Language Radio Programme for the Geneva Area," *EBU Review* XXXIV(3), May 1983, p. 46.

[108] Paulu, p. 460. Cf. Note 58.

[109] *Information please . . .* , pp. 277–278.

[110] Gertrude Joch Robinson, *Tito's Maverick Media: The Politics of Mass Communication in Yugoslavia* (Urbana: The University of Illinois Press, 1977), p. 191.

[111] David M. Abshire, *International Broadcasting: A New Dimension of Western Diplomacy* (Beverly Hills, CA: Sage, The Washington Papers, No. 35, 1976), p. 73.

[112] Paulu, p. 476.

[113] Robinson, pp. 6 and 206ff.

[114] WRTH 1984, pp. 151–153 and 410–411.

[115] Paulu, pp. 465–470 and 474ff.

[116] Tomo Martelanc, "Television in Yugoslavia: Content and Usage," *InterMedia* 13(4/5), July/September 1985, pp. 79–80.

[117] "Yugoslavia Cuts Imports," *TV World*, December 1983/January 1984, p. 5.

[118] Sydney W. Head (Ed.), *Broadcasting in Africa: A Continental Survey of Radio and Television* (Philadelphia, PA: Temple University Press, 1974), pp. 350–351.

[119] *Ibid.*, pp. 406–411.

[120] Douglas A. Boyd, *Broadcasting in the Arab World: A Survey of Radio and Television in the Middle East* (Philadelphia, PA: Temple University Press, 1982), p. 5.

[121] Prosser, pp. 104–105. (Cf. Note 2).

[122] R. Arnold Gibbons, in Head, pp. 107–113.

[123] Christopher Kolade, in Head, pp. 78ff.

[124] WRTH 1984, pp. 168 and 414.

[125] *Ibid.*, pp. 177 and 416.

[126] Edward M. Moyo, in Head, pp. 72–74.

[127] John Kugblenu, in Head, pp. 78 and 89ff.

[128] WRTH 1984, pp. 162 and 412.

[129] Gibbons, pp. 113–114.

[130] WRTH 1984, pp. 169 and 414.

[131] Timothy Green, in Head, pp. 11ff.

[132] Head, pp. 399 and 403.

[133] Boyd, p. 24.

[134] "Tunisia Inaugurates Second Channel," *TV World*, July 1982, p. 8.

[135] T. L. de Koning, "Broadcasting in the Republic of South Africa," in McCavitt, pp. 9–24. (Cf. Note 18).

[136] "Trilingual South African Service," *TV World*, May/June, 1983, p. 30.

PART III

PREVIEWING AND REVIEWING
WORLD BROADCASTING

Telecommunication toward the Twenty-First Century: International Broadcasting via Shortwave and Satellite

The communication satellite is revolutionizing broadcasting everywhere in (and indeed beyond) the world. National broadcasters and policymakers are understandably ambivalent, however, about the proliferation of direct broadcast satellites. Most see DBS as having a number of strengths and weaknesses. Their advantages include: cost-effectiveness in reaching large masses of people spread over great distances and many time zones; high quality transmission of scores of audio and video channels, independent of location or terrain conditions and relatively free from sunspot interference; and unexcelled viability as a mode for facilitating international understanding. Among the disadvantages of DBS are: inaccessibility in case of repair; the necessity for relatively expensive receiving equipment; inequities in national allocations of orbits and spectrum space; unsuitability for serving local programming needs or providing public participation; and a host of thorny political problems attending their ability to intrude into sovereign territories and assault national cultures with competing sources of foreign programming.[1]

The implications of communication satellites in general, and the direct broadcast satellite in particular, are far reaching. Political and cultural response time worldwide lags far behind the pace of technological innovation and diffusion, in telecommunication as in other fields. Consider these points. Each nation has, by international agreement, sovereign control over its own broadcasting services and territory; hence, many nations want veto control over all programming reaching their citizens via satellites. Third World countries, for example, are concerned about the one-way nature of programming flow and news coverage from the industrialized nations. And the communist states are particularly reluctant to have their people exposed to Western life styles, values, and ideology.

Historically, problems of interference, propaganda, and the protection of programming content have been mostly bilateral concerns, typically between adjacent states. With DBS, nations will be able to send programs around the world, but with no intervening ground control over their reception. Relatedly, the DBS will impact significantly on national television systems, by competing with them and lessening the need for earth stations and rebroadcasting transmitters to a great degree.[2]

This chapter addresses in some detail the technical, legal, cultural, and operational aspects of shortwave and satellite broadcasting—the two most effective media of international mass communication. Specifically, it

1. examines the uses of shortwave radio as a means of external broadcasting and propaganda by selected nations;
2. surveys the global, regional, and national broadcast satellite systems now in operation or planned for the near future;
3. discusses the regulatory issues and framework guiding the allocation and use of the electromagnetic spectrum and outer space for international broadcasting purposes;
4. identifies and compares the most significant policy implications of DBS for national broadcasters, cultures, audiences, and governments.

THE TECHNICAL PARAMETERS
OF SHORTWAVE BROADCASTING

Shortwave broadcasting uses a dozen bands of frequencies between 2,300 KHZ and 26,100 KHZ. The four bands at the lower end of the frequency range are called the Tropical Bands, in that they are used mainly for domestic broadcasting by a belt of nations on either side of the Equator in Latin America, Africa, Asia, and the Pacific.[3] The next eight bands of ascending SW frequencies are occupied increasingly by powerful international broadcasters. These stations are usually operated by national governments interested in reaching foreign audiences with programming in the various languages of the targeted listeners. It should be noted that the *higher* frequencies provide more effective conditions for transmission and reception during *daylight* hours, while the *lower* frequency bands are better *after dark*. Table 8-1 lists the HF bands assigned for Shortwave broadcasting, including the additional 850 KHZ allocated by the ITU in 1979 but not for use until the late 1980s or early 1990s.

Shortwave, despite enjoying the advantages of being a truly global medium of mass telecommunication, is plagued with a number of constraints associated with the earth's rotation cycle. Several of these need to be explained, since the vagaries characteristic of SW transmitting and receiving have precursory relevance to direct satellite broadcasting.

First, the problem of time zone differentials between countries and continents, broadcaster and listener, require that programming schedules adhere to a standardized and international measure of time—a kind of world clock. SW broadcasters have overcome this constraint by using a world time standard called Coordinated Universal Time (UTC), formerly known as Greenwich Mean Time (GMT).

A second problem is that SW broadcasters must continually switch frequencies and activate alternative transmitters at various locations every few hours, as a means of adapting to the constant changes in ionospheric conditions caused by

Table 8-1   Present and Future Shortwave
Broadcasting in MHZ and Meter Bands
and Ranges in KHZ

KiloHertz	MegaHertz Band	Meter Band
H.F. Broadcasting Bands		
2,300–2,495	2	120[a]
3,200–3,400	3	90[a]
3,900–4,000	4	75[b]
4,750–5,060	5	60[a]
5,950–6,200	6	49
7,100–7,300	7	41[c]
9,500–9,775	9	31
11,700–11,975	11	25
15,100–15,450	15	19
17,700–17,900	17	16
21,450–21,750	21	13
25,600–26,100	26	11
WARC-79 Additional High Frequency Broadcasting Allocations[d]		
9,775–9,900		
11,650–11,700		
11,975–12,050		
13,600–13,800		
15,450–15,600		
17,550–17,700		
21,750–21,850		

[a]Tropical Bands, for use only in designated tropical zones.

[b]Not used for broadcasting in the Western Hemisphere. Only the segment 3,950–4,000 kHz is used in Europe and Africa.

[c]Not used for broadcasting in the Western Hemisphere.

[d]The Conference reduced the present 26 MHz band by 70 kHz to 25,670–26,100 kHz.

Source: World Radio TV Handbook 1982, p. 44.

the earth's daylight and darkness rotation cycle. This is particularly critical to the major international operations like the Voice of America, Radio Moscow, and the BBC World Service, who routinely transmit on several frequency bands at once, often with different programs in several different languages. As their target areas of coverage alternate between daytime and darkness, the SW broadcaster must shift to frequencies and transmitters appropriate to reaching their audiences.

Finally, sunspot activity, which runs in cycles of approximately 11 years, directly affects the High Frequency band and the effectiveness of SW broadcasting. The relationship is a direct one: high sunspot activity improves Shortwave reception, and low activity diminishes it. The current activity cycle is rated accordingly: 1976 Low/Minimum . . . 1980–81 High/Maximum . . . 1987 Low/Minimum.[4]

Obviously, these complications also make SW listening (called DX-ing, for long distance reception) more difficult than the passivity apropos of listening to AM and FM broadcasts. DXers likewise must follow a particular station's frequency changes throughout the 24-hour broadcast day by scanning the appropriate SW bands until optimal reception is achieved. And SW reception is seldom as "clear and clean" as listening to AM and FM stations. But such inconveniences are part of the DX-ing ethos, and are usually regarded as challenges. The serious SW hobbyist may collect QSL verification cards by writing to SW stations and confirming the frequency, time (in UTC), and date a program was received. Often a formal reception report is used, providing the broadcaster with valuable engineering and coverage information about the proportionate signal strength, interference, atmospheric noise, propagation, and overall merit of the broadcast. The payoff comes when someone in, say, Buffalo QSLs a broadcast in English from Radio Baghdad.

SHORTWAVE AND PROPAGANDA

International shortwave broadcasting historically has been used for promotional and propagandistic purposes. Of course, the world's nearly 150 international radio stations serve all manner of masters—political, religious, military, commercial—through programming intended to inform, educate, entertain, advance foreign policy, project positive national images, convert listeners to causes and faiths, coerce, threaten, boast, intimidate, and sell goods, services, and ideas.[5] It is the latter item, the promotion of ideas or ideologies, that distinguishes propaganda from the other forms of communication.

Propaganda, the word and the deed, has been defined many ways over the years.[6] This book regards *propaganda as the systematic attempt though mass communication media to influence and manipulate the thinking and behavior of target audiences in the interests of an organized ideological group.*

The late John Whitton organized propaganda into categories based on various purposes or normative subdivisions. One was *Subversive Propaganda,* which may be used for revolution, liberation, and disruption by inciting the status quo. A second kind, called *Defamatory Propaganda,* is used "to degrade, revile, or insult foreign states, their institutions, leaders, and people." This was typical of Nazi propaganda, but is still found today among the most primitive and fanatical of ideological and religious groups, as well as some major world leaders. *Propaganda For War,* a third category, is used to incite factions within other nations to overthrow their governments or to rally forces within one's own nation to support a foreign war effort that the leadership is committed to. Whitton's last type is *Private Propaganda,* meaning hostile communication by individuals or groups independent of government and thus legally free to publicly attack and "defame foreign states, their leaders, peoples, and institutions" through the mass media. Whitton cites support for the Irish Republican Army by some American media as an example of private propaganda with international ramifications.[7]

Two examples of Defamatory Propaganda were provided by President Reagan during his first term in office. Following the 1983 downing of a Korean airliner by Soviet jets over their own territory, Reagan went on American TV and denounced the USSR as "an evil empire." Then, during a warm-up for his weekly radio polemics on August 11, 1984, The "Great Communicator" tested his microphone levels with the following statement: "My fellow Americans, I am pleased to tell you I have signed legislation to outlaw Russia forever. We begin bombing in five minutes." He later dismissed the quip as a "joke," but the USIA regarded it as a propaganda faux pas of the first order, the proof being supplied by press reactions from America's closest allies.

Lawrence C. Soley has made some important legal distinctions between clandestine stations and other types sometimes confused with them. *Clandestine* stations operate illegally and broadcast political/revolutionary messages. *Pirate* stations are also illegal, but usually apolitical. *Foreign service* broadcasts are political or revolutionary in nature but are transmitted by legally licensed stations, such as international shortwave operations. Finally, *de facto administration* stations may be legal or illegal and invariably transmit political messages, but they are operated by governing bodies whose legality may be doubtful, like governments-in-exile.

There were 43 clandestine radio stations operational in the world during 1981. Only two were in Europe: Our Radio (Voice of the Turkish Communist Party), and Radio Solidarity in Poland. Africa had eight such stations, and Asia nine. Of the ten clandestine stations on the air in Latin America, seven were in Cuba, two in El Salvador (Radio Venceremos and Radio Liberacion), and one in Nicaragua (the anti-Sandinista station, Radio 15 de Septiembre). The Middle East claimed the most clandestine broadcasters, with 14—three Afghan Mujahedin stations in Afghanistan, three revolutionary operations in Iraq, and eight political and religious stations in volatile Iran.[8]

A contemporary though more subtle brand of propaganda being practiced with some success by the USSR in the 1980s is *disinformation* (dezinformatsia). This may be defined as efforts to control media in foreign countries through the use of communist parties and front organizations, clandestine radio broadcasting, personal and economic blackmail, and political influence operations. These active measures of disinformation are planned and implemented by an organized structure designed to be used in pursuit of Soviet foreign policy and strategic objectives. Examples range from the planting of false stories in Western news media, to covert involvement in the European peace movement, to coercing Soviet exiles—like Stalin's daughter and Red Army disserters—into returning home to Mother Russia if they valued the lives of their loved ones.[9]

Table 8-2 lists 31 countries in order of the number of hours each devotes to external broadcasting annually. A brief summary and comparison of the top five nations' SW services follows.

Table 8-2   Estimated Total Program Hours per Week of External Broadcasters in Selected Nations from 1950 to 1982

	1950	1960	1965	1970	1975	1980	1981	1982
USSR	533	1015	1417	1908	2001	2094	2114	2180
United States of America	497	1495	1832	1907	2029	1901	1959	1975
Chinese People's Republic	66	687	1027	1267	1423	1350	1304	1423
German Federal Republic	—	315	671	779	767	804	786	786
United Kingdom (BBC)	643	589	667	723	719	719	741	729
North Korea	—	159	392	330	455	597	581	587
Albania	26	63	154	487	490	560	567	578
Egypt	—	301	505	540	635	546	518	544
Cuba	—	—	325	320	311	424	459	420
East Germany	—	185	308	274	342	375	427	415
India	116	157	175	271	326	389	396	396
Australia	181	257	299	350	379	333	336	336
Poland	131	232	280	334	340	337	130	335
Nigeria	—	—	63	62	61	170	342	322
Netherlands	127	178	235	335	400	289	290	293
Bulgaria	30	117	154	164	197	236	289	289
Czechoslovakia	119	196	189	202	253	255	283	283
Iran	12	24	118	155	154	175	238	280
France	198	326	183	200	108	125	125	275
Spain	68	202	276	251	312	239	253	274
Japan	—	203	249	259	259	259	263	259
Turkey	40	77	91	88	172	199	206	221
Portugal	46	133	273	295	190	214	214	214
Israel	—	91	92	158	198	210	210	212
South Africa	—	63	84	150	141	183	205	205
Romania	30	159	163	185	190	198	204	201
Italy	170	205	160	165	170	169	169	169
Canada	85	80	81	98	159	134	143	147
Sweden	28	114	142	140	154	155	145	144
Hungary	76	120	121	105	127	127	127	127
Yugoslavia	80	70	78	76	82	72	72	72

i)   USSR includes Radio Moscow, Radio Station Peace & Progress and regional stations.
ii) USA includes Voice of America (996 hours per week), Radio Free Europe (544 hours per week) and Radio Liberty (465 hours per week). (1982 figures).
iii) German Federal Republic includes Deutsche Welle (533 hours per week) and Deutschlandfunk (253 hours per week). (1982 figures).
iv) The list includes fewer than half the world's external broadcasters. Among those excluded are Taiwan, Vietnam, Sourth Korea, and various international commercial and religious stations, as well as clandestine radio stations. Certain countries transmit part of their domestic output externally on shortwaves: these broadcasts are mainly also excluded.
v)   All figures for December or nearest available month.

Source: BBC Annual Report and Handbook 1984, p. 143

The Voice of America

While most international shortwave radio services evolved out of their nation's domestic broadcasting organizations, the Voice of America (VOA) was created by the state for the separate and express purpose of being the official propaganda station of the U.S. government. The VOA began operations in February 1942 as an instrument of the Office of War Information, established by President Franklin D. Roosevelt to assist American efforts during World War II.

A scaled down version of the VOA continued to offer international broadcasts in various languages after WWII under the control of the U.S. State Department. As the Cold War with the USSR heated up and the U.S. became involved in combat in Korea in the early 1950s, official interest in the VOA's propaganda value peaked.[10]

The United States Information Agency (USIA) was created in 1953 by the Eisenhower Administration to convey a true picture of American society, culture, institutions, and governmental policies to the rest of the world through personal contacts, cultural and educational exchanges, and a wide variety of electronic and print media. Under the Carter Administration it was renamed the U.S. International Communication Agency (USICA), but reverted to its former USIA designation after President Reagan took office in 1981.

The VOA's programming mission was clarified by a 1976 act of Congress. Its three principles mandated the VOA to: (a) be a consistent, reliable, and authoritative source of accurate, objective, and comprehensive news; (b) represent all of American society by presenting a balanced and comprehensive range of thought and activities in the U.S.; and (c) present U.S. policies clearly and effectively, including responsible discussion and opinion on American policies. Besides information, VOA programs feature sports, humor, interviews, popular music, and jazz.[11]

The VOA became a revolving door under the Reagan regime, going through four directors in as many years. The first, James Conkling, was not appointed until 5 months into the Reagan Presidency, and left in March 1982. His successor, John Hughes, headed VOA only 5 months before becoming the State Department's chief spokesman. Next came Kenneth Tomlinson, a 39-year-old neoconservative who resigned in July 1984 to return to the *Reader's Digest* as editor. Former NBC newsman Gene Pell took Tomlinson's place at the helm.

During President Reagan's first term, the VOA underwent a facilities facelift, had its annual budget increased to over $100 million, and saw its programming mission greatly politicized. Examples of the latter came in the form of censored newscasts and commentaries in lieu of straightforward journalism.[12] These practices were initiated by Charles Wick, a millionaire friend of President Reagan and head of the United States Information Agency which runs the Voice.

Similar censorship also has infected Radio Free Europe (RFE) and Radio Liberty (RL), both of which failed to report Reagan's September 1984 microphone test "joke" about outlawing and bombing Russia. As a result, listeners behind the Iron Curtain heard the story first from Radio Moscow and stations in Eastern Europe, thus enhancing their credibility at the expense of the American SW services. The blatant ideological tone of the VOA and RFE/RL has many people worried, since the trend away from objectivity will render these U.S. voices no more believable to foreign audiences than the propaganda broadcasts from totalitarian states.[13]

But the politicalization also spread to VOA's news division, which witnessed the systematic replacement of career journalists by inexperienced Reagan-appointed ideologues during 1981 and 1982. News items reported domestically—such as the CIA sending arms to Afghanistan, and the assassination of a Turkish diplomat in San Francisco—were censored from VOA's airwaves because they contradicted U.S. policy or embarrassed the Administration. Furthermore, official memos implored VOA news writers always to take the "national interest" into account when writing news stories. Hence, U.S.-backed guerrillas were called "freedom fighters," American fighter planes became simply "Air Force jets," and the Soviet President had to be referred to as a "ruler."[14]

Perhaps the most heavy-handed American attempt at propaganda was the international TV spectacular, "Let Poland Be Poland," an idea again hatched by Charles Wick following the 1981 declaration of martial law in that country by Premier Jaruzelski. Wick, who wrote and produced "Snow White and the Three Stooges" for Twentieth Century Fox years earlier, brought together a cast of old and new Reaganites—ranging from Bob Hope, Frank Sinatra, Margaret Thatcher, and Helmut Schmidt—to produce a 90-minute videotape for airing abroad. As propaganda, however, "Let Poland Be Poland" proved to be an embarrassingly bad melodrama which missed its target literally as well as figuratively, since the program was seen only in Western Europe, which hardly needs to be lectured about the evils of communism by Hollywood producers. Audiences behind the Iron Curtain heard only the show's truncated sound track via VOA transmitters.

Television critics in both Britain and France panned the extravaganza. The BBC said it "raised smiles in sophisticated Europe;" the London *Times* called it "almost as dull as an East European propaganda film;" France's *Le Monde* labelled it "a bore." Veteran VOA staffers were appalled at such efforts to turn the agency into a propaganda machine in violation of its long tradition of travelling the high road of credibility.[15]

Another mission of the USIA and VOA was to design a public relations campaign in 1983 to win support for President Reagan's nuclear arms policies among West European youth. The goal was to get this "successor generation" to forget America's bad Vietnam and Watergate image and, instead, to view Reagan as a kind of prince of peace.[16]

By 1984, the VOA was broadcasting an average of 950 hours per week in English and 41 other languages to over 80 million listeners via a satellite-fed global network of some 105 transmitters. It maintains 32 domestic studios—26 at Master Control in Washington, DC, three in New York City, and one each in Chicago, Los Angeles, and Miami. The VOA has 16 domestic transmitters in Greenville, North Carolina, eight in Delano, California, six near Bethany, Ohio, and one in Marathon, Florida.[17] The latter site is used by the Voice's latest acquisition, Radio Marti, whose 50-kilowatt AM transmitter targets broadcasts to Cuba on 1180 KHZ.

Radio Marti

Radio Marti, a pet project of the Reagan Administration, was put before Congress in the form of a bill in early 1982 asking that $10 million be authorized to establish a U.S. propaganda station named after Jose Marti, a Cuban patriot. Congress approved $7.5 million in August to start Radio Marti, providing it be operated under VOA control and broadcast on 1180 KHZ.[18]

Radio Free Europe and Radio Liberty

Two other prominent voices of America heard abroad via shortwave are Radio Free Europe (RFE) and Radio Liberty (RL). Though sometimes confused with the VOA, RFE and RL began in 1950 and 1951, respectively, as supposedly unofficial instruments of U.S. foreign policy that relied upon private contributions from American citizens wishing to support their efforts to free listeners behind the Iron Curtain from communist domination. This early portrayal of the two stations being privately funded turned out to be a lie. In reality, the RFE and RL operations were both secretly financed and directed by the Central Intelligence Agency until 1971, when the CIA was forced to sever its ties with both stations following several years of Congressional investigations.[19]

In 1976, Radio Free Europe and Radio Liberty merged into a consolidated organization RFE/RL, Inc., though each remains a separate broadcasting division. The new entity operates under the authority of the Board of International Broadcasting, which receives an annual allocation from Congress.[20] RFE/RL received over $90 million in 1984 to broadcast nearly 1100 hours in 21 languages via 46 transmitters located in West Germany, Portugal, and Spain. Their corporate headquarters and news bureau are in Washington, and program production centers are maintained in New York and Munich. Radio Free Europe broadcasts to Eastern Europe in six languages—Bulgarian, Czech, Slovak, Hungarian, Polish, and Romanian. Radio Liberty targets its programs only to the people of the Soviet Union, in Russian and 14 other major regional languages. Most announcers heard on both services are natives of East Europe and the USSR who have immigrated to the West; thus, they speak in the common vernaculars of their listeners. Jamming RFE/RL broadcasts is commonplace, but also tends to ebb and flow in response to East–West relations and tensions.[21]

But the Soviets have used other methods besides jamming to hamper the missions of RFE and RL. The most successful has been pressuring the International Olympic Committee into banning RFE/RL reporters from the 1976 Winter

Olympics in Innsbruck, Austria and again at the 1984 games at Sarajevo, Yugoslavia. The president of RFE/RL, former U.S. Senator and State Department official James Buckley, stated in 1984 that the Soviet Union objects to their sports coverage mainly on the grounds that it breaks the state monopolies on information inside the Eastern Bloc. However, the Soviets claim that RFE/RL are not legitimate broadcasting organizations, since they transmit only into foreign countries rather than to listeners in their homeland.[22]

The BBC External Services
The British Broadcasting Corporation began the world's first regularly scheduled international radio station in late 1932. Called the Empire Service, it offered programs in English via shortwave to listeners, particularly British subjects, living outside the UK. The service took on a more explicit political mission in 1938 as the propaganda and military machinery of Nazi Germany moved into high gear. Several foreign language services were developed as part of the BBC's external broadcasting activities during World War II. In 1948, the BBC's Overseas and European operations were merged to form the External Services, a permanent international SW system to be funded on a grant-in-aid basis by Parliament. Being independent of government ownership makes the BBC External Services unique among the world's international broadcasters. This, no doubt, also helps explain its exalted reputation for accurate, impartial, and credible newscasts, as well as the wide variety of quality entertainment programming. Nevertheless, the BBC's foreign operations work closely with the British Foreign Office to insure that the government's official policies are correctly presented to the outside world.[23]

The current program schedule of the BBC External Service is dominated by news, editorials, commentaries, sports, popular and classical music, comedy, and drama, both light and serious. Besides broadcasting the most authoritative and trusted news reports of any international SW service in the world, BBC external programming is distinguished by its high performance, production, and technical standards. It is one of the few SW broadcasters to present request music shows, excellent radio drama, documentaries, in-depth interviews, and features on cultural and artistic topics. And where else can a SW DX-er hear an author such as John Le Carre do a serialized reading of one of his novels?[24]

By the mid-1980s, the BBC External Services division was receiving an annual income from the Treasury of 63 million pounds, a sum equivalent to that allotted to VOA but considerably less than Radio Moscow's yearly stipend. The BBC's budget allows its 24-hour English-language World Service and ten other regional services to broadcast approximately 730 hours per week in 39 languages. Financial restrictions under the Thatcher government had clouded the future of external broadcasting by 1984, although the BBC enjoys continued support by Parliament, the press, and the public abroad.

The BBC maintains what is perhaps the world's best Monitoring Service of international broadcasting besides the Foreign Broadcast Information Service (FBIS) in the United States. Radio and TV programs are monitored, taped, translated, analyzed, and excerpted for rebroadcast by listening stations in Britain and elsewhere. Foreign governments often call upon the BBC Monitoring Service for information about events in nations diplomatically closed to them.

The BBC also commissions audience research and opinion surveys about SW listening in many parts of the world. This is done primarily to ascertain the popularity of the BBC External Services, but also generates much data of interest to other international broadcasters. Recent results show the BBC leads the world's major SW stations in listenership by rating ahead of the VOA, Radio Moscow, Deutsche Welle, and Radio Peking in most of Africa, Asia, and the Middle East. In Latin America, however, the BBC Spanish Service placed third behind the VOA and Radio Moscow in a 1980 survey, but tied with VOA in English-language broadcasts. The BBC receives over 350,000 letters from listeners each year. In addition, it sends questionnaires out to audience samples each year, with nearly 20,000 completed and returned in 1980.[25]

Deutsche Welle

Deutsche Welle ("German Wave") was established in 1953 as a kind of first cousin to the BBC World Service. DW began broadcasting only in German, but programs in English, French, Spanish, Portuguese, and Arabic were added within 5 years. Its foreign services output grew to 26 languages during the 1960s.[26]

By 1984, DW was offering 93 programs daily in 34 languages via its two domestic (Julich and Wertachtal) and six foreign-based SW transmitters (in Rwanda, Portugal, Antigua, Malta, Monserrat, and Sri Lanka.) Its programs emphasize domestic and world news, West German culture and music, and features about economic and social life within the country.[27]

DW's annual budget is authorized by the federal parliament and allocated through the Interior Ministry. This amounted to about $100 million by the mid-1980s. Despite this direct funding from government, it is interesting to note that DW enjoys more autonomy from officialdom than most other shortwave services, including the VOA and even the BBC.[28]

Radio Beijing

The PRC's only overseas SW service, Radio International, is known to the world's DX-ers by its identification, "This is Radio Peking." Having begun broadcasting in seven languages in 1950, Radio Beijing was second only to Radio Moscow as an international SW station by 1984—transmitting over 1400 hours a week in 39 foreign languages and four Chinese dialects. Its biggest problem today is a lack of places around the world to locate transmitters. Since breaking off relations with Albania in recent years, China has found it difficult for Radio Beijing to cover Europe with its remaining relay stations in Xingian and Tibet.

Radio Beijing devotes about 80% of its programming to cultural information about China, news, and commentary. The rest is indigenous music. Its foreign programming sections, in order of importance, are Japanese, English, and French. Two things distinguish Radio Beijing from its communist counterparts: it rarely discusses politics, and its "air personality" is pleasant and upbeat.[29]

Radio Moscow

Radio Moscow is the most extensive and best-financed SW broadcasting service in the world today. Having begun in 1929 with broadcasts in Russian, German, French, and English, it was transmitting in 75 foreign languages to all continents and virtually all nations by 1984. Radio Moscow defines its mission as striving "to promote mutual understanding and strengthen good relations between the USSR and all nations and to inform the world public about the Soviet Union, about its domestic and foreign policies, about the Soviet way of life." Through a vast global network of SW transmitters, Radio Moscow was broadcasting an estimated 178 hours of programming daily, or nearly 2200 hours a week, as of 1984.[30] The annual budget is roughly three times that of the VOA, and RFE/RL.

Radio Moscow's programming is dominated by news and information, most of it provided by the TASS news agency and NOVOSTI correspondents around the world. Music is used primarily for continuity between program segments or as brief interludes. Much of it is classic Russian, but one increasingly hears ersatz jazz and rock. Features on Soviet achievements and lifestyles are common and rarely last longer than 15 minutes. Missing are live or taped news reports by correspondents stationed around the USSR or in other countries. Listeners will hear very little spontaneous conversation on Radio Moscow; virtually every word aired has been scripted. One notable exception is the program "Moscow Mailbag," in which announcers Vladimir Posner and Joe Adamov answer letters from foreign listeners in perfect U.S.-English, using an ad lib style and often resorting to frankness and humor.[31]

Another shortwave outlet, Radio Station Peace and Progress—called "The Voice of Soviet Public Opinion" because it nominally is run by "Soviet public organizations"—broadcasts about 160 hours weekly in a dozen languages and three Chinese dialects to Europe, Asia, Africa, the Near and Middle East, Latin America, and mainland China. It uses SW frequencies occupied at other hours by Radio Moscow is and targeted to the same geographic areas.[32]

One of the more interesting public gaffes on Radio Moscow occurred in May of 1983 when an English-language announcer, Vladimir Danchev, startled listeners by referring to the Soviet Troops in Afghanistan as "invaders," a term he used twice in 5 days. He was finally removed from Radio Moscow's airwaves after saying: "The population of Afghanistan plays an increasing role in defending the country's territory against Soviet occupiers." How the blunder happened is open to speculation. One rumour had it that Danchev might have been ordered to read the bogus bulletin by the internal political enemies of Konstantin Chernenko, propaganda chief of the Politboro, in hopes of getting him fired. Cherenko not only survived the incident but went on to succeed Premier Yuri Andropov as head of state.[33]

Some Comparisons and Contrasts

International broadcasting scholar Donald Browne studied the similarities and differences in the organizational structure, function and news selection process of newsrooms at the VOA, BBC, and Deutsche Welle in 1980. He found that all three had centralized news operations and faced two common problems: (a) accurately translating news into dozens of languages, and (b) recruiting journalists with competence in international affairs so as to avoid "domestic bias" in their newscasts. The VOA and BBC speak to the world in scores of languages but with a unified news voice, while DW's various program units have more latitude in choosing which of the central newsroom's stories will be aired. Also, all three SW broadcasters have editors-in-chief, writing staffs, and reporters, although the BBC's newsroom staff of 120 is twice the size of the VOA's and over three times that of DW. Each relies heavily on similar news sources, such as various national and regional wire services, their own reporters, and reports gleaned from monitoring other international and domestic broadcasts from around the world. All are likewise plagued by news staff turnovers and the recruitment pressures they create.

Browne was surprised that many news personnel had little or no foreign travel experience, except for the BBC, which provides continual if brief trips abroad to its staff on a rotating basis. Differences also exist in terms of how each reviews its programming for accuracy, quality, and effectiveness. DW hires outside program reviewers. The VOA has an internal review procedure that sometimes relies on outside authorities. The BBC allows each program unit to evaluate scripts and tapes of its broadcasts, but has no formal reviewers per se. The study confirmed that the BBC is held in the highest esteem by SW broadcasters in other countries for its excellence as a source of information.[34]

The 1984 selection of Gene Pell, a veteran broadcasting professional, to head the VOA signals that the Reagan Administration finally realized the agency's severe morale problem after 3 years of incompetent stewardship under a trio of ideologues. The turnover also created a public relations problem for VOA, as outside observers and listeners worldwide have sensed its instability and diminished political influence as a credible international radio station. Pell will be supported by two deputies—another professional broadcaster from outside VOA, and a career foreign service officer.[35] The VOA also contracted in 1984 to build new transmitters in five countries as part of a $1.5 billion expansion program designed to extend its coverage into territories previously not reached, overcome jamming, and increase the number of foreign languages it broadcasts from 42 to 60 within 5 years.[36]

Julian Hale, in his classic book *Radio Power,* examined the use of radio for propaganda purposes by Nazi Germany and traced its influence to the contemporary styles employed by Soviet and Western governments. Although Soviet propaganda has improved greatly since the Stalinist era, Hale assesses Radio Moscow as still suffering "from ponderousness, parochialism and partiality." It also sounds "defensive." As a vehicle of propaganda, Hale claims that Radio Moscow "has never tried to build up a faithful audience through achieving high standards of credibility like the BBC has." On the contrary, the Soviets condemn the term "objective," preferring instead to propagate a kind of socialist truth based on their own perceptions rather than on "the facts of the case." In this respect, Hale equates Radio Moscow with Radio Vatican. The VOA and RFE/RL fall somewhere between partisanship and objectivity, a practice Hale suggests has had "unhappy results."[37]

External Broadcasting By Satellite

It is inevitable that the world's major international shortwave broadcasters have shown unusual interest in broadcasting satellites as a means of enhancing the coverage of their shortwave services and supplementing them with transnational and intercontinental television transmissions. The USIA, in fact, entered the world of foreign television in 1983 by initiating a weekly 30-minute news feed, *TV Satellite File,* to broadcasters in other countries. Clients for the program include networks in Austria (ORF), Brazil (Globo and Manchete), Britain (BBC and ITN), Canada (CBC and CTV), France (TF-1 and Antenna-2), Germany (ARD and ZDF), Israel (IBA), Italy (RAI-1), Japan (NHK, Fugi, Nippon, Asahi, and TBS), Mexico (Televisa), Norway (NRK), Venezuela (Venevision) and Yugoslavia (TV Belgrade).

Material for *TV Satellite File* is produced by local TV stations in America and purchased by the USIA on a negotiated "fair payment" basis. The idea was the brainchild of Director Charles Wick, and is intended to involve U.S. commercial stations in telling "America's story" to the world. Wick also convened a group of Hollywood filmmakers and corporation executives to procure and send American films and TV programs to U.S. embassies around the world, for showing to foreign audiences in hopes of giving them "a more complete picture of American society."[38]

In the wake of President Reagan's 1984 re-election, renewed attention is being given by NASA to the possible use of direct broadcast satellites in elliptical, polar, subsynchronous, and geostationary orbits to beam VOA programming to 15 designated zones worldwide. The use of satellites operating in the HF band could enable VOA and RFE/RF to improve the quality of their signals and override skywave jamming by the Soviet Union. The subject of jamming by the USSR, which renders half of the HF radio spectrum unusable, has been a highly sensitive one at the ITU—causing Western SW broadcasters to greatly increase their transmitting power to overcome it.

A 1983 study by the Massachusetts Institute of Technology points to the dilemma inherent in using the 26 MHZ band for DBS-radio broadcasting—namely, that it is wide open at present but there are few 26 MHZ receivers in the world. Another MIT report on the subject is forthcoming. One prospect is for converting up to 100 UHF channels now reserved for DBS telecasting to a multi-nation radio common carrier system. The U.S. is, further, thinking of developing commercial international broadcasting carriers.[39] Imagine hearing: ''We'll be right back with more propaganda after these messages from our sponsors.''

Douglas Muggeridge, Managing Director of the BBC's External Services, announced an ambitious plan for a world satellite TV service in 1984. The first phase of the Muggeridge Plan would have the BBC broadcast 2 hours of programming daily to Europe and North America, 20 minutes of which would be news, via a fixed satellite system like Intelsat. The second phase would have the service extended worldwide via DBS, with 24 hours of programming each day. Muggeridge feels that the opposition to international satellite broadcasting will only grow in the UN and elsewhere, and that the BBC must not give in to misguided information policies of foreign countries but, instead, must ''add pictures to overseas broadcasting.''[40]

The USIA demonstrated a similar system in late 1983 called *Worldnet,* a global hookup of five satellites and a dozen earth stations capable of two-way video broadcasts. Worldnet, which received $7.6 million in funding in 1984, is divided into four regional systems—Euronet (Europe), Arnet (Latin America), Eanet (East Asia), and Afnet (Africa).[41]

TECHNICAL PARAMETERS OF BROADCAST SATELLITES

Communication satellites may be distinguished according to their respective functions. The *fixed satellite system* (FSS) relays telephone, data, and radio signals from one point to another (point-to-point) or to many other ground stations (multipoint). A *broadcast satellite system* (BSS) transmits radio and TV signals from a number of originating programming services to other terrestrial broadcast or cable transmitters. *Direct broadcast satellites* (DBS) beam radio and TV program signals from originating stations directly to homes via high-powered satellite transmitters. DBS thus allows people within the coverage area (*footprint*) of the satellite's broadcast signals to receive programming through their own umbrella-sized dish antenna directly from the satellite transmitter, rather than through the terrestrial transmission of a local station.

What makes DBS reception possible with a small parabolic dish antenna only 18 inches in diameter is the presence of a high-powered transmitter aboard the satellite with the capacity to deliver high quality program signals to every home within its footprint. The earlier FSS and BSS birds had much smaller transmitters, and thus larger dish antennas (from 6 to 30 feet in diameter) were required for adequate signal reception.[42]

DBS has been defined by the ITU as a ''radio-communication service in which signals transmitted or retransmitted by space stations are intended for direct reception by the general public.[43] Direct reception may occur through either an *individual* rooftop dish or by a *community* antenna.

The beaming of program signals from the originating stations up to the satellite is called *uplink;* the amplification and retransmission of the program signal from the satellite down to the ground stations or earth antenna is the *downlink.* Three Super High Frequency bands of the spectrum are currently used in satellite broadcasting—the C-Band (4/6 GHZ), the Ku-Band (11/14 GHZ) and the Ka-Band (18/30 GHZ). The lower of the two frequencies performs the Uplink Segment, and the higher ones are used in the Downlink Segment. The earliest genre of satellites can be found in the C-Band. Most current DBS utilize the Ku (pronounced as "cue") Band. The next generation will move up to the Ka-Band, though the range may extend much higher.

By 1984, the following DBS frequencies had been assigned on a worldwide basis:

11.7–12.5 GHZ to *Region 1* (Europe, Africa, the USSR, and Mongolia)
12.2–12.7 GHZ to *Region 2* (the Americas)
11.7–12.2 GHZ to *Region 3* (Asia and the Pacific)

Table 8-3 indicates how Europe's 11.7–12.5 GHZ band translates into 40 TV channel allocations.

Each information-carrying channel aboard a satellite is referred to as a *transponder.* The average broadcast satellite has capacity for 24 TV channels. It is not unusual for a DBS to require from 100 to 200 watts per transponder in order to deliver a quality TV signal (suitable for home viewing) to a small rooftop antenna, though some state-of-the-art DBS models perform well with far less amplification (20- to 30-watt channels). A simple relationship thus exists when it comes to space transmission and reception: the more powerful the satellite's transmitter, the smaller the earth station antenna can be.

Home reception requires that one be located within the footprint of a DBS, have a clear line of sight orientation between the rooftop dish antenna and the satellite, and be equipped with a *down converter* that changes the high-frequency microwave signals from the satellite into the lower frequencies used by conventional TV channels.[44] But new TV reception technologies are also on the way.

DBS, HDTV, and Enhanced Television

High Definition Television (HDTV) was developed in Japan several years ago by the SONY Corporation and NHK, its national broadcasting service, for use with DBS telecasting. HDTV technology is based on an 1125-line transmission standard that produces a TV picture as sharp as 35mm film on a theatre-size TV screen, having a larger width-to-height aspect ratio (5:3 instead of 4:3) than a regular TV picture tube. Despite offering a wider screen and stereophonic sound equal to a typical movie theatre, HDTV also has a number of disadvantages.

Table 8-3   TV Channels and Bands Allocated to DBS:
The European Example[a]

Ch	GHz	Ch	GHz	Ch	GHz
1	11.727 48	15	11.996 00	28	12.245 34
2	11.746 66	16	12.015 18	29	12.264 52
3	11.765 84	17	12.034 36	30	12.283 70
4	11.785 02	18	12.053 54	31	12.302 88
5	11.804 20	19	12.072 72	32	12.322 06
6	11.823 38	20	12.091 90	33	12.341 24
7	11.842 56	21	12.111 08	34	12.360 42
8	11.861 74	22	12.130 26	35	12.379 60
9	11.880 92	23	12.149 44	36	12.398 78
10	11.900 10	24	12.168 62	37	12.417 96
11	11.919 28	25	12.187 80	38	12.437 14
12	11.938 46	26	12.206 98	39	12.456 32
13	11.957 64	27	12.226 16	40	12.475 50
14	11.976 82				

[a]The band allocated to Direct Broadcasting Satellites (DBS) is in the range 11.7–12.5 GigaHerz. This is divided into 40 channels as follows (the freq. indicated is the Vision Freq):

Europe: Each ch. is allocated to a group of countries, which share the frequency by using different orbital positions and polarity. The following is a list of assignments mainly in We. & So. Europe.

France, San Marino, Turkey: Ch's 1, 5, 9, 13, 17.
Ireland, Germany (F.R.): Ch's 2, 6, 10, 14, 18.
Greece, Lichtenstein, Luxembourg, Portugal: Ch's 3, 7, 11, 15, 19.
Andorra, Austria, U.K.: Ch's 4, 8, 12, 16, 20.
Belgium, Cyprus, Monaco: Ch's 21, 25, 29, 33, 37.
Switzerland: Ch's 22, 26, 30, 34, 38.
Denmark: Ch's 12, 16, 20, 24, 36.
Finland: Ch's 2, 6, 10, 22, 26.
Iceland: Ch's 21, 23, 25, 27, 29, 31, 35, 37, 39.
Sweden: Ch's 4, 8, 30, 34, 40.
Norway: Ch's 14, 18, 28, 32, 38.
Italy: Ch's 24, 28, 32, 36, 40.
Netherlands/Spain/Vatican: Ch's 23, 27, 31, 35, 39.
Source: *World Radio TV Handbook 1984,* 397.

First, consumers will find it very expensive, two to three thousand dollars more than today's TV sets. Next, regulators will be faced with having to reallocate TV frequencies, since HDTV takes up to five times the spectrum space of current TV systems, with bandwidths of 30 MHZ instead of 6 MHZ. And broadcasters would have to purchase all new transmission equipment. Nevertheless, SONY has invested heavily in HDTV and plans to market it worldwide by 1990. Whether broadcasters and regulatory agencies adopt it for DBS use or not, HDTV will no doubt have playback value through cable, home video, and theatre systems.[45]

Another problem is that nations may have a difficult time agreeing to a world

HDTV production standard. Japan is on the cutting edge of an 1125 scanning line system with a 60 HZ field rate. America's standards-setting body, the Advanced Television Systems Committee (ATSC), has endorsed the SONY system, as has CBS. However, this 60 HZ version is being opposed in Europe by the EBU and the BBC, which prefer an 80 HZ field rate more compatible with the 50 HZ field frequencies used by their PAL and SECAM color standards. Moreover, the challenge of converting wideband HDTV into the narrower UHF and VHF channels of existing TV sets also needs to be met.[46]

America is facing this challenge through upgrading its antiquated 525-line/NTSC standard for TV signal and color transmission, in order to produce a new generation of receiver that hopes to compete favorably with HDTV without requiring a massive retooling of its current broadcasting infrastructure. In 1984, the ATSC studied ways to improve the NTSC standard. The group recommended that an "enhanced" 525-line system—based on the British MAC signal format and called "straw man"—be developed as the U.S. satellite broadcasting standard. A report on the Straw Man standard was sent to the International Radio Consultative Committee (CCIR), the ITU body charged with setting a world production standard for HDTV.[47]

Enhanced 525 offers multichannel TV sound capacity and digital circuitry. These two advances will allow for stereophonic telecasting, a third audio channel for a second-language translation of a soundtrack, and a computer-generated 1050-line TV picture being produced from a 525-line transmission. This is not to say that HDTV will not be available in the U.S. and other 525-line countries, but that Enhanced TV will be a transitional and supplementary format. HDTV is still widely considered as the TV standard of the 1990s, when DBS becomes more commonplace. West Germany and France also are working on a "higher resolution" TV system compatible with their 625-line transmission standard.[48]

Types of Orbits, Launching Vehicles, and Communication Satellites

Today's communication satellites travel in one of five orbital configurations: *sun-synchronous, polar, equatorial, elliptical, and geostationary*.[49] Almost all of the world's broadcast satellites use geostationary (i.e., synchronous) orbits, since they rotate with the earth in arcs 22,300 miles over the equator and thus remain in fixed positions relative to geographical points on earth. Soviet satellites are the best known exception to this rule. Their FSS Molniya and DBS Ekran satellites orbit every 12 hours in elliptical arcs that range in altitude from more than 24,000 miles over Siberia to less than 300 miles over North America. Elliptical orbits are best suited to the USSR, since its northern latitudes and 11 time zones would not be served as effectively by broadcast satellites moving in equatorial geostationary orbits.

The main providers of launch vehicles for placing satellites in orbit are the American and European space agencies, NASA and ESA. NASA has used the Atlas, Delta, and Atlas Centaur rockets to put satellites into geostationary positions around the planet, while ESA has relied mainly on the French-built missles of Arianespace. The spacecrafts most in use in the mid-1980s were NASA's Space Shuttles and ESA's Ariane 1, 2, and 3 series. NASA's 1984 loss of Westar 6 and Palapa B-2 satellites, which it later recovered, nonetheless left egg on the faces of NASA and McDonnell Douglas Astronautics, and gave an unwitting boast to Arianespace's international reputation as being a more reliable launch system. NASA still hopes to capture 75% of the commercial satellite launching market in the free world, but Ariane's lower pricing structure and waxing image promise to give the Space Shuttles a run for their money in the coming decade.[50]

Broadcast satellites have evolved through four stages of development. The *first* of these produced small, cost-efficient birds that required large and expensive earth stations to receive their low-power transmissions. The *second* generation saw the advent of the DBS, with its high-powered transmitters, increased channel capacity, and better quality signals—all making it possible to reduce the power, size, and construction and operating costs of earth terminals. The *third* stage of satellite development, planned for the late 1980s, will have on-board switching capabilities to enable the use of multibeam signals—if various international issues and conflicts can be resolved. The decade of the 1990s will usher in the *fourth* generation of broadcast satellites, characterized by orbital antenna farms and gigantic space platforms. These will be transported piecemeal by the Space Shuttle and erected in space. Just one of these huge platforms could supply the Western Hemisphere with all its communication needs.[51]

Although there are many satellites in orbit today, all derive from three generic communication spacecrafts built by RCA, Hughes, and British Aerospace/Matra. The *RCA Satcom* flew first in 1975 and later had 24-channel C-Band capacity, with K-Band versions being produced in the mid-1980s. The *Hughes HS 376* satellite began operating in 1977 and today also comes in 24-channel C-Band and K-Band formats. The *British-Aerospace/Matra ECS* also appeared in 1977 as part of the ESA's Orbital Test Satellite (OTS) project. France has based its TELE-COM-1 satellite on the OTS/ECS model, as has Eutelsat. Ford is now joining this triumvirate with its new Supersat model, patterned after the Intelsat V design.[52]

DBS technology has many applications other than transmitting radio and TV programs from satellites directly to homes. These include personal cellular radio communication (via a cordless wrist-size telephone), high-speed facsimile transmissions of newspapers and electronic mail, teletext information, teleshopping, telebanking, telemedicine, teleducation, and simultaneous translation of languages between nations and continents.[53]

Other types of communication satellites are being used to transmit computer data, digital voice signals, facsimile reproductions (hardcopies) of documents and photographs, as well as for teleconferencing, air and sea navigation, scientific exploration of the universe, military surveillance verification of weapons and test ban treaties, and remote sensing of the earth's surface for geological, agricultural, bathymetry, land use, and weather forecasting purposes.[54] Still, it is satellite broadcasting that has captured the attention and sparked the imaginations of people around the world.

A WORLD SURVEY OF BROADCAST SATELLITE SYSTEMS, CIRCA 1984

Broadcast satellite operations may be classified as being *global, regional,* or *domestic.* Global satellites can broadcast between continents; regional satellites have a more limited yet multinational coverage area; domestic satellites usually confine their broadcasts to a single nation. Domestic broadcast satellites are designated as either *dedicated systems,* those owned by public or private entities within the nation, or *shared use systems,* in which a national organization leases transponder time on another owner's satellite—typically INTELSAT's space segment facilities.[55]

GLOBAL/INTERCONTINENTAL BROADCAST SATELLITE SYSTEMS

Only two truly global systems of satellite broadcasting were operational in the mid-1980s, INTERSPUTNIK and INTELSAT. The INTERSPUTNIK Satellite System was created by the USSR in 1968 and was registered by U.N. Agreement in 1971 when several East European countries and Cuba officially joined the system. INTERSPUTNIK today serves about a dozen communist-bloc member-states via leases on interconnected Soviet communication satellites and ground stations.[56]

The INTERSPUTNIK system is comprised of an intercontinental *space segment* and a network of local *earth stations.* The space segment is cooperatively administered by all member states and consists of both communication satellites and a terrestrial guidance system. Each state builds and owns its own earth stations for receiving transmissions from INTERSPUTNIK's satellites. The INTERSPUTNIK organization is governed by a policy and oversight board comprised of one representative from each member state, and is financed from a statutory fund to which all members contribute on a pro rated basis according to how much they use the system's channels.[57]

INTERSPUTNIK began providing telecommunications services to Eastern Europe, Cuba, and Mongolia through Soviet MOLNIYA 2 and 3 satellites in the mid-1970s, and has since established global coverage with the deployment of the Statsionar-T and 1-10 series of C-Band satellites, designed for community DBS reception rather than point-to-point, like most INTELSAT payloads.[58]

The International Telecommunication Satellite Organization, INTELSAT, is the largest and oldest global satellite broadcasting system in the world. It became a U.N. agency in 1964 (see Chapter 2) under early management of the American Communications Satellite Organization (COMSAT). INTELSAT launched its first satellite, Early Bird, in 1965 and followed it with the INTELSAT II through V series from 1966 to 1984.

Its most sophisticated communication satellite series, INTELSAT V-A, was inaugurated in 1984, having 15,000 voice circuits and two video circuits. The INTELSAT VI series, scheduled for launching in 1986, will more than double V-A's capacity by providing 36,000 voice and two video circuits.[59] A new Business Service satellite, INTELSAT V (F-8), was positioned over Brazil in 1984 and will serve almost a third of the earth's surface, from the Americas to Africa and Europe, with a range of digital communications—TV, voice, teletext, facsimile, and data transmissions—via the Ku-Band.[60]

INTELSAT celebrated its twentieth anniversary on August 20, 1984. What began with 14 national signatories now has 109 member-states and links together some 170 territories with a global system of 16 satellites over three oceans in shared geostationary orbits. The INTELSAT system is accessible to virtually all countries and users, due to its nondiscriminatory worldwide price averaging and economies of scale. INTELSAT used its birthday occasion to announce Project Share (Satellite for Health and Rural Education), a new program it is cosponsoring with the International Institute of Communications to provide 16 months of free satellite testing by scores of developing countries wishing to experiment with new telecommunication technologies for social purposes.[61]

To date, INTELSAT has invested over $3 billion in its space and ground facilities that handle two-thirds of the world's telephone and data communications and virtually all live TV transmissions. INTELSAT's telecommunication traffic doubled between 1980 and 1984, while its communication charges actually decreased. In the coming decade, it expects this traffic to grow eight-fold, since the number of transponders dedicated to TV will increase from 5 to 35 channels. Yet, INTELSAT is worried about the deregulation and competition trends in American telecommunications, since they contradict the U.S. government's treaty obligations to INTELSAT by working against its long-standing practice of averaging rates so that the heavily used routes subsidize the "thin routes" used by the developing nations.[62]

Many changes and trends marked satellite communications in the early 1980s. INTELSAT lost its monopoly status as regional and national satellite systems appeared and began moving into the 11/14 GHZ band. DBS technology also became operative. Access to space improved as new spacecrafts and launcher concepts made satellites more efficient and economical to operate. And policymakers scrambled to keep pace with technical innovations and the multitude of competing program services occuring worldwide. These events and others are affecting INTELSAT materially, especially the presence of public and private rivals.[63]

The first regional satellite venture to challenge INTELSAT came in 1980, when 21 nations of the Arab League decided to develop the ARABSAT system, which was launched in 1984. In 1983, 20 European countries formed Eutelsat and built a K-Band satellite service to cover most of the continent and distribute TV signals as far as Africa and the Middle East. INTELSAT also appears to be losing the opportunity to link Mexico and Canada with the U.S.[64]

Bureaucratic in-fighting within the Reagan Administration during 1984 prevented the U.S. government from establishing a policy to guide applications to the FCC by domestic companies wishing to offer international telecommunication satellite services. INTELSAT is concerned that it, as an international organization with delicate relations to balance worldwide, has to compete with private users for orbital slots. INTELSAT's director general, Richard Colino, criticized the attitude of the Reagan Administration in a 1984 speech before the International Club, saying that INTELSAT was born of an idealism and altruism no longer in vogue in America. In his words: "INTELSAT couldn't happen in 1984, only in the sixties. We live in an interdependent world. The U.S. should understand it is *more* dependent on that world, not less."[65]

INTELSAT's monopoly position in international satellite communications appeared to be shaky at the end of 1984, when the Reagan White House gave the FCC the go ahead to consider five applications for separate satellite services that would operate outside of the U.N. agency which the U.S. helped to create two decades earlier. Such a move, if and when it should occur, would open up space to free market entreprenurialism and introduce INTELSAT to private competition. The U.S. government reasoned that separate systems "are required in the national interest."

Many of INTELSAT's 109 member nations registered concern with the U.S. State Department and the FCC, fearing that economic harm would be done to the global satellite system that two-thirds of the world relies on for all of its overseas telecommunications. President Reagan assured INTELSAT that the proposed system would be barred from providing telephone service, which accounts for 75% of INTELSAT's income.

INTELSAT began facing challenges from private satellite services in the early 1980s. The two applicants most eager to begin international services are Orion Satellite Corporation and the Pan American Satellite Corporation. Orion hopes to sell transponders to clients wishing to offer communication services between the U.S. and Europe, while PanAmSat plans to link together the countries of the Western Hemisphere and provide Latin America with a domestic satellite service.[66] None of these developments should threaten INTELSAT's existence, but its future in space will be one of confusion and competition rather than of orderliness and domination.

REGIONAL/MULTINATIONAL BROADCAST SATELLITE SYSTEMS

Two regional satellite systems for broadcasting were operational in 1984: Indonesia's PALAPA series (1, 2, A, and B), serving Southeast Asia; and Western

Europe's Eutelsat/ESA bilateral projects. In addition, several systems are scheduled to be launched between 1985 and 1990. These include the Arab League's ARABSAT, the Scandanavian NORDSAT project, Africa's AFROSAT, and an Andean satellite system for Brazil, Chile, Colombia, Ecuador, and Peru. NORDSAT is being planned by five Nordic nations—Denmark, Finland, Iceland, Norway, and Sweden—and hopes to be operational by the end of the decade. AFROSAT, still under consideration, is intended to serve the 38 members of Africa's Panaftel group. And ARABSAT's launching is imminent.[67]

A group of Mid-Eastern nations have already contracted with a French consortium to build a DBS for launching in 1985. The satellite is to be operated by ARABSAT, a multinational organization based in Riyadh, Saudi Arabia. It is intended for the exclusive use of member Arab broadcasters. Squabbles between sparing countries may still sabotage the project, or oil-rich Saudi Arabia may preempt ARABSAT by putting its own DBS into orbit.[68]

World broadcasting's most ambitious regional satellite system is the one operational over Western Europe. Eutelsat was formed in 1968 as the satellite coordinator for the consortium of West European PTTs known as CEPT (Conference Europeene des Postes et Telecommunications). Eutelsat at first shaped and directed the communication satellite activities of the European Launcher Development Organization (ELDO), which was established in 1961 to coordinate the development of the continent's aerospace and telecommunications industry. When ELDO was replaced by the European Space Agency (ESA) in 1973, Eutelsat then spearheaded ESA's communication satellite projects by helping to design and later manage a series of bilateral satellite systems. The Eutelsat/ESA projects have included the Orbital Test Satellite (OTS) series, the current European Community Satellite (ECS) program, the defunct H-SAT bird, and the planned L-SAT project. ("H" and "L" stand for Heavy and Large Telecommunications Satellite.)

A K-Band OTS was launched in May of 1978, and carried two television channels: France's TDF network and a British commercial DBS service, Sky Channel. An ECS-F1 K-Band satellite with a capacity of 12 channels was launched in 1983 by Eutelsat and quickly gained two customers. The first was the UK's private Sky Channel service, which did not renew its lease with the weaker OTS-2 bird. The second was TV 5, a French-language programming service jointly produced by the broadcasting organizations of France, Belgium, and Switzerland. Another channel may be used by the Swiss until their own DBS is ready. Eutelsat put ECS-F2 into orbit in late 1984, with one transponder reserved for TV and five for business purposes. The latest Eutelsat/ESA bilateral project is a large DBS planned for 1987, L-SAT OLYMPUS. One of its TV transponders is earmarked for Italy's RAI system, and the other for the European Broadcasting Union's Pan European TV service.

Eleven nations belonged to the ESA in 1984: Austria, Belgium, Denmark, France, the Netherlands, Ireland, Italy, Spain, Sweden, the United Kingdom, and West Germany, with Canada and Norway having observer status. ESA has earth stations in Belgium, West Germany, Italy, and Spain. Besides its DBS projects with Eutelsat, it controls space research and application activities, including the Ariane Launcher.[69]

NATIONAL/DOMESTIC BROADCAST SATELLITE SYSTEMS

By 1984, many nations had committed themselves to communication satellite systems. Eighteen countries had so-called Dedicated Systems—national satellites for domestic telecommunication purposes—and over 40 others had Leased/Shared Use Systems—23 operational and 18 planned—on INTELSAT's facilities. A half dozen nations (Canada, France, Italy, Japan, U.S., and West Germany), along with the West's two major space agencies (NASA and ESA), sponsored a total of 14 experimental satellite systems. Of these, only Japan's BSE, the French-German SYMPHONIE series, Italy's SIRIO, and the ESA's Orbital Test Satellites (OTS) were being used for television transmission. In addition, nine military satellite systems were also operational in 1984: four American, three Russian, one British, and the NATO Phase series.[70]

Following an overview of 12 nations with planned or operational domestic satellite systems, the six countries most active in satellite broadcasting—France, West Germany, Japan, Britain, U.S., and the Soviet Union—are examined more closely.

Australia planned to put two 15-channel Ku-Band satellites into orbit in 1985 using a Hughes HS-376 launching vehicle: AUSSAT-1 in July, and AUSSAT-2 in December. Likewise, *Brazil* planned two launches in 1985: a 24-channel C-Band satellite, SBTS-1, in February, and a Ku-Band SBTS-2 version in August. *Canada,* a pioneer in satellite broadcasting, had six birds in orbit by the end of 1984—the Anik-A, B, C, and D series, positioned since 1980 and covering both C- and Ku-Bands with from 12 to 24 channels each, as well as the new TELE-SAT-1 and H satellites that went up in June and October of 1984. A Canadian DBS prototype, the Communications Technology Satellite (CTS), set the pace in world broadcasting when it was first developed in 1976. *Colombia* has let a contract for the construction of a domestic FSS broadcast satellite, SATCOL.

India has used satellites for a decade to provide people in half a million remote villages with instructional TV programming. ITV activities began in 1975, when the Indian government leased a transponder on the American ATS-6 satellite, used originally in the Satellite Instructional Television Experiment (SITE) project to reach rural areas in six American states. This led India to commission its own satellites—INSAT-1A in 1982, and INSAT-1B a year later—to be received via community TV sets supplied by the government. The first one failed to work, but the 1B satellite now broadcasts two TV channels: one in local languages to isolated states like Andhra Pradesh, and a second national service in Hindi and English. Programs teach children and adults agricultural skills and health care habits, but also feature local news and cultures.[71]

Indonesia's national satellite system, PALAPA A and B, has also been in service nearly a decade and, as mentioned earlier, covers the entire region of Southeast Asia. The A series was launched in 1976, and the B in June of 1983. The B-2 is perhaps best known as the satellite that was lost at the time of its launching in February 1984, but was recovered the following fall by the U.S.-manned Space Shuttle, Discovery.

Italy planned its own DBS payload, SARIT, for launching in late 1985, and a telecommunication satellite, ITALSAT, to be operationalized a year later. Neighboring *Luxembourg* might be considered "the mouse that roared" in West European broadcasting, since its popular private commercial station, Radio Luxembourg, is heard throughout the continent and the British Isles. The satellite plans of Radio-Tele-Luxembourg (Campagnie Luxembourgeosie de Telediffusion) are no less great. Although DBS plans were not finalized at the end of 1984, RTL is seriously considering a regional satellite service for the late 1980s. Known as LUXSAT, it would offer two domestic TV channels and would lease three transponders to commercial entertainment interests in adjacent countries. Possible clients are a West German company, BDZV, which would program a German-language channel, and firms to operate French-language channels for Belgium and France.[72]

Mexico was scheduled to put two satellites into orbit during 1985: MOR-ELOS-A, with 18 C-Band channels and 6 Ku-Band channels, in May; and MORELOS-B, of similar capacity, in November. *Sweden* hopes to launch TELE-X sometime in 1987. Three of its transponders would be used for broadcasting purposes, in cooperation with Norway and Finland. *Switzerland*'s DBS decision had not been made as of 1984, but the mountainous nation seems committed to its HELVESAT project. And, in the Middle East, the Saudi Arabian Broadcast Satellite System, SABS, hopes to put a DBS bird in flight around the globe in the late 1980s.

Japan: First in DBS and HDTV

Japan's National Space Development Agency launched that nation's first DBS in January of 1984. The BS-2a satellite was placed in geostationary orbit 22,300 miles above the equator over New Guinea, and began rebroadcasting NHK's two national TV networks in color the following May.[73] Although Japan has run an experimental broadcast satellite service, BS-1 ("Yuri"), since 1978, the BS-2a bestows upon NHK the honor of being the world's first national broadcaster with its own DBS service. Moreover, the BS-2a is experimenting with high-definition TV technology. Domestic manufacturers like Matsushita, NEC, and Toshiba are cooperating with NHK by developing inexpensive HDTV receivers in anticipation of a growth in the world DBS-HDTV market. A BS-2b spare was being planned for the mid-1980s. The BS series is an outgrowth of the earlier FSS Communication Series of satellites, CS-2a and 2b. Japan also has a more advanced generation of DBS on the drawing boards, the (CS-3) SAKURA sequence.[74]

The USSR: First in Space, Last in the Marketplace

The Soviets have shown a keen interest in satellites since their launching of Sputnik nearly three decades ago. Being both the world's largest geographic nation and a superpower, the USSR has applied satellite technology largely to domestic telecommunication purposes and global military strategies. This combination has led the Soviet Union to develop a technically sophisticated system of communication satellites. But, as a closed society, the Soviet leadership is threatened by the individualism and freedom inherent in the programming and home-based technologies being marketed throughout much of the world.

The FSS solar-powered MOLNIYA series of satellites began broadcasting across the USSR in 1965 and has been augmented since the 1970s by the EKRAN generation, which today has DBS capabilities. Two other operational FSS satellites systems, LOUTCH and RADUGA, are also used for TV distribution, although the latter is used for military purposes as well.[75] Another Soviet satellite system, GORIZONT, has been developed to offer television services to viewers in border regions, Eastern Europe, Scandanavia, and parts of Western Europe.

France and West Germany: Space Partners and Competitors

France and West Germany, together and separately, have been in the forefront of broadcast satellite activities on the European continent. Their collaboration began with the SYMPHONIE 1 and 2 series in 1974 and 1975. These were experimental satellite services operating over the Atlantic and Indian Oceans. France uses its component to reach Francophone populations in Africa, the Caribbean, and North America. In 1979, the two countries abandoned their support of the ESA's H-SAT project and entered into a twin DBS enterprise which resulted in each developing its own satellite—TDF-1 for France and the West German TV-SAT.[76]

In the spring of 1984, France reversed an earlier decision for the TDF satellite system to offer a single service, and opted instead for a full commercial service. Europe, in fact, is becoming somewhat leery of multi-channel international DBS television after several decades of very limited program options via their own national broadcasting organizations. The possibilities of going from a handful to literally dozens of channels requires some analysis of programming needs and technological regulations.[77]

By the end of 1984, France had rescheduled the launching of TDF-1 for the fall of 1986. The satellite's programs will reach 100 million Europeans by offering two national DBS channels and a cultural service in French to France and its adjacent neighbors. However, TDF-1 may find itself in competition with Coronet, a joint U.S.–Luxembourg project planning also to offer DBS programming in both French and German. Luxembourg's national broadcaster, RTL, has already agreed to lease two DBS channels on TDF-1 for broadcasts in two languages.[78]

France's PTT initiated its own satellite venture, TELECOM-1, in 1979.[79] It was finally launched in mid-1984 and will serve France's overseas territories (called Departments)—Guadelupe, Guyana, Martinique, Mayotte, Reunion, and Saint-Pierre-et-Miguelon—as well as Corsica.[80] TELECOM-1 has four C-Band, six Ku-Band, and two Ka-Band channels. A five transponder TELECOM-2 is being planned for television.[81]

The first series of West Germany's TV-SAT is designed to transmit the three national television channels (ARD, ADF, and the Third Program) to every household in the country equipped with a small and inexpensive parabolic antenna. Its funnel-shaped footprint is contoured to also cover West Berlin. A solar-powered TV-SAT-2 will carry five additional channels when operationalized in 1986 or 1987. Austria may use one of its transponders as well. The West Germans also are planning another national satellite for broadcast service, DFS/KOPERNICUS, for launching later in the decade.[82]

DBS in the United Kingdom: From Controlled Competition to Confusing Cooperation

A noted observer of British media activities, Brenda Maddox, has been sharply critical of the Thatcher government's handling of telecommunications policy in general ("it is preaching competition and practicing control") and DBS policy in particular ("it's more of a farce than a tragedy"). Her displeasure is understandable.

In 1982, the government awarded Britain's impending DBS service to the BBC instead of ITV. In time, it became clear that the satellite venture would bankrupt the BBC, so ITV was invited to participate. When the two broadcasters could not come to terms on price and programming, the government then heeded the cries of private outside interests by allowing them into the DBS project.[83] The British government finally killed the UNISAT DBS project in mid-1985 due to exorbitant cost projections of 80 million pounds annually. Although UNISAT appears to be dead, a brief obituary is of historical value.[84]

UNISAT was to have been built and maintained by United Satellites Limited (USL), a company formed by British Aerospace, Marconi Electonics, and British Telecom. Three satellites were slated for the UNISAT-I series: the first scheduled for launching in 1986 or 1987; a second "flying spare;" and the third to be held in reserve on the ground.

UNISAT's three DBS channels were to be programmed by a tripartite consortium jointly owned by the BBC (50%), the ITV network companies (30%), and a group of 21 private companies (20%). The latter partner, dubbed the "21 Club," included Granada TV Rentals, Thorn EMI, Pearson, Ltd. (which publishes the *Financial Times* and owns Virgin Records), and Consolidated Satellite Broadcasting (whose principal owner is Radio-Tele-Luxembourg).[85]

A new Authority, the Satellite Broadcasting Board, drawn from IBA members and the BBC Governors, also was being planned to decide the standards, content, and transmission specifics of UNISAT's programming.[86]

The historical rivalry between Britain's two broadcasting organizations surfaced in early 1984, when the BBC announced that it would not lease a whole satellite system from the UNISAT consortium because the estimated cost of a DBS receiver was too great to attract a large enough audience. The BBC blamed the government's decision to use IBA's MAC-C signal standard as the reason for pricing DBS sets out of the reach of most people. The BBC and ITV companies finally agreed in April 1984, after government-mediated discussions, to form a jointly-run enterprise to operate the UNISAT System and to offer two DBS channels each.[87]

By 1985, the BBC had estimated it would that it would incur additional yearly costs of 75 million pounds just to provide programming for UNISAT. When the BBC suggested that it might have to resort to advertising rather than increase license fees in order to fund its DBS service, both the public and ITV objected strenuously. Given the economic and regulatory problems facing DBS in the United Kingdom, the government withdrew its support.[88] UNISAT could still fly if all parties agree to a less expensive version.

Britain's DBS future will rely now on the privately-backed BRITSAT vehicle, the recently legalized SMATV operations fed by low-powered communications satellites, and on foreign DBS facilities. ITV, in fact, has planned a so-called Superchannel service, comprised of its members' best programming, to be transmitted via France's TDF-1 satellite in competition with Rupert Murdoch's Sky Channel. Eutelsat's medium-powered satellites will open up several dozen new transponders to broadcasters, including the BBC, by 1991. BRITSAT emerged in late 1984 claiming it could build a cheaper satellite than UNISAT, and faster, with bank backing and access to American (RCA) DBS technology.[89]

Satellite Broadcasting in America: Open Skies and a DBS Shakeout

America's first domestic communication satellite was WESTAR I, launched by Western Union from NASA's Kennedy Space Center in April 1974. After WESTAR I came the geostationary SYNCOM satellites and the INTELSAT series. A decade later, nearly two dozen similar satellites orbited along side it in space. These spacecrafts have affected U.S. broadcasting in numerous ways, particularly in terms of electronic news gathering and new distribution to local stations, program feeds to cable systems across the country, and now direct telecasts.

From the mid-1970s forward, traditional broadcasting has increasingly leaned on satellites for distributing network and syndicated programming to affiliated local outlets across the country.

The use of satellites to interconnect TV network affiliates was inaugurated in the U.S. by the Public Broadcasting Service (PBS) during 1978 and 1979. The PBS distribution system was utilizing four transponders and 179 earth stations in 1984, while the commercial TV networks were only beginning to link their local affiliates by satellite feeds. NBC contracted Comsat General to create a satellite distribution network by 1985, while ABC and CBS have leased positions on AT&T's TELSTAR system. NBC's satellite network will use the Ku-Band rather than the lower-frequency C-Band. CBS is making the transition more gradually, linking only nine stations in the southwestern states by satellite in 1984 and adding affiliates region by region until the whole network is satellite interconnected in 1987. ABC had made no commitment to complete satellite distribution as of 1984, but was planning some feeds to its western stations by year's end.

American radio networks were quick to begin adapting to satellite-delivered programming, due to its flexibility, high-quality sound specifications, and economy. Between 1978 and 1979, Mutual, National Public Radio, RKO Radio, and the AP Radio networks became the first to offer their affiliates programming feeds from satellites. ABC, CBS, and NBC radio networks moved more slowly into satellites, not completing the transition from landlines until late 1983. RCA has designated its SATCOM-I-R as its "radio bird" in that ABC, CBS, NBC, and RKO are now using it, with Mutual and several radio syndicators ready to hop aboard. In fact, over 3500 radio stations had dishes aimed at SATCOM I-R in 1984.[90]

Satellites have also revolutionized local TV news by making it feasible to import video clips and hardnews feeds from anywhere in the country or the world, and integrate them into their local newscasts. American TV networks routinely use COMSAT or INTELSAT to transmit news stories home from overseas. Because of the expense involved—$150 per minute—ABC, CBS, CNN, and NBC often share satellite time and fees. U.S. news bureaus sometimes request access to foreign TV facilities and usually are granted it, even in the Soviet Union. Satellites thus not only expedite live coverage of events anywhere in the world but also encourage international cooperation between broadcasters of adversarial nations.[91]

Four companies owned America's principal broadcasting satellites as of 1984: *Comsat/AT&T* (COMSTAR I-IV and TELSTAR 301); *Hughes Communications* (GALAXY I and II); *RCA* (SATCOM I-V); *Western Union* (WESTAR II-V); and *Satellite Business Systems* (SBS I-III). Seven satellite service companies function as brokers, by finding customers to lease the hundreds of transponders on these 21 satellites. The seven are: Bonneville Satellite Systems, Hughes Television Network, Netcom, Public Service Satellite Consortium, Group W's

Television Videotape Satellite Communications (TVSC), VideoStar Connections, and Wold Communications.[92]

The inventory of clients using America's 21 satellites to supply programming services to cable systems for broadcasting purposes included 34 basic channel services, four "superstations" (WTBS-Atlanta, WGN-Chicago, WOR-New York, and WIPX-New York), and 11 Pay TV services (viz., HBO, Showtime, Cinemax, The Movie Channel, The Disney Channel, The Playboy Channel, Home Theatre Network, Bravo, American Movie Classics, ON Satellite TV, and GalaVision).[93]

America's DBS Scene, Circa 1984

The FCC began accepting DBS applications in 1981. The first approved, in June, was the Satellite Television Corporation (STC), a subsidiary of Comsat. The Commission authorized eight other U.S. companies in October, granting the DBS Construction Permits for 1982.[94] Within 2 years, these nine original DBS applicants (*) had been joined by 13 others—although not all of them would prove to be legally and/or financially qualified. By the end of 1984, the tally sheet of America's possible DBS players read:[95]

*Advanced Communications Corporation
*CBS Satellite Systems
*Direct Broadcast Satellite Corporation (DBSC)
*FOCUS Broadcast Satellite
*Graphic Scanning Corporation
Home Box Office
Home Broadcasting Television Partners
Hughes Communications Galaxy Incorporated
National Christian Network
National Exchange Incorporated
Private Satellite Network
*RCA Americom Incorporated
Satellite Development Trust
Satellite Syndicated Systems Incorporated
*Satellite Television Corporation (STC)
Skyband, Incorporated
Space Communications Services
United Satellite Communications Incorporated (USCI)
*United States Satellite Broadcasting (Hubbard Broadcasting Company)
Unitel
*Video Satellite Systems (Dominion Video)
Western Union

The first DBS service in America was begun by United Satellite Communications Incorporated in November 1983. With financial backing from General

Instrument and Prudential Insurance, USCI acquired a transponder on Telesat Canada's ANIK-C-II domestic satellite and—after initial coverage of Indianapolis and metropolitan Washington, DC—expanded its Pay TV service to two dozen northeastern states. For just under $40 a month and a one-time $150 installation charge, USCI offered its customers five channels—two movies, general entertainment, children's programs and ESPN sports.[96] USCI's fast start startled the DBS competition, especially STC, but proved also to be premature.

STC had planned to put its own DBS into orbit in 1986 and offer a multichannel service for 20 to 30 million viewers. To remain competitive with USCI, STC revised its timetable and subsequently announced that it would offer five channels of first-run movies, sporting events, cultural programs, and teletext via an SBS-IV bird to viewers in the eastern states by late 1984 at a monthly fee lower the USCI's. However, a partner was needed to help finance the expensive venture. CBS, who had scaled down its own DBS plans by early 1984, expressed interest in joining STC in a DBS project but later backed out.[97]

Meanwhile, USCI was close to bankruptcy after only 8 months of operation, having enrolled less that 15,000 subscribers in 26 states. Since it too needed a partner in order to survive, USCI and STC decided to merge in August of 1984. Their joint company would closely follow STC's original and more ambitious plan: to launch two three-transponder satellites in 1986, high-powered enough to cover the entire continental U.S. (CONUS) with six channels receivable by relatively inexpensive 30-inch dish antennas.[98]

But the DBS picture in America was far from clear at the end of 1984. On the bright side, some optimists estimate that $100 billion will be spent on building and launching communication satellites in the next 15 years. In fact, the number of domestic satellites serving the U.S. may double (from 20 to 40) between 1985 and 1995. Predictions of such growth have been bolstered by a recent FCC decision to allow U.S. satellites to orbit closer together (only two degrees apart rather than four) after 1987 in order to accommodate the demands of applicants wishing to telecommunicate from space. Relatedly, new transmission techniques will increase the channel capacity of satellite transponders.[99]

Applications for orbits in 1981 resembled a kind of gold rush into space, but DBS turned out to be "fool's gold" for many during 1984. The first bad omen came in February, when Indonesia's PALAPA-2B and Western Union's WEST-AR-VI fell into low orbit after launching and were rendered useless. Fortunately, both were recovered 9 months later by a NASA Space Shuttle team aboard Discovery, which also successfully deployed two new satellites—Telsat Canada's ANIK D-II and the Hughes LEASAT I. Despite the retrieval, NASA lost both reputation and business to Europe's Arianespace as an Ariane 3 rocket put GTE's SPACENET II into orbit and won the bid to launch SPACENET III for the American company in 1985.[100]

The second bad omen can be seen in the year's DBS shakeout figures. Of the eight applicants granted DBS construction permits by the FCC for 1982, only four were still in the game by mid-1984—STC, Dominion Video, DBSC, and Hubbard's USSB. CBS and Western Union both dropped their plans for entering the DBS business. RCA Americom modified its original proposal and will reapply for a new permit to launch two less-costly, 16-channel satellites later in the decade. Graphic Scanning also plans to go ahead with a two-channel national service at some future date, but will confine its coverage to the western half of the CONUS during the first phase of its operations after 1986.[101]

A third telling omen came in late 1984, when the board of Comsat, the owner of STC, voted against entering into DBS partnership with Prudential Insurance and USCI, despite having invested $40 million in the idea. The decision does not bode well for the future of either STC or USCI, together or separately. That two dominant forces in the U.S. marketplace for direct satellite broadcasting should be vascillating so erratically likewise does not auger well for all the earlier promises of DBS pie in America's sky.[102]

REGULATING INTERNATIONAL BROADCASTING AND OUTER SPACE

The organizations most involved in developing policy and making laws to regulate the spectrum and assign the orbital positions in outer space for communication satellites are the U.N. General Assembly, UNESCO, the outer Space Division of the U.N. Secretariat, and the International Telecommunication Union (ITU). International attention to communication satellites galvanized quickly following the launching of Sputnik in 1957. The UN General Assembly established its Committee on the Peaceful Uses of Outer Space in late 1958, and reconstituted it as a permanent U.N. committee (known as UNCOPUOS) a year later. Early regulatory discussions centered on *legislative* versus *operational* approaches to direct satellite broadcasting.

The five basic principles underpinning the legal framework regulating human activities in outer space, such as satellite communication, are:[103]

1. *free use* (all states are free to explore and use space);
2. *sovereign equality of states* (all states have equal rights of access to explore space and establish systems, and should also have equal access to the economic and technological resources to do so);
3. *prohibition of national appropriation* (no state can claim sovereignty in its use of space or occupation of a given orbital position);
4. *state responsibility* (all states are responsible for activities in space carried out by their government or nongovernmental entities);
5. *common interest of all humankind* (space may only be used to benefit individuals and countries, irrespective of their stage of economic or scientific development).

The ITU grouped its Member Nations into five geographical areas at its 1959 Plenipotentiary in Geneva. There were: Region A (The Americas), Region B (Western Europe), Region C (Eastern Europe and Northern Asia), Region D (Africa), and Region E (Asia and Pacific Oceania).[104] These would later be streamlined into just three regions.

The UN pursued an active agenda on broadcasting from space during the 1960s. The General Assembly passed Resolution 1721 in late 1961, stating that outer space be used only for the betterment of humankind and for the benefit of all states, regardless of their level of development. A year later, the passage of Resolution 1802 committed all U.N. agencies to grant member nations technical and financial assistance in developing satellite communication facilities.

At the ITU's specialized WARC in 1963, the French delegation, fearing the spread of pirate broadcasting, attempted to add the word "satellites" to a previous ITU regulation (Article 422) which prohibited broadcasting from ships and aircrafts. This was rejected by the convention. Brazil asked for a ban on using satellites for encouraging class, racial, or national rivalries. The U.N. responded with a Declaration of Legal Principles Governing Activities of States in the Exploration and Uses of Outer Space.

Two years later, UNESCO sponsored a meeting of space experts to discuss the political and cultural aspects of satellite broadcasting. Attention was focused on the troublesome dilemma of trying to adhere to the U.N.'s free flow of information doctrine while, at the same time, being sensitive to the fears of some nations that their sovereign rights would be threatened by broadcasts from space.

These issues and others formed the agenda of the U.N.'s ensuing discussions and culminated in 1967 with passage of the Outer Space Treaty by the U.N. General Assembly.[105] The accord defined the rights and obligations of nations in space and, although it did not mention DBS by name, implicitly permitted space broadcasting with the proviso that some programming constraints were possible. For example, the treaty's language requires that all nations' space activities be of benefit to, and considerate of, the "corresponding interests of all other states' parties." Nevertheless, it gave states the freedom to conduct activities in space, as long as international laws were observed, and explicitly condemned the use of satellites for provocative and unpeaceful propaganda.[106]

The ITU identified three critical DBS issues: (a) coordinating their use with existing terrestrial broadcasting systems, (b) assuring their interference-free operation in space, and (c) advising and aiding the developing countries in the use of the new technology.[107] At the 1971 World Administrative Radio Conference for Space Telecommunications, the ITU's revised Radio Regulations were adopted. Aiticle 7, 428A stated:[108]

In devising the characteristics of a space station in the broadcasting-satellite service, all technical means available shall be used to reduce, to the maximum extent practicable, the radiation over the territory of other countries unless an agreement has been previously reached with such countries.

The West insisted that this regulation only relates to the *technical* aspects of satellite operations, not to the *program content* of DBS signals, but UNESCO closed the loophole in that interpretation the following year.

Satellite broadcasting was again the centerpiece at UNESCO's 1972 General Conference, and the U.N. General Assembly the same year. The UNESCO biennial adopted a Soviet-sponsored Declaration of Guiding Principles on Satellite Broadcasting by a vote of 55 for, 7 against (including the U.S.), and 22 abstentions. It read in part: "It is necessary that states, taking into account the principle of information, reach or promote prior agreements concerning direct satellite broadcasting to . . . countries other than the country of origin of the transmission." The Declaration, in stressing national sovereignty and the equality of all states, placed many restrictions on satellite broadcasting. These included requirements that news broadcasts be accurate and programming be apolitical; that each country could decide the content of educational programs broadcast to it, in order to preserve its indigenous culture; that broadcasters should respect other countries' laws and cultural distinctiveness; and that prior consent agreements be made between sending and receiving nations, especially with respect to commercial advertising.[109]

A Working Group on Direct broadcast satellites—set up in 1969 to study the new technology's technical, political, and legal implications—met in mid-1973 to forge specific principles agreed to by UNESCO's DBS declaration the previous year. Three conflicting positions were staked out by the participating parties. The first was the side favoring UNESCO's *prior* agreement between sending and receiving nations, which was backed by the USSR, most of the Third World, and some Western members, including France. The middle approach, co-sponsored by Sweden and Canada, advocated prior consent on satellite transmissions but not on content. The third position, advanced by the U.S., suggested that the principles guiding DBS be nonbinding since satellite technology was not yet fully developed.

More exacting technical solutions to transnational signal spillover by satellites were offered in 1974 by the U.N.'s DBS Working Group. They included:[110]

> beam shaping and satellite stability, reducing signal amplitude in border areas, antenna directivity and shielding in the direction of unwanted transmissions, use of separate frequency assignments to adjacent countries, and the use of special transmissions requiring signal decoders.

The Working Group also considered a host of legal principles in formulating the following guidelines for direct broadcasting via satellite:[111]

* *rights and benefits of states* (to send and receive DBS signals)
* *prior consent and participation* (Second and Third Worlds favor it, West doesn't)

- *spillover* (should be avoided where technically possible)
- *program content* (must respect laws and culture of receiving states)
- *illegality of broadcasts* (such as propaganda and pornography)
- *duty and right to consult with each other* (sending and receiving states)
- *peaceful settlement of disputes* (through direct talks or UN or ITU)
- *copyright, neighboring rights, and protection of TV signals* (as per current law)
- *notification* to the U.N. and its agencies when problems with DBS arise
- *interference* with a nation's sea, air, and radio communication (is illegal).

The ITU, which had always allocated spectrum frequencies and geostationary orbits on a first-come-first-served basis, began recognizing the need for more equitable access to these limited natural resources at its 1971 WARC for Space Telecommunications and its 1973 Plenipotentiary Conference. About 100 communication satellites were in geostationary orbit by 1977, when the RARC for Planning Broadcast-Satellite Service Frequencies was convened. The resulting "Geneva Plan of 1977" contained several important ITU decisions relative to defining different satellite services and assigning them orbits and frequencies good for 15 years.[112]

First, *direct* satellite broadcasting was officially defined in terms of *reception* rather than *transmission*, since transmissions had always been direct but reception was heretofore relayed to home viewers indirectly via local broadcast or cable stations. The ITU further specified two kinds of direct reception: individual and community. *Individual reception* refers to broadcasts received by way of a small rooftop dish antenna for use by a person or family unit living in a single dwelling. *Community reception* indicates satellite programming that is received by larger parabolic antennas for distribution through cable systems to groups of viewers living in an apartment complex or a limited geographic area like a municipality or rural village.[113]

Second, the Geneva Plan admonished that DBS signals of domestic satellites ideally should conform to the national boundaries of the sending nation. Exceptions were recognized for political entities smaller than a DBS footprint—such as the Vatican State, San Marino, Andorra, Monaco, Luxembourg, and Liechenstein.

Third, additional spectrum bands and orbital slots were assigned by the ITU for BSS, FSS, and DBS services in two of the world's three geographic areas on the basis of its "equal rights to all countries" principle. Specifically, *Region 1* (Europe, Africa, the USSR, and Mongolia) was assigned the 11.7–12.5 GHZ segment of the spectrum, while *Region 3* (Asia and the Pacific) received the 11.7–12.2 GHZ Band. The assignments for *Region 2* (the Americas) were postponed for 5 years, until the 1983 RARC, by request of the United States. The DBS of all European countries were grouped together in five orbital positions, between 37° West and 5° East.

Lastly, all European countries, regardless of size, were allocated five TV channels each for DBS—except for Denmark, Finland, Norway, and Sweden, which were given three channels each for national coverage and will share two extra channels among themselves.[114]

The 1979 World Administrative Radio Conference, one of ITU's general WARCs held every 20 years, took place in Geneva during the fall. WARC-79 brought together some 2000 delegates from 142 member nations to revise and update radio regulations, pass a number of resolutions, and plan the future use and allocation of the spectrum and orbital space. The decisions reached were of critical importance to high-frequency broadcasting services like shortwave and DBS, since the regulations enacted at WARC-79 are intended to remain in force until the year 2000.

The Third World nations challenged the ITU's first-come-first-served practice at the 1979 WARC, on the grounds that it violated the 1973 International Telecommunication Convention requiring equitable access to frequencies and orbits, and that it favored the developed countries. The developing states feared that all of the geostationary orbital positions and radio frequencies would be allocated away by the time they were ready and able to use them. The Third World therefore asked that orbits and frequency bands to be assigned on an *a priori* basis—meaning that they be allocated to all nations in advance and in effect be reserved for future use. The U.S. and its Western allies opposed the a priori scheme because, in their judgment, spectrum space would be wasted and technological development arrested.[115]

Also discussed at WARC-79 were the need for cooperation between nations in the areas of direct satellite broadcasting, transborder data flows, and remote satellite sensing across national frontiers. Such topics blur the previous distinctions made between technical and political matters. Nevertheless, a resolution was adopted favoring the principle of equitable access by all nations in the planning and use of space and spectrum alike. Another resolution opened up 30% more of the spectrum for High Frequency (SW radio) use (See Table 8-1), and also made more frequencies available for fixed satellite service (FSS) broadcasting in the four bands below 10 GHZ, in the 10–15 GHZ range, and on selected frequencies between 35 and 275 GHZ.[116] The conference further proposed that a special WARC be held within 5 years to set allocation and utilization principles and procedures for guaranteeing equal access to HF bands by all nations.[117]

Other items on the Third World's agenda at WARC-79 were calls for access to unused HF assignments, assigning other frequencies according to national need, assistance from the International Frequency Registration Board (IFRB) in reducing their interference problems and giving them new frequencies, asking developed nations to minimize their utilization of the spectrum and space, and allowing Third World countries to rent or lease their a priori-assigned frequencies and orbits to users from the developed world until they are ready and able to use them.[118]

The U.S. gained nearly all of its technical goals at WARC-79, but was outmaneuvered by the Third World forces on controversial policy issues like spectrum planning for space services. Much of what happened can be explained by a simple power equation: although a relative handful of Western nations dominate 90% of the international spectrum while having only 10% of the world's population, the developing countries control the voting majority within the ITU and also proved superior to procedural wisdom at the 1979 WARC.[119]

Regulatory Conference For the 1980s

Matters pertaining to international shortwave and direct satellite broadcasting will be discussed in Geneva and elsewhere throughout the decade following WARC-79. The U.S., however, boycotted most of the preparatory meetings held in 1981 for the U.N.'s scheduled Unispace 82 conference in Vienna, due to anger over the appointment of key personnel considered to be hostile to American interests in outer space.[120] A special U.N. political committee approved a Resolution in November 1982 banning DBS transmissions across international frontiers, without obtaining the prior consent of the receiving nation's government. The vote was 88 to 15, with 11 countries abstaining. It was solidly opposed by the Western nations. Backing for the proposal came mainly from the UN's Third World members (on cultural grounds) and from the Communist countries (for political reasons).

The resolution means that satellite service rights would have to be negotiated between sending and receiving nations, in conformity with ITU technical requirements, yet also would have to respect "the political and cultural integrity of states" and adhere to the "principles of nonintervention." Further, governments would be legally responsible for all DBS signals broadcast by services under their jurisdiction. The issue may be moot, however, since nonconsensual DBS television service appears to be unlikely in much of the world. Europe and Asia, for example, have already apportioned their satellite frequencies and orbital slots to countries in their parts of the world (Regions 1 and 3) for domestic use exclusively. The nations of the Western Hemisphere (Region 2), including the U.S., developed their DBS plan in June of 1982, which will utilize segments of the 12 GHZ band. The U.N. prior-consent decision reinforced another proposal—namely, apportioning frequencies and orbits a priori to nations regardless of their immediate needs, rather than on the first-come-first-served basis favored by the U.S. and other Western nations with birds ready to fly.[121]

The principles guiding satellite broadcasting, which had been vigorously debated for a decade, finally reached a consensus in the December 1982 U.N. General Assembly by a vote of 107 to 13, with 13 members not voting. Those voting against the measure were the same states that had opposed it in the Outer Space Committee: namely, Belgium, Denmark, West Germany, Iceland, Israel, Italy, Japan, Luxembourg, the Netherlands, Norway, Spain, UK, and U.S. New U.N. principles require DBS operators to notify and consult with receiving nations prior to directly transmitting international TV signals, so that sovereign national rights and the tenets of nonintervention may be observed. Like the ITU's 1977 prior agreement regulation, the U.N.'s guidelines do not apply to those satellites (FSS) distributing TV programming to cable systems in America and many European nations.[122]

A Regional Administrative Radio Conference (RARC) was held in the summer of 1983 in Geneva to plan broadcasting and satellite service in the Americas. The Final Acts of RARC-83 adopted an a priori plan for the DBS band and assigned orbital positions and frequency channels for the countries in Region 2. The conference also adopted detailed technical standards for DBS operations in the Western Hemisphere, including parameters such as frequency plan, channel bandwidths, polarization, signal levels, and interference ratios.[123]

RARC-83 netted the U.S. eight orbital positions, each having enough spectrum space (500 MHZ) to provide up to 32 channels of service in the 12.2–12.7 GHZ band. Only five of the orbits, however, are in locations capable of covering the entire continental U.S.—known as full CONUS coverage. America lost out to Canada and Brazil on a vote of adopting a high-power versus low-power DBS standard. The U.S. wanted the former, which is best for home reception in remote places, but Canada and Brazil, having clustered populations, favored the less expensive low-power standard most suitable for large-dish reception by cable systems such as SMATV (Satellite Master Antenna Television) units.[124]

FM broadcasting in the VHF band was planned for Regions 1 and 3 at the Second Session of RARC in late 1984. The First Session of the 1984 RARC reallocated the HF bands for broadcasting, set limits in shortwave transmitter power, and exhorted all nations to not jam or otherwise interfere with SW frequencies not assigned to them. Future plans for HF Band allocations to SW broadcasting were scheduled for a 1986 WARC. Satellite broadcasting and geostationary satellite orbits for use by space services will be planned at two WARC sessions in 1985 and 1988. Other ITU conferences during the decade will plan for the regional and global utilization of mobile services (1987), AM radio frequencies (1986 and 1988), and the VHF/UHF bands for Africa (1987 and 1989).[125]

The 1984 High Frequency WARC put jamming on its agenda, since nearly half of Europe's SW frequencies are still being rendered useless because of deliberate interference by Eastern Bloc countries, despite the fact that jamming has been declared illegal by international agreement. By 1984, 163 countries of the world were operating a total of 1500 SW transmitters an average of 16 hours a day via the 448 channels available in the HF Band, spaced 5 KHZ apart. At any minute, day or night, approximately 1,000 SW transmitters are on the air.[126]

In a departure from past practice, representatives from the private sector worked closely with government officials during 1984 in preparation for the ITU's 1985 Space WARC in Geneva. Such cooperation enabled the U.S. government's policy apparatus—the State Department, NTIA, and, in particular, the FCC—to use private section technical information to its best advantage in formulating America's official policy positions for planning the future uses of space services in the international forum. Questions discussed at the 1985 meeting include planning frequencies and orbital assignments, the economic impact of the new space technologies, and deciding whether international and regional "common user" systems like INTELSAT and Eutelsat should have priority over systems wanted by individual countries. One challenge is to resolve the Third World's demand for guaranteed access to the orbital arcs vis-a-vis the West's wish to assign orbital slots on the basis of stated needs. The U.S. hoped that each nation would be flexible in determining its space requirements, since some might benefit from a conventional satellite system, others from a regional approach, and still others from terrestrial microwave or undersea cable networks.[127]

The August 1985 WARC for Space Systems was scheduled for the purpose of incorporating the frequency and orbit allocation plans developed at the 1977 and 1983 RARCs into coherent international radio regulations. In late 1984, however, the British criticized the Western Hemisphere's satellite plans, drawn up at RARC-83 for Region 2, for possibly interfering with Region 1's 1977 DBS plan for Europe and Africa. The UK further challenged the authority of Space WARC-85 to incorporate the DBS plans of Regions 1, 2, and 3 (Asia and the Pacific), since it is only the first of two such sessions scheduled for that purpose—the next to be held in 1988. Interference is a likelihood, since the three regions have developed different DBS downlink and feeder-link provisions. Talks between the affected governments ensued in hopes of resolving the issue.[128]

A REVIEW OF WESTERN DBS POLICIES

At the dawn of the 1980s, policymakers in the West began worrying about the threats that DBS pose to the cultural autonomy and national identity of their countries, much as the Third World has for a decade. Telecommunications policy expert Don LeDuc finds that parallel approaches to DBS technology are being pursued in Western Europe, North America, and Japan as the policy community in each region faces a common dilemma: "how to satisfy public demand for a wider range of television viewing alternatives without sacrificing the cultural integrity of each nation which is preserved and reflected by its own mass media."[129] He sees only two choices in resolving the dilemma: *either* keep commercial mass entertainment from the U.S. off European DBS channels and risk public discontent, *or* accept it and endanger their national cultures and the autonomy of their own broadcasting services that have nurtured it.

LeDuc has identified a number of factors that have limited Europe's DBS policy options over the years.[130] First of these is that European satellite technology was developed to be sold in global markets rather than merely be used specifically in Europe. The push behind today's European DBS hardware came from the Common Market's aerospace and telecommunication industries, not from the region's national broadcasters. These cooperative production and marketing ventures gradually were undermined by the limited demand of the European DBS market and by competing self-interests of the major national satellite developers in France, West Germany, and Britain.

The competition between nations also has negatively affected DBS frequency allocations for Region 1, set at the ITU's 1977 RARC. Concerns of the national broadcasting organizations in Western Europe regarding overlapping coverage and proper satellite usage were ignored at RARC-77 in the rush to allocate DBS frequencies and orbits. The resulting plan, good for 15 years, gave every nation of the continent, regardless of size, five DBS television channels, and also assigned them the same orbital slot in space. These hasty decisions seem certain to make trans-border TV signal spillover unavoidable—especially with respect to Austria, Belgium, France, Luxembourg, the Netherlands, Switzerland, and West Germany. Programming targeted to any one of them from DBSs clustered together in orbit above will inevitably blanket their neighboring countries as well.

Broadcasters in Western Europe have not enjoyed much clout in formulating DBS policies, in part because of the power and centralized structure of their national PTTs. In most countries, the PTT owns and operates the transmission networks and sometimes the facilities used by the national broadcasting services. They also control all public and common carrier channels, enabling them to extract high fees from their broadcasters and use the money to subsidize unprofitable postal and telephone systems. Add to this the fact that the PTT is typically the largest market for telecommunication equipment in the nations of Western Europe, as well as being the primary source of funding for telecommunication research and development.

In recent years the region's PTTs have consolidated their power by forming an organization (CEPT) with its own satellite consortium (Eutelsat), which, together with the ESA, have great leverage over individual national broadcasters and their regional fraternity, the European Broadcasting Union (EBU). To illustrate the collective power of the PTTs, they can charge their national broadcasters excessive rates to lease the DBS channels which they control through Eutelsat. If their broadcasters refuse to pay the asking rates, then the channels would be leased to private firms eager to offer advertiser-supported entertainment programming in competition with the national broadcasters. Most broadcasting systems in Western Europe have traditionally operated as public services dependent on license fees or taxes more than on advertising. Their programming has therefore tried to serve all segments of society and maintain cultural standards. Commercial competition would tend to threaten their public service missions as the public is fed a diet of mass-appeal entertainment.

Some Comparisons With American DBS Policy

When the FCC undertook its inquiry into DBS regulations in the fall of 1980, it did so without either reviewing Western Europe's DBS policies or evaluating the long-term potential of DBS in public interest terms. The FCC actually accepted a dozen DBS applications, and even approved one (STC), during 1981 before deciding on its own regulatory rules and policy for the new technology. It adopted a set of "interim" rules in 1982 that were essentially the same ones its own staff had recommended 20 months earlier without any public hearings. Le Duc characterized them as follows:[131]

> The DBS regulations enacted by the Commission impose very few restrictions upon those who will be receiving its five-year licenses. No limitation has been placed upon the number of DBS channels or systems that can be owned by a single entity, no technical standards must be observed except those required by international law and none of the agency's own rules will be binding upon system operators except for equal employment opportunity standards that must be followed by "broadcast" type operators.

American DBS policy proposals, according to Le Duc, "seem to promise the public nothing more than access to an increased number of pay television and commercial television viewing alternatives." These in effect forsake the traditional American concept of localism in broadcasting and, as in Western Europe, void traditional concerns with public service and culturally balanced programming.

Why did the FCC choose to give away America's DBS resources to the commercial marketplace rather than husband it so both public and private interests could share in its potential? The answer lies in the political climate of the moment and its mania for deregulation. Le Duc sees a bitter irony in the contrast between the FCC's treatment of cable vis-a-vis direct broadcast satellites.[132]

> A Commission that only a decade ago had spent seven years to develop "modern" cable television rules had in this case selected its DBS applicants within a year of the time it began its inquiry and issued rules for those licenses to be issued to these applicants only eight months after they had been selected.

Even *Broadcasting* magazine accused the Reagan Administration of spinnings its wheels on DBS matters, saying it is being forced by events rather than its own self-initiative to develop a coherent international policy for satellite communication. This was sorely apparent in the procedural impasse which surfaced between the White House, the State Department, the FCC, and the Commerce Department's National Telecommunication and Information Administration when attempting to decide if private satellite operators would be allowed to compete with INTELSAT.[133]

CONCLUSION: SOME IMPLICATIONS OF DIRECT BROADCASTING BY SATELLITE

Direct satellite broadcasting brings with it a multitude of positive and negative implications worthy of serious consideration.[134] Many feel that popular support for national broadcasting entities may be eroded by DBS competition, causing further resentment and evasions in paying receiver license fees. This would no doubt diminish the cultural and informational programming roles of classic "public service" operations like the BBC as satellite and cable services deliver more TV programs than the traditional broadcasters can afford to match. The result could be private entreprenuers leasing unused channels and filling them with advertiser-supported mass-appeal productions from foreign sources like America.

Inter-country rivalries could be stirred up as spillover from orbiting DBS transmitters and terrestrial stations in adjacent nations fragment audiences and compete for the same viewers who support domestic radio and TV services through their license fees, taxes, and purchases of advertised items. Spillover might also force noncommercial broadcasters to fallback on advertising and mass entertainment in order to attract more viewers and better compete with private programmers. DBS spillover poses the greatest problems in Western Europe, where nations are clustered closely together and commonly share the same orbital slots.

However, a partial solution to spillover lies in *beam-shaving,* which allows DBS transmitters to cast an ellipse-like footprint over a geographical area so that no (or only minimal) spillover occurs—except along borders. Signal spillover will also be curbed by language barriers and by cultural and time zone differences, as well as by natural obstacles like mountains or technical factors, such as incompatible receivers and limited antenna directionality.

Nevertheless, developing satellite technology is far easier than implementing DBS programs services, since the latter requires international agreements that can only be enacted if nations are willing to change the structure and policies of their broadcasting systems and PTT monopolies. The European Common Market nations, in particular, see satellite broadcasting creating problems in the legal areas of copyright, advertising, and public morality. How can the copyright jurisdiction of materials be adhered to in cases where TV signals carry into unlicensed territories? And how can copyright fees be collected? Although goods are allowed to move freely across the borders of EEC Member States, would advertisers also have the freedom to provide services and communicate across national frontiers? Will nations be able to regulate the content and flow of morally objectionable TV programs and films entering their sovereignties via DBS?[135]

Questions such as these were addressed by the Commission of the European Communities in a 1984 Green Paper entitled *Television Without Frontiers,* a document that proposed a set of legislative regulations and practical measures for establishing a so-called common market for broadcasting.[136] The overall strategy is to create an integrated European TV network service whose programs would be co-produced by EBU members in various languages.[137] The Commission made clear that Europe's broadcasters must work together to remove the legal and economic barriers hindering the free flow of TV programming if they are to be competitive producers and distributors in the international market as satellite and cable technologies develop.[138]

On the brighter side, DBS could free up many terrestrial transmitters now being used by national TV systems for use tomorrow as local or regional stations. Ironically, although DBS may localize West European broadcasting, it conversely threatens to undercut localism as the historic cornerstone of U.S. broadcasting by reducing many stations to mere outlets for nationally distributed programs.

DBS technology may help Third World countries to reach their rural majorities with useful development information instead of continuing to serve only affluent urban dwellers a diet of foreign entertainment and news through their Westernized TV operations. Few advancing nations have the money to build adequate systems of satellite ground stations and programming services, nor do they have the capital formation capacity to keep them running. Further, the "first-come-first-served" practices of the UN and ITU have denied them sufficient access to frequencies or orbits. It is their hope that the switch to an a priori allocation procedure, together with aid targeted to DBS development, will resolve these chronic problems.

Lastly, the totalitarian states of the Second World are more threatened by than optimistic about direct satellite broadcasting. Although the Soviet Union has a sophisticated and extensive system of relay, distribution, and broadcast satellites, officialdom in communist countries fear their citizens having direct access to foreign programming—particularly Western popular culture, news, and advertising. Governments in both the East and the West almost certainly will use DBS to disseminate propaganda and eventually may resort to jamming each other's satellite transmissions.

CHAPTER 8 NOTES

[1] B. H. Burdine, "Satellite Communications," in Maxwell Lehman and Thomas J. M. Burket (Eds.), *Communication Technologies and Information Flow* (New York: Pergamon Press, 1981), pp. 35–36.

[2] Benno Signitzer, *Regulation of Direct Broadcasting From Satellites: The UN Involvement* (New York: Praeger, 1976), pp. 7–8.

[3] *World Communications,* Annual (New York: Davis Publications, 1981), p. 21.

[4] *World Radio TV Handbook,* Annual (New York: Billboard Publications, 1982, 36th. Edition), pp. 42–46.

[5] Donald R. Browne, *International Radio Broadcasting: The Limits of the Limitless Medium* (New York: Praeger, 1982), pp. 30–37.

[6] Michael Choukas, *Propaganda Comes of Age* (Washington, DC: Public Affairs Press, 1965), p. 37.

[7] John B. Whitton, "Hostile International Propaganda and International Law," in Kaarle Nordenstreng and Herbert I. Schiller (Eds.), *National Sovereignty and International Communication: A Reader* (Norwood, NJ: Ablex, 1979), pp. 217–229.

[8] Lawrence C. Soley, "The Political Context of Clandestine Radio Broadcasting in 1981," *Journal of Broadcasting,* 27(3), Summer 1983, pp. 233–250.

9 *Chronicle of International Communication,* V(7), September 1984, p. 10.

10 Browne, *op. cit.,* pp. 93–100.

11 Information provided to the author by Rogene M. Waite, PIO, Voice of America, May 1982.

12 "Third VOA Chief in Three Years Resigns," *Broadcasting,* July 16, 1984, pp. 50–51.

13 "Keep News Objective in US Overseas Radio," *Buffalo* (NY) *News,* September 9, 1984, p. F-2.

14 Robin Grey, "Inside the Voice of America," *Columbia Journalism Review,* May/June 1982, pp. 23–30.

15 *Ibid.*

16 "The Talk of the Town," *The New Yorker,* April 18, 1983, p. 39.

17 Information provided to the author by the VOA.

18 "House ODs Radio Marti Funds," *Buffalo* (NY) *Courier-Express,* August 11, 1982, p. A-5.

19 Browne, *op. cit.,* pp. 135–136.

20 "Overseas Units Now Under Joint Structure," *Broadcasting,* October 18, 1976, p. 35.

21 Information provided to the author by RFE/RL, Incorporated.

22 James L. Buckley, "To the Soviets, Name of Games Was More Suppression," *Broadcasting,* March 19, 1984, p. 18.

23 Burton Paulu, *Television and Radio in the United Kingdom* (Minneapolis, MN: University of Minnesota Press, 1981), pp. 373ff. (See: Chapter 21).

24 Browne, *op. cit.,* Chapter 6, pp. 161–189.

25 *BBC Annual Report and Handbook 1984,* pp. 61–75, 111 and 119.

26 Browne, *op. cit.* pp. 190–198.

27 WRTH 1984, pp. 88–89.

28 David M. Abshire, *International Broadcasting: A New Dimension of Western Diplomacy* (Beverly Hills, CA: Sage, 1976), pp. 22–25. See also: Arthur Williams, *Broadcasting and Democracy in West Germany* (Philadelphia, PA: Temple University Press, 1976), pp. 23ff and 35ff.

29 John Howkins, *Mass Communication in China* (New York: Longman, 1982), pp. 59–64.

30 Information provided to the author by Radio Moscow in 1984.

31 Browne, *op. cit.,* pp. 230–234; and SW monitoring by author.

32 WRTH 1984, p. 149.

33 "Radio Moscow's Blooper," *Newsweek,* June 6, 1983, p. 56.

34 Donald R. Browne, "The International Newsroom: A Study of Practices at the Voice of America, BBC, and Deutsche Welle, *Journal of Broadcasting,* 27(3), Summer 1983, pp. 205–231.

35 "Saga of Super Sound: Act IV Scene I," *Chronicle of International Communication,* V(7), September 1984, pp. 4–6.

36 "Voice of America Aims to Expand, Improve Signal," *Buffalo* (NY) *News,* December 26, 1984, p. A-5.

37 Julian Hale, *Radio Power: Propaganda and International Broadcasting* (Philadelphia: Temple University Press, 1975), pp. 20–21.

38 "USIA Solicits Material to Present US to World," *Broadcasting,* August 15, 1983, p. 60.

39 "Saga of Super Sound," op. cit. (Cf. Note 35.)

40 "World: BBC Proposes a World TV Service by Satellite," *InterMedia,* 12(2), March 1984, pp. 3–4.

41 Rod Townley, "This Is One Show That's Driving the Russians Crazy," *TV Guide,* December 22, 1984, pp. 40–42.

42 Rolf T. Wigand, "Direct Satellite Broadcasting: Selected Social Implications," in Michael Burgoon (Ed.), *Communication Yearbook 6* (Beverly Hills, CA: Sage, 1982), p. 253.

43 Thomas F. Baldwin and D. Stevens McVoy, *Cable Communication* (Englewood Cliffs, NJ: Prentice-Hall, 1983), pp. 322ff.

44 *Ibid.,* pp. 322–325.

45 Lynne Schafer Gross, *The New Television Technologies* (Dubuque, Iowa: Wm. C. Brown,

1983), pp. 148–151. See also: "HDTV: Resolution for the 90's," *Channels*, November-December 1983, p. 56.

46 "HDTV, DBS Standards Dominate Discussion at IBC," *Broadcasting*, October 1, 1984, pp. 41–42.

47 "Better Pictures," *Broadcasting*, July 30, 1984, p. 7.

48 "Enhanced TV: Set for the Future," *Channels*, Field Guide '85, p. 12.

49 Thomas Y. Canby, "Satellites That Serve Us," *National Geographic*, 164(3), September 1983, pp. 329.

50 "NASA's Loss is Arianes' Gain," *Connections: World Communications Report*, No. 13, August 13, 1984, pp. 3–4.

51 Wigand, *op. cit.*, pp. 276–279.

52 Albert D. Wheelon, "The Future of Communication Satellites," *InterMedia*, 12(2), March 1984, pp. 41ff.

53 Wigand, *op. cit.*, p. 275.

54 *Ibid.*, pp. 256–269; Joseph N. Pelton and Marcellus S. Snow (Eds.), *Economic Policy Problems in Satellite Communications* (New York: Praeger, 1977), pp. 175ff and 217; George Gerbner and Marsha Siefert (Eds.), *World Communication: A Handbook* (New York: Longman, 1983, pp. 517–521.

55 Rolf T. Wigand, "Direct Satellite Broadcasting: Definitions and Prospects," in Gerbner and Siefert, *op. cit.*, pp. 246–253.

56 Pelton and Snow, *op. cit.*, p. 217.

57 Benno Signitzer, *Regulation of Direct Broadcasting from Satellites: The UN Involvement* (New York: Praeger, 1976), p. 7.

58 Roberto Guido and Guiseppe Richeri, "Western Europe: The Development of DBS Systems," *Journal of Communication*, 30(2), Spring 1980, pp. 169ff.

59 John R. Bittner, *Broadcasting and Telecommunication* (Englewood Cliffs, NJ: Prentice-Hall, 1985, Chapter 7.

60 "Intelsat Opens New Bird to Comsat Competitors," *Broadcasting*, April 2, 1984, p. 56.

61 "Birthday Pat on the Back for Intelsat," *Broadcasting*, August 20, 1984, pp. 36–38.

62 Wheelon, *op. cit.*, pp. 40ff.

63 *Ibid.*, p. 40.

64 *Ibid.*, pp. 40–41.

65 *Broadcasting*, August 20, 1984, pp. 37–38.

66 "President Extends Free-Market Doctrine to Space," *Broadcasting*, December 3, 1984, pp. 37–38.

67 Wigand, *op. cit.*, 1982, pp. 251–252; See also: Gerbner and Siefert, p. 517.

68 Douglas Boyd, *Broadcasting in the Arab World* (Philadelphia, PA: Temple University Press, 1982), p. 5.

69 Grandi and Richeri, *op. cit.*, pp. 169–177.

70 "Appendix Four: Global Satellite Systems," in Gerbner and Siefert, pp. 517–521.

71 James Traub, "Beaming the World to Andhra Pradesh," *Channels*, May/June 1984, pp. 41–43.

72 Don Le Duc, "Direct Broadcast Satellites: Parallel Policy Patterns in Europe and the United States," *Journal of Broadcasting*, 27(2), Spring 1983, pp. 110–111.

73 "Japan Launches Satellite for TV," *The Buffalo News*, January 24, 1984, p. B-12.

74 *InterMedia*, 12(3), May 1984, p. 8.

75 Pelton and Snow, *op. cit.*, p. 215. (Cf. Note 56)

76 Wigand, 1982, *op. cit.*, p. 264.

77 *InterMedia*, May 1984, p. 8.

78 "TDF Hitch, Coronet Struggles," *TV World*, November 1984, p. 6.

79 Grandi and Richeri, *op. cit.*

[80] "Demand Lifts Off," *TV World,* May/June 1984, pp. 41 and 49.

[81] Wheelon, *op. cit.,* pp. 45ff.

[82] *TV World,* May/June 1984, *op. cit.*

[83] Brenda Maddox, "In Pursuit of the Unviable," *Connections: World Communications Report,* No. 13, August 13, 1984, pp. 2–3.

[84] "UNISAT: UK Kills Off Its DBS Project," *InterMedia,* July/September 1985, 13 (4/5), pp. 7–8.

[85] "HDTV, DBS Standards Dominate Discussion at IBC," *Broadcasting,* October 1, 1984, pp. 41–42.

[86] "DBS for Britain by 1990," *TV World,* May/June 1984, p. 11.

[87] *InterMedia,* May 1984, *op. cit.,* p. 8.

[88] Andrew Waller, "UK: Regulators' Nightmare," *InterMedia* 13(3), May 1985, p. 7.

[89] *InterMedia,* July/September 1985, *op. cit.*

[90] "After 10 Years of Satellites, the Sky's no Limit," *Broadcasting,* April 9, 1984, pp. 43–68.

[91] "Good Connections Needed for TV Satellite Hookup," *The Buffalo News,* June 11, 1984, p. D-9.

[92] *Broadcasting,* April 9, 1984, *op. cit.,* pp. 56–58.

[93] "Satellite Channels: A Guide," *Channels,* 1985 Field Guide, pp. 53–62.

[94] Le Duc, *op. cit.,* pp. 112–113. See also: Bittner, pp. 151ff.

[95] "DBS Players Chart," *DBS News* (Bethesda, MD: Phillips Publishing, 1984).

[96] "DBS Off the Ground, Up in the Air," *InterMedia,* 12(3), May 1984, pp. 7–8.

[97] Richard Barbieri, "DBS: If Wishes Were Dishes," *Channels,* Field Guide '85, p. 48.

[98] STC Asks for Modification in DBS Plans," *Broadcasting,* July 23, 1984, pp. 99–100.

[99] Jonathan Miller, "Satellites: A Global Reach, For Better or Worse," *Channels,* Field Guide '85, pp. 50–51.

[100] "Rescuing Wayward Birds," *Broadcasting,* November 19, 1984, pp. 40–41.

[101] "Thinning Ranks of DBS Pioneers Heads for July 17," *Broadcasting,* July 16, 1984, pp. 30–31.

[102] "Another Nail in the DBS Coffin: Comsat Bows Out," *Broadcasting,* December 3, 1984, p. 36.

[103] Signitzer, *op. cit.,* pp. 22ff.

[104] George A. Codding, Jr., "The 1982 Plenipotentiary Conference," An IIC Briefing Paper (Geneva: ITU), 1982.

[105] Signitzer, pp. 26ff., *op. cit.*

[106] Wilson P. Dizard, "The US Position: DBS and Free Flow," *Journal of Communication,* 30(2), Spring 1980, pp. 157–168.

[107] Signitzer, *op. cit.,* pp. 34–55.

[108] "Summary of the Geneva Conference by the UN Working Group on DBS," *Control of the DBS: Values in Conflict* (Aspen Institute, 1974), p. 126.

[109] Ithiel de Sola Pool, "Direct Broadcast Satellites and the Integrity of National Cultures," in *Control of the DBS: Values in Conflict* (Palo Alto, CA: Aspen Institute Program on Communications and Society, An Occasional Paper, 1974), p. 37.

[110] "Summary of the Geneva Conference," *op. cit.,* p. 120.

[111] *Ibid.,* pp. 120–130.

[112] Stephen Gorove, "WARC: Some Legal and Political Issues on Space Services," in Gerbner and Siefert, *op. cit.,* pp. 418–423.

[113] Thomas F. Baldwin and D. Stevens McVay, *Cable Communication* (Englewood Cliffs, NJ: Prentice-Hall, 1983), pp. 322ff.

[114] Grandi and Richeri, *op. cit.,* pp. 169–171; and Le Duc, *op. cit.,* pp. 104–106.

[115] Gorove, *op. cit.,* pp. 420–422.

[116] "WARC '79 Doubles FSS Spectrum," *Interlink,* 1(6), First Quarter 1980, p. 1.

117 Syed A. Rahim, "International Communications Agencies: An Overview," in Gerbner and Siefert, *op. cit.*, pp. 391–399.

118 Harvey J. Levin, "US Communication Policies at Home and Abroad: Are They Consistent?" in Gerbner and Siefert, *op. cit.*, pp. 433–444.

119 William H. Melody, "The Radio Spectrum: Principles for International Policy," in Gerbner and Siefert, *op. cit.*, pp. 229–235.

120 *Chronicle of International Communication*, III(3), April 1982, p. 3.

121 "UN Resolution Would Limit Distribution of DBS Signals," *Broadcasting*, November 29, 1982, pp. 30–31.

122 "UN: New Satellites Principles," *InterMedia*, 11(1), January 1983, pp. 9–10.

123 "DBS: What Has Gone Before," *Television/Radio Age*, May 28, 1984, p. 45.

124 "Coming to Consensus in Geneva," *Broadcasting*, July 18, 1983, pp. 24–26.

125 "ITU: A New Convention is Agreed," *InterMedia* 11(1), January 1983, pp. 6–8.

126 Jim Vastenhoud, "WARC 1984," in WRTH 1984, *op. cit.*, p. 45.

127 "Cooperation is the Key Word in Preparation for Space WARC," *Broadcasting*, August 13, 1984, pp. 67–68.

128 "DBS Plan Hits Snag," *Broadcasting*, December 10, 1984, pp. 95–96.

129 LeDuc, *op. cit.*, p. 100.

130 *Ibid.*, pp. 100–112.

131 *Ibid.*, p. 113.

132 *Ibid.*, p. 114.

133 "Wheel-Spinning on International Policy," *Broadcasting*, June 4, 1984, pp. 98–99.

134 Wigand, 1982, *op. cit.*, pp. 261–275; and Le Duc, *op. cit.*, p. 100; and Ronald E. Rice and Edwin B. Parker, "Telecommunications Alternative for Developing Countries," in Gerbner and Siefert, *op. cit.*, pp. 270ff; Grandi and Richeri, *op. cit.*, pp. 169ff.

135 Scott Crosby and Alastair Tempest, "Satellite Lore: Copyright, Advertising, Public Morality, and Satellites in EEC Law," *EBU Review*, XXXIV(3), May 1983, pp. 30–38.

136 Commission of the European Communities, *Television Without Frontiers: (Green Paper on the Establishment of the Common Market for Broadcasting, Especially by Satellite and Cable)*, COM(84) 300 Final, Brussels, 14 June 1984.

137 Carlo Ripa di Meana, "A Blueprint for European Television," *Europe 85*, No. 5, May 1985 (a monthly publication of the Commission of the European Communities), p. 7.

138 For another perspective, see the following publications of The European Institute for the Media, University of Manchester, England: Anthony Pragnell, *Television in Europe: Quality and Values in a Time of Change* (Media Monograph No. 5, January 1985), pp. 19ff; Dr. Elaine Couprie, *Advertising, Cable and Satellite: The Elements of the European Debate* (Media Monograph No. 3, August 1984), pp. 29ff.

National Comparisons and Global Trends in Broadcasting, Cable, and the VCR

This book has taken us through four worlds of broadcasting and into outer space. Evidence presented in the preceding chapters demonstrates that practically every country on earth has undergone changes in its national broadcasting policy, structure, and practices. These changes are being made in response to technological advances, foreign competitive pressures, and demands from their own people for more channels, program diversity, and localism. The final chapter highlights cable TV developments, surveys the worldwide growth and implications of the video cassette recorder (VCR), reviews the internationalization and cultural ramifications of television programming and advertising, and offers a comparative summary of trends in world broadcasting in the age of the satellite.

THE DEVELOPMENT OF CABLE TELEVISION IN WESTERN EUROPE

Cable is growing faster in Western Europe than in any other region of the world except North America, where two-thirds of Canadian and 40% of U.S. TV households receive from 12 to 50 channels via hundreds of local franchises. Although the 1984 cable penetration figures in Belgium (82%) and the Netherlands (70%) look impressive, it is difficult to draw genuine analogies between the structure and function of cable communication on the two continents. This is due to several factors—one being definitional.

A far greater percentage of Europeans live in apartments than is the case in North America, and most of them receive their local television signals via *collective* antenna systems equivalent to MATV. In addition, there are *community* antenna systems (CATV), which connect individual houses to cable networks, offering extra channels of programming, often from neighboring countries, to larger numbers of subscribers throughout a wider area. Depending on whether these two types of reception are tabulated separately or together, the number of TV households having "cable" in a given country may differ widely.

To illustrate, West Germany makes legal distinctions between four types of reception: *individual* by a single antenna (48.7%), *collective* to *less* than 100 units (30%), *collective* to *more* than 100 units (20%), and by *cable* networks (1.3%). As a result, cable statistics for the FRG have been reported as high as 51.3% and as low as 1.3%. Most European countries (France is one exception) distinguish between *collective* and *community* cable hookups, but often combine the two counts when citing national cable penetration data. These variances—together with statistical discrepancies over how many people would be willing to pay how much for what kinds of new programs from satellites and other sources—have made life difficult for cable operators and market researchers in Europe.[2]

Cable TV systems in Europe and North America also differ in terms of channel capacity and of the sources, types, costs, and distribution patterns of programming. Most cable subscribers in North America, in addition to their local channels, have access to TV signals imported from distant cities as well as premium packages of over 30 national programs and about a dozen Pay-TV services like HBO that are distributed nationally via satellite and microwave relay. By contrast, most European systems average from 6 to 12 channels and carry only their national terrestrial TV networks and perhaps those from an adjacent country. Some older CATV systems have capacity for only three or four channels of programming that are also available to viewers over-the-air.

By the mid-1980s, the typical European CATV operations could handle about 12 channels, but several nations were installing or planning new switched systems with channel capacity twice to six times as great. These technological improvements, along with the public's appetite for additional program choice, have put pressures on governments to draft new policies and laws for fostering the development of cable. The cable policy approaches taken by the nations of Europe are similar in most respects, yet each reflects its own cultural and sovereign needs.

European cable operations are largely financed by the viewer through monthly fees that range from $1.15 to $8.40, with the average charge being about $3.80 for 10 channels. Britain depends mainly on private investment and competition to create a free market environment for cable, while France, Germany, and Sweden rely on their public PTTs to install and supply most of the funding for new cable expansion. Belgium, Holland, and Switzerland are steering a middle course by allowing cable systems to be built, managed, and funded by either private companies, public authorities, or semi-private entities. The purchase of advertising time on cable is banned in almost all European countries. Britain is the prime exception, and West Germany limits commercial programming to 20% of a cable station's total output.

Program origination by cable companies has been prohibited in all European countries until recently. By 1984, all but Austria were allowing some level of local production—with the British and Dutch doing the most to encourage private participation. This will create a market for new program sources, both domestic and foreign, and should give an impetus to satellite distribution. Moreover, cable operators in all nations but the Netherlands have "must carry" rules requiring them to distribute the program services of their national broadcasting organizations. Only Austria and Switzerland allow their cable systems to interconnect and form national networks, but this no doubt will take place in other countries during the coming decade. A look at cable activities around the continent points up the nationalistic complexities of the burgeoning medium as they existed at the end of 1984.

Cable operators in *Austria* are pressuring the government for permission to fill their free channels with local programs, relays from satellites—particularly West Germany's TV-SAT, Britain's Sky Channel, and a pending Swiss service via ECS—as well as a domestic Pay TV service. Rupert Murdock, a media magnate in Anglophone societies, introduced his commercial Sky Channel service in early 1984 for reception by Austrian cable systems. Sky Channel was originally a private UK operation called Satellite Television Limited. The nation's cable industry had been ailing, due to a number of government restrictions and poor program selection. Only 12% of Austria's TV households subscribed to cable by mid-decade, well below the West European average.

Vienna's cable system had 90,000 customers, yet two-thirds of the homes it passes were not connected by 1984. The reasons have to do with costly installation and subscription fees, and with a limited service of only six channels—two from the national ORF, three West German programs, and the German-language network from Switzerland. Also, cable operators have been forbidden to originate local programming. Sky Channel could usher in a whole new era of diversification, specialization, and commercialization in Austrian media.[3]

Belgium's huge cable population (82%) is wired to nearly 200 local and regional companies or networks. The only satellite service licensed by the PTT is TV5, although some systems carry Soviet TV from its GORIZONT satellite. TV5 is the joint program service that the French-language networks in France (TF1, A2F, and FR3), Switzerland (SSR), and Belgium (RTBF) transmit to their respective cable companies via the French ECS transponder. A new Pay TV service in French, produced by RTBF, was under consideration in 1984. Private cable operators are hopeful of carrying a combined Swiss and TV5 program in French, along with developing and distributing their own cable channel using Belgium's transponder on the ECS bird.

The government of *France* approved a set of new regulations for cable development in April 1984 which pleased all parties involved—the PTT, programmers, and system operators. The PTT will have the monopoly on providing a switched-star/optical fiber cable network, except for the headend—meaning the PTT will be a common carrier, but not a programmer. Private programmers will receive 30% of a system's revenues to help fund domestic production, which should be sizeable since imported programming is limited to 30%. Cable companies will be jointly owned by the local municipalities and private interests, with neither having majority control. To insure that cable companies remain local and apolitical, outsiders will be prohibited from buying up cable franchises and forming empires, and an already-elected local official will be named as chairman of each municipal cable firm. The new rules are deliberately flexible enough to allow each locality to arrange its own mix of public and private interests. They also encourage satellite feeds and a healthy portion of original programming, to help make cable attractive and accessible to as many subscribers as possible.[4]

Even though 38% of France's TV households had cable by 1984, only about half a million of these were connected to CATV systems. The government plans to lay enough new cable to pass 1.4 million French homes; its long-range goal is to connect 4.5 million households to the PTT's optical fiber network by 1992. No advertising is permitted to be sold by cable firms, but they can carry commercial programs from outside broadcast sources.

Helmut Kohl's Christian Democratic government has changed the course of *West German* broadcasting since coming to office in 1983, and also has infused the cable industry with a new spirit of entrepreneurialism. Among the most eager investors are the publishing companies. The government's PTT has invested $3.2 million in laying cable for four pilot projects and other systems elsewhere in the country. Only 20% of cable's airtime can be commercially sponsored; hence, subscribers will make up the difference through monthly fees of less than three dollars.

The new cable systems will offer a wide variety of programs up and above the three terrestrial channels they must carry, including the UK's Sky Channel, a national satellite service just for cable (PKS—Programs Kabel und Satellite), regional and local programming, education, music, and a public access channel. In response to the growth and popularity of cable, ARD and ZDF have purchased unprecedented numbers of foreign TV series and feature films.[5]

The freedom to carry satellite feeds and originate programming on cable stems from the FRG's 1983 Telecommunication Regulation. The four cable pilots in Berlin, Dortmund, Ludwigshafen, and Munich were operational by the end of 1984. The Ludwigshafen scheme is the most advanced broadband cable system in West Germany, having capacity for 22 TV and 22 radio channels. It will be coordinated by the Cable Communication Institute (abbreviated as AKK in German), comprised of 40 representatives from various cultural, political, and religious groups in the Land. Eleven of Ludwigshafen's TV channels will carry the present national, regional, and adjacent foreign stations; the other 11 channels are earmarked for new programming services as authorized by the AKK Committee. They will include videotex, interactive television, and satellite feeds.

Over two-thirds of *Holland*'s nearly 5 million cable subscribers receive from 6 to 12 channels, via collective rather than community antennas. Newer cable systems have capacities as high as 30 and even 72 channels, though 18 is the norm. The Dutch authorities are the most adamant in Europe about not allowing time to be bought on cable channels. All cable systems can be financed only by subscription fees and by their communities. One company was refused permission to carry the Sky Channel, but satellite programming will be allowed on cable in the future providing that no advertising is aimed directly at the Dutch audience. A 1983 government White Paper proposed the introduction of Pay TV in the Netherlands under certain conditions. These include a ban on advertising, that all programming be targeted to individual paying subscribers (addressability), that a "reasonable" amount of Pay TV's content be domestically produced, and that the public broadcaster's right of refusal for certain program categories be respected. The banning of advertising on pay-cable may be only temporary, but the decision was based on fierce opposition from both the broadcasters (who rely on it for a quarter of their income) and the press (which doesn't need the competition).[6]

A channel on the ECS satellite has been reserved by the Netherlands for a possible pan-European service called Eurikon, but private firms also are showing interest in using it. One of them, Euro TV, appeared certain in late 1984 to receive a license from the Dutch government to supply Holland with its first pay-cable programming service.

Roughly half of *Swiss* homes have cable and receive an average of 8 to 12 channels of programming from the national networks and those in contiguous countries, as well as from TV5 and the British Sky Channel. An experimental pay service called Teleclub has been authorized for Zurich and was offering mainly feature films for $10.65 a month in 1984. Two subscription TV companies were granted 6-year licenses in 1984—an international satellite service in German (Pay-Sat) via ECS-1, and a cable service (Telecineromandie) in French for Swiss audiences.

In *Sweden,* 60% of TV households are linked to collective antenna systems—many limited to only three to six channels. A Committee on the Mass Media studied the new technologies in 1983 and subsequently forwarded policy recommendations on cable, satellites, and videotex to the government for enactment of new legislation in 1985. A pilot cable system in Lund, built and funded by the PTT, began serving nearly 6,000 homes in late 1983. A second experimental cable operation is planned for the Stockholm suburb of Skarpnack.

Future plans call for CATV systems in Sweden to distribute the national TV networks of SR (SVT 1 and 2), those of Denmark (DR) and Germany (ARD and ZDF), a pay-TV service, and a community channel. Cable operators may also be required to carry the domestic (TELE-X) and regional (NORDSAT) satellite services. A private cable company, Telelex/VIP Media (TVMS), will be sending over 500 hours of programming to all Nordic cable systems after 1985. Moreover, the Soviet DBS satellite, GORIZONT, covers all of Sweden, as does Britain's Sky Channel.[7]

Elsewhere in Scandanavia, *Norway* is considering lifting its ban on commercial TV and has proposed satellite pay-TV. *Finland* has fewer restrictions on cable than almost any European nation, and introduced a two-way pay-cable service to over 20,000 homes in 1985. *Denmark,* too, has removed many shackles from cable, paving the way for a $420 million investment in a national, wide-band cable network. Satellite transmissions by cable are prohibited, however, until the late 1980s.

Spain has very low cable and VCR penetration for Europe, but pilot cable systems are planned for Madrid and Barcelona in the coming decade. *Italy*'s plethora of private television stations has kept it virtually uncabled, a situation unlikely to change in the near future.

Cable is undergoing a rapid transition in the *United Kingdom*, from former, low-capacity systems, usually carrying only the four national networks, to a bold new era of private and commercial multi-channel companies. The change was spawned by the 1982 Hunt Committee Report and the government's 1983 White Paper, *The Development of Cable Systems and Services*. These documents erected the policy framework for the 1984 cable and broadcasting legislation.

Britain's Home Office approved 11 of 37 applicants for cable operations in November 1983, granting them interim licenses pending discussions with each concerning managerial and financial viability audits. These franchises will operate in Aberdeen, Ealing (London), North Glasglow, Coventry, Craydon, South Liverpool, Guildford, Swindon, Belfast, Westminster (London), and Windsor-Slough-Maidenhead.

A new Cable and Broadcasting Act set up a Cable Authority in 1984 and followed closely the recommendations of the 1982 Hunt Report (see Chapter 3). Licensed cable companies must promise to offer a range and diversity of programming, including healthy levels of British and Common Market products, public access and participation programs, educational content, and third-party services. Licensees must be either UK or EEC residents. Those not eligible for licenses include local authorities and political or religious organizations. ITV companies, local radio stations, and newspapers cannot hold cable franchises in areas where their businesses are located.

Some wonder if cable will succeed in Britain, since 98% of the population already receive excellent quality TV programming from four national networks (two paid for by a mandatory license fee), and VCRs are in more than a quarter of the homes. Research indicates that the British watch more TV and own more receivers and VCRs than viewers in Europe. And how much could and would Britons be willing to pay for additional, untested programming? Costs are being estimated at $13 a month for basic cable service and $25 for the premium tier. Also, cable is unlikely ever to penetrate more than half of the nation's TV households—probably less. Lastly, there will be competition from DBS after 1987. For the other half who will not have access to cable, paying $200 for a rooftop dish to receive dozens of channels will be considered a bargain.[8]

The Thatcher government has an aggressive strategy for developing a privately-financed, wideband cable system having minimal and flexible regulations, yet insuring the preservation of the existing BBC and IBA broadcasting structure. Twelve-year licenses will be granted to pilot and tree-and-branch cable systems, and 20-year licenses to the more elaborate star-switched, optical fiber systems. Both types are eligible for 8-year renewals.

Unlike most of Europe, Britain will allow advertising on cable at the same level as exists for the ITV companies (6 minutes per hour). Pay-per-view programs will also be permitted, providing they are not events normally aired by the public service broadcasters. Cable systems are required to have a capacity of 25 channels and must relay the BBC and ITV networks. They may also carry foreign channels and satellite services—the latter including Britain's two ECS clients (Sky Channel and British Telecom) and the three UK transponders on INTELSAT-V (one with HBO).

Research into the European potential for cable has indicated that many people (especially the French and Germans) are unhappy with their current TV services and want more choices; but they do not want to pay more than $10 a month for new programs. It was estimated in 1984 that only 20 million European households were connected to cable systems having more than 300 subscribers and offering more than six channels. When contrasted with the 84 million cabled households in the U.S., the figure sheds some doubt as to whether the potential audience for satellite-fed cable programming is large enough to be economically viable. One forecast suggests that cable penetration in Europe could reach 27%, or nearly 34 million homes, by 1992—three times that of DBS users. But, while most eyes have been on DBS and cable, VCR has proven to be the darkhorse of the new telecommunication technologies.

THE VCR: ITS USES, ABUSES, AND WORLDWIDE IMPACT

It has been said that television "goes in one eye and out the other." It did, anyhow, until the arrival of the home video cassette recorder (VCR). By 1984, over nine million households in America owned a VCR. Its primary uses are for (a) recording programs off the air or cable and replaying them at the user's convenience (i.e., "timeshifting"), (b) recording material (especially movies) for saving (i.e., "library building"), and (c) playing rented and purchased tapes in the comfort and privacy of one's home[9]—thus, erotic content rivals movies, classic films, and "live" concerts in VCR popularity.

Home video technology decreases the transience of television broadcasts and shifts much of the control over choice of programming and viewing time from the broadcaster to the user of the TV receiver. This user control also allows the TV set to be utilized in a variety of active rather than passive ways—video games, computer displays, homemade videos, home theatrical screen—which transform television into a medium more akin to books, magazines, records, and movies.

The VCR has been called "the hottest thing since television." Nearly one in every five American homes had one by the end of 1984. In that year alone, Americans bought over seven million VCRs and more than 100 million blank video cassettes, with the VHS (Video Home Service) format outselling Beta about three to one. Although VCR sales were expected to level off in 1985, it is estimated that 51% of American homes will have a home video recorder by 1990—about the same penetration as predicted for cable. Most people buy a VCR for timeshifting, but research has shown that owners quickly discover the benefits of renting or buying pre-recorded tapes, particularly recent feature films. In fact, about 80% of those with VCRs did so in 1984. But among Americans, the third most popular use of VCRs is video photography—making home "movies" on tape with add-on video cameras—instead of building video libraries. Thus, the portable VCR is putting a huge dint in sales of 8mm motion picture equipment. Both Kodak and Polaroid are fighting back with a new line of 8mm video tape units called "camcorders." Other video improvements are also on deck. A higher quality "super VCR" machine is scheduled to appear as prices for regular home video units fall below $200. More than 30 VCR brands are on the U.S. market—led by RCA (22%), Panosonic (18%), and Sony (13%).[10]

Only a few countries have substantial VCR manufacturing capacity: those being Austria, West Germany, the Netherlands, and Japan. Other countries, including the U.S., merely assemble recorders from imported kits. Japan is the birthplace of the VCR, with Sony inventing the Betamax home video system in 1975 and JVC (Japan Victor Corporation) developing the longer-playing VHS standard a year later. The VHS system dominated the Beta format in worldwide sales by roughly a three to one ratio (72% to 28%) as of 1985.

Unknown to most people is the fact that the British actually made the first video recorder intended for home use in 1960. It was called the Telcan, and used quarter-inch audio tape to produce fuzzy black-and-white pictures at a speed allegedly known only to the manufacturer. It never reached the marketplace. America also had two early home video failures: Cartrivision by Avco Embassy, and RCA's original SelectaVision, a holographic tape system served before its time.[11] A Dutch firm, Philips, has succeeded with its V2000 VCR format.

Over 100 companies met in Tokyo in 1983 and agreed on a new standard format for home video cassettes. It would be 8mm wide, about the same as an audio cassette, rather than the present 12 mm size. Sony and Philips of Holland strongly supported the new standard, while JVC and others, who use the 12mm VHS format, opposed it. The marketplace will decide which standard prevails.[12]

The penetration and regulation of the VCR differ widely from country to country. *Belgium,* for example, bans pornographic tapes, while *France* requires a license to own home VCRs.[13] The worldwide popularity of the VCR is caused by many factors. The availability of Western entertainment and erotic material accounts for the high level of VCRs in countries where television programming is limited or heavily censored, such as the Middle East and the Second World. The movies-on-tape industry is blossoming. In *Canada,* for instance, a Toronto firm (VTR Productions) turns out 70,000 movie cassettes every month by running its 700-deck facility around the clock.[14]

In *France,* moves by the Mitterand government to make French TV more uplifting by limiting the number of imported (mostly American) shows has been a boon to VCR sales despite an annual tax being levied on the owners of home video equipment.[15] And perhaps *Sweden's* long winters account for a third of the cassettes on sale being pornography. The remainder are crime, adventure, comedies, thrillers, and family programs.[16] About 25% of *Ireland's* TV households owned a VCR by 1984. Sales were motivated by several factors: the Western half of the population having fewer channel options and less exposure to British television than their Eastern compatriots; the liberalizing impact of British culture on Irish youth and those returning home from work stints in England; and public reaction to the prudishness of Church and state officials. Ironically, violent and erotic tapes are the viewing favorites in country pubs and among young people in Ireland.[17]

Italy has a VCR penetration of only 2%. Why so low? Two reasons stand out: the first being the 16% sales tax the government imposed on VCRs in late 1982; the second (more important) being the cornucopia of over-the-air channels available to Italian viewers. With the private and RAI networks airing an average of 35 to 40 films every day, who needs to tape movies on a $400 machine?[18]

It is precisely the user-control potentials of the VCR that makes it, the computer, and other telecommunication technology so threatening to officials in closed societies like the *Soviet Union.* Data is scarce on the availability of VCRs within the Second World, but it is safe to assume that some machines and tapes have been smuggled in from outside and can be purchased underground. In fact, VCRs sell on the Soviet black market for about $5000 each, and foreign tapes can be had for $200 apiece—roughly the average monthly wage in the USSR. Only high state officials and members of the professional elite can afford such a luxury.

Not surprisingly, the Soviets, who have previously accused capitalist societies of using VCRs to "enslave man spiritually" and "manipulate people's thoughts," began manufacturing their own VCR in 1984. Video is now seen by the Kremlin as a more cost-effective way of getting state propaganda across in more remote villages, given the shortages of both projectors and films. The Russians are turning out only 75 VCRs a month and will sell them for $1500 per unit at new video shops opening up in Moscow, Leningrad, and Minsk—half the price of an "under the counter" Japanese model. It should also surprise no one that Soviet VCR decks have a technical standard that is incompatible with the West's VHS and Beta formats.[19]

Australia had no cable as of 1984, though a report by the Australian Broadcast Tribunal recommending its commencement was under active consideration by Parliament at year's end. However, VCRs were already in nearly one of every three homes, and the figure is growing. Unfortunately, so is video piracy. It is estimated that a quarter of all pre-recorded tapes sold in Australia are illegal. The practice is so efficient that films like "Ghandi" and "E.T." appeared on cassette within weeks of their theatrical showings. But this kind of copyright abuse of VCR technology is not limited to a few countries; indeed it has become a global problem.[20]

Video Piracy Around The World

Perhaps the most negative impact of the VCR is the practice of video piracy. Those who produce, distribute, exhibit, and hold copyrights to television programs and motion pictures are losing millions of dollars worldwide or, in the case of many British cinema proprietors, going out of business. Piracy involves making and selling unauthorized mass duplications of movies, TV programs, and other types of productions on video cassettes. It was estimated in 1984 that nearly half of all pre-recorded video cassettes in circulation in the UK are pirated copies. The figure is 30% in America, where the U.S. film industry lost about $700 million in retail sales in 1984 alone. In the six largest European countries, with a combined VCR population of 12.5 million, over 100 million blank tapes were sold in 1983.[21]

Part of the problem lies in weak or outdated copyright laws. In Britain, for example, video pirates, if caught, face only an $82 fine under the country's 1956 Copyright Act. By contrast, the penalty is $10,000 or 6 months in prison under Australia's Copyright or Trade Mark Act.[22] Also, not enough countries have become signatories to international copyright treaties to wage a concerted battle against the theft of intellectual property.

But several strategies are being tried to fight video piracy. West Germany and Austria require VCR and videotape manufacturers to pay a royalty tax prior to the retail sales of their products. The fund would then reimburse the creators and owners of the original productions. American and British filmmakers, distributors, and video companies have formed the Federation Against Copyright Theft (FACT), and funded it with a $1.5 million war chest to fight illegal taping.

It has been suggested that the copyright holders are partially to blame for failing to serve the low price end of the video market. People seem willing to pay the pirate's price ($15 to $20) for a movie tape, but feel that the legitimate company's price ($60) is a rip-off. As a short term tactic, film producers and distributors have been forced to shorten the time lapse (or "window") between a film's release to theaters and its legal availability on cassette. The longer the interval, the more likely the pirates will steal the march on the copyrighted movie's market.[23]

Video piracy is gaining momentum in the USSR as well. Among the most popular pirated Western films on tape are "Apocalypse Now," "The Godfather," "A Clockwork Orange," "The Deer Hunter," and "Emmanuelle." Soft porn is also in demand.

Russians are willing to pay dearly for even third- and fourth-generation dubs, but the risks are considerable. The *Evening Standard* of London reported in 1983 that a 47-year Moscow artist almost received an 8-year prison sentence for charging $50 a head to see pirated Western porno and horror films in his studio. How did he beat the rap? It seems that Moscow's chief of police, an Inspector Kupriyanov, was one of his customers.[24]

Another breed of video pirate exists in Denmark. A pirate TV station there called "Channel 3" began broadcasting tapes of West German and Swedish programs in 1981 to the 20% of the population which cannot directly receive its neighbors' signals. Officials had trouble catching the outlaw broadcaster, largely due to tip-offs from its viewers—which included journalists, local police, and even government officials. The way the scheme worked was that Danes in border areas made video cassettes of popular German and Swedish shows, and sent them to the TV pirate at an address in East Jutland.[25]

With nearly 50 million VCRs in use in practically every nation on earth, it is no wonder that video piracy has become a worldwide phenomenon. Repressive cultures and governments of all political flavors find it especially hard to control. American TV accounts of the assassination of Benigno Aquino were passed from house to house in the Philippines on tapes showing an opposite version from the story being peddled by the Marcos regime over state-owned news media. A Catholic social club in South Africa was raided by government police in February 1984, and 740 illegal video cassettes were confiscated, including the U.S. mini-series "The Thorn Birds."

Racy Western material is forbidden by Moslem law in Arab countries such as Saudi Arabia and Kuwait, where movie theaters, bars, and even on-screen kissing are prohibited. Ironically, VCR penetration is highest in the Middle East, where almost all of the relatively few TV sets are owned by uppercrust elites with a taste for Western pop culture artifacts like "Dynasty" and "Magnum, P.I." In Iran, where the Ayatollah Khomeini led a successful revolution via audio-cassette while in exile in Paris, foreign videotapes with dubbed Farsi sound tracks are the rage among underground video clubs.

In a 1984 article in *TV Guide,* Joanmarie Kalter aptly summed up the global impact of video piracy on broadcasters and sovereign cultures alike:[26]

> A world on fast-forward is not easily controlled. Where information flows more freely, cultures become more homogenized, and piracy, running unchecked, wears down the very industry it feeds on. Still, new developments in technology cannot be rewound.

What American TV viewers consider a VCR asset is seen by advertisers as a serious problem—the ability to delete or "zap" commercials while taping, or by fast-forwarding through them during playbacks of timeshifted programs. Nielsen research in 1984 showed this to be the case 65% of the time. Of course, viewers have always been able to change channels to avoid commercials, but zapping can shorten a 3-hour broadcast of a movie to 2 hours. It's too soon to tell what if any damage this may do to the TV advertising business, but Madison Avenue is nervous.

VCRs have also begun to affect cable by slowing down subscription growth and causing some customers to disconnect. Pay-per-view programming via cable and satellite could hurt VCR sales in the future or, conversely, VCRs may torpedo pay-per-view's success, since VCR penetration in the U.S. was four times that of addressable cable homes in 1984.[27] VCRs were originally feared as a threat to the American film industry, but movie house attendance in the U.S. has actually been stimulated by the VCR, in much the same fashion as Music Television (MTV) fuels the sale of rock records and videos.

Worldwide, the VCR may have the following impacts:

1. Viewer support for the national television network services may dwindle as tape rentals, cable, and DBS programming offer more and better opportunities for viewing and timeshifting.
2. The VCR has affected the broadcaster's program scheduling strategies, since viewers can tape shows at hours when they are not at their sets and can watch one program while taping another program on a competing channel.
3. National laws and broadcast policies prohibiting certain types of content and subject matter can be easily circumvented by VCR owners.
4. Home video hardware and software pose further challenges to Third World countries trying to protect their national cultures from Western media influences.
5. Rulers in totalitarian societies may be forced to let home video exist on a controlled basis rather than continue their futile attempts to supress it.
6. Efforts to use radio and television in Fourth World settings to save and revive authentic cultures and folk languages could be undermined as their younger generations succumb to the VCR as a purveyor of Anglo-American rock concerts and youth-oriented movies.

Table 9-1 summarizes the status of the VCR, cable, and broadcast satellites in selected countries around the world in 1984. These new technologies are contributing to an emerging trend toward co-productions between national broadcasters and freelancers, and toward a general internationalization of television programming.

TELEVISION PROGRAMMING AS AN INTERNATIONAL PRODUCT

International feeds of television programming used to be the sole preserve of the big American networks, and was limited mostly to transatlantic spot news coverage of events of great interest to American if not always to world audiences. The new technologies of the satellite age have created the means necessary for truly international and reciprocal exchanges of all kinds of TV programming by broadcasting organizations in nations the world over. Subtitling by character generators is one key to international programming, as are dubbing and computer-

Table 9-1 The Status of Cable, VCR, and Broadcast Satellites in Selected Countries: 1984

Country	Cable	% of Penetration By: VCR	(VHS/Beta/V2000)	Broadcast Satellites: Operational or Planned
Australia		30	(69/29/ 2)	AUSSAT
Austria	12	6	(40/10/50)	
Belgium	82	7.7	(70/25/ 5)	
Brazil		3.6	(95/ 5/)	BRAZILSAT
Canada	66	12	(65/35/)	ANIK A-D & TELESAT-1 & H
Colombia		11.6	(40/60/)	SATCOL
Denmark	58	9	(64/26/10)	
Finland	68	15	(70/20/10)	NORDSAT & Tele-X Partner
France	53	9.7	(80/13/ 6)	SYMPHONIE & TDF & TELECOM
India		4.5		INSAT
Indonesia		10		PALAPA A & B
Ireland	27	15	(75/15/10)	
Italy	2	5	(56/23/21)	ITALSAT & SARIT
Japan	12	21	(66/34/)	BS-1 & 2, CS-2a & b, SAKURA-2
Luxembourg				LUXSAT
Mexico		2.8[a]		SATMEX
The Netherlands	70	16	(55/25/20)	
New Zealand		18	(90/10/)	
Norway	31	16	(80/13/ 7)	NORDSAT & Tele-X Partner
Peru		17.5	(15/85/)	Andean Satellite Project
Saudi Arabia		19.3		SABS
Singapore		54	(95/ 5/)	
South Africa		6	(70/30/)	
Sweden	51	22	(80/10/10)	Tele-X & NORDSAT
Switzerland	60	15	(70/10/20)	HELVESAT
USSR		.01		EKRAN, GORIZONT, LOUTCH, MOLNIYA, RADUGA, VOLNA
United Arab Emirates		75[b]	(55/45/)	
United Kingdom	13	23	(67/27/ 6)	UNISAT
USA	40	19	(77/23/)	RCA/GTE/STC/SBS/WU/ATT/HCI/ASC
West Germany	21.3	22	(50/15/25)	SYMPHONIE, TV-SAT, DFS-KOPERNICUS

[a]Mexico City only
[b]only 100,000 TV sets in the country

Sources: InterMedia 11(4/5), July/September 1983, pp. 38–75; TV World, May/June 1984, "World Program Prices & TV Statistics"; TV World, October 1984, "World Home Video Chart" (compiled by DMM: D'Arcy, MacManus, Masius)

assisted simultaneous translation. Subtitling, however, is a turn-off for most viewers, except those who patronize minority-interest cultural services like the BBC-2, Channel Four, and PBS in America. Some countries forsake subtitling altogether. France, Italy, and West Germany only dub sound tracks, at a cost of about $600 for a 100-minute film, while British viewers favor subtitles over dubbing.[28]

An exemplar of transnational television cooperation was initiated in April 1984 through a contract between the world's largest satellite transmitter of radio and television programs, Wold Visnews Broadcast Services of America, and a consortium of major broadcasters in Japan—NHK, TBS, Nippon, Fuji, Asahi, and TV Tokyo—known as the Japanese International Satellite Joint Users Organization (JISO). This binational collaboration established a 24-hour pipeline of news, sports, and entertainment programming from America to viewers of the six Japanese channels via Wold's three technical centers in Los Angeles, New York, and Washington and a series of uplinkings and downlinkings involving Telstar 301, Comsat, and the Pacific INTELSAT IV-F4 satellites.

JISO's broadcasting partners, which are in stiff competition with each other in Japan, actually save money by sharing expenses for the 28 hours of collective programming they receive and schedule autonomously each week.[29]

Another binational agreement was signed in August of 1984 by West Germany's second channel, ZDF, and Gosteleradio of the USSR. The Soviet state broadcasting service will help ZDF produce a dozen programs on economic reform and the leisure lifestyles of young people in Soviet society. In return, ZDF will give technical and organizational assistance to Soviet TV production teams working in the FRG.[30]

International conventions for marketing television programs have taken place for many years in both Western and Eastern Europe. Representatives from Western, communist, and developing countries meet each year to buy and sell programming product for their national television services. Among the most prominent affairs are the Market for International Productions (MIP-TV), held since 1964 in Cannes, France; the London Multi-Media Market (LMMM); and the International Broadcasting Convention (IBC), which exhibits TV equipment as well as programming. Many other marketing conventions were started in Europe in the mid-1980s.

The counterpart in the Second World is the annual Intervision Teleforum held in Moscow. The main purpose of Teleforum is to view and select TV programs for exchange between the communist bloc countries that comprise Intervision, but a number of Western and Third World broadcasters usually attend.[31]

There are hopeful signs that the American TV market may be opening up to foreign programming, due largely to the rapid growth of DBS and cable channels. The American Market for International Programs (AMIP) held its first annual convention in 1983, with the purpose of promoting and facilitating the sale of foreign-produced TV programming in the U.S. AMIP, a joint venture of

American, French, and British program distributors, brings U.S. buyers and foreign sellers together under one roof for a week of bartering. The 1984 AMIP meeting in Miami Beach was attended by about 250 American commercial broadcasters and program sellers from 44 countries.

Foreign-made TV programming is gradually finding its way into U.S. television, and the AMIP participants feel the future market will be even healthier. One problem is that American audiences are generally put off by "foreign" accents (like British and especially Australian) and locations. Another drawback is that many foreign programs are exactly 30 or 60 minutes long, having been produced for noncommercial broadcasts; thus, editing them for U.S. advertising spots is rough on programmers as well as the program's integrity. Dramas and some comedies have the best chance of acceptance by American audiences, documentaries the least. A compromise strategy for successfully internationalizing TV programming is co-production—programs made by broadcasting companies from two or more countries and often featuring well known American or British stars.[32]

Some foreign TV programs were already making their way onto American TV and cable outlets by the early 1980s. A French production company has begun making programs in English for an American audience and marketing the service as TeleFrance USA. Its cultural output includes French cooking shows, plays by Moliere, and films by Francoise Truffaut. TeleFrance USA was reaching 7.5 million cable households in the U.S. by 1983, but its survival is in doubt.

The Satellite Program Network in Tulsa was devoting a quarter of its programming to international productions in 1983. SPN's other foreign programs in English included an NHK production, "Japan 120," a joint Nordic nation show, "Scandanavian Weekly," "Mediterranean Echoes" from ERT in Greece, and "Hello Jerusalem," made by Israel's IBA.[33]

A number of British TV series were sold to American commercial stations in 1983. A combined total of 125 episodes from three series—"Man About The House," "Robin's Nest," and "George and Mildred"—were bought for off-network syndication. "Man About The House" even placed first in the ratings in New York City against the 6 pm local news and American reruns when aired by WNET-TV.[34] The bulk of British TV programs seen in the U.S. are imported by Public Television, but the BBC's cable partnership with America's Arts and Entertainment Network helped bring its 1984 sales to at least 200 hours of programming. BBC Enterprises Limited sold 7000 hours, or $43 million worth, of programs overseas in 1984.[35]

One of West Germany's regional TV companies, Westdeutscher Rundfunk (WDR) in Cologne, began a weekly program in 1983 in which various segments from CBS shows are broadcast in English with German subtitles. The excerpts come from "60 Minutes," "CBS Reports," "Universe," and "CBS News Specials."[36] American TV shows are a big hit across the border in East Germany, where about 90% of the viewers turn their antennas toward the West German stations. The practice used to be illegal; it was also risky, since westward-pointed antennas were often torn down by Party stalwarts. By 1984, however, "Dallas," "Dynasty," and "The Streets of San Francisco" were favorites—along with West German commercials. The lure of Western TV is so great that government officials in East Germany have been known to fight transfers to the country's "dead corners" of the northeast and southeast where TV reception is poor.[37]

As part of China's new open door policy to the West, Central Television placed an order with the BBC in 1981 for the 37 plays of Shakespeare, "The Mayor of Casterbridge," "The Old Curiosity Shop," "The Voyage of Charles Darwin," and 115 hours of classic music concerts and ballets. The CCTV network also purchased 65 hours of TV programming from CBS, including the "Walter Cronkite's Universe" series.[38] Other popular imports are "The Man From Atlantis" and "Anna Karenina." Domestic productions include variety shows, dramas, cartoons, and even soap operas. Several classic Chinese novels are being produced as mini-series. The government of the PRC created a new Ministry of Television and Radio in 1982, which has authorized regional stations to purchase foreign programs and to enter into co-production agreements with other nations.[39]

China opened its first TV picture tube factory in late 1981 in Xianyang, Shaanxi Province, using equipment imported mainly from Japan. The plant turned out 100,000 tubes in 1982 and hopes to produce a million color tubes for receiver factories in Peking, Shanghai, and seven other cities. There were about 20 million sets for 400 million Chinese viewers by 1984. The government gives away TV sets as worker incentives—a ploy that works well, since a black-and-white receiver costs $200, about the annual income of many peasants.[40]

AMERICAN TV PROGRAMMING AS A GLOBAL ECONOMIC AND CULTURAL FORCE

Many Americans have become hypersensitive of late to the influx of foreign products into the domestic economy and the resulting trade deficit. Conversely, very few Americans are aware of the imbalance of trade which exists in the world economy of television programming, perhaps because it is a market that the U.S. completely dominates. Afterall, competition is so much more fun when your side is "number one." And when it comes to TV programs, global trade is a one-way street outbound from America. Measuring the traffic in dollars and hours of production tells the story.

By 1984, U.S. firms like MCA, Viacom, Paramount, MGM/UA, Embassy, Lorimar, and others totalled nearly 3 billion dollars a year in TV program sales— a fifth of it to foreign buyers. American sitcoms, crime dramas, and prime time soap operas have found popularity in practically every nation on earth—led by such hits as "I Love Lucy," "Bonanza," "Kojak," "Dynasty," and "Dallas." Why such an international demand for U.S. programming?

Perhaps the main reason is practical economics. Many foreign broadcasters lack the money, facilities, and talent to match the output and populist slickness of the American studios. As one U.S. producer put it: "Italy can't duplicate 'The A-Team.' And why should they? For $30,000, we can sell them an episode that cost us nearly a half million to produce."[41] And herein lies another reason: the American ability to produce mass appeal entertainment whose production values include opulence, fast-action, built-in suspense, and sex designed to capture and hold the attention of the most dull-witted viewers and of far too many smart ones.

Improved dubbing and subtitling technologies make American programs easily translatable into virtually every language. Much of the production if not message quality of the U.S. television product stems from the fact that most of the popular TV hits in America are made by major Hollywood film companies. This is not done in other countries, as a rule.

By contrast, American broadcasters buy and show very little foreign TV programming—only about 3%. This is because American viewers apparently will not accept dubbing or subtitling, have little tolerance for British accents or slower paced storytelling, and regard anything "foreign" as inferior or irrelevant. But are these the only reasons, or is it also because U.S. commercial broadcasters are ruled solely by marketplace competition as measured by the "ratings"? Much foreign TV programming is excellent, but probably would not play well in Peoria. One notable exception is the British show, "Benny Hill," which enjoyed success on many commercial U.S. TV stations. Numerous examples can be cited on PBS, where the best of British television finds a small but loyal American audience and the multinational corporations who underwrite them score important public relations points. The presumption that pay cable and satellite services would accommodate an even richer menu of foreign programs does not seem to be panning out. By 1984, three pay-TV operations with a variety of international offerings in their schedules—CBS Cable, TeleFrance, and The Entertainment Channel—had folded for lack of sufficient subscriptions. The latter merged with another cultural service to form the Arts and Entertainment channel, which offers many BBC programs via satellite to hundreds of U.S. cable systems.

More and more foreign countries were taking steps to curtail or limit imported programming on their domestic TV services by 1984. Some have set legal quotas on the percentage of foreign production that can be transmitted. Their motives for doing so range from economic to cultural. Obviously, TV schedules are finite, so the more programming a nation imports, the less airtime is left for its own productions.

A compromise strategy being employed more frequently in the 1980s uses contracts between program companies in several nations to coproduce material that can be seen in both countries as "home-made" content, yet also marketed abroad. Recent examples of co-national productions are "The Body Machine" (France's Antenna 2 and Goldcrest of the UK), "The Far Pavilions" (America's HBO and Goldcrest-UK), and "Marco Polo" (a U.S.-Italian-Chinese tri-production). Such international ventures are mutually advantageous in that they spread the costs, circumvent home content quotas, and, by making multiple soundtracks, become marketable in several major languages—especially the world media language, English.[42]

But the most volatile aspect of the one-way flow of U.S.-dominated TV programming is its effects on the cultures of importing nations, particularly in the Third World. American TV programming has been condemned for its preoccupation with sex, violence, and materialistic values. This can be especially insidious if it is perceived as stimulating the sale of American products in the host economy. Moreover, Western programs depict affluent lifestyles, celebrate the status quo, and parade the values of vanity, competition, and greed which are patently offensive to many traditional cultures in the developing and Fourth Worlds. On the other hand, these same elements make U.S. programs very attractive to the majority of Third World peoples, particularly youth, because the plots are simple and predictable, the stars are appealing, and the visual and sound qualities are emotionally provocative and professionally rendered.[43]

The output of TV programming from the U.S. is so prodigious that many Western countries find themselves alongside Third World nations in a shared concern for their national cultures. This somewhat shopworn issue was discussed again at a fall 1984 seminar at London's National Film Theatre. Nigerian broadcasters complained that 60% of their current schedule was foreign, and that much of the rest is prescribed by its government, which owns all 32 of the nations TV stations. Televisa Mexico feels the pinch in terms of competition, since massive amounts of U.S. programming are carried by Mexico City's cable networks.

The root of the problem lies in the fact that slick American productions can be bought for as little as $200 an hour by poor Third World countries, and may generate a hundred times that amount or more in advertising. On the other hand, an hour of local production would cost more than it could recoup in commercial revenue. And the problem of TV imperialism will only worsen during the 1990s. The nearly 70% of the world's population that had little or no real access to television in 1984 will be blanketed by foreign DBS footprints by 1994.[44]

Television Imperialism: The Special Case of "Dallas"
No television program in the history of the medium has attracted as much international attention as "Dallas." The American prime-time soap opera, produced by Lorimar Productions for CBS, has captured audience ratings, the contempt and praise of critics, and the wrath of politicians in virtually every country it has been aired. During 1984, it was rated among the top 10 TV programs in West Germany (third on ARD), Britain (second on BBC-1), Canada

(first on CBC), and the Netherlands (third on TV-1)—to name a few. In fact, the show is syndicated in over 60 countries and has achieved top ratings on every continent.[45] One American journalist in Europe described the phenomenon this way:[46]

> On almost any evening of the week, somewhere between the Berlin Wall and the western shores of Ireland, living rooms are taken over by J. R. Ewing, showing off a world of money and raw power that, to the average European mind, is the essence of America.

In an intercontinental empirical study of "Dallas," Katz and Liebes conducted interviews to determine how demographically similar viewers (lower-middle class, high school educated or less) in two different cultural settings (Israel and Los Angeles) made sense of the show, and whether viewer understanding differs from culture to culture. The researchers' premise was that "Dallas" has certain universal themes about kinship, id, and superego relations that viewers selectively perceive, interpret, and evaluate in terms of their local cultures and personal experiences.

From the interviews, it was concluded that the focus groups of "Dallas" viewers selectively understood the narrative outlines and relationships between characters, and that culturally divergent viewers will differ in the extent to which they generalize or personalize the characters and issues depicted in a TV program. In other words, while there may be less "social distance" between the Ewings and TV audiences around the world than previously thought, viewers will nevertheless either accept or reject the values in "Dallas"—family life versus business success, money versus happiness, law-abiding civilization versus frontier lawlessness—depending on their personal value systems. Finally, Katz and Liebes suggested "that television programs do not impose themselves unequivocally on passive viewers. The reading of a TV program is a process of negotiation between the story on the screen and the culture of the viewers."[47]

In the sampling of TV program ratings shown in Table 9-2, "Dallas" appeared among the most popular shows in 6 of the 10 countries. Thirty-two of the 121 rated programs were American productions—or 26%. Canada had the highest proportion—12 of 20 (60%)—and Brazil had none.[48]

ECONOMIC AND CROSS-CULTURAL ASPECTS OF TRANSNATIONAL BROADCAST ADVERTISING

Exporting advertising from one culture to another is more problematic than program exchanges in more ways than one. Local customs, cultural taboos, and complex language differences must be taken into consideration and overcome if a business expects to successfully advertise and sell its goods or services overseas. Literal translations of advertising copy, for instance, can result in nonsensical mumbo-jumbo, especially in Asia.

Table 9-2   A Sampling of TV Program Ratings Around the World in 1984

Country		Program	Channel	Rating %	Viewers (millions)
Australia (Week ending	1	Sale of the Century TCN-9			
July 30, 1983)	2	60 Minutes TCN-9			
	2	Movie (Escape from Alcatraz) TEN-10			
	2	Knight Rider TCN-9			
	2	Quincy ATN-7			
	2	Rugby League Football TEN-10			
	3	A Country Practice ATN-7			
	4	News ATN-7			
	4	Sale of the Century TCN-9			
	4	Sons and Daughters ATN-7			
	4	News TCN-9			
Argentina (September	1	Las 1001 de Sapag			
1–21 1984)[a]		(local humor)	9	34.5	
	2	Amo y Senor			
		(domestic soap)	9	27.9	
	3	A Brigade	9	27.8	
	4	Sabados de la Bondad			
		(2nd edition)	9	20.2	
	5	Yolanda Lujan			
		(domestic soap)	11	19.9	
	6	Sabados de la Bondad			
		(1st edition)	9	19.6	
	7	Michael Jackson show	9	19.5	
	8	Matt Houston	9	18.5	
	9	Sabados de la Bondadel.7			
	10	Domingos para la Juventud			
		(2nd edition)	9	17.5	
Britain (Week ending		BBC1			
March 25, 1984)[b]	1	World Figure Skating			
		Championships			13.75
	2	Dallas			11.85
	3	A Question of Sport			11.50
	4	Jim'll Fix It			10.65
	5	Top of the Pops			10.50
		BBC-2			
	1	Sporting Chance			6.70
	2	Fainthearted Feminist			4.35
	3	Marti Caine			3.85
	3	M.A.S.H.			3.85
	5	Call My Bluff			3.55
		ITV			
	1	Coronation Street (Wed)			16.60
	2	Minder			15.90
	3	Coronation Street (Mon)			15.80

(*continued*)

Table 9-2 (continued)

Country		Program	Channel	Rating %	Viewers (millions)
	4	Duty Free			15.65
	5	This Is Your Life			15.45
		CHANNEL 4			
	1	Treasure Hunt			3.65
	2	Brookside (Wed)			2.90
	2	Skating - World Championship Gala			2.90
	4	Brookside (Tue)			2.65
	5	Cheers			2.50
Belgium (Week ending January 8, 1984, excluding news programmes)c	1	Hoger-Lager		38.2	
	2	Dallas		33.9	
	3	Sportweekend		32.0	
	4	Panorama		28.9	
	5	I.Q.		26.4	
	6	Juke-box special		23.8	
	7	Benny Hill Show		22.5	
	8	Een Ruiter wild en vrij		21.9	
	9	Dynasty		20.7	
	10	Geschiedenis mijner jeugd		19.0	
Brazil (Week ending August 1, 1983)	1	Journal Nacional (news)	Globo	63	
	2	Guerra das sexes (soap opera)	Globo	62	
	3	Louca Amour (soap opera)	Globo	61	
	4	Fantastico (variety)	Globo	55	
	5	Pao, Pao, Beijo, Beijo (soap opera)	Globo	51	
	6	Trapalhoes (comedy)	Globo	48	
	7	Chico Anisio (comedy)	Globo	44	
	8	Viva O gourdo (comedy)	Globo	43	
	9	Gols do Fantastico (football)	Globo	42	
	10	Quarto Nobre (weekly play)	Globo	35	
Canada (Week ending March 27, 1984)d		CBC			
	1	Dallas			2.88
	2	H.N.I.C.			2.43
	3	Three's Company (Tues)			2.28
	4	Walt Disney			2.13
	5	Sportsweekend: Brier			2.03
		CTV & Supps			
	1	Miss Teen Canada			3.01
	2	Magnum P.I.			2.99
	3	Knight Rider			2.95
	4	Hotel			2.29
	5	Academy Performance			2.06
		Global			
	1	60 Minutes			0.94
	2	Dynasty			0.83

Table 9-2   (continued)

Country		Program	Channel	Rating %	Viewers (millions)
	3	Knots Landing			0.61
	4	Suzanne Pleshette			0.61
	5	Love Boat (Sat)			0.52
		Radio-Canada			
	1	Oiseaux se Cachent			2.41
	2	Temps d'une Paix			2.16
	3	Terre Humaine			2.06
	4	Poivre et Sel			1.87
	5	Beaux Dimanche			1.83
Greece (Week ending February 4, 1984)e	1	Ierosili (Greek series)	ERT 2	59	
	2	It happens everyday (Greek series)	ERT 1	52	
	3	Shining Stars (Greek series)	ERT 2	50	
	4	Greek film	ERT 2	46	
	5	Greek film	ERT 1	43	
	6	Hart to Hart	ERT 2	45	
	7	Greek cinema	ERT 1	43	
	8	Western	ERT 2	42	
	9	Please swear (Greek series)	ERT 2	40	
	10	Dynasty	ERT 2	38	
The Netherlands (Week ending May 13, 1984)f	1	Hoger-Lager	BRT TV-1		35.2
	2	IQ	BRT TV-1		33.4
	3	Dallas	BRT TV-1		31.5
	4	Sportsweekend	BRT TV-1	31.0	
	5	Panorama	BRT TV-1	27.8	
	6	Football: Anderlecht v. Tottenham	BRT TV-1	25.5	
	7	The Jewel In The Crown	BRT TV-1	24.9	
	8	Banana Splits Show	NED 1	23.8	
	9	The Benny Hill Show	BRT TV-1	22.5	
	10	Stick Together	NED 2	22.1	
South Africa (TV1 Programmes, Week ending February 26, 1984)g	1	A-Team			
	2	Dallas			
	3	Fynbos			
	4	Private Benjamin			
	5	Skooldae			

(continued)

Table 9-2   (continued)

Country		Program	Channel	Rating %	Viewers (millions)
	6	Murder by Natural Causes (feature film)			
	7	Star Trek			
	8	Under the Mountain			
	9	Campbell Koninkryk			
	10	Newhart			
West Germany (Week ending September 9, 1984)[h]	1	Tatort	ARD	16.27	
	2	Someone Must Win	ARD	14.54	
	3	Karl May: The Oil Prince	ZDF	12.45	
	4	Get Set, Go XY	ZDF	12.23	
	5	Dallas	ARD	11.89	
	6	What Am I?	ARD	11.42	
	7	The Slow Poison	ARD	9.38	
	8	Sports (Saturday)	ARD	8.84	
	9	The Beautiful Wilhelmine	ZDF	8.58	
	10	The Two	ZDF	8.21	

[a]*Source:* Mercados y Tendencias S. A.
[b]*Source:* BARB
[c]*Source:* BRT
[d]*Source:* A C Nielsen
[e]*Source:* ERT
[f]*Source:* BRT Kijk & Luisteronderzoek
[g]*Source:* SABC
[h]*Source:* ARD/ZDF
Note: Reprinted by permission from *TV World.*

The "Come alive with the Pepsi generation" slogan in Taiwan came out as "Pepsi will bring your ancestors back from the dead." The use of sex appeal, scantily-clad women, and intimate details of hygiene in ads are turn-offs in more traditional societies. In China, where the odor of dairy products is considered offensive and getting one's head wet every day is believed to cause illness, it is obvious that ads for pre-dinner cheeses and a shampoo "gentle enough to use every day" were less than effective.

Cross-cultural advertising often reflects alien value systems which, even if successful in the marketplace, may cause resentment. This is most true when younger viewers become Americanized and turn against their own heritage as being old fashioned or obsolete.[49]

As the decade of the 1980s began, the top ten U.S. advertising agencies dominated not only 40% of the North American market, but 38% of Australia's, 43% of Holland's, and over 70% of the national advertising markets throughout the Third World. The degree and direction of transnational advertising flow from the West, primarily America, to the rest of the world, especially the developing countries, carries with it a number of ramifications. Several have been advanced by the Dutch critic, Cees Hamelink.[50]

First, transnational advertising is basically North American propaganda designed and packaged by their largest ad agencies to sell the output of their biggest transnational corporations. Second, most transnational advertising is persuasive rather than informative, and promotes the sale of consumer goods (prepared foods, cosmetics, and household products) instead of capital goods (like office equipment, trucks, and machinery). Third, advertising has been exported along with the transfer of the American commercial broadcasting model to other countries in the Third World and elsewhere. In fact, broadcast advertising occupies a larger average percentage of the airtime among Third World radio and TV stations (15.8%) than is the case in either the Second World (1.6%) or even the First World (5.4%). Fourth, American advertising helps define the basic needs in developing countries in terms of goods and services that are inappropriate to the local needs of a developing society. In Hamelink's words:[51]

> Products are not adapted to suit local needs; local needs, through advertising, are adapted to the products. Thus, consumption patterns are being created that lead to a wasteful spending of what little is available. The poorest in Third World countries spend a considerable part of their income for products which make them even poorer.

Examples of this practice can be seen in peasants buying advertised products like seltzers and colas in place of traditional herbal medicines and mint tea— which are cheaper and just as effective. A particularly terrible example has been the advertising campaign by Western baby food producers to convince Third World mothers to buy and use powdered milk in place of breast-feeding. Illiteracy and poor water supplies have led to the improper and unhygenic preparation of the advertised milk formula, resulting in increased baby deaths. Thus, Hamelink concludes, an "effective, adequate, and cheap method has been exchanged for an expensive, inadequate, and dangerous product."[52]

Perhaps the most insidious aspect of transnational broadcast advertising is the capacity of commercials to peddle dreams and fantasies along with the goods being sold. The poorest consumers in the Third World are most susceptible to and exploited by foreign TV commercials depicting an affluent lifestyle that they can never hope to achieve. Such ads, by promoting consumerism, help to diminish the national wealth of developing countries by making their affluent elites part of the international economy while distracting the struggling majorities from genuine needs like health care and education.

Broadcast Advertising in Europe

Despite the aforementioned negatives, advertising is certain to be a major ingredient in the future financing of national broadcast systems everywhere in the world. This is particularly true in Western Europe, where the traditional public service model has reached its limits on increasing receiver license fees or relying much further on public tax treasuries. Advertising is the most painless way to enhance the financial support of broadcasting systems, in the eyes of most broadcasters and audience members.

The dependence of all mass media on advertising has been growing steadily for a decade and will continue to do so for the rest of the century. By 1984, the annual worldwide expenditure on advertising had reached $64 billion. Half of the total was spent in the U.S. alone, with Britain, France, West Germany, Japan, and Canada accounting for over a billion dollars each. This trend can be interpreted for good and for ill.

One advantage of advertising as a source of media revenue is that it comes from many individual sources, therefore concerted or unified pressure on media gatekeepers is less likely or effective than when a single entity like government supplies all or most of the money. Another advantage is that advertising has come to be preferred by most Europeans to paying ever-increasing license fees which still cannot seem to generate enough income to keep pace with broadcast expenses during these inflationary times.

Advertising's disadvantages stem from the negative impacts it tends to have on programming standards and formats, as ratings dictate production and scheduling decisions. The needs of sponsors to reach the largest possible audiences with their commercial messages inevitably dilute programming standards as the lowest common denominator becomes the broadcaster's target in order to maximize audiences and profits. Commercials interupt programs and become an annoyance to viewers. Program-makers are forced, therefore, to produce the show around commercials by placing artificial breaks in the storyline so that ads can be inserted during broadcasts.

European advertising matured during the 1970s and today rivals the North American industry in sophistication, if not volume. Service industries have replaced manufacturers as the dominant advertising clients on the continent, and public service advertising, especially by government and semi-state entities, is on the increase. The fledging cable TV industry in Western Europe is beginning to siphon advertising dollars away from the more costly over-the-air networks.

Europeans are looking forward to wider program choices as cable and satellite services appear, but some research suggests that they do not want to pay directly for it, that advertising is a welcome alternative to Pay TV or license fee hikes. Moreover, Europe faces many complex questions, since the laws and policies governing broadcast advertising differ from country to country, yet signal spillover is commonplace. These issues include copyright control, royalty payments, libel and slander, national security matters, and public morality.

Generally speaking, there are two levels of broadcast advertising control in Europe: (a) the amount of airtime allowed for commercials; (b) the content of the ads themselves. Furthermore, some countries have unique policies or bans. West

Germany, for instance, does not allow advertising on Sundays and holidays; nor does Holland, which also requires that short cartoons be run between spots. Greece only allows 30 minutes of TV advertising a day, and Sweden bans it altogether. Many broadcasters have strict controls on comparative advertising, or prohibit certain products (liquor, cigarettes) and services (prostitution, money-lending) from the airwaves. Britain disallows advertising by charities, religions, and political parties or candidates.

In short, Europe needs to standardize broadcast advertising practices and laws, especially in the age of the satellite. Transnational control is vital in the areas of *trade protection* (relating to specific professions, industrial competitions policies, and protectionism from foreign goods) and *consumer protection* (in matters of taste, decency, truthful claims, and health). The EBU, European Court, Council of Europe, and the Common Market (EEC) have all addressed continent-wide advertising regulations, but none had been formally agreed upon as of 1984. EEC lawyers have warned against any country banning the advertising of products on foreign DBS services if the product is advertised on its own national channels. The EEC's 1984 Green Paper on Europeanizing advertising control urges nations to be flexible and change their laws in order to achieve harmony and ensure the free flow of goods, television programming, and information (including advertising) across each other's borders.

The current trend in Europe is toward liberalizing advertising regulations and allowing it on television. The Netherlands increased its commercial airtime 100% between 1976 and 1984; public service advertising was introduced on Belgian TV in January 1984; Denmark is slated to start a second commercial TV network; and West Germany has plans for more advertising on ARD, as well as for new private TV and cable stations in the late 1980s.[53]

Table 9-3 compares TV advertising statistics in 17 European countries, based on 1981 practices. Given current trends, these figures will multiply in the decade ahead.

By 1982, a total of $3.8 billion was being spent in TV advertising in Europe, and $14.3 billion in the U.S. With the addition of TV-am and Channel Four in Britain, the ITV's advertising revenues peaked to an all time high in 1984 of over $1.1 billion.[54]

A COMPENDIUM OF COMPARISONS, CONTRASTS, AND TRENDS IN WORLD BROADCASTING

Having looked fairly closely at national broadcasting systems, policies, and issues throughout the Four Worlds, and at the new technologies that will shape the future of mass telecommunication, we conclude by summarizing world broadcasting's emerging patterns of ownership, organization, financing, control, policy, programming, and technical development.

Table 9-3   TV Advertising in Western Europe in 1981

Country	Channel(s)	Maximum advertising airtime (minutes per day)	Percentage of channel's revenue
Austria	ORF-1/ORF-2	20	42
Belgium	RTBF-1,2		non-commercial advertising began January 1984
	BRT-1,2	none	—
Denmark	Radio Denmark	none	—
Finland	MTV/YLE-1	16	80
	MTV/YLE-2	9	80
France	TF-1	18	53
	A-2	18	54
	FR-3	18	?
Germany	ZDF	20	40
	ARD-1	20	40
	ARD-2	—	40
Greece	ERT-1	30	25
	ERT-2	variable	?
Iceland	Rikisutvaspid-Sjonvarp	16.4 (average)	33.7
Italy	RAI-1	28	23.8
	RAI-2	28	23.8
	RAI-3	—	—
	Private stations	15% per hour	100
Luxembourg	RTL	68	100
Netherlands	NOS-1	15	25
	NOS-2	15	25
Norway	NRK	none	—
Portugal	RTP-1	83	43
	RTP-2	45	43
Spain	TVE-1	57	74
	TVE-2	42	74
Sweden	STV-1,2	none	—
Switzerland	SRG (German)	20	35
	SRG (French)	20	35
	SRG (Italian)	20	35
UK	BBC-1,2	none	—
	ITV	90	100
	Channel 4	50	100

Source: InterMedia, 12(2), March 1984, p. 16. Reprinted by permission.

Ownership

Private ownership is growing throughout the First and Third Worlds in competition with the public corporations of Western Europe and the government-owned systems in Africa, Asia, and the Middle East. Private radio and TV services have started or are under consideration in Spain, Austria, West Germany, Denmark, New Zealand, and Greece. In the Third World, private broadcasting is strongest in Latin America and is gaining in the Caribbean and Pacific Oceania, and will spread as developing economies form capital bases.

By contrast, public service broadcasting organizations around the world are in trouble. The BBC is underfinanced; the NHK in Japan faces growing commercial competition; Italy's RAI is awash in a sea of virtually unregulated private stations; the CBC is up against the American services, an aggressive private rival (CTV), an expanding cable environment, and several dozen North American satellite services; Holland's NOS is being downgraded; West Germany's ARD confederation will soon see private TV cable competition; and America's PBS may have to accept some form of advertising to supplement insufficient government support.

Government ownership of broadcasting is still solidly entrenched throughout the Second World and most of Africa and Asia, although the latter two regions are becoming more commercialized—a forerunner to privatization.

Organization

As the policies and laws governing ownership and financing change, so too will the organizational structure of a nation's broadcasting system. The most obvious trend worldwide is toward decentralization and localism. The West European trend away from monopolistic and duopolistic market structures, toward private competition, will no doubt continue and may spread to other regions. This shift will bring with it a new responsiveness to local interests and needs, greater pluralism in programming, more opportunities for public access to telecommunication channels, renewed possibilities for private station ownership, and an accompanying need for new sources of income through advertising. And as cable, DBS, and home video offer more and diversified programming options, it is fair to say that the days of the public service monopoly and media nationalism are numbered.

The decentralization of broadcasting services is also taking place in Second and Third World countries, where ethnic minorities and language groups have been successful in winning culture-specific radio and TV stations. Such Fourth World broadcasting services have spread from nation to nation, saving authentic cultures and ancient tongues from extinction.

Financing

Advertising is on the ascendancy as a means of broadcasting support in virtually all regions of the world. It is increasingly being relied on in Western Europe to supplement license fee income, which may have reached the limits of public tolerance or affordability. Third World countries are also airing more commercial content. Even Second World broadcasters are finding advertising an efficient way to enhance state-run enterprises and to augment broadcast revenues.

Commercial broadcasting typically offers popular programming free of direct charge to mass audiences that are undifferentiated as to social, cultural, economic, educational, and intellectual status. Nations having advertiser-supported broadcasting thus have need for an extensive advertising industry, which in turn is a source of employment for creative talent like copywriters, graphic artists, illustrators, filmmakers, video producers, and actors. Thus, advertising stimulates the national economy. As a by-product, TV ads become highly salient artifacts within the popular culture.

But advertising also has the most direct influence on a broadcasting system's programming. Since sponsors supply the money to make and broadcast programs, they also decide what gets and stays on the air. Programs are thus the means (audience bait) to an end (sales and profit), meaning their success is totally determined by ratings. The result is populist, simplistic, safe, trendy, and disposable programming aimed at the lowest common denominator in order to maximize audiences and profits.

License fees provide a more direct and democratic means of support for a broadcasting system than any other financing scheme—advertising, taxes, subscriptions, or donations—since all viewers pay the same stipend and receive a balanced menu of programs uninterrupted by commercials, uncensored by government or sponsors, and less susceptible to cancellation by the tyranny of a majority.

One weakness of fee-based broadcasting systems is that operational costs are outstripping the public's ability and willingness to pay for the same number of channels and types of programming in the age of cable, DBS, and VCRs. Further, fees have been increasing without a corresponding improvement in program services or quality. This has bred public resentment and, in the extreme, evasion of payment. Some viewers find fees a form of taxation, since they are mandatory, but a voluntary system would be as ineffective and degrading as the tin-cup appeals by American public broadcasters. Ironically, most Americans would protest or simply refuse to pay a receiver license fee for ad-free TV, but think nothing of paying much more for pay-cable and home video.

Control

Broadcasting always serves the ideological and practical objectives of the power elite in each country, regardless of which philosophy it is based on—Authoritarian, Western, Communist, Developmental, or Revolutionary. In every nation, broadcasting is controlled by either big business or big government, with some public body charged with licensing and regulating the uses of the spectrum and common carrier facilities. The key to control lies in the relationship between the regulatory body, the government, and the broadcaster. When governments control telecommunication, they also control the messages. When broadcasters are publicly chartered, they have more operational autonomy. When an independent regulatory agency of government is responsible for licensing and guiding the activities of private broadcasters, the public interest becomes secondary to the private interests of the channel owners.

The modes of social and operation control are changing most radically in the United States, where *deregulation* is leaving most programming decisions to market forces, and the ownership of telecommunication services is becoming concentrated in fewer and fewer hands. In Western Europe, the PTTs still reign supreme over telecommunication transmissions and policymaking, but private competition in broadcasting and cable will gradually increase the marketplace's influence.

State control inevitably leads to the bureaucratization of the broadcasting organization, which becomes top heavy with administrators from the ranks of civil service instead of broadcasting. The result is a lack of flexibility in planning and unimaginative programming. Radio and television are used for short-term political gain by government and are generally unresponsive to the needs and interests of the public. Moreover, the news loses credibility.

Policy
National broadcasting policies reflect the people and process that produce them. Two policy patterns are common in the First World. The traditional public service broadcasting policies of Western Europe are arrived at through a series of government commissions, committees of public inquiries, and carefully tested pilot projects. The process is directed by the national PTTs, with the broadcasting organizations having minor input. Conversely, American broadcast policy is influenced primarily by the commercial broadcasting industry, which works outside of the public interest arena by lobbying legislators, contributing vast amounts of money to the political campaigns of friendly politicians, and pressuring weak federal bodies like the OTP, NTIA, and FCC. The resulting program practices serve mainly commercial and private objectives rather than the interests and needs of all segments of the public.

Broadcast policy in communist countries is made by Party officials who simultaneously operate the radio and TV system and generate programming designed to meet ideological goals and divert public attention away from governmental failings. Policy making in the Third World is shaped by officials purportedly interested in using broadcasting as an instrument of national development. Their chronic insistence on importing massive amounts of Western content, and misguided attempts to offer full schedules of TV programming, run counter to stated policy objectives. Radio, however, is used much more purposefully as a genuine domestic medium to meet legitimate local and cultural needs.

Programming

Entertainment is the most salient type of programming to be found on national TV schedules anywhere in the world. It dominates the Western airwaves, is imported more than any other type of content by Third World broadcasters, and is simultaneously denounced and gratuitously scheduled by TV gatekeepers in communist countries. American program formats (co-anchored newscasts, made-for-TV movies, sitcoms), themes (sex, crime), and production values (fast-paced action and rock music backgrounds) are being imported and emulated by foreign broadcasters in vastly differing cultures. But it is the flow of news and information that is perhaps most controversial.

The production and global flows of information and television programming are controlled by the U.S. and a handful of other Western countries. They also dominate most of the electromagnetic spectrum and orbital positions in space. The existing lines of communication are vertical, running North (Euro-American) to South (the developing world), with very little news flowing in the opposite direction or even between Africa and Asia. This inequity, which negatively affects the advancing Third World nations, may be somewhat redressed by the ITU's coming a priori space allocation plans or could worsen by the 1990s, given the foundering state of UNESCO and the New World Information and Communication Order strategy. The withdrawal of America and Britain from UNESCO will materially damage the credibility and solvency of the U.N. agency in the short run. It may not survive were several other Western nations to leave, since the USSR lacks both the resources and will to make up financial losses of this magnitude.

Soviet TV programming will continue to be the handmaiden of a hierarchy of official values that puts propaganda ahead of entertainment, and the needs of the state before the desires of the audience. Programs that are most popular with viewers may be cancelled, while those frought with ideological significance remain on the air despite their lack of audience support. The State TV and Radio Committee conducts audience research through its Scientific Programming Center, but the results are not made public, nor do they appear to influence programming decisions. Internal research suggests that TV has a greater psychological impact than radio or newspapers in terms of building viewer confidence in the Soviet system.

The USSR's telecommunication policy goals for the rest of the decade call for an upgrading of the national radio and TV system with coloration and stereophonic sound but with no explicit plans for developing cable. This official policy is based on ideological reasons rather than a lack of technical competence. Although cable and compatible VCR services would offer Soviet citizens wider program choices, such changes would lessen the centralized broadcasting system's capacity to present uniform information and influence popular tastes from above. Of course, it is also easier to control viewing with only three or four channels. Programs with heavy political value can be scheduled opposite each other, and the audience has no place to hide except to push the "off" button. Cable systems, however, would be not only expensive to install but nearly impossible to program without resorting to counter-scheduling entertainment against news and propaganda.[55]

Governments throughout the world tend to use the mass media to achieve propaganda objectives by inserting information into national channels of communication, through outright censorship, or by manipulating news agencies and journalists who nevertheless masquerade as independent brokers of information. News management through the use of leaks, trial balloons, background briefings, photo opportunities, carefully staged news conferences, and presidential addresses to the nation are particularly common techniques used in the West. In the U.S. for example, the competition for ratings makes TV newscasts highly susceptible to manipulation by politicians and groups with media savvy. Ronald Reagan has brought the art of controlled news media access to the presidency to an unprecedented level. In short, while the First World has competing news media that are freer of government control than those in the Second and Third Worlds, Western journalists are nevertheless subject to manipulation by official and private forces.

Broadcasters in all three worlds define news differently. Westerners see news as a commercial product that is sold to them by information brokers at a profit. Communists interpret this kind of "news for profit" as inherently favoring those who own and pay for the news media rather than aiding the public interest. Third Worlders also have a problem accepting news as a commodity since, in their view, news controlled by big business is no better than news controlled by the state. Neither source is impartial, they would argue, and both place their own interests ahead of the people's.

An American philosopher, Paul Kurtz, has drawn another interesting parallel between Eastern and Western television:[56]

> In totalitarian societies, the media serve as the vehicle of propaganda and indoctrination. In democratic societies television, radio, films and mass publishing too often cater to the lowest common denominator and have become banal wastelands. There is a pressing need to elevate standards of taste and appreciation. Of special concern to secularists is the fact that the media (particularly in the United States) are inordinately dominated by a proreligious bias. The views of preachers, faith healers, and religious hucksters go largely unchallenged, and the secular outlook is not given an opportunity for a fair hearing. We believe that television directors and producers have an obligation to redress the balance and revise their programming.

The state of children's television in America is also a national disgrace. The U.S. is the world's only nation that doesn't officially recognize children as a unique category of TV viewer. The commercial networks are guilty of a kind of child abuse by allowing more advertising (12½ minutes per hour) in children's programming than during adult primetime (9½ minutes per hour). Some nations do not allow advertising within children's TV shows.[57] The real question is: why advertise to children under 12 years of age who are dependent minors without incomes and lacking in critical and consumer skills? Fortunately, the Corporation for Public Broadcasting is tripling its budget for children's educational programming from $2 million in 1984 to $6 million in 1986.[58]

Technical Developments

The decade from 1985 to 1995 will be one of transition from traditional national broadcasting structures to new configurations based upon competing new technologies like cable, direct satellite broadcasting, and home video devices. These developments are forcing nations to rethink the rationale for their present broadcasting organizations as the market forces of competition demand a restructuring of distribution, financing, regulation, and programming mechanisms. But the changes required by the new technologies differ from country to country.

Cable is having the greatest impact in North America and a lesser yet significant impact in Europe. It is relatively insignificant in the Second and Third Worlds, but for different reasons. Satellite broadcasting, direct and distributed, is experiencing a shakeout in North America, where it has grown and failed the fastest.

DBS is developing more modestly and more steadily in Europe, but also faces numerous obstacles associated with spillover—such as transborder advertising, copyright, language barriers, public morality, and competition with national broadcasting organizations and emerging cable operations. DBS is viewed as a threat to cultural sovereignty and national development by the Third World, and as an ideological threat if not provocation among Communist Bloc countries.

But it is the VCR that is proving to be the most revolutionary of the new technologies. Affordable, portable, user-controlled, the VCR allows viewers to program their own TV sets by timeshifting, renting or buying prerecorded tapes for playback, developing personal cassette libraries, and making their own home productions with videocameras. Another aspect of the VCR that makes it revolutionary is its availability and popularity in all regions of the world. The VCR is the only new telecommunication technology to have made its way into the Third World, especially the Middle East and South America.

And whereas cable and DBS are either unfeasible to develop or seen as negative intrusions in many societies, the VCR can liberate individual viewers from limited or unsatisfactory TV environments and has the potential to liberate entire nations from oppressive or fanatical regimes.

If the new technologies present challenges to national broadcasters in the First World and national cultures in the Third World, they threaten the very existence of the ideology and structure of Second World societies. Information technologies like computers, cable television, DBS, and VCRs are not neutral. The mass production and diffusion of affordable digital and telecommunication hardware and its attending software will put information, ideas, and popular alien cultures in the hands and minds of citizens of closed societies. This is inimical to the social structure of the Eastern Bloc nations. It will be impossible for police states to justify their controls over the people, let alone to convince them that their system is better than all others.

The Second World may be faced with no less a dilemma than the choice between adapting to the new technologies and abandoning totalitarian ideals and practices, or rejecting the new technologies and losing the economic race with the West and eventually the obedience of their own people.[59] The Second World may in fact be fighting a losing battle in trying to control new technologies like the computer, DBS, and VCRs. Marx's view of labor producing the wealth may be obsolete in the information age, where wealth is generated by high technology and a service economy rather than by manufacturing and heavy industry. Moreover, the marketplace values the simple, the convenient, the quick, and the inexpensive. When ideas become commodities, it stands to reason that simple ideas are easier to peddle than complex ideas. TV and advertising are essentially emotional modes of communication, and emotions flow more easily than does the intellect.

The new technologies promise to wreak havoc with the American network oligopoly. The commercial networks' share of the total TV audience in the U.S. was 91% in 1978 but only 81% in 1982. With pay cable, their share slipped to 60% by 1985. By 1990, it is estimated that the networks' will collectively reach under half (46%) of the total TV audience, due to the fragmentation caused by competion from pay-cable, DBS, MDS, and home video.

It is estimated that there will be 89 million TV households in the U.S. by 1988. A DBS operation needs only 5% of that total (4 to 5 million) to be profitable. Also, cable penetration may be 50% and home dish antennas 10%, meaning DBS could reach 60% of the TV homes in America by the end of the decade—most of them outside of the Top Ten markets.[60]

But will the new technologies reach their cultural potentials? Will more channels mean better programming or simply a cornucopia of tasteless mass entertainment, sensationalistic news, and crass commercial clutter? One haunting thought that intelligent TV viewers harbor is whether the best of traditional public service programming will survive. In a recent speech before Britain's Cable Television and Satellite Broadcasting Conference, the Director-General of the BBC, Alistair Milne, questioned the validity of the phrase "widening choice," if it means doubling the number of channels and putting "Dallas" on all of them. He offered this challenge to his audience:[61]

> Try switching from channel to channel in the United States and make up your own mind whether the fare offered there is as varied as the programming our four national television channels provide. . . . For instance, in America very little television drama, as we understand it, is being written or produced. Feature film

material made for television in Hollywood, yes; soap opera, yes; television drama, no! There is very little documentary, a form of programming in which we particularly excel.

Milne concluded with what could be the prophecy for world broadcasting in the age of the satellite: "You can 'widen' viewer choice over four networks and narrow choice over 40." It is something to think about.

CHAPTER 9 NOTES

[1] All cable information comes from these sources: "An EBU Survey on Cable Television in Europe," *EBU Review,* XXXV(1), January 1984, pp. 31–42; Tony Pearson, "Heavier Cable Penetration in Larger European Countries Seen As Possible Deterrent to DBS," *Television/Radio Age,* May 28, 1984, pp. 43ff; *Channels,* '85 Field Guide, p. 34.

[2] *TV World,* May/June 1984, p. 61.

[3] "Austria: Seeking an Answer to Sky Channel," *InterMedia,* 12(3), May 1984, pp. 6–7.

[4] "Cable and Electronics Have a Bright Future," *InterMedia,* 12(3), May 1984, pp. 3–5.

[5] Paul Barrett, "Government Encouragement for New Cable Initiatives," *TV World,* August 1984, pp. 44–45.

[6] Piet te Nuyl, "Sowing the Seeds for Pay-TV," *InterMedia,* 12(1), January 1984, pp. 9–11.

[7] *TV World,* August 1984, p. 2; "Swedish TV: Under Pressure," *TV World,* May/June 1984, pp. 52–54.

[8] "Cable: UK Government Plans Eleven Interim Licenses," *InterMedia,* 12(1), January 1984, pp. 3–4.

[9] Mark R. Levy and Edward L. Fink, "Home Video Recorders and the Transience of Television Broadcasts," *Journal of Communication,* 34(2), Spring 1984, pp. 56–71.

[10] David Lachenbruch, "VCRs: The Hottest Thing Since Television," *Channels,* '85 Field Guide, pp. 6–8.

[11] John Chittock, "Why Britain Sets the Pace," *InterMedia,* 11(4/5), July/September 1983, pp. 72–73.

[12] "Video: Agreement on a New Format," *InterMedia,* 11(3), May 1983, p. 3.

[13] Francoise Lerusse, "Cable is More Attractive," *InterMedia,* 11(4/5), July/September 1983, p. 42.

[14] Jack Miller, "Low Prices, High Sales," *InterMedia,* 11(4/5), July/September, pp. 43–44.

[15] Annette Suffert, "Gunfight at the Poitiers Corral," *Ibid.,* p. 50.

[16] Stig Svard, "VCR Penetration to Reach 17%," *Ibid.,* pp. 69–70.

[17] Desmond Fisher, "Across the Border," *Ibid.,* pp. 54–55.

[18] Alessandra Silj, "The Football Factor," *Ibid.,* pp. 56–57.

[19] "Kremlin Has Eye on Videocassettes," *Buffalo* (NY) *News,* September 9, 1984, p. C-10.

[20] Stewart A. Fist, "The Suburban Dream," *InterMedia* 11(4/5), *op. cit.,* pp. 41–42.

[21] Stephen Schiffman, "Video Piracy's Real Winners and Losers," *TV World,* March 1984, pp. 32–33.

[22] "Piracy in Australasia," *TV World,* July 1983, pp. 25–26.

[23] Schiffman, *op. cit.*

[24] Richard Owen, "An Elite Revolution," *InterMedia,* 11(4/5), July/September 1983, p. 75.

[25] "Danes 'Protect' Pirate TV Station," Buffalo (NY) *Courier-Express,* August 25, 1981, p. B-11.

[26] Joanmarie Kalter, "Why Some Nations Fear The Great American Tape Invasion," *TV Guide,* July 28, 1984, pp. 33–34.

[27] "VCRs," *Broadcasting,* August 20, 1984, pp. 42–50.

[28] Howard Keen, "The New Generation," *TV World,* October 1984, pp. 62–64.

[29] Charla Foster, "Pipeline to Tokyo," *TV World,* August 1984, pp. 37–38.

[30] "Russo-German Deal," *TV World,* August 1984, p. 6.

[31] "Success for Socialist Market," *TV World,* November 1984, p. 37.

[32] "AMIP #2: Selling in the Sunshine," *Broadcasting,* November 26, 1984, p. 40.

[33] David Purcell, "Telefrance, Japan 120: Foreign TV Comes to US," *The Christian Science Monitor,* February 16, 1983, p. 2.

[34] "Imports," *Broadcasting,* August 15, 1983, p. 7.

[35] "Rise in Sales of BBC Programmes," *TV World,* August 1984, p. 6.

[36] "German News," *Broadcasting,* August 15, 1983, p. 74.

[37] "East Germany Called a Hotbed of U.S. TV," *Buffalo News,* April 4, 1984, p. D-9.

[38] "China to Run a CBS Series," *Buffalo News,* TV Topics, August 28, 1983, p. 16.

[39] Larry Rohter, "The Biggest TV Audience," *Newsweek,* August 16, 1982, p. 44.

[40] "TV Tube Factory Opens in China," *Buffalo Courier-Express,* December 31, 1981, p. A-4.

[41] Peter Caranicas, "American TV Tightens Its Grip on the World," *Channels,* January/February 1984, pp. 27–30.

[42] *Ibid.,* p. 30.

[43] Elihu Katz and George Wedell, *Broadcasting in the Third World: Promise and Performance* (Cambridge, MA: Harvard University Press, 1977), pp. 157ff.

[44] Kim Lerner, "Cultures Under Threat," *TV World,* November 1984, p. 17.

[45] *World Press Review,* August 1982, p. 6.

[46] Marcus Eliason, "Europe Still a Captive Audience for All Things American," *Buffalo News,* June 10, 1984, p. A-3.

[47] Elihu Katz and Tamar Liebes, "Once Upon a Time, In Dallas," *InterMedia* 12(3), May 1984, pp. 28–32.

[48] All data in Table 9-2 is from the following issues of *TV World:* September 1983, p. 69; March 1984, p. 45; April 1984, p. 149; August 1984, p. 47; October 1984, p. 65; November 1984, p. 48.

[49] Ann Scott, "Asian Advertising Loses Something in Translation," *Buffalo News,* January 7, 1984, p. B-6.

[50] Cees J. Hamelink, *Cultural Autonomy in Global Communication* (New York: Longman, 1983, 1983), pp. 10–16.

[51] *Ibid.,* p. 14.

[52] *Ibid.,* p. 15.

[53] Alastair Tempest, "Why We Need Advertising," *InterMedia,* 12(2), March 1984, pp. 14–19.

[54] *Television/Radio Age,* September 3, 1984, p. A-16.

[55] Badhnaseeb Shahzad, "TV is the Opium of the People," *InterMedia* 12(3), May 1984, pp. 24–25.

[56] Paul Kurtz, *In Defense of Secular Humanism* (Buffalo, NY: Prometheus Books, 1983), pp. 20–21.

[57] "Kidvid: A National Disgrace," *Newsweek,* October 17, 1983, p. 46.

[58] "Children's Programming Doubled by Public Broadcasting Group," *Buffalo News,* January 18, 1985, p. C-9.

[59] Rex Malik, "Communism VS the Computer: Can the Soviet Union Survive Information Technology?" *InterMedia,* 12(3), May 1984, pp. 10–23.

[60] Stephen A. Sharp, "The US Networks May Not Need Their Affiliates," *InterMedia* 11(2), March 1983, pp. 6–8.

[61] Alistair Milne, "A View from the Brits: Westward No!" *Channels,* July/August 1983, pp. 63–64.

Author Index

Subject Index